The English-Speaking Alliance

By the same author:

'Appeasement' and the English Speaking World. Britain, the United States, the Dominions and the Policy of 'Appeasement', 1937–1939 (1975)

The Origins of the Arab–Israeli Wars (1984)

The Foreign Policy of the British Labour Governments, 1945–1951, editor (1984)

The English-Speaking Alliance

Britain, the United States,
the Dominions and the Cold War
1945–1951

Ritchie Ovendale
University College of Wales, Aberystwyth

London
GEORGE ALLEN & UNWIN
Boston   Sydney

**George Allen & Unwin (Publishers) Ltd,
40 Museum Street, London WC1A 1LU, UK**

George Allen & Unwin (Publishers) Ltd,
Park Lane, Hemel Hempstead, Herts HP2 4TE, UK

Allen & Unwin, Inc.,
8 Winchester Place, Winchester, Mass. 01890, USA

George Allen & Unwin Australia Pty Ltd,
8 Napier Street, North Sydney, NSW 2060, Australia

First published in 1985

British Library Cataloguing in Publication Data

Ovendale, Ritchie
The English-speaking alliance: Britain, the
United States, the Dominions and the Cold War,
1945–1951.
1. World politics—1945–
I. Title
327′.09′04   D840
ISBN 0-04-327078-6

Library of Congress Cataloging-in-Publication Data

Ovendale, Ritchie.
The English-speaking alliance.

Bibliography: p.
Includes index.
1. Great Britain—Foreign relations—1945–
2. Commonwealth of Nations—Foreign relations.
3. United States—Foreign relations—Great Britain.
4. Great Britain—Foreign relations—United States.
5. World politics—1945–1955.   I. Title.
DA588.O89 1985   327.73041   85-11075
ISBN 0-04-32078-6 (alk. paper)

Set in 10 on 11½ point Palatino by V & M Graphics Ltd, Aylesbury, Bucks
and printed in Great Britain by Billing and Sons Ltd,
London and Worcester

3-31-87

To withstand the great concentration of power now stretching from China to the Oder, the UK and Western Europe must be able to rely on the full support of the English speaking democracies of the Western Hemisphere; and for the original conception of Western Union we must now begin to substitute the wider conception of the Atlantic Community. (Ernest Bevin, 8 May 1950)

The people in this country were pinning their faith on a policy of defence built on a Commonwealth–U.S.A. basis – an English-speaking basis. People here were frankly doubtful of Europe. How could he go down to his constituency – Woolwich – which had been bombed by Germans in the war, and tell his constituents that the Germans would help them in a war against Russia? Londoners would not rely on the Germans; if the Germans come in to help, so much the better. But reliance must be placed on America and the Commonwealth. Similarly in regard to France, the man in the street, coming back from a holiday there, was almost invariably struck by the defeatist attitude of the French. (Ernest Bevin, 23 August 1950)

Contents

Acknowledgements

Part of the research for this book was made possible by grants from the British Academy and its Small Grants Fund in the Humanities, and a visiting research fellowship from the American Council of Learned Societies tenable at the University of Virginia, Charlottesville. The Australian National University, Canberra, kindly elected me a visiting research fellow in the Department of International Relations attached to the Research School of Pacific Studies.

I should like to thank the following for assistance: Dr Christopher Andrew, Sir Harold Beeley, Peter L. Boulting, Gillian Bromley, Professor Inis Claude, Professor D. K. Fieldhouse, Professor John Garnett, Professor Agnes Headlam-Morley, Professor Ieuan John, Professor James Joll, Professor Nicholas Mansergh, Professor J. D. B. Miller, Professor Ian Nish, the late Professor F. S. Northedge, Dr James Piscatori, Sir Frank K. Roberts, Professor Keith Robbins, Professor Jack Spence, Lucy Seton-Watson, Anthony Short, David Steeds, Professor Geoffrey Warner, Professor D. Cameron Watt and Dr Moorhead Wright.

I am grateful to the library staffs of many institutions and archives for their expertise. In particular I should like to thank the following and, where appropriate, acknowledge permission to quote from collections in their custody: Churchill College, Cambridge and the Earl Attlee for the *Attlee Papers*; the British Library for the *Oliver Harvey Diaries*; the British Library of Political and Economic Science for the *Dalton Papers*; the Western Manuscripts Department of the Bodleian Library, and the Master and Fellows of University College, Oxford, for the *Attlee Papers*; the Guy W. Bailey Library, the University of Vermont, for the Warren R. Austin and Ernest Gibson Jr's papers; the Alderman Library, University of Virginia, for the Edward R. Stettinius Jr and J. Rives Childes' collections; the Robert Muldrow Cooper Library, Clemson University, for the *James F. Byrnes Papers*; the George C. Marshall Library, Virginia Military Institute, for George C. Marshall's papers and other collections housed there; Princeton University Library; the Harry S. Truman Library, Independence, Missouri; the Franklin D. Roosevelt Library; Georgetown University Library for the *Robert*

F. Wagner Papers; the Library of Congress Manuscript Division; the National Archives in Washington together with the National Records Centre at Suitland, Maryland; the Australian Archives in Canberra; and the Australian National Library, Canberra, for the papers of Sir Percy Spender and Sir Robert Menzies. The staff of the Public Record Office, London, was always obliging and courteous; copyright material housed there appears by permission of Her Majesty's Stationery Office. Mrs Chris Chadwick, Mrs Kathy Hamilton and the staff of the Hugh Owen Library, University College of Wales, Aberystwyth, were willing and cheerful.

Some of the material used in this book originally appeared in: *International Affairs*, the quarterly journal of the Royal Institute of International Affairs, London, published by Butterworths; the *Historical Journal*, published by Cambridge University Press; *History*, published by Longman; and *The Foreign Policy of the British Labour Governments, 1945-1951*, published by Leicester University Press. I appreciate permission from the respective editors to incorporate that work.

PART ONE

Introduction

1

The Inheritance

Late in the 1930s, while he was Prime Minister, Neville Chamberlain laid the foundations of the English-speaking alliance. It was this alliance that enabled Britain to fight the Second World War and emerge victorious. Immediately after assuming office Chamberlain chaired the Imperial Conference which met in London in May 1937 amidst the patriotic fervour of King George VI's coronation. From 1934 the British government, and Chamberlain in particular, had been conscious of the weakness of Britain's defences and the need to rearm. Indeed on 22 March 1934 the Cabinet decided that a policy designed to keep Britain out of all war in Europe and the Far East would mean adopting too narrow a view: Britain could not restore international peace and confidence by 'backing out of Europe and leaving others to take the consequences'. Britain was an imperial power with worldwide responsibilities. This meant that successive British governments had to weigh carefully the opinion of the Dominions. During the second half of 1934 Sir Maurice Hankey, the secretary to the Cabinet and to the Committee of Imperial Defence, visited South Africa, Australia and New Zealand to sound out those countries on defence matters. As Chancellor of the Exchequer in Stanley Baldwin's government Chamberlain overheated the economy by accelerating rearmament. Against the background of Mussolini's activities in Abyssinia, Hitler's occupation of the Rhineland and the Spanish Civil War, the Dominion Prime Ministers were alerted to the seriousness of the European situation. Even before the Imperial Conference of 1937 Chamberlain had decided on a policy of trying to preserve peace in Europe. At this meeting the Prime Ministers of South Africa, Australia and Canada remained opposed to European commitments. Chamberlain was convinced that his approach was right.

Chamberlain also pursued a foreign policy designed to win the sympathy of the United States: he did everything he could to mollify a difficult and isolationist American public opinion. The policy of his government is summed up in a memorandum of 1938 written by F. Ashton-Gwatkin, the head of the economic relations section of the Foreign Office:

> In a play which I saw in London some years ago, a young Foreign Office secretary finds himself by an accident, at a full meeting of the Cabinet. ... He is asked by the philosophical Prime Minister what he thinks is the most important thing in the world and he replies without hesitation: – 'Love – and Anglo-American relations'.
>
> I am glad to think that my department is popularly considered to have its fundamental policy so firmly based.

President Franklin D. Roosevelt had consistent plans for aiding Britain, but knew that he was tied by the attitude of the American Congress and public. During the Munich crisis he warned the British ambassador, Sir Ronald Lindsay, that in indefinable circumstances the United States might again find itself involved in a European war, but so strong was isolationist opinion that even in such a case he thought it 'almost inconceivable' that he would be able to send American troops across the Atlantic. If Britain were invaded, however, it was possible that a wave of emotion would send the American army overseas.

The Chamberlain Cabinet was conscious that the only countries that could oppose the growing strength of the dictators were those of the English-speaking world. Malcolm MacDonald, the Secretary of State for the Dominions, on 30 August 1938 warned a meeting of ministers considering the question of whether Britain should go to war if Czechoslovakia were invaded by Germany:

> The result of consultation with the Dominions would probably be that we should not be in a position to utter the threat. If, nevertheless, we made the threat, we should put a great strain on the loyalty of the Dominions and might break up the Commonwealth. The British Commonwealth of Nations and the United States of America together were the only force which could eventually check the progress of dictatorship; one day this combination might have to fight to defeat the growing evil. His Majesty's Government should not take a step now which would break the Commonwealth.

At Munich Chamberlain managed to avert war, and for a short time became the 'man of the hour' in the United States. On his return he told the Cabinet that he was 'more hopeful', but it would be madness to stop rearming until Britain's deficiencies had been made good: 'In our foreign policy we were doing our best to drive two horses abreast: conciliation and rearmament.' In pursuing this policy Chamberlain tried to carry the Dominions along with him. But after Hitler's invasion of Prague in March 1939 Britain guaranteed Poland without consulting the Dominions: it was felt that the Dominions 'would not have wished that the United Kingdom should invite them to share responsibility for the decision'. Roosevelt wanted to reinforce the new British policy of deterrence by repealing the neutrality acts. He hoped that he would be able to present this to King George VI during the royal visit to the United States in June. Congress thwarted him. At this time Japanese intransigence and maltreatment of British subjects in the Tientsin concession in China meant that for a time it seemed as if war would start in the Far East and not in Europe. This meant a serious rethinking of British contingency planning. If war did start in the East, it was unlikely that Germany and Italy would be able to resist the temptation to move in Europe. Britain might have to fight on three fronts simultaneously. Chamberlain's cautious policy – successful in the end – was hampered by the attitude of the United States: that country favoured Britain's taking a firm stand against Japan. On the eve of war, however, Roosevelt did indicate his willingness to apply pressure on Japan if that country became hostile.

In September 1939, largely as a consequence of Chamberlain's astute diplomacy, Britain only faced war on one front. Canada, Australia, New Zealand and South Africa joined the mother country. The people of the Dominions fought for Britain, for their kith and kin. Chamberlain also knew that he had the support of a sympathetic American President. Indeed, by that time the exchange of information between Britain and the United States was such that it could be argued that a special relationship existed between the two countries. Defence co-operation and joint planning had also been initiated with the visit of Captain R. E. Ingersoll of the United States Navy to London in January 1938, and of Commander T. C. Hampton to Washington in June 1939.[1]

With the American entry into the war in December 1941, following the bombing of Pearl Harbor by the Japanese, the United States and the countries of the British Commonwealth faced the dictators in Europe and the Far East. The English-speaking alliance, envisaged by the Chamberlain Cabinet, was in operation.

Britain fought the Second World War as an imperial power with worldwide commitments. Looking back on this experience, at a time when the Labour government was considering once again the need for Britain to undertake responsibilities for European defence, Sir John Cunningham warned the Chiefs of Staff on 2 February 1948 that it had been Britain's traditional policy in the past to avoid continental commitments: 'Twice in the past we had given a guarantee to assist a continental nation to the limit of our power by the provision of land forces. On both occasions we had suffered severely, first on Mons and more recently at Dunkirk.'[2] As the Second World War progressed, however, Britain's geographical position meant that its preoccupation with the envisaged alignments of power on the European continent grew. Winston Churchill became increasingly worried that he could not persuade the United States to take a sufficiently long-term view of postwar problems. During 1943 Anglo-American military co-operation was close, both in the Mediterranean theatre and in preparations for the second front. But Roosevelt wanted Marshall Stalin as the close ally, and the President was worried that the Russian leader might suspect that Britain and the United States were 'ganging up' on him.[3]

On his way to the Tehran Conference at the end of 1943 Churchill told Harold Macmillan: 'Germany is finished, though it may take some time to clean up the mess. The real problem now is Russia. I can't get the Americans to see it.' By that time statesmen in Britain and the United States had significantly different perceptions of Russian intentions for the postwar world. Roosevelt probably envisaged Russia and the United States working for peace together. When these two countries were fighting side by side this vision was enlarged: Russia and the United States would manage world affairs under the aegis of the United Nations. Roosevelt, unlike Churchill, feared Nazi aggression more than Russian expansionism. Even after the Yalta Conference Roosevelt, in April 1945, appeared not to share Churchill's fears of a communist take-over in Europe: he urged the Prime Minister to minimize the Russian problem and things would straighten out.[4] The United States had started planning for the postwar world before Pearl Harbor. This was shown by Sumner Welles's mission to Europe in 1940, and the Atlantic charter of 1941 which embodied those freedoms the Americans considered basic to the continuance of international society. The United Nations declaration was signed as early as January 1942. The general American attitude was that there was a need to move away from the old system of the balance of power, and allied blocs, and into the new era of efficient world organization. The prospective United Nations appeared to be more important than alliances. Colonialism had to go, and this meant conflict with Britain. By 1942 Britain suspected that the United States was trying to overthrow British rule in India.[5]

Britain was, perhaps, more pragmatic, and more concerned with the realities of power on the European continent. This meant an increasing suspicion of Russian intentions, and an anxiety over seeming American blindness to them. Differences in attitude between Britain and the United States towards Russia were evident at the Cairo meeting in November 1943 which preceded that at Tehran. Churchill had to face suspicions that British military planning in the Mediterranean and the Far East was a scheme to defend or recapture Britain's imperial possessions. The United States also feared that Britain was trying to trap its allies into activities in the Balkans. Lord Moran, Churchill's doctor, recorded in his diary that 'to the Americans the P.M. is the villain of the piece; they are far more sceptical of him than they are of Stalin'. Because of the attitude of the United States, the two countries went to face Russia at Tehran without a common policy. Evidently the President played the role that he had envisaged: a sort of arbiter between Churchill and Stalin. On Eastern Europe Churchill had a proposal to create a Danubian confederation. Stalin did not like this, as it seemed to imply that Britain would re-establish the balance of power in Europe. Roosevelt supported Stalin who insisted that Romania, Austria and Hungary should become independent powers again. Churchill resisted, as he felt that Stalin was aiming at the Balkanization of Eastern Europe. Roosevelt and Stalin agreed on the need to keep Germany weak. Churchill was probably more concerned that Russia would become too strong. In his private conversations with Stalin Roosevelt discovered common ground that separated the two men from the British: they were both concerned to liquidate Western colonial empires, and agreed that Indo-China should not be returned to France. Churchill was appalled by his impotence at Tehran: he realized that he could not rely on Roosevelt's support and that the Russians knew this.[6]

But there was little that Churchill could do. By the time of the next meeting of the big three a year later, Britain and the United States had still not co-ordinated their policies. There were even military differences between the two countries: on the issue of the second front, it was the United States and Russia that were in step. Roosevelt suspected British efforts to carve a sphere of influence in Eastern Europe. Because of Anglo-American closeness the differences between the two countries were accentuated. It was general American policy that no decisions on frontiers should be made until the end of the war, when divisions would be settled by a world organization. Russia was free to pursue its special interests in Eastern Europe. Britain's lack of faith in the prospective world organization focused American resentment on Britain rather than Russia. Churchill, anxious to stop the Russians and to bring the United States around to his view of the postwar problems, could do neither.[7]

The Italian campaign revealed real differences between Britain and the United States. But for British statesmen what mattered more was their influence on affairs in central Europe. Churchill and Anthony Eden, the Foreign Secretary, wanted to exploit the victory in Italy to play a more influential part in central Europe. The United States opposed this, using strategic arguments. Churchill and Eden felt that political inhibitions about becoming involved in the Balkans were the real reason. In 1944 Eden advised that the only way of checking Russian influence in the Balkans was to consolidate Britain's position in Greece and Turkey.[8] The British Cabinet had no doubts over Russia's intentions in Eastern Europe. On 25 January 1944 Eden told it that what Russia had in mind for Poland was probably 'a puppet Government under Russian control and a Soviet Republic'. In May Churchill, referring to disagreements over Romania, admitted that Molotov's attitude 'led him to despair of the possibility of maintaining good relations with Russia'. On 9 October 1944 Churchill met Stalin in the hope of securing British control in Greece, and some influence in Bulgaria, Hungary and Yugoslavia. The Prime Minister suggested an informal division of influence in Eastern Europe. Stalin agreed. For Churchill, this was, apparently, only a guide, and did not set up a rigid sphere of interest. This 'percentage split' agreement did not commit the United States.[9]

By early 1945, however, despite earlier differences, Britain and the United States did achieve agreement on the Polish question. Roosevelt's attitude was that the United States should continue to recognize the London Poles, as both the government and people of the United States had no evidence that the Lublin committee as it was constituted represented the people of Poland. The leader of the London Poles, Stanislaw Mikolajczyk, was the only man who seemed to 'offer the possibility of a genuine solution of the difficult and dangerous Polish question'. Eden told the Cabinet on

2 January that British and American policy over Poland was 'closely in line' and he and Edward R. Stettinius, the secretary of state, decided at Malta on 1 February 1945 that the Russians should be asked to agree to an interim government in Poland with a council including Mikolajczyk.[10]

Britain, by the beginning of 1945, had also secured American acquiescence in its policy in Greece, the only means it had of checking Russian influence in the Balkans. Stalin seemed prepared to accept British primacy in the area. Stettinius, however, stated in a memorandum of 8 November 1944 that in East and south-east Europe and the Near East the United States should not assume that 'the American interest requires it at this time to identify its interests with those of either the Soviet Union or Great Britain'. As early as 9 August 1944 Eden had considered the need to dispatch troops to Greece to avoid a *coup d'état* by EAM, the communist guerillas, when the Germans withdrew. In December the activities of EAM, possibly inspired by Stalin but probably more as a result of a decision taken on a local level, threatened an uprising in Greece. Subsequent strong action taken by Churchill, supported by Ernest Bevin who handled trade union criticism, was effective. But EAM was able to publicize the State Department's comment that in the liberated territories the United States expected that the problems of government would be worked out on democratic lines without interference from outside. Roosevelt was furious with British action in Greece, as he felt that it involved shooting those Greek communists who had been allies in the fight against Nazism. Churchill, with his assurance that elections would be held at some fixed date, did manage to secure a more conciliatory attitude from the President, and, on the whole, there was little American criticism of British policy in Greece before Yalta.[11]

Poland and Greece, however, were isolated instances where agreement between Britain and the United States was achieved by consummate diplomacy rather than through a similar assessment of Russia's intentions. Roosevelt was still inclined to view the world rather than the European situation. When the big three met at Yalta in February 1945 Anglo-American policies were not co-ordinated, and this lack was largely through American engineering. Churchill found the President unreceptive to the idea that 'only a solid understanding between the United States and Britain could keep Stalin's appetite under control'. At Yalta Churchill and Roosevelt did not work easily together, and the Prime Minister saw that 'the map of Europe will be redrawn in red ink'. There was nothing that Churchill could do about it.

Roosevelt was preoccupied with the idea of the United Nations. With his worldwide view, he was determined to maintain co-operation with Russia as the key to world peace. Immediately, he wanted Moscow's agreement to American proposals for voting at the United Nations. On this issue, the Russians gave in to his ideas: as Churchill told the Cabinet on 19 February 1945, he 'had been struck by the desire of the Russians to meet the President half way on points to which they thought he attached real importance'. Churchill appeared uninterested and showed his lack of faith in the world body. Roosevelt was under the influence of Admiral William D. Leahy, who thought Europe unimportant, and the Far East more an American concern. The President negotiated in secret with Stalin, without consulting his Chinese or British allies, and reached an agreement to cover the Far East. Eden was opposed to signing this agreement, but Churchill thought it necessary to try to safeguard British authority in the Far East. Britain and the United States fell out over the issue of a world charter to deal with territorial trusteeships and dependent areas. Churchill would tolerate no interference with the British empire and won his point: the allies would not interfere with one another's sphere of influence. But this victory was double-edged. It virtually left Russia free to do what it liked in the occupied territories of Eastern Europe. There was no real agreement over Poland, though a rift was avoided. Britain could not push the Polish case because of what it had done in Greece, and, as Churchill told the Cabinet, Stalin 'had most scrupulously respected his acceptance of our position in Greece'. On Eastern Europe generally, Russia would not give way and Britain evidently had little support from the United States. The declaration on liberated Europe which pledged the allies to work for the establishment of democractic institutions in the freed territories was only a paper agreement.[12]

Initially there was some optimism, even in Britain, over the Yalta declaration. But the weeks following the Yalta communiqué showed the markedly different assessment of Russian intentions on the two sides of the Atlantic. Roosevelt maintained his anti-colonial stance – possibly weakening only on his deathbed – and his insistence on independence for such territories as French Indo-China. This stand, however, was personal, and in making it Roosevelt was not supported by his bureaucracy or by his national security advisers, who were concerned that such a stand would threaten American rights to its Pacific possessions.[13] Indeed on 2 April the research and analysis branch of the Office of Strategic Services argued in a memorandum that after the war the United States would be confronted with a situation potentially more dangerous than any preceding one. Russia would emerge by far the strongest nation in Europe and Asia. If the United States stood aside, Russia would be able to dominate Europe, and at the same time establish its hegemony over Asia. Russian material resources and manpower were so considerable that in a relatively few years it could become more powerful than Germany or Japan had ever been. In military potential Russia could outrank the United States in the 'easily foreseeable future'. Russia should be convinced of American 'unaggressive intentions', and of its readiness to understand Russian problems. At the same time the United States should demonstrate its determination to safeguard its own position. The United States should persuade other powers, such as Britain, to adopt a similar policy. Moreover, it was also in the American interest that the British, French and Dutch colonial empires be maintained. The United States should encourage the liberalization of colonial regimes 'in order the better to maintain them, and to check Soviet influence in the stimulation of colonial revolt. We have at present no interest in weakening or liquidating these empires or in championing schemes of international trusteeship which may provoke unrest and result in colonial disintegration, and may at the same time alienate from us the Empire states whose help we need to balance the Soviet power.' Furthermore, the United States should do everything possible to encourage and support the development in West European states of independent, economically prosperous democratic regimes which could, in alliance with Britain and the United States, serve as 'a counterweight to Russian power and a bulwark against further Russian expansion'.[14]

There was also division in Britain between the leadership and some of the bureaucracy. For Churchill, the test seemed to be Poland: he told the Cabinet on 21 February that the acid test of Russian intentions in this regard would be whether they raised objections to Mikolajczyk returning. By 6 March it was evident that Vyacheslav Molotov's attitude on this matter was unsatisfactory. Then in Romania, two weeks after the Yalta communiqué, the Russians engineered a *coup d'état*. This must have been planned either before or during the Yalta Conference. The Foreign Office argued that little could be done to change Russian control and that an obstinate British policy might wreck the

11

chance of Russian co-operation on other matters. In Bulgaria the Russians obstructed the British mission and the Foreign Office could not obtain American support for a protest to Moscow. In April Roosevelt wrote to Stalin that he could not see why events in Romania should not be regarded as falling within the terms of the agreement on the declaration of liberated Europe. The Foreign Office, perhaps, like Roosevelt, viewed the Russian objectives as limited. Churchill did not. He hoped for Western democratic institutions in South-Eastern Europe, and was unwilling to believe that Russian control could not be stopped. The Post-Hostilities Planning Committee, on which both the Foreign Office and the Chiefs of Staff were represented, as late as March 1945 tentatively accepted that Britain should not oppose any reasonable Russian demands, provided that these did not conflict with vital British interests.[15] But on 2 April a Foreign Office minute by Sir Orme Sargent suggested that it should be made 'abundantly clear' to Russia that the policy of Anglo-Soviet co-operation had to apply fully in central and south-eastern Europe, as in the rest of the world.[16]

On 3 April Churchill addressed a meeting of the War Cabinet attended by Commonwealth dignitaries and outlined his vision of the postwar world. The 'dominating facts' in the world situation were the position of Russia and the United States. Relations with Russia were less cordial: there were grave difficulties over the Polish question; Russia might not give full co-operation to the new world organization:

> It was by no means clear that we could count on Russia as a beneficient influence in Europe, or as a willing partner in maintaining the peace of the world. Yet, at the end of the war, Russia would be left in a position of preponderant power and influence throughout the whole of Europe. In the western hemisphere, the United States had made enormous strides during the last two years, and had built up a military machine and supporting war production which was maintaining a vast military effort, not only in Europe but in the Pacific theatre. The resources in men and material commanded by the United States were vastly superior to our own; and they had acquired during this war a new capacity and experience in marshalling these resources in war.

In this new situation the British Commonwealth could only hold its own by unity, and superior statecraft and experience.[17]

American support was essential to halt Russian advances in Europe. This action had to be taken quickly at a time when Anglo-American military strength in Europe was at a maximum. Churchill wanted a meeting of the big three at which the United States and Britain would face Russia with the threat that if the Russians did not honour their agreements at Yalta, the Anglo-American armies would stay their ground. The Prime Minister's wish for a stronger bargaining position against the Russians was thwarted by the United States, and especially General D. D. Eisenhower. In Churchill's estimation what was needed was a rapid military advance on Berlin. Eisenhower had other plans, of which he informed the Russians, without authorization from the combined Chiefs of Staff, on 28 March. To the United States, Berlin was not a particularly important objective. The American Chiefs of Staff also supported Eisenhower's plan not to advance his troops across the Elbe in mid-April. The new President, Harry S. Truman, would not consider Churchill's view of the political consequences of the military objectives. The pattern was repeated in Czechoslovakia. On 13 April Eden sent a message to the American ambassador in London urging the United States to liberate Prague before the Russians. The message took time to reach Washington, and Eden raised the matter with Stettinius at San Francisco on 28 April. In the British view, the liberation of Prague and as much as possible of western Czechoslovakia might influence not only the postwar situation in Czechoslovakia but also that in nearby countries. Otherwise, Western influence would be lost there as it had been in Yugoslavia. Churchill repeated the message to Truman but General G. Marshall and the American Chiefs of Staff were opposed to operations conducted with a political rather than a military purpose. Eisenhower, after a protest from the Russian high command, halted his troops when they could easily have entered Prague and at a time when there were no Russian troops in Bohemia. Later in 1945 the United States withdrew even from the positions that it did hold in Czechoslovakia. Seemingly it did not share Churchill's fears of exposing the country to Russian influence, and anticipated that Czechoslovakia would develop as an independent state not subject to pressures from either East or West.

Truman, even more that Roosevelt, was determined that there should be no Anglo-American collaboration against Russia. Instead of accepting Churchill's plan to negotiate a real settlement with the Russians, he delayed the next meeting of the big three and tried a unilateral approach to Stalin with the mission of Harry

Hopkins to Moscow. The Hopkins mission did secure a paper agreement on Poland, but it appeared to the British, and especially to Churchill, that the United States was not alive to the dangers of a Russian advance in Europe. Churchill seemed to be concerned that Truman, like Roosevelt, would not want to commit American forces to a long stay in Europe, especially if it appeared that they were going to be used in what seemed to be the British interest. On 12 May Churchill sent a telegram to Truman about his fears for Europe when there might be only a few French divisions against two or three hundred Russian. The Prime Minister saw an 'iron curtain' being drawn down upon the Russian front. He felt that it would soon be open to the Russians to advance to the North Sea and the Atlantic. It was necessary to achieve a settlement with Russia before British and American strength was dissipated.[18]

It could be argued that Truman's cancellation of Lend Lease to Russia on 11 May 1945 showed a hardening of attitude on the part of the new President. Perhaps he considered economic pressure as an option to use against Russia. More likely, Truman thought that he was giving in to anticipated congressional pressure: Lend Lease was intended only to help fight the war and not for reconstruction. Though Russia was affected, Britain also suffered from the cancellation.[19] Truman, initially, had made some sort of stand against the Russians on the Polish issue before the meeting at San Francisco to prepare the Charter for the United Nations. This was probably because of his inexperience and his consequent reliance on certain sources of advice. In late April Truman told Molotov that the United States wanted friendship with Russia but not 'on the basis of a one-way street'. Molotov protested that he had never been talked to like that in his life. Although Eden would have preferred the weighting of American policy to be towards a strong stand against Russia, the success of plans for the United Nations still had top priority. There were difficulties at the conference on the issue of the veto and the seating of Argentina, but the American policy of giving priority to the idea of the United Nations and conciliating Russia lest it walk out was successful in that the Charter was finally drawn up on 26 June.[20]

The big three finally met at Potsdam in July. The British Cabinet on 20 June had considered asking for a postponement until after the results of the British general election were known. Churchill felt that a Labour government would maintain continuity in British policy if it were determined by those ministers who had been part of the wartime coalition. Statements by the Labour Party chairman, Professor Harold Laski, suggested, however, that there would be no such continuity and that policy might be determined by the executive committee of the Labour Party. The meeting was not delayed.[21] Eden had hoped for a preliminary exchange of views with the new American Secretary of State, James F. Byrnes. This did not materialize, but there were talks between Foreign Office and State Department delegates on 14 July. Before leaving for Potsdam, Eden wrote to Churchill that he found the 'world outlook gloomy and signs of Russian penetration everywhere'. In the Foreign Office, William Hayter suggested that the Americans should be persuaded to adopt the procedure that even if the Russians should make reasonable requests, these should not be granted except 'in return for their agreement to reasonable requests on our part'.[22] At Potsdam, while British and American policies often had the same objectives, there were still important differences of emphasis. On Eastern Europe, however, Truman gave Churchill the impression over lunch on 18 July that he agreed that matters had to be settled as a whole, and that he intended 'to press with severity the need of their true independence in accordance with free, full and unfettered elections'.[23] Stalin refused supervised elections, and the proposals for political freedom were, in effect, worthless. After the news of the successful explosion of the atomic bomb, Churchill, presumably with some relief, noted on 23 July that 'the United States do not at the present time desire Russian participation in the war against Japan'.[24] Churchill was anxious that the Russians should not acquire so much German territory. The Americans did not appear so concerned. Britain was worried about the political dimension of some of the economic proposals for the management of Germany. Sir David Waley of the Treasury pointed out to Byrnes: 'if a line is drawn across the middle of Europe so that there is a frontier with Russia on one side and the Western Powers on the other side, this has an importance far transcending reparations'.[25] The Americans, though ready to resist Russian pressure in Iran and Turkey, were less concerned about Russian claims to be a trustee of an Italian colony in North Africa, a prospect which alarmed Churchill as it seemed to threaten British interests in the Mediterranean. In any case Churchill felt that it was too late: 'the time to settle frontiers has gone. The Red Army is spreading over Europe. It will remain.'[26]

Churchill, together with Attlee, returned to London for the result of the general election. By early afternoon on 26 July it was evident that the Labour Party had won a landslide victory.

15

Churchill went to Buckingham Palace around seven o'clock that evening and advised King George VI to ask Attlee to form a new government. In the House of Commons, Labour held 393 seats, as against just under 220 by the Conservatives and their allies. Foreign policy was hardly an issue in the election campaign. Conservatives, however, had suggested that Churchill's knowledge of it made him indispensable. But Churchill had invited Attlee, his close colleague in the wartime coalition government, to accompany him to Potsdam: Churchill explained that he and Attlee 'thought alike' on foreign affairs, and it would show that the two British leaders stood together on some of the main aspects of foreign policy.[27]

Attlee at 62 was virtually an Establishment figure. A public school Oxbridge product, he represented intellectual rather than working-class socialism. His attitude towards Russia was that of a traditional conservative: he regarded Russia as 'a great continental power with an immense heritage in Asia to be developed, but with ambitions in Europe which are essentially imperialist, whether ideological or territorial whether derived from Lenin or Peter the Great'.[28] It was thought by some that Hugh Dalton would be Attlee's obvious choice for Foreign Secretary. Attlee's own drafts for his government, however, do not list Dalton as a possibility. The first plan assigned Hector McNeil to this post, but a revised version replaced him with Ernest Bevin.[29] The strained relationship between Bevin and Herbert Morrison meant that the two men had to be kept apart. King George VI is supposed to have told Attlee on 26 July that he hoped that Bevin would take over responsibility for foreign affairs.[30] Dalton recorded the next day, however, that before lunch Attlee told him that he would almost certainly be wanted at the Foreign Office, and advised him to prepare to leave for Potsdam. But shortly after four that afternoon Attlee called Dalton to Great George Street and said that he had reconsidered the matter: it had better be the Exchequer; Morrison and Bevin had to be kept apart and the latter would go to the Foreign Office.[31] Bevin did not know until a quarter to five that he was to be Foreign Secretary. Until that time he had expected to be Chancellor of the Exchequer. He did not object, however, at the age of 64 to taking over the Foreign Office.[32]

Unlike Attlee, Bevin was a self-made man who had risen from the working classes, through the trade unions to the hierarchy of the Labour Party.[33] Bevin never tried to pretend that he was anything else. When Foreign Secretary he continued to drop his

16

'h's' and refused to assume Establishment mannerisms. He had a temper which he did not always moderate, and a blunt turn of phrase: his was not always the language of diplomacy. Bevin's health was not good: he sometimes showed obvious signs of exhaustion.[34] In negotiations he was often long-winded, and some thought him rather vain.[35] But, as his private secretary, Frank Roberts, has observed, 'he brought to diplomacy a robust and practical commonsense, not always found in Foreign Ministers or professional dipomats'.[36] Attlee entrusted foreign affairs to Bevin. In April 1944 Bevin had said that he could never accept the notion that Britain could use Germany against Russia. As Foreign Secretary Bevin changed his mind, and showed himself to be well suited by temperament for dealings with 'unco-operative' Russian leaders. Through the offices of Pierson Dixon, Bevin consulted with Eden on the problems of foreign policy, ensuring its continuity. If it had been hoped that left would be more easily able to speak with left in other countries, that expectation faded rapidly. Though it pursued ideals of socialism at home, the British Labour government did not extend these to foreign policy. Indeed Bevin was little influenced by left-wing criticism from within his own party, though he did publicly denounce as a 'stab in the back' the backbench revolt in the House of Commons of November 1946: a foreign affairs amendment to the address called for 'a socialist alternative' to the Super-powers.[37]

Given his background it was widely expected that Bevin would make changes in the Foreign Office, and it was alleged that senior officers like Sir Alexander Cadogan and Sir Orme Sargent expected to be replaced. But Bevin made no such alterations. Even Lord Halifax, the former Conservative Foreign Secretary, remained as ambassador in Washington well into 1946. Possibly Bevin, when he assumed office, did not know the personnel of the Foreign Service well enough to make the changes, even had he wanted to do so. In a short space of time it was evident that Bevin 'became more devoted than any of his predecessors for a generation to the Career Diplomat and all the Old Boys in the F.O., so that "now all the old nags are going back to the old stables"'.[38]

The term 'Superpower' was gaining currency in 1945, and then it was applied to Britain as well as to the United States and Russia. Bevin assumed office at a time when Britain's position at the conference tables of world diplomacy obscured the reality of Britain's diminished power. As Churchill told Stalin at Potsdam

17

on 22 July 1945, Britain 'came out of this war as the greatest debtor in the world'.[39] Britain was, in effect, bankrupt. But at the same time it had worldwide commitments. To continue fighting the Second World War Britain had had to sell almost everything it had, including £1,118 million of foreign assets. Even when fighting it seemed that Britain did not have sufficient manpower and economic resources for a world role. As late as March 1945 British cities were still being hit by Nazi bombs. The Germans destroyed or damaged over 4 million houses in Britain. Perhaps rationing of the armed forces' diet ensured that the British people enjoyed better health than in the prewar years, but the government White Paper of November 1944 pointed to a drop in butter consumption from 1939 of almost two-thirds, while meat consumption fell by one quarter, and significantly lower levels of fruit, tea, eggs and sugar were being eaten. Shortly after the German surrender in April 1945 there was a further reduction in the food allowance: it looked as if peace promised no relief. Rebuilding a scarred Britain, and improving living standards, was only part of the problem faced by the postwar administration. With victory came new responsibilities. British forces occupied parts of Europe and the Far East: Britain had to see that peoples in these areas did not die of starvation even if this meant greater austerity at home.[40] Britain no longer had significant dividends from foreign assets to pay for imported food and raw materials. Indeed to fight the Second World War Britain had accumulated debts around the world totalling £2,723 million. Repayment seemed impossible at a time when there was no money to buy from abroad raw materials needed to revive the British economy. At the end of the Second World War it was estimated that exports would have to be increased between 50 and 75 per cent just to finance the prewar scale of imports. It was thought that that would take between three and five years.[41] As well as its responsibility to the 49 million Britons at home, the new Labour government also had commitments to many more millions abroad either in the Empire-Commonwealth or in occupied territories. In August 1945 Britain sat at diplomatic tables as an imperial and world power. But, as Orme Sargent observed in October of that year, Britain's position in relation to Russia and the United States was 'Lepidus in the triumvirate with Mark Antony and Augustus'.[42]

It was the United States that emerged from the Second World War in a powerful economic position. Britain and the United States had pooled their economies during the war. Initially Lend

Lease enabled Britain to continue the fight against the dictators. This developed into Mutual Aid and the Combined Boards with the intention of merging the production programmes of Britain and the United States into 'a single integrated programme, adjusted to the strategic requirements of the war'.[43] Some British officials anticipated that the arrangement could continue after the war to enable Britain to rebuild its economy. Washington hoped for multilateral trade in the postwar world: this meant a relatively smaller British share of trade than before 1939, though one which would be larger in absolute terms. An alternative, favoured by some British experts, was a sterling area extended to include not only the Dominions, but possibly Africa, the Middle East and Western Europe. This bloc would be self-sufficient and protect British firms at a time when Britain could no longer compete as a low-cost manufacturer because of the lack of technical innovations and the work force's demand for a higher standard of living.[44] These ideas alarmed Washington. But in the end, if Britain was to sustain the illusion of being a world power, it could only do so with American economic backing. London also had to ensure that it did not just become Washington's appendage. Financial independence was thought to be an essential basis for an individual foreign policy. Only the United States could provide Britain with this. That overriding economic reality confronted the new Labour government.

Britain could only maintain the illusion of being a world power with American money: a vast loan was needed to sustain Britain's economic viability. The war in the Far East ended with the dropping of the second atomic bomb on Nagasaki, and almost immediately, on 17 August 1945, Truman – as he later claimed, without reading it – approved a memorandum ending Lend Lease to Britain. The new Chancellor of the Exchequer, Hugh Dalton, observed later that Britain was faced with 'total economic ruin'. Lord Keynes, in his negotiations, tried to convince the Americans that London could participate in Washington's scheme of multilateral trade only if financial arrangements were made to enable Britain to survive the following three to five years. Bevin insisted that Britain had to achieve financial independence. Indeed, initially Keynes expected an outright gift from the Americans, based on the assumption of the greater British sacrifice during the war. But Keynes soon discovered that there was a gulf separating Washington from London. The American administration and its 'immeasurably remote public opinion' were not interested in British 'wounds, though incurred in the common cause', but in British 'convalescence'. In the end, in December 1945, London accepted a $3·75 billion loan at 2 per cent interest. At the same time British debts under Lend Lease were effectively written off. Given the state of public and congressional opinion in the United States the terms were generous: no other nation was treated in such a favourable way. But Parliament and the British public viewed the agreement in a sour mood. When the loan went to Congress the American administration endorsed the British cause at a time when Washington was beginning to stand against Moscow. Many Americans thought that London could use the money to sustain the British Empire, or implement the socialist programme of nationalization, or fight the Zionists in Palestine, all of which they disapproved. Increasing Russian intransigence, however, helped the administration's case, and Truman was finally able to sign the agreement on 15 July 1946. The freezing winter of 1946–7 in Britain brought that country more effectively to a standstill than had the Nazi bombs, and waiver clauses over the interest payments of the loan had to be operated. London effectively broke the agreement by suspending the convertibility of the pound sterling. Britain did not have the money to sustain its worldwide obligations: Britain's deficit in 1946 could be attributed to military payments. Increasingly, however, in American eyes, British weakness was a threat to American security: an economically strong Britain was seen as politically necessary for the United States. With this prevailing mood, Britain managed to preserve a system of imperial preference and the sterling area. Despite Marshall Aid, however, London was forced to devalue the pound sterling against the dollar in 1949. The Labour governments of 1945 – 51 implemented their Cold War foreign policy against a background of continuing economic crises. They were able to do this only with American backing.[45]

Against the background of the overriding need to rebuild Britain economically, Attlee's government faced a new strategic situation. Jet engines, rockets, guided missiles and the atomic bomb practically eliminated the sea as a significant defence. If Russia was the most likely enemy, the British navy would be of limited use against a land-locked power. This meant that, despite the financial straits, the army would have to be maintained. In addition Britain had the victor's obligations to occupy Japan, Germany, Austria, Venezia Giulia and Greece. Troops were also needed to keep order against terrorism in Palestine. The Labour governments retained conscription in peacetime. This was seen as necessary. By December 1946 Britain needed 400,000 more troops than had been anticipated; the

British military establishment totalled almost 1,500,000. During the fiscal year of 1946, 18·7 per cent of men were in military service; in comparison only 10 per cent of American men were under arms. That year Britain's defence expenditure accounted for 18·8 per cent of the national income; in the United States it was only 10·6 per cent. Attlee was even forced to slow down demobilization.[46]

In August 1945 Britain, if it was to remain a significant force in the world, was faced, in effect, with three options: it could try to lead a united Europe as a force in world politics; it could develop the Commonwealth as an alternative power bloc, a course often favoured by the Labour left; or it could revive the wartime Anglo-American alliance to stand against Russia. These alternatives were not mutually exclusive, and Churchill spoke of them as being interlocking.[47]

The European option was not acceptable: indeed until 1948 the Middle East rather than Europe was considered to be Britain's first line of defence. During the Second World War, Attlee had had hopes of the Commonwealth. But it was evident at the conference of Commonwealth leaders in London held during April and May 1946 that although there might be agreement as to the nature of the Russian threat, the Dominions were reluctant to compromise their independence in any way. The 1948 Commonwealth Conference evidenced a similar hesitation. It was only really in 1949, following the election of the anti-communist Afrikaner Nationalist government in South Africa, and with the joining of the Cold War in Asia, that Britain was able to enter into bilateral defence discussions with the old 'white' Dominions. Until then Bevin chose to stress the Anglo-American special relationship. As the Cold War was joined in Europe he manoeuvred the United States, Canada, and the West European powers into a defence system with which to face the threat of Russia. As the Cold War spread to the Middle East, Asia and the African continent, Bevin broadened the emphasis on the Anglo-American special relationship to embrace, possibly in a looser form, and through bilateral discussions, the old 'white' Dominions. In the end his vision of Britain's position in the world was not very different from that of Neville Chamberlain's Cabinet in 1938. To meet the threat of the the Cold War the Labour governments opted for the English-speaking alliance.

Notes: Chapter 1

1 R. Ovendale, *'Appeasement' and the English Speaking World. Britain, the United States, the Dominions and the Policy of 'Appeasement', 1937–1939* (Cardiff, 1975); 'Britain, the Dominions and the coming of the Second World War, 1933–9', in W. J. Mommsen and L. Kettenacker (eds), *The Fascist Challenge and the Policy of Appeasement* (London,1983), pp. 323–8.

2 Public Record Office, London, FO 800/452, fol. 34, Def/48/5A, COS(48) 16th Mtg. Confidential Annex, 2 February 1948.

3 E. Barker, *The British between the Superpowers, 1945-50* (London, 1983), p. 4.

4 J. Wheeler-Bennett and A. Nicholls, *The Semblance of Peace* (London, 1972), p. 290; J. M. Burns,*Roosevelt: The Soldier of Freedom 1940–1945* (London, 1971), pp. 103, 596. A critique of Burns is offered by Robert Dallek: see R. Dallek, 'Franklin D. Roosevelt as world leader', *American Historical Review*, vol. 76 (1971), pp. 1503-13; *Franklin D. Roosevelt and American Foreign Policy 1932--1945* (New York, 1979); see also J. Bishop, *FDR's Last Year, April 1944–April 1945* (London 1974). Terry H. Anderson argues that during his last few days Roosevelt was being moved towards taking a tougher stand against the Russians. See T. H. Anderson, *The United States, Great Britain, and the Cold War 1944-1947* (Columbia, Miss., 1981), pp. 49–51.

5 S. Wells, *The Time for Decision* (London, 1944) pp. 61–117; W. H. McNeill, *America,Britain and Russia. Their Co-operation and Conflict 1941–1946* (London, 1953), pp. 164–5; W. R. Louis, *Imperialism at Bay: The United States and the Decolonization of the British Empire, 1941–1945* (London, 1978); C. J. Bartlett, 'Inter-allied relations in the Second World War', *History*, vol. 63 (1978), pp. 390–5.

6 *Foreign Relations of the United States, 1943–51* (Washington, DC, 1961–83) (hereafter cited as FRUS), *The Conference at Cairo and Tehran* (Washington, DC 1961); C. M. W. Moran, *Winston Churchill. The Struggle for Survival, 1940–1965* (London, 1966), p. 132, 25 November 1943; p. 140, 29 November 1943; p. 144, December 1953; Wheeler-Bennett and Nicholls, *The Semblance of Peace*, pp. 142–67; McNeill, *America, Britain and Russia*, pp. 348–68; L. Woodward, *British Foreign Policy in the Second World War*, Vol. 3 (London 1971), p. 104; V. Mastny, 'Soviet war aims at the Moscow and Teheran Conference of 1943', *Journal of Modern History* vol.47 (1975), pp. 481-504; Frank Spencer, 'The United States and Germany in the aftermath of war, II: The Second World War', *International Affairs*, vol. 44 (1958), pp. 48–62; V. H. Rothwell, *Britain and the Cold War, 1941–1947* (London, 1982), pp. 107–23.

7 McNeill, *America, Britain and Russia*, pp. 402–11; E. Barker, *Churchill and Eden at War* (London, 1978); G. Warner, 'From Teheran to Yalta: reflections on F. D. R.'s foreign policy', *International Affairs*, vol. 43 (1967), pp. 530–6; G. Ross (ed.), *The Foreign Office and the Kremlin. British Documents on Anglo-Soviet Relations 1941–45* (Cambridge, 1984), pp. 41–51.

8 A. Eden, *The Reckoning* (London, 1964), pp. 460–7; T. Higgins, *Soft Underbelly: The Anglo-American Controversy over the Italian Campaign, 1939–1945* (New York, 1968); L. Morton, 'World War II: a survey of recent writings'. *American Historical Review*, vol. 75 (1970), pp. 1987-2008 at p. 1997; Public Record Office, London, FO 381/43335, Foreign Office paper on postwar Soviet policy, 29 April 1944, printed in part in Ross (ed.), *The Foreign Office and the Kremlin*, pp. 147–55.

9 Public Record Office, London, CAB 65/45, fol. 21, WM(44)11, Most Secret, 25 January 1944; 46, fol. 41, WM(44)63, Top Secret, 11 May 1944; E. Barker, *British Policy in South–East Europe in the Second World War* (London,1976); A. Resis, 'The Churchill–Stalin secret "percentages" agreement on the Balkans,

Moscow, October 1944', *American Historical Review*, vol. 83 (1978), pp. 368–87; J. M. Siracusa, 'The meaning of Tolstoy: Churchill, Stalin, and the Balkans, Moscow, October 1944', *Diplomatic History*, vol. 3 (1979), pp. 443–63; Rothwell, *Britain and the Cold War*, pp. 128–36.

10 CAB 65/48, fos 86–7, WM(44) 169, Top Secret, 16 December 1944; 51, fol. 4, WM(45)1, Top Secret, 2 January 1945; Woodward *British Foreign Policy*, Vol. 3, pp. 154–252; G. V. Kacewicz, *Great Britain, the Soviet Union and the Polish Government in Exile (1939–1945)* (The Hague, 1979); R. C. Lukas, *The Strange Allies: The United States and Poland, 1941–1945* (Knoxville, Tenn., 1978).

11 CAB 65/47, fol. 31, WM(44)103, Top Secret, 9 August 1944, H. Macmillan, *The Blast of War 1939–1945* (London, 1967) pp. 604–13; CAB 65/48, fol. 105, WM(44)175, Top Secret, 29 December 1944; Woodward, *British Foreign Policy*, Vol. 3, pp. 383–453, 460–1; C. M. Woodhouse *The Struggle for Greece 1941–1949* (London, 1976); L. S. Wittner, 'American policy towards Greece during World War II', *Diplomatic History*, vol. 3 (1979), pp. 129–50; J. O. Iatrides, *Revolt in Athens: the Greek Communist 'Second Round', 1944–1945* (Princeton, NJ, 1972); L. S. Wittner, *American Intervention in Greece, 1943–1949* (New York, 1982), pp. 1–35.

12 FRUS, *The Conferences at Malta and Yalta* (Washington, DC, 1955); Moran, *Winston Churchill*, p. 232, 11 February 1945; p. 237, 13 February 1945; CAB 65/51, fos 78–9, WM(45)22, Top Secret, 19 February 1945; A. Theoharis, 'Roosevelt and Truman on Yalta: the origins of the Cold War', *Political Science Quarterly* vol. 87 (1972), pp. 210–41: K. Sainsbury, 'British policy and Germany unity at the end of the Second World War', *English Historical Review*, vol. 94 (1979), pp. 786–804; Louis, *Imperialism at Bay*, pp. 448–60; R. M. Hathaway, *Ambiguous Partnership. Britain and America 1944–1947* (New York, 1981), pp. 112–31.

13 D. C. Watt, *Succeeding John Bull. America in Britain's Place 1900–1975* (Cambridge, 1984), pp. 194–219; C. Thorne, 'Indo-China and Anglo-American relations, 1941–1945', *Pacific Historical Review*, vol. 45 (1976), pp. 73–96; D. Halberstam, *The Best and the Brightest* (London, 1974), pp. 102–3; W. La Febre, 'Roosevelt, Churchill and Indochina: 1942–45', *American Historical Review*, vol. 80 (1975), pp. 1277–94; E. R. Drachman, *United States Policy towards Vietnam 1945–1965* (Cranbury, NJ, 1970); G. Warner, 'The United States and Vietnam 1945–1965, I: 1945–54', *International Affairs*, vol. 48 (1972), pp. 379–94.

14 George C. Marshall Library, Lexington, Va, Joint Chiefs of Staff White House Records of Fleet Admiral William D. Leahy 1942–1949, Folder 88, Research and Analysis Branch of OSS: Problems and Objectives of United States policy, 2 April 1945.

15 Woodward, *British Foreign Policy*, Vol. 3, pp. 515–16; Peter G. Boyle, 'The British Foreign Office view of Soviet-American relations, 1945–46', *Diplomatic History*, vol. 3 (1979), pp. 307–20; CAB 65/51, fol. 82, WM(45)23, Top Secret, 21 February 1945; fol. 93, WM(45)26, Top Secret, 6 March 1945; Barker, *The British between the Superpowers*, pp. 6–11; Ross (ed), *The Foreign Office and the Kremlin*, pp. 147–99.

16 Public Record Office, London, FO 371/47881, Minute by Sargent, 2 April 1945, printed in part in Ross (ed.), *The Foreign Office and the Kremlin*, pp. 199–204.

17 CAB 65/52, fol. 3, WM(45)39, Top Secret, 3 April 1945.

18 S. E. Ambrose, *Eisenhower and Berlin, 1945: The Decision to Halt at the Elbe* (New York, 1967); W. Ullmann, *The United States in Prague, 1945–1948* (New York, 1978); Woodward, *British Foreign Policy*, Vol. 3, pp. 490–578.

19 G. C. Herring, Jr, *Aid to Russia 1941–46* (New York, 1973); H. S. Truman, *Years of Trial and Hope* (London 1956), p. 108; R. N. Gardner, *Sterling-Dollar Diplomacy* (London, 1969).

20 D. Yergin, *Shattered Peace* (Boston, Mass., 1977), pp. 79–86; Wheeler-Bennett and Nicholls, *The Semblance of Peace*, pp. 311–14, 547–51; J. Tillapaugh, 'Closed hemisphere and open world? The dispute over regional security at the U.N.

Conference, 1945', *Diplomatic History*, vol. 2 (1978), pp. 25–42; W. D. Miscamble, 'Anthony Eden and the Truman–Molotov conversations, April 1945', *Diplomatic History*, vol. 2 (1978), pp. 167–80; Rothwell, *Britain and the Cold War*, pp. 140–4.

21 F. Williams, *A Prime Minister Remembers: The War and Post-War Memoirs of the Rt. Hon. Earl Attlee* (London, 1961), p. 5; CAB 65/54, fos 23–5, CM(45) 10, Top Secret, 20 June 1945; K. O. Morgan, *Labour in Power 1945–1951* (Oxford, 1984), pp. 37–9.

22 *Documents on British Policy Overseas*, Series 1, Vol. 1 (hereafter cited as *DBPO*) (London, 1984), pp. 212–14, Eden to Churchill, 12 July 1945; pp. 284–8, Record of a preliminary meeting with the United States delegation held in Berlin on 14 July 1945, 15 July 1945.

23 *DBPO*, pp. 367–71, Note of conversation between Truman and Churchill, 18 July 1945.

24 ibid., p. 573, Churchill to Eden, 23 July 1945.

25 ibid., pp. 1049–51, Waley to Sir W. Eady, 31 July 1945.

26 *FRUS, The Conference of Berlin (Potsdam)* (Washington, DC, 1960); E. Mark, '"Today has been a historical one": Harry S. Truman's diary of the Potsdam Conference', *Diplomatic History*, vol.4 (1980), pp. 307–26; T. D. Burridge, *British Labour and Hitler's War* (London,1976); C. L. Mee, Jr, *Meeting at Potsdam* (London, 1975); Moran, *Winston Churchill*, p. 282, 23 July 1945; p. 279, 22 July 1945; p. 284, 24 July 1945.

27 A. J. P. Taylor, *English History 1914–1945* (Oxford, 1965), pp. 594–600; F. S. Northedge and A. Wells, *Britain and Soviet Communism: The Impact of a Revolution* (London, 1982), pp. 103–4; K. Harris, *Attlee* (London, 1982), pp. 255–62.

28 Churchill College, Cambridge, Attlee Papers, 1/17, Labour in Power; Rothwell, *Britain and the Cold War*, p. 226.

29 Bodleian, Oxford, Attlee Papers, 2, Plans for New Government 1945; List A; Next Draft.

30 J. Wheeler–Bennett, *King George VI, his Life and Reign* (London, 1958), p. 636, diary, 26 July 1945

31 British Library of Economic and Political Science, London, Dalton Diaries, 33, fol. 4, 27 July 1945.

32 British Library, London, Oliver Harvey Diaries, 8, 28 July 1945.

33 A. Bullock, *The Life and Times of Ernest Bevin*, 3 vols (London, 1960-83); F. Williams, *Ernest Bevin, Portrait of a Great Englishman* (London, 1952).

34 Dalton Diaries, 35, fol.2, 17 January 1947; fos 16–18, 24 February 1947.

35 Princeton University Library, Forrestal Diaries, Box 4, 7, fol. 160, 28 April 1947.

36 F. K. Roberts, 'Ernest Bevin as Foreign Secretary', in R. Ovendale (ed.),*The Foreign Policy of the British Labour Governments, 1945–1951* (Leicester, 1984), p. 25.

37 Rothwell, *Britain and the Cold War*, pp. 222–35; P. Dixon, *Double Diploma: The Life of Sir Pierson Dixon, Don and Diplomat* (London, 1968), pp. 179, 198–9; Morgan, *Labour in Power*, pp. 62–9; A. Bullock, *Ernest Bevin. Foreign Secretary 1945–1951* (London, 1983), pp. 394–9.

38 Dalton Diaries, 34, 25 February1946.

39 *DBPO*, pp. 530–47 at p. 540, Record of Sixth Plenary Meeting, 22 July 1945.

40 Northedge and Wells, *Britain and Soviet Communism*, p. 105; Rothwell, *Britain and the Cold War*, p. 3; Hathaway, *Ambiguous Partnership*, pp. 23–4.

41 British Parliamentary Papers, Cmd 6707, *Statistical Material Presented during the Washington Negotiations* (London, 1945).

42 Quoted by Anderson, *The United States, Great Britain and the Cold War*, p. 84.

43 H. G. Nicholas, *Britain and the United States* (London, 1963), p. 33.

44 Hathaway, *Ambiguous Partnership*, pp. 28–9.

45 G. C. Herring, 'The United States and British Bankruptcy, 1944–1945; responsibilities deferred', *Political Science Quarterly*, vol. 86 (1971), pp. 260–80; Truman, *Years of Trial and Hope*, p. 108; H. Dalton, *High Tide and After: Memoirs, 1945–1960* (London, 1962), p. 68; United Kingdom Parliamentary Debates, House of Lords, 138, cols 777–8, 18 December 1945; Gardner, *Sterling–Dollar*

Diplomacy, pp. 259–385; Hathaway, *Ambiguous Partnership*, pp. 182–201; Anderson, *The United States, Great Britain and the Cold War*, pp. 130–2; H.L. Roberts and P. A. Wilson (eds), *Britain and the United States. Problems in Co-operation* (London, 1953), pp. 62–86; R. Clarke, *Anglo-American Economic Collaboration in War and Peace 1942–1949*, (ed.) A. Cairncross (Oxford, 1982).

46 Hathaway, *Ambiguous Partnership*, pp. 36–7, 297; Anderson, *The United States, Great Britain and the Cold War*, p. 157.

47 R. Ovendale, 'Britain, the U.S.A. and the European Cold War, 1945–8', *History*, vol, 67 (1982), pp. 217–36 at p. 231.

PART TWO

The Cold War in Europe

2

Bevin and the Russians

On 28 July Attlee and Bevin flew to Berlin. The big three still had to decide on reparations and the western frontier of Poland. British policy did not change. On Poland Britain wanted to stand on the eastern Neisse, but 'the Americans rather suddenly gave way'. The boundary had to be the western Neisse. Britain also had to concede higher reparations deliveries from Germany than it wanted. Attlee was not dissatisfied with the overall result. Indeed, the new British Prime Minister thought Truman 'very co-operative', though he found that the President showed a certain lack of interest in the later stages of the conference. Bevin, however, 'picked up all the points extremely quickly and showed his quality as an experienced negotiator in playing his hand'.[1] At the meetings Bevin, it seems, effaced Attlee, and did all the talking while the Prime Minister convulsively nodded his head and smoked his pipe. In the Foreign Office, Alexander Cadogan was convinced that Bevin was 'very wise and sound'.[2]

From the beginning Bevin was determined to maintain an independent British policy. He wrote to Attlee on 6 September that he had 'long held the view that for defence purposes the British Empire ought to be divided into zones and the main policing responsibilities should be undertaken by the different constituents integrated with the Imperial forces'.[3] The Foreign Secretary insisted that Britain had to 'stand up for herself': the world should realize that despite the terrible price Britain had paid in the war, it was not 'down and out'; Britain would survive. Despite its economic dependence on the United States, Britain had to surmount the tremendous pressure 'to alter our way of life and economy to meet the desires of the worst elements of American capitalism'. The Americans had to be convinced that Britain, in proportion to its population, had made the supreme effort in the war, and was ready to co-operate to the fullest possible extent in the peace. If this were

29

done the policy of the two countries could 'be harmonised and brought on the right lines'.[4] In reality British independence was only possible with American support, and for the second half of 1945 the United States did not always seem a reliable ally. Britain, however, refused to act as a suppliant. Attlee complained frankly to Truman about the three biggest British ships, the Queens and the *Aquitania*, being in the American service when British troops were awaiting repatriation. Truman immediately instructed the Joint Chiefs of Staff to provide Britain with the requisite personnel lift.[5] Churchill endorsed this sort of approach. On the issue of the joint occupation of bases by the United States and the countries of the British Commonwealth, he advised Bevin that this would strengthen both the power of the United States and the safety of Britain. And although the United States was far more powerful than the British Commonwealth, 'we must insist upon coming in on equal terms'.[6]

From the British angle it was policy towards Russia in particular that needed to be harmonized with the Americans. On 15 August Bevin sent his fraternal greetings to Molotov: the two men would have to collaborate to make conditions in the world worthy of the sacrifice of the magnificent people who had supported them.[7] Only five days later Bevin told the House of Commons that the governments of Bulgaria, Romania and Hungary did not represent the majority of their people; one kind of totalitarianism was replacing another. On 27 August he bluntly warned the new Polish ambassador that the assurances he had been given at Potsdam that had led him to acquiesce in the extension of the Polish zone to the western Neisse were not being honoured: it was unfortunate that inquiries about free elections, the press, arrests and the treatment of the German population were regarded as 'foreign interference'.[8] From Moscow the ambassador, Sir Archibald Clark Kerr, suggested that, for the moment, Russia was enjoying 'the good humour of repletion': it had achieved the security it had been striving for in Europe. The danger–spots in Anglo–Soviet relations, however, remained in the Middle East: Russia had not renounced its claims upon Turkey and the Straits, and was 'embarrassingly active' in Persia.[9] Molotov's demands at the first meeting of the Council of Foreign Ministers (set up at Potsdam) in September at Lancaster House suggested that the Russians also wanted a base in the Mediterranean: a 'corner' of Tripolitania would do, and Britain could have Cyrenaica. Bevin refused to allow a new military power into an area that was a lifeline of the British Empire. As Pierson Dixon recorded, the Russians knew that Britain was dependent on the United States, that the Americans had a phobia about the British Empire, and calculated that Britain could not depend fully on American support when defending its imperial interests. Bevin was prepared to be accommodating over issues such as the recognition of Bulgaria and Romania, but two private meetings with the Russian statesman showed that Molotov would not deal. From the embassy in Moscow, Frank Roberts suggested that Britain should try to reach agreement with the Russians on their respective interests in Europe. Such bilateral conversations were ruled out: they would be bad tactics at a time when Molotov's behaviour had aligned the other four powers in opposition to Russian aims.[10]

At the end of October Roberts reported from Moscow that Russian suspicions of the West had revived since the end of the war. The vigorous Anglo-American policy in eastern Europe, followed by unilateral American action in the Far East with the ending of hostilities against Japan, and the 'apparent Anglo-Saxon preference for wide international co-operation instead of the Big Three procedure favoured by the Russians' were largely responsible. He did not think that the atomic bomb had influenced the prevailing international problems, but advised that the Anglo-American attitude towards giving Russians the 'Know-How' would be a factor in determining general Russian policy.[11] Truman was also preoccupied by this thought. He told the British ambassador, Lord Halifax, that he was conscious of all the arguments in favour of trying to get some explicit arrangement with the Russians: it seemed impossible that the scientific secrets could be kept for more than a very short time. The President wondered whether it would be possible to distinguish between passing on scientific knowledge – which the Russians would probably soon acquire anyway – and 'industrial know how'.[12] At that time the British suspected that the Americans were excluding them from information on research and development. Initially the development of the atomic bomb had been regarded as an equal partnership, and Roosevelt and Churchill had agreed at Quebec in 1943 that the collaboration should continue after the end of the war. This was reaffirmed in 1944. Prompted by the Chiefs of Staff, Attlee raised the issue with Truman on 17 August, 1945, urging that means should be sought to enable the frank collaboration and exchange of information to be continued. Attlee hoped that they could both issue directives authorizing this, and instructing their representatives to get together to work out methods for the solution of commercial difficulties.[13]

On 11 October Bevin told the relevant British committee,

General 75, that there was everything to be gained from letting Russia into the secret of the bomb. A week later he had changed his mind. The Foreign Secretary had the same view as Roberts: recent difficulties with Russia could not be attributed to the bomb. Attlee told the Cabinet on 5 November that the best solution would be to build an effective organization before the Russsians could make their own bomb. Later in the month he discussed the matter with Truman and William L. Mackenzie King, the Canadian Prime Minister, in Washington. Truman agreed that 'full and effective' co-operation should be continued along the lines of Roosevelt's promise to Churchill at Hyde Park in September 1944, and instructed that his Cabinet policy committee should recommend arrangements. A draft agreement was drawn by a sub-committee to the Combined Policy Committee which provided for full and effective co-operation in the exchange of information required for the development programmes of the two countries. The British programme would include the construction of large-scale plants in that country. When the Combined Policy Committee met, however, the Americans made it clear that they would not enter into any agreement. Attlee rejected Truman's argument that such a move would be inconsistent with the public declaration made by both leaders and Mackenzie King in November 1945 about the international control of atomic energy. Bevin and the Chiefs of Staff discounted Truman's case that a plant in Britain would be vulnerable, presumably either from enemy attack or sabotage. But the Foreign Secretary was prepared to consider the erection of the plant elsewhere, if not in Canada possibly in Africa taking advantage of the water power of the Victoria Falls, or possibly in Australia. At the beginning of May 1946 Bevin told Attlee that he held 'the view strongly that our main atomic energy development ought to be placed at the Victoria Falls'. As a location it was protected. Such a move would also enable Britain 'to assure the safety of Pacific and Indian Oceans'. Attlee agreed.[14] The American administration, however, lent its support to the McMahon Bill in Congress which proposed restrictions on the disclosure and exchange of information on atomic energy. The Bill became law on 1 August 1946. Britain felt that this Bill went back on the undertakings that had been given. It went ahead and developed its own bomb at immense cost, and this was a decision taken and implemented by a socialist administration which feared Russia. Even with the formation of the North Atlantic Treaty Organization (NATO) the United States did not relent. It was not until attempts to reconsolidate the Anglo-American relationship in the aftermath of the Suez crisis of 1956 that the McMahon Act was repealed. For Britain, the American refusal to share the military and industrial secrets of atomic energy, to the development of which Britain had significantly contributed, was the major shortcoming of the Anglo-American relationship during the years of the emergence of the Cold War.[15]

When the Foreign Ministers of the big three met again in Moscow in December 1945, Russia seemed to be on the advance. Communist support in Eastern Europe at this time, however, was weak; in the election in Hungary in November 1945 the communist vote was 17 per cent against 57 per cent for the Small Farmers' Party; in Poland Mikolajczyk's Peasant Party was thought to have similar support. Roberts reported that the Russian authorities probably realized that the local reactions to the presence of the Red Army in Eastern Europe was doing that country harm even in friendly countries, but the Russians were strangely impervious to psychological considerations of that kind and would not risk losing their firm grip on a country on that account. The Russians might even feel that 'since they are unlikely to inspire affection, salutary respect is a good substitute'.[16] Despite rhetoric, it appears that Britain and the United States accepted Russia's apparent need for a rim of friendly states on its borders. In a memorandum of 18 October Charles E. Bohlen, who was special assistant to Byrnes, drew obvious parallels with the Monroe doctrine. He observed that while the United States had not tried to deny Russia 'the legitimate prerogatives of a great power in relation to smaller countries resulting from geographic proximity', it seemed that Stalin was seeking 'complete Soviet domination and control over all phases of the external and internal life' of neighbouring states. The Russians had to be made to understand the difference between domination and 'legitimate influence' confined to the 'politico-strategic aspect' of foreign relations. While the United States would 'oppose and even forbid the conclusion of military and political alliances between a Latin American state and a European or Asiatic power', it did not on the basis of that 'right' attempt 'to dictate their internal life or to restrict their intercourse with foreign nations except in that limited sphere'. Britain and the United States could not challenge Russia's position in Eastern Europe: they wanted some influence to try to secure a democratic framework. Russian occupation forces enabled the communists to prevail in all these areas, except for Czechoslovakia, and by the end of 1946 the resistance of independent political forces was broken.[17] On 19 November 1945 the Turkish ambassador warned Bevin that the

Russian 'war of nerves' over Turkey was aimed at forcing Turkey out of the British and into the Soviet orbit: it was Russian policy to exert constant pressure on Turkey through the backdoor of Iran and in the provinces of Kars and Ardahan; Russia also encouraged Kurdish opposition to the Turkish government; it was not just a question of the Straits.[18] In Iran Britain and Russia had been eyeing one another suspiciously since the Anglo-Russian-Iranian agreement of 1942. This agreement established a Russian zone in the north, a British zone in the south and joint occupation of Tehran. Logistic difficulties in the British zone led to the United States undertaking certain transport arrangements. But these were not American occupation troops. On 28 August 1945 the United States announced that its troops would be withdrawn from Iran by 1 November 1945. At this time, Russia was separating the northern provinces from the rest of the country and appeared to have ambitions in the area. The original treaty had provided for the evacuation of British and Russian troops within six months of the end of the war. Bevin feared that this unilateral American withdrawal left Britain in a weak position for his proposal to the Russians that occupation forces should be withdrawn by mid-December except for British troops in the southern oilfields and Russian troops in Azerbaijan which might remain until 2 March 1946. In November autonomists in this region of Iran with the support of the Russian army staged an open revolt. In reacting to this the United States would not co-operate with Britain. It ordered the evacuation of American troops, and Byrnes urged Britain and Russia to do likewise. Britain favoured rapid evacuation as well, but not at the risk of the Russians overrunning Iran.[19]

Against this background Byrnes, without consulting Bevin, suggested to Molotov that the big three should meet again. Bevin did not want this meeting to take place as he felt that Russia would be the only gainer. The Foreign Secretary's relations with Byrnes were increasingly strained. In Washington, Halifax objected to Byrnes that Bevin had been put 'in a bit of a hole' by this. Byrnes was mildly apologetic: it would have looked a bit funny to Molotov had he told the Russian that he was consulting Bevin about making a joint request for an invitation to Moscow. Halifax retorted that he rated the American's diplomatic skill higher than to suppose that he needed to have handled it in just that form. On 5 December Halifax warned Bevin that the President and Byrnes had made up their minds and would not be swayed by British protests. The Americans wanted the first meeting of the United Nations Organization to be a success: to do this it was necessary to ease the prevailing tension with the Russians. The most important item on the agenda, in Byrnes's view, was the atomic bomb. If the tripartite proposals of Truman, Attlee and Mackenzie King went to the United Nations before they had been explained to the Russians, the West would be courting a fiasco like that of the Council of Foreign Ministers in London.[20]

At this time Bevin was not liked in Russia. Stalin later protested to Clark Kerr that the Foreign Secretary did not 'treat the Russians as allies'. About a fortnight before the meeting at Moscow Bevin, in the House of Commons, had accused the Russians of territorial ambitions which they did not have. Stalin complained that this was 'rough' and had given offence: Bevin was free to hate Russia, but he wished that Bevin would not express his feelings in such a way as to give pain to him and his people. One Russian source pointed out that there were people in the Kremlin who could not forget that Bevin was a man of the 'old International' which had been against the Bolsheviks in 1917. In Britain the *Daily Worker* carried a cartoon headed 'Good Relations with Russia' with Bevin explaining 'I aint done nothing – 'cept kick her in the teeth'.[21]

Before the Moscow meeting the American ambassador in Moscow observed that the Russians had been advancing their own interests in the Far and Near East, and in the Balkans, in previous weeks, regardless of American views. Clark Kerr reported that the atomic conversations in Washington had been interpreted in Moscow as the 'formation of an Anglo-Saxon "bloc"', but there was a tendency to single out the British government and Bevin in particular as 'the villains of the piece who are hostile to the Soviet Union at every turn'. The British ambassador speculated on the impact the atomic bomb had had in Russia: with the final defeat of Germany it had seemed that Russia could be made safe at last. From behind its three hundred divisions Russia 'could stretch out her hand and take most of what she needed and perhaps more. It was an exquisite moment.' Then came the bomb: Russia was balked by the West when everything seemed to be within its grasp. The disappointment of the Russian people was tempered by the belief that their Western comrades in arms would surely share the bomb with them. It seemed that the Kremlin shared this expectation. When it was not fulfilled it seemed that the West did not trust them. The old suspicions were justified and quickened.[22] Clark Kerr also warned Bevin in advance that Byrne's main preoccupation was likely to be securing a Far Eastern settlement satisfactory to the Americans, leaving undiscussed the questions in Europe and the Near and Middle East of more immediate concern to Britain. Britain could be particularly exposed to Russian pressure.[23]

In Moscow, on 17 December Bevin warned Byrnes that it looked as if the Russians were trying to undermine the British position in the Middle East, particularly in Greece, Turkey and Iran. Byrnes told the Foreign Secretary that he did not intend to raise the question of the Straits. Relations between the two men deteriorated. Bohlen and the American ambassador, Averill Harriman, admitted to P. Dixon of the Foreign Office that Byrnes had let the Foreign Secretary down. Byrnes had put forward the American proposals on atomic energy a day earlier than had been agreed, and without having cleared them with the British. The explanation offered was that an American official had assumed that Byrnes had cleared the paper with the British and had not stopped the action. Furthermore Byrnes had genuinely believed that Bevin had said that he would not press for the inclusion of India at the peace conference, though he had subsequently realized that he had been mistaken. Harriman attributed Byrnes's mistakes to impulsiveness and inexperience: they were not administration policy. Byrnes was new to international negotiations and did not understand the need for caution and forethought. Roberts, however, minuted that George Kennan, the American Counsellor in Moscow, and other American officials had tried to influence Byrnes, but had failed. In Kennan's words, they hoped 'Mr. Bevin will fight his battle personally with Mr. Byrnes'. There was also a report from a member of the British staff in the United States, Isaiah Berlin, that Byrnes arrived in Moscow with a sense of grievance against Britain, partly inspired by alleged Foreign Office propaganda against the establishment of the seat of the United Nations in the United States. The American embassy in London had reported that this 'propaganda' had stressed that the minorities – in particular the Jews, Poles and Irish – had a dominant influence on American policy, and that the United Nations would be subject to similar disturbing influences if established there. Nothing annoyed the Americans more than the suggestion that they were scarcely able to control their own destiny, that they were not a nation but 'a conglomorate of ill-assorted groups'. Memories of Churchill's 'spheres of influence' deal with Stalin in October 1944 still rankled with Americans, and Byrnes occasionally referred to this as typical of what Britain did when it was not watched. Britain and the United States seemed further apart than they had been during the days of Churchill and Roosevelt, 'despite all the friction which occasionally occurred in that relationship'. Bevin minuted that Dixon's and Berlin's reports should only be seen by Attlee.[24]

Bevin told Stalin personally about British fears of Russian intentions in Iran and Turkey. Stalin spoke of the provinces of Turkey inhabited by Georgians and Armenians where the old frontier had to be restored. With regard to the Straits the Russian claim for a base still stood. Russia did not claim the right to close the Straits, but did not want Turkey to be able to do so either. Bevin proposed a three-power commission on Iran. On Christmas Eve Stalin complained to Bevin that Britain was not prepared to trust Russia in Tripolitania. Furthermore Britain had India and its possessions in the Indian Ocean in its sphere of interest; the United States had China and Japan; but Russia had nothing. Bevin retorted that the Russian sphere extended from Lubeck to Port Arthur. Stalin observed that he was not particularly anxious to see Britain leave certain territories and mentioned the British presence in Egypt during the war as having been of considerable value. In reply Bevin spoke of Britain's duty to police that part of the world, and hoped that in doing this it could count on Stalin's sympathetic consideration. The generalissimo indicated his assent.[25] Afterwards Stalin complained to Clark Kerr that his impression of Bevin had not been good: he did not understand why it had not been possible to arrive at a good official and personal relationship with the British Foreign Secretary. Stalin had achieved that with the previous British government. The generalissimo had been offended by Bevin's approach on Turkey. The British ambassador, however, gave as good as he got, and retorted that there were many things that the Russian government did that were incomprehensible to Britain.[26]

On 6 January 1946 Clark Kerr wrote to Bevin:

You will remember that from out of the darkness of Moscow I have tended to give the Russians here and there the benefit of the doubt on the matter of good faith, but my visit to the Balkans has allowed me a peep, as it were, under the skirts of the Soviet policy as it manifests itself in the fringes of the Russian sphere of influence. This has not been edifying and it would be disingenuous in me if I were not to admit that I am somewhat shaken.[27]

After reading the communiqué of the Moscow Conference Truman recorded: 'There was not a word about Iran or any other place where the Soviets were on the march. We had gained only an empty promise of further talks.' He noted down to inform Byrnes on 5 January 1946: 'I do not think we should play compromise any longer. ... I'm sick of babying the Soviets.'[28]

37

In Moscow, Kennan and Roberts, friends from the Second World War when they had both been in Lisbon, discussed Russian policy together. Indeed co-operation between the staffs of the British and American embassies in that city was close. The new American ambassador, Walter Bedell Smith, came to regard Roberts and his wife 'almost as members of our family'.[29] On 31 December 1945 Roberts warned that Russia was integrating Eastern Europe into its own system of planned economy, establishing 'a series of small economies working largely for the benefit of the Soviet Union, and isolated so far as possible from the outside world, and even from each other'. In the new year he expanded his analysis: Russia would be active in countries on its borders not yet under communist control. In the Middle East Russia had the old tsarist ambitions in a heightened form, and there the only obstacle to its expansion was Britain. There Russia was using the 'Sudeten' technique, posing as the protector of minorities in Turkey, Iran and Afghanistan. Britain had to be resolute in its determination to keep Russia out of Turkey and Iran. American support would make this more effective.[30]

That support came in the form of a telegram from Kennan to the State Department on 22 February explaining Russia's behaviour. The timing was strategic: six months earlier the views would have met with disapproval; six months later they would have appeared as preaching to the converted. By then, Truman had decided that he was no longer prepared to leave foreign policy to Byrnes. The President was more sure of himself, and the State Department was consequently feeling for a new and realistic policy towards Russia. The State Department fixed on the Kennan dispatch. Kennan suggested that in Russia there was a 'political force committed fanatically to the belief that with U.S.A. there can be no permanent modus vivendi, that it is desirable and necessary that the internal harmony of our society be disrupted, our traditional way of life be destroyed, the internal authority of our state be broken, if Soviet power is to be secure'. Kennan argued that the United States should be prepared to guide the peoples of Europe, because if it did not, Russia would. Later, in June 1947, Kennan played a role in putting across this new policy to the American public with his 'X' article in *Foreign Affairs*. This article, excerpts from which were printed in wide circulation magazines like *Reader's Digest* and *Life*, also stated the specific doctrine of containment: 'It is clear that the main element of any United States policy towards the Soviet Union must be that of a long-term, patient but firm and vigilant containment of Russian expansive tendencies.'[31]

If the American administration was to have a new policy towards

38

Russia it first had to educate public opinion to the realities of the Russian threat. The 'bring back daddy' clubs, mutiny by enlisted men in the armed forces and threats by Congress that it would take matters into its own hands showed that American citizens would not serve in mass military units in peacetime. The old republican tradition was too strong. Overnight, people in the United States returned to peacetime thinking. The administration had little option other than to bring the boys back home. Forces in Europe were withdrawn in relation to length of service rather than strategic needs. This recalled Churchill's fears that there would be little in Europe to stop the onslaught of the Russian armies. There were debates about the size of Russia's armed forces and the extent to which they were employed in occupation duties. But these were battle-hardened troops and considerably larger in numbers than their American equivalents. American forces were largely newly inducted and inexperienced. In January 1947 Truman assured Congress that the army would be reduced to 1,070,000 men. By 1948 the active army was only 554,030 strong. Despite a campaign by top military and civilian officials to retain the draft and universal military training a combination of religious, pacifist, educational, farm and labour organizations kept this proposal from serious consideration.[32]

American opinion at this time can be gauged from the reaction to Churchill's speech of 5 March 1946. Speaking at Fulton, Missouri, in the company of the President, he stated: 'From Stettin in the Baltic to Trieste in the Adriatic, an iron curtain has descended across the Continent. ... This is certainly not the Liberated Europe we fought to build up.' Churchill not only referred to Russia by name but called for the unity of the English-speaking peoples to meet the menace. The immediate reaction of the Foreign Office, though not the Cabinet, was consternation. In the United States the speech was widely misinterpreted as an expression of official British opinion and the reference to 'fraternal association' was taken to mean an attempt to manoeuvre the United States into an alliance. Churchill reassured Attlee and Bevin on 7 March that Truman had read a mimeographed copy of the final draft of the speech and had said that it would 'do nothing but good though it would make a stir'. Byrnes and Leahy had also seen it and were enthusiastic. But such was the reaction of isolationist sentiment in the United States that Truman had publicly to dissociate himself from the speech.[33]

Shortly after Churchill's speech, Roberts warned from Moscow that 'there was a limit beyond which we could not tolerate continued Soviet infiltration and undermining of our position'. Earlier that month he had précised Kennan's telegram to the Foreign Office, mentioning the analysis that Russia was not out to destroy the West, and that provided that it maintained its strength there was no reason why the West could not live in peace with Russia. In his missive of 14 March, however, Roberts pointed to mounting evidence of Russian subversion in the Middle East, and in India. There was even the suggestion of a Russian base in the Dodecanese which would pose a threat to Greece, Turkey and to British interests in the eastern Mediterranean. Russia was ruthlessly excluding all Western influence from Eastern Europe, and there were signs that it wanted to control all of Germany. But Roberts thought that Russia was just being its usual opportunist self: it would avoid a clash, especially if there was a chance that the United States might side with Britain. The Russians, however, wanted to gain every 'advanced position' they could before the international situation became less fluid. Fortunately for Britain the Russians were acting with such clumsiness and greed that they were arousing the deepest suspicions in Washington. Internally the Russians were promoting a propaganda campaign emphasizing a Messianic conception of a Russian world mission, and a revival of orthodox Marxist ideology. Roberts speculated as to whether the prevailing reckless mood was tactical, and the extent to which it 'represented the first steps in a carefully considered long-term offensive strategy'. A few days later Roberts observed that Russia had interests everywhere. Its policies were flexible and could 'be pressed, adapted or temporarily shelved to suit the needs of the moment'. 'In the long run she thinks she is bound to win out and can afford to be patient, provided always that she can defend herself against what she regards as a potentially hostile world.' Russia was dynamic and expanding. Its long-term ambitions were dangerous to vital British interests 'as we now see them'. The Russians felt that Britain would not be able to fight for at least five years and that the Americans were reluctant to do so. Russian moves would be affected by their assessment of Anglo-American relations.[34]

At this time, however, Attlee favoured a policy of considerable disengagement from areas where there was a risk of Britain clashing with Russia. In February he argued that it was useless to pretend that Britain could keep the Mediterranean route open in wartime. Britain could not defend Turkey, Iraq, or Iran against the pressure of the Russian land masses. The situation would only be different if the United States became interested, and that country was withdrawing into isolation. Towards the end of March he told the Defence Committee that Britain should withdraw from the Middle East and concentrate on a line of defence across Africa from Lagos to Kenya. Captain B. H. Liddell Hart endorsed this view in a memorandum of 20 March: Russia and Britain would be likely to clash in the Mediterranean and the Middle East; it would be preferable to consolidate and strengthen Britain's position in Africa.[35]

Attlee's proviso, however, was met: the United States did become interested. The new American policy of standing up to the Russians was first evident in Iran in March 1946. On 22 February Bevin wrote to Attlee that the treaty date for the completion of the withdrawal of British forces from Iran was 2 March: he wanted to be in a position to state publicly that all British forces had left. The matter was 'of such political importance that there must be no possibility of things going wrong'. The Russians broke their undertaking to withdraw troops. R. G. Howe of the Foreign Office suggested that it might be desirable to take the matter to the Security Council. The United States finally associated itself with the British stand in the United Nations. The Russians withdrew. At this time Bevin even had reason to believe that Russian action could be explained through its oil interests rather than a desire to acquire territory or warm-water ports. Britain had considerable commercial interests in the area, which the United States did not. To some extent the American approach was legalistic: it only acted when Russia was in the wrong. But when it did act, the administration was aware of the need to stop Russian expansion.[36]

The pattern was repeated in Turkey. Late in 1945 Turkey, backed by Britain and the United States, refused Russia special rights to garrison the Straits area. In March 1946 Washington considered sending a powerful fleet into the Straits. On 7 August 1946 Russia requested joint Turkish-Russian defence of the Dardanelles. Truman's military and diplomatic advisers concurred: Russia intended to dominate Turkey. If it succeeded, it would be difficult to stop it from gaining control of the Near and Middle East. Russia could only be deterred by the threat of force. The United States used a show of gunboat diplomacy: units of the American fleet, including the most modern aircraft carrier, sailed to the eastern Mediterranean. The Truman administration was willing to risk war to block Russian expansion.[37] Britain was not involved in this American response. Indeed F. B. A. Rundall of the North American Department of the Foreign Office doubted whether the American public realized that war was possible, or that it was psychologically prepared for it.[38]

At the Council of Foreign Ministers which met to draw up the peace treaties in Paris from March to September 1946, Britain and the United States stood solidly together against Russia, a solidarity only marred by criticism of the 'get tough with Russia policy' by Henry A. Wallace, Truman's Secretary of Commerce, who was required by his President to resign. The negotiations were marked by clashes between Molotov and Byrnes.[39] Molotov wanted maximum reparations from Germany, which in effect meant from the highly industrialized British zone. Bevin thought that Molotov wanted to strip industry in the west and build it up in the east under Russian control. The British Foreign Secretary told the meeting that if an agreement could not be obtained to treat Germany as an economic whole, his government would have to seek co-operation between the British and other zones so as to relieve the British taxpayer. Byrnes responded appropriately, and suggested privately to Bevin that preparations should be made immediately for the British and American zones to co-operate to the exclusion of the Russian. Bevin was hesitant about this in the Cabinet discussion in July.[40]

Britain was uncertain as to how long the Americans would stay in Europe. Bevin had mentioned to the Cabinet on 11 March his worries about an early American withdrawal from Germany. The Foreign Office referred to the Russian zone as a 'walled-off area' with the Russians living off the land. Refugees had swollen the population in the British zone to 21,000,000: it would cost Britain at least £100 million in 1946 to feed them at subsistence level. It hinted that if there were war against Russia there should be as many Germans as possible on the side of the West. The Chiefs of Staff early in April 1946 considered Russia a more dangerous potential enemy than Germany: British policy should be shaped to allow the rebuilding of Germany at a later date. If Bevin had hesitations about abandoning the prospect of a united Germany, these were seriously challenged late in July by the grain shortage and the bread rationing in Britain. In a paper of 23 July he urged the Cabinet to accept Byrnes's offer of uniting the American and British zones as a means of solving the difficulties over food production for the British zone. That same day he told General Sir Brian Robertson, the deputy military governor in the British zone, and J.B. Hynd of the Foreign Office about his anxieties in dealing with the Americans 'lest they should suddenly change their minds and leave him in the lurch'. Then, on 6 September, in a speech at Stuttgart, Byrnes mentioned a provisional government for an economically self-supporting Germany and stated that American forces would remain in occupation. This was the first indication that American troops were going to stay in Europe. Early in October Byrnes apprised Bevin of information he had from reliable sources that the Russians appeared to be consolidating in Europe and were determined to increase the grip on the satellite states and to hold on to their zone in Germany for as long as they could so as to extract consumer goods for Russia. There were difficulties with the Americans in the talks as to how to fuse the two zones together, particularly on economic matters, but the single economic and political unit, the Bizone, was formed on 1 January 1947. The United States was preparing to block Russian expansion in Europe. Byrnes's Stuttgart speech signified that Roosevelt's grand design of co-operation with Russia had failed.[41]

While in New York for the signing of the peace treaties at the end of the year Bevin met Molotov privately and found the Russian for once 'amiable and inquisitive'. Molotov wondered why it was that the Labour government was pursuing the same foreign policy as Churchill had. Bevin retorted that Churchill's government had been a coalition in which the Labour ministers had had great influence: 'The British public realised this and it was for that reason four square behind the present government's continuation of the Coalition's foreign policy.' Later Molotov asked why Britain kept in such close touch with the United States and not with Russia. Bevin explained that this was so because it was possible to exchange views and ideas between British and American statesmen and officials. If Britain had doubts about some action taken by the United States, 'we expressed the doubts and discussed the problem'. The American government acted in the same way. But it had proved impossible to get relations on the same basis with the Russian government. The Russian ambassador in London had only visited Bevin a few times, and then to discuss trivial matters. It was ridiculous to think that the British Empire wanted to attack the Soviet Union: 'We wanted to be friends. It was the Soviet Government which was making things difficult.' Bevin wondered whether the Soviet government did not dislike social democracy more than it disliked capitalism. Molotov denied this.[42]

Bevin told Molotov that the British people were 'four square' behind his government's foreign policy. On 18 November, however, in the House of Commons, Richard Crossman and the Labour left-wingers had tried to undermine this with their amendment arguing for a 'third Force' to stand between Russia and the United States. Attlee stamped on it but athough the amendment was defeated by 353 votes to nil, around a hundred

Labour members abstained. Stalin possibly thought that he could use this mood to weaken Bevin's position and the emerging Anglo–American alliance. When Field Marshal L. Montgomery visited Moscow early in January 1947 there was a 'flurry of Anglo–Soviet goodwill'. The generalissimo and the field marshal spoke together on 10 January. At that time Britain and the United States were making arrangements to standardize their armaments. Montgomery told Stalin to ignore newspaper reports on this: there was no Anglo–American alliance. Stalin, however, said that such an alliance was perfectly acceptable, provided that it was not aimed at Russia and if he were consulted: after all he had alliances with France and other countries. Montgomery asked whether Stalin felt there should be an alliance between Britain and Russia. Stalin responded: 'That is what I would like, and I think is essential.' He felt that the Anglo–Soviet treaty of 1942 had been 'suspended in the air'. Bevin did not have the same view of the alliance as himself. Presumably referring to Bevin's statement on 22 December 1946 that 'Britain does not tie herself to anyone except in regard to her obligations under the Charter', Stalin complained that, as he understood it, Bevin took the view that the World Organization was now in being, and that the Anglo–Soviet alliance had therefore, in effect, lapsed.[43] Stalin forced the issue: on 15 January *Pravda* said that Bevin had repudiated the Anglo–Soviet treaty. Bevin denied this, but Stalin pressed the matter: the generalissimo wanted, in the words of the American ambassador in Moscow, Walter Bedell Smith, 'to split the Anglo–American front'.[44] That the British Foreign Secretary would not allow. On 27 January he recorded that Britain should handle the approach of the Russian government in such a way that 'it does not affect our relations with the Americans'. Recent manoeuvres of that government and of the 'Communist Party' in Britain were aimed at denying the British government the support of public opinion, and at sowing distrust between London and Washington, so that Western resistance would be weakened over the discussions on Germany in Moscow. Bevin thought it necessary to consider the connection between proposals for the revision of the Anglo–Soviet treaty, including the military clauses, and the conversations which the Chiefs of Staff had been having with the Americans about standardization of military equipment and exchange of information. The American Chiefs of Staff had approved the proposals of the Ministry of Defence on this, and were ready to implement them. Bevin felt that if Britain started negotiations with the Russians, and at the same time stalled on the talks with Washington, the Americans would 'conclude that we have gone over definitely to the Russian camp and have lost interest in military co-operation with them'. This was not acceptable: 'This might mean that we should lose the agreement with the Americans altogether. I feel that this would be a disaster. I believe that arrangements of this kind with the Americans are essential to our security and that they are in no way in conflict with the United Nations Charter.'[45] The new American Secretary of State, George C. Marshall, was reassured that Bevin was particularly anxious that he should not think that London was weakening in any way in its desire for the closest Anglo–American collaboration.[46]

Britain stalled in its negotiations with Russia. Domestically the Labour Party leadership answered the 'third Force' pamphlet, *Keep Left*, with its own *Cards on the Table* which denied that Bevin's foreign policy was indistinguishable from that of Churchill. Privately Foreign Office officials explained to the Americans that Anglo–American solidarity against Russia was the Foreign Secretary's top priority, but the government's education campaign still had to protect Bevin from his 'third Force' critics rather than emphasize the dangers of the Russian threat. At the Labour Party conference in Margate, at the end of May, Bevin blamed the Russians for provoking the British and Americans and forcing them together. It was the Russians who would have to change their policy. The delegates gave Bevin an overwhelming vote of confidence. The Russians stopped pressing for discussions on the Anglo–Soviet treaty, and at the beginning of August 1947 the Foreign Office was able to inform the American embassy that these negotiations were dormant.[47]

Bevin chose the Anglo–American alliance. As early as 13 February 1946 he had written to Attlee:

I believe that an entirely new approach is required, and that can only be based upon a very close understanding between ourselves and the Americans. My idea is that we should start with an integration of British and American armaments and an agreement restricting undesirable competition between our respective armament industries. The next step would be the adoption of parallel legislation in both countries to give their governments real control over the production of arms. The final stage would be the necessary ... conventions.[48]

Talks towards this end took place in the United States in September 1946 between Montgomery, by then Chief of the Imperial General Staff, and the American Chiefs of Staff. These were partly a result

45

of the Dardanelles crisis in August and a suggestion from the Joint Chiefs of Staff that British representatives should attend their meetings. At such a meeting on 30 August Admiral Leahy asked for contingency plans for Anglo–American forces in case of Russian attack. Mackenzie King agreed with Montgomery that there should be discussions covering the whole field of defence, and when Montgomery saw Truman on 11 September the President okayed the idea. On a cruise on the Potomac the American chiefs agreed with Montgomery that talks covering the strategic concept of the West in a third world war should start: that day they looked at what parallel action might be possible for British and American forces in Europe if there were a sudden attack by Russian armies.[49] The talks between Britain and the United States about bases had not led to anything, but on 20 August Byrnes suggested that there should be a 'common user' policy between the United States and the British Commonwealth for the reciprocal use of ports, and possibly air bases. Bevin took this to mean that the Americans were worried about Russia, and aware of the possibility of war. It was thought that there should be no formal written agreement, and further discussions led to the arrangement, accepted early in December 1946, that the wartime practice of American and British naval vessels using each other's ports should be continued indefinitely. Where similar arrangements existed for aircraft they should continue.[50] By the end of 1946 the British and American air forces were exchanging officers to study tactics and equipment. With the co-operation of Mackenzie King recommendations were made for the exchange of personnel, the reciprocal use of military facilities, adoption of standard equipment and joint military projects. The Joint Chiefs of Staff on 29 November 1946 approved a British proposal for Anglo–American–Canadian long-term military planning. In Washington, American, British and Canadian military experts discussed arms standardization, weapons research and common tactical doctrines. Britain had offices in the Pentagon, close to the Joint Chiefs of Staff: the British Joint Staff Mission handled matters of common interest. The Combined Chiefs of Staff, in some ways the only Anglo–American organization that survived the end of the Second World War, continued until 1949 when the North Atlantic Treaty Organization was formed. Britain and the United States had an informal military alliance by December 1946.[51]

Bevin, in shaping this alliance, however, was challenged by Attlee. On 1 December the Prime Minister wrote to his Foreign Secretary in New York speculating on the extent to which Russian policy was dictated by expansionism, and how far 'by fear of attack' by Britain and the United States. 'Fantastic as this is, it may very well be the real grounds of Russian policy. What we consider merely defence may seem to them preparations for an attack. The same kind of considerations apply to the proposals by the U.S.A. for Air bases in Canada which the Russians might regard as offensive in intention.' Attlee felt that there was a tendency in the United States to regard Britain 'as an outpost of America, but an outpost that they will not have to defend'. Attlee was disturbed by signs that the United States was trying to make a safety zone around itself, while leaving Britain and Europe in no man's land. While it was important to find out what the Americans were prepared to do, Britain should not commit itself. Britain had to consider its commitments carefully, lest it try to do more than it could.

Greece, in particular, troubled Attlee. He did not like the suggestion of the Chiefs of Staff that British forces had to remain there for at least another year. Support was expensive, the Greeks did nothing but quarrel amongst themselves and Britain was 'backing a very lame horse'. Attlee reiterated his conviction that British military advisers overrated the strategic importance of the Mediterranean. The Middle East was only an outpost position and the real line of the British Commonwealth ran through Lagos to Kenya. In any case the Prime Minister doubted whether the countries bordering on 'Soviet Russia's zone' – Greece, Turkey, Iraq and Iran – could be made strong enough to form an effective barrier. Britain did not have the resources to achieve this. It would be greatly to Britain's advantage to reach an agreement with Russia that 'we should both disinterest ourselves as far as possible in them so that they become a neutral zone'.[52]

Pierson Dixon drafted a response: a neutral zone might be an obvious solution on paper, but it was not practical politics.'Nature abhors a vacuum, or to change the simile, the protective pad would not be a dry pad: it would soak up. In other words, Russia would certainly infiltrate into a "neutral zone".' A neutral zone would mean the loss of the British position in Egypt and Arabia. The line of the British Commonwealth from Lagos to Kenya would not hold. It would bring Russia to the Congo and the Victoria Falls. Dixon conceded that the Mediterranean was no longer any use as a communications route in war. But others had to be kept out. With Russia in the Mediterranean Britain would lose its influence in Italy, France and North Africa. He doubted whether, even in the atomic age, Britain could risk having no first line of defence between Central Africa and Russia. And British defence of Central Africa, in any case, existed only on paper.[53]

If Britain left Greece, only the United States could take its place. In the second half of 1946 American scouts in Greece had warned of imminent collapse and rumours of British withdrawal. On 25 November Bevin told Byrnes that economies might force Britain to leave.[54] Christopher F. A. Warner suggested from the Foreign Office that the Americans should be told what Britain could do, and that they would have to be prepared to do the rest. During the second week of December Bevin told the Secretary of State that Britain would continue to help with military equipment, but that he hoped that the United States would provide economic assistance. On 20 December Byrnes reported to Truman that the British should continue 'primary responsibility for supply'; the Americans, however, would provide Britain with the appropriate weaponry. Bevin urged the Americans to dispatch a promised economic mission immediately. Early in the new year that mission arrived in Greece headed by Paul A. Porter, assisted by Mark F. Ethridge. On 17 February Ethridge warned that the Russians thought of Greece as a 'ripe plum ready to fall into their hands'. Two days later Porter told the State Department that economic and political stability would only be possible if there was an all-out effort on the part of the United States. On 21 February, before the arrival of Britain's message that it would have to leave by 31 March, Marshall instructed Dean Acheson to prepare the 'necessary steps for sending economic and military aid' to Greece.[55]

It was against the background of these developments in American policy that Bevin fought his battle with Attlee. The Foreign Secretary and the Prime Minister met at Chequers on 27 December. Attlee wanted to withdraw British forces from Greece. The re-equipment of the Turkish armed forces was not even discussed. Afterwards Bevin said that he could no longer fall in with Byrnes's proposal that Britain should look after Greece's and Turkey's military requirements, while the Americans looked after their economic needs. There was a danger that Britain could incur the odium of Russia and its satellites for bolstering Greece and Turkey, while the Americans could protect themselves with economic statistics and just concentrate on the bread and butter needs of the people. Bevin wanted to tell Moscow that a British withdrawal from Greece would be dependent on a Russian withdrawal from Bulgaria.[56]

Attlee persisted that he wanted to try for an accommodation with Russia. He sent his thoughts to the Foreign Secretary on 5 January. Using a historical analogy he mentioned Britain's conflicts with

France all over the world at the end of the nineteenth century. Within a short time there was the Entente Cordiale. Similarly, bad relations with Russia after the Russo–Japanese War, and alarm over Russian designs over Afghanistan, had not stopped Britain and Russia fighting side by side during the First World War. In both instances a common fear of Germany had been a powerful factor in bringing allies together, 'but to–day there is a common fear of what another world war may bring to us all'. In 1946 it was, as Attlee understood it, not considered possible for Britain to place sufficient forces on the European continent to support the Western bloc of powers. Only the countries of Western Europe could, therefore, stop Russia from advancing rapidly to the Atlantic coast. Attlee thought such resistance only possible after Europe had revived economically. That would take some years. At the same time there would be a lessening of the attraction that communism offered to countries in economic depression. The Western conception of democracy would grow. A lessening of international tension would make it more difficult to maintain in Russia the war mentality and war economy that had persisted since the revolution. The best hope of peace lay in a change in the character of the Russian regime. Unless Britain believed that Russia was committed to a policy of world domination, and that there was no possibility of change, before adopting what Attlee considered 'a strategy of despair', Britain should seek to come to an agreement with Russia after a discussion with Stalin of all points of conflict.

The strategy of despair, disliked by Attlee, was that offered by the Chiefs of Staff and the Imperial Defence College. It was based on the assumption that Britain, the heart of the Commonwealth, was vulnerable to modern attack by long–range weapons. There was no effective method of passive defence. The only way to prevent such an attack was by a threat of counter–attack, so formidable that a potential enemy would be deterred through fear of its own losses. The only possible enemy was Russia. The only bases from which Russia could be attacked were situated in the Middle East. It was therefore essential to maintain British influence and forces in that area. Oil supplies and communications through the Mediterranean also had to be secured if at all possible.

This strategy meant heavy military commitments which had to be considered in relation to manpower and economic resources. Britain had to support a number of states in the Middle East – Turkey, Greece, Iraq, Persia, the Lebanon, Syria, Egypt and Transjordan – and maintain its position in Palestine. That meant competition for political and economic influence with Russia. What might be considered necessary defence to Britain could be regarded by Russia as the preparation for an offensive, a natural course according to Russian ideology that would be adopted by any state that did not accept the communist philosophy. The Russians could react by mounting a westward penetration so as to be able to strike more effectively at Britain than Britain could at them, or penetrate the Middle East to deny Britain a possible base for attack against their vulnerable points. The Russians could pursue both policies. The countries of the Middle East were weak. Greece was hopelessly divided. The other countries had essentially reactionary governments, and were 'excellent soil for the sowing of communist seed'. Britain, in trying to keep its influence over these weak, backward and reactionary states had to face Russia, 'organised under an iron discipline, equipped with the weapon of a revolutionary doctrine liable to attract the masses, strategically well placed for penetration or attack and with only a limited number of its key points open to our attack'.

Attlee speculated on the chances of negotiating with Russia. He wondered whether it was possible to convince Russia that Britain had no offensive intentions against it. A Foreign Office minute commented 'No'. How far was the ideology of the rulers of Russia committed to the conception of the necessity of world revolution? A Foreign Office response was: 'Completely'. The Prime Minister wondered what the prospects were of changes in the Russian mentality: if it were agreed that Russia was not prepared for a major war for some years, what likelihood was there that an easing of its internal economic situation would lead Russia to be less ready to throw away what it had gained? The Foreign Office notation read: 'Very few'.

Attlee wondered whether it would not be possible to get an agreement on oil rights in Iran. The Dardanelles issue could be settled on principles applicable to all major international waterways. The German issue could be handled on the basis of mutual interest in seeing that the German nation did not again become a threat to either Britain or Russia. Britain and Russia might work together to secure some degree of unity and economic co-operation in Europe. Britain could also try to dispel Russia's fear of the United States: that fear seemed to be the mainspring of Russia's policy in the Far East.[57]

In response Dixon prepared a note to be discussed by Sir Orme Sargent, R. G. Howe, C. F. A. Warner, William Hayter and himself. Dixon argued that the Russians saw British predominance in the Middle East as part of the 'British imperial setup'. A British withdrawal from that area would be 'Munich' and an incentive to ultimate Russian world domination rather than a sedative. The countries of the Middle East might be poor, but if Britain left it would be making a gift to Russia of the manpower of the region: a difference of 100 million men in the balance sheet. To attempt an agreement with Russia then would be arguing from weakness; the time to try for such an agreement would be when Britain could bid from strength. If the Middle East became a 'neutral zone', Russia would infiltrate into the vacuum. A British withdrawal from the Middle East would be disastrous for the neighbouring countries and Europe. The United States would despair of Britain and the world would effectively be divided into an American and Russian bloc. This would heighten the probability of a world war in which Britain would be massacred. Even if Russian world domination could be discounted, the 'bear will certainly not resist pushing paw into soft places'.[58]

The Chiefs of Staff decided to point out to Attlee the importance of Palestine in any Middle East defence scheme. Furthermore, they felt that the Prime Minister did not understand that their plans were defensive as well as offensive. Their plan envisaged small military establishments to be increased in case of emergency. In this regard the friendship of the Arab world was essential to assure the stability of British bases. Attlee was, in their view, misguided in thinking that all Britain's oil stores could be kept in the United Kingdom.[59]

On 9 January 1947 Bevin informed the Prime Minister that the political arguments against his proposals were overwhelming. Attlee was trying to reverse the Middle East policy Bevin had pursued since taking office. Britain had to accept that the rulers of Russia were committed to the belief that there is a natural conflict between the capitalist and communist world. The Russians thought that they had a mission to work for a communist world. They preferred to achieve that through infiltration rather than armed conflict. Bevin thought that it would be idle to place reliance on gaining British security by large-scale one-sided concessions to Russia. Even if Britain reduced itself to impotence and so convinced Russia of its pacific intentions, Russia would remain suspicious of American intentions to use the British Isles in a war against Russia. Bevin thought that an improvement in Russia's internal situation would make it more not less aggressive. That was shown by the published intentions of Russia's Five Year Plans to strengthen her military and industrial potential. Russian propaganda was trying to keep alive the bogey of a capitalist war. The Foreign Secretary

51

thought that the Russian leaders believed that war with the United States was inevitable. Britain could not disillusion them. Only the Americans could do that, if it could be done at all. Negotiations of the sort envisaged by Attlee were not likely to be successful. There were many objections to withdrawal from the Middle East. If Britain left, Russia would fill the gap whatever it had promised. The Americans would write Britain off entirely. Britain was dependent on the United States economically, and without its help could not maintain the standard of life of its people. Britain also depended on the United States militarily. And at last the United States had been persuaded that their strategic interests involved the maintenance of Britain's position in the Middle East. If the Russians created a further batch of satellite states in the Middle East the United Nations would be imperilled. After the British abandonment of India and Burma, a retreat from the Middle East would appear to the world as the abdication of Britain's position as a world power and encourage India to gravitate towards Russia. Egypt could soon fall under communist control, and Britain's position in the Sudan would become untenable. The effect would be felt throughout Africa, and Britain's project for a base in East Africa and any prospect of holding North Africa would be threatened. The effect on the Dominions would be incalculable. South Africa would thoroughly dislike the prospect of the Russians in Africa, and Australia and New Zealand would hardly welcome the Russians in the Indian Ocean. Bevin concluded that only when Britain had consolidated its economy, when Europe had revived, when the Russians realized that they could not drive a wedge between London and Washington, would Britain be in a position to negotiate with Stalin from strength. There was no hurry. Everything suggested that the Russians were 'drawing in their horns' and had no immediate aggressive intentions. 'Let us wait until our strength is restored , and let us meanwhile, with American help as necessary, hold on to essential positions and concentrate on building up U.N.O.'[60]

Bevin won. On 9 January, together with the Minister of Defence, A. V. Alexander, he saw Attlee. It was agreed that Bevin's general policy would be followed. There would be no withdrawal of British forces from the Middle East in excess of the programmes already contemplated. There would be an investigation into the possibility of building up underground stores of crude oil in Britain. Attlee, however, was still not satisfied about the maintenance of the prevailing policy in the Middle East.[61] He wanted a meeting with the Chiefs of Staff. They were adamant. Air Marshall Arthur William

Tedder told the Cabinet on 15 January that there were three cardinal requirements for the future defence of the British Commonwealth: the defence of the United Kingdom and its development as a base for air offensive; the maintenance of sea communications; and the retention of Britain's existing position and influence in the Middle East. These were the three 'vital Props' of Britain's defensive position. They were all interdependent, and if any one were lost, 'the whole structure would be imperilled'. These fundamental principles would be unaffected by any change in the nature and use of weapons, or assumptions made about the potential enemy. It was essential for Britain's defence that it could fight from the Middle East in war. This meant that Britain had to maintain a foothold there in peace. Though lightly manned in peace these bases could be used for the rapid deployment of greater force against a threat of war. India would no longer be available for such bases so the retention of those in the Middle East was essential. Palestine was of special importance. Britain's strategic policy for the Middle East was not wholly dependent on preserving the friendship of Spain, Italy, Greece and other countries bordering the northern seaboard of the Mediterranean. The line of communication through the Mediterranean would still be of substantial value, even if one of those countries were hostile, provided the countries on the southern shore of that sea were not also hostile.[62]

Against the background of the freezing winter of 1947, economic chaos and disruption, Bevin, despite the opposition of his Prime Minister, chose to emphasize the Anglo–American special relationship as the foundation-stone of British foreign policy. Convinced of Russia's expansionist intentions, the Foreign Secretary was determined that nothing should endanger the development of an alliance which he saw as being essential for Britain's security. He realized Britain's dependence on the United States, but felt that Britain had to maintain its independence and its seat at the table of great powers. He was conscious of the difficulties of American public opinion. George Kennan, in March 1947, thought that Britain tried to lessen the stigma of being an imperial power with this in mind. On 28 January of that year Britain announced the future constitution of an independent Burma; on 14 February it was known that Britain would refer the Palestine question to the United Nations, an issue on which there had been major Anglo–American disagreement; on 20 February Attlee said that India would be independent no later than June 1948; negotiations with Egypt were in progress.[63] By 11 February Bevin had concluded that policy towards Greece had to be reviewed. On 18 February he decided to send 'a strong telegram to the United States asking them what they were going to do and on the other hand telling the Greeks that we could not continue'. This was for 'the sole purpose of bringing matters to a head'. On 21 February the First Secretary of the British embassy in Washington gave Loy W. Henderson, the director of the Office of Near Eastern and African Affairs, two messages. The first noted the strategic importance of keeping Greece out of the hands of Russia and suggested that the British and American Chiefs of Staff urgently consider the situation in the eastern Mediterranean. British aid to Greece would have to end on 31 March: 'His Majesty's Government trust that the United States Government may find it possible to afford financial assistance to Greece on a scale sufficient to meet her minimum needs, both civil and military.' The second note said much the same about Turkey.[64] Earlier that day Marshall had given instructions for the necessary preparations to be made for sending aid to Greece and Turkey.

Notes: Chapter 2

1   *DBPO*, pp. 1143–3, Attlee to Churchill, 1 August 1945; pp. 1151–2, Attlee to Eden, 1 August 1945.
2   D. Dilks (ed.), *The Diaries of Sir Alexander Cadogan, 1938–1945* (London,1971), p. 778, Cadogan to Theodosia Cadogan, 31 July 1945; p. 781, diary, 14 August 1945.
3   Public Record Office, London, FO 800/451, fos 9–10, Def/45/3, Bevin to Attlee, 6 September 1945.
4   FO 800/512, fos 36–8, US/45/25, Bevin to Cripps, 20 September 1945.
5   FO 800/512, fos 52–3, US/45/34, Attlee to Truman, Telegram no. 9908, Personal and Top Secret, 3 October 1945; fol. 59, US/45/37, Truman to Attlee, Telegram no. 10018, Personal and Top Secret, 5 October 1945.
6   FO 800/512, fos 151–4, US/45/110, Churchill to Bevin, Most Secret, 13 November 1945.
7   FO 800/501, fol. 10, SU/45/9, Bevin to Clark Kerr, Telegram no. 4559, 15 August 1945.
8   FO 800/490, fol.5 Pol/45/3, Bevin to Cavendish–Bentinck, no. 452, Confidential, 27 August 1945.
9   Public Record Offic, London, FO 371/47883, Clark Kerr to Bevin, 6 September 1945, printed in part in Ross (ed.), *The Foreign Office and the Kremlin*, pp.226–8.
10 FO 800/501, fos 20–4, SU/45/10, Minutes by Clark Kerr of conversation between Bevin and Molotov on 23 September 1945; Ross (ed.), *The Foreign Office and the Kremlin*, pp.228–63.
11 FO 371/47883, Roberts to Bevin, 26 October 1945, printed in part in Ross (ed.),*The Foreign Office and the Kremlin*, pp. 263–5.
12 FO 800/512, fos 41–2, US/45/27, Halifax to Bevin and Attlee, Telegram no. 6422, Top Secret, 25 September 1945.
13 FO 800/512, fol. 8, US/45/7, Attlee to Truman, Telegram no. 8463, Personal and Top Secret, 17 August 1945.
14 FO 800/438, fos 100–3, Ate/46/5, Truman to Attlee, Telegram no. 3779, Top Secret and Personal, dated 20 April 1946, sent 23 April 1946; fos 104–6,

Ate/46/6, Bevin to Attlee, Top Secret, 24 April 1946; fol. 107, Ate/46/7 Bevin to Attlee, 1 May 1946; fos 110-16, Ate/46/9 Attlee to Truman, Personal and Top Secret, 6 June 1946.

15 Wheeler–Bennett and Nicholls, *The Semblance of Peace*, p.290;FO 800/438, fol. 125, Ate/46/13, Bevin to Attlee, Telegram no. 1454, Top Secret, 5 November 1946; Nicholas, *Britain and the United States* pp.58–69; M. M. Gowing, *Independence and Deterrence: Britain and Atomic Energy, 1945–52*, 2 vols. (London,1974); Bullock, *Ernest Bevin*, pp.184–9; J. L. Gormly 'The Washington declaration and the "poor relation"'; H. Macmillan, *Riding the Storm* (London, 1971) pp. 313–41; Anglo-American Atomic Diplomacy, 1945–46', *Diplomatic History*, vol. 8 (1984), pp. 125–43.

16 FO 800/501, fos 40-2, Roberts for JIC, Particular Secrecy, 23 October 1945.

17 McNeill, *America, Britain and Russia* p. 700; J. L. Richardson, 'Cold–war revisionism: a critique', *World Politics*, vol. 24 (1972), pp. 578–612 and pp. 583–9; H. B. Hammett, 'America's non–policy in Eastern Europe and the origins of the Cold War', *Survey*, vol. 19, no.4 (1973), pp. 144–62: R. Garson, 'The role of Eastern Europe in America's containment policy, 1945–1948' *Journal of American Studies* vol. 13 (1979), pp. 73–92; L. E. Davies, *The Cold War Begins: Soviet–American Conflict over Eastern Europe* (Princeton, N. J. 1974); G. Lundestad, *The American Non–Policy towards Eastern Europe* (New York, 1975); R. L. Messer, 'Paths not taken: the United States Department of State and alternatives to containment, 1945–1946', *Diplomatic History*, vol. 1 (1977),pp. 297–319; E. Mark, 'Charles E. Bohlen and the acceptable limits of Soviet hegemony in Eastern Europe: a memorandum of 18 October 1945', *Diplomatic History*, vol. 3 (1979), pp. 201–14; 'American policy towards Eastern Europe and the origins of the Cold War, 1941–1946: an alternative interpretation', *Journal of American History*, vol. 68 (1981), pp. 313–36; W.A. Harriman and E. Able, *Special Envoy to Churchill and Stalin, 1941–1946* (London, 1976), *passim*.

18 FO 800/507, Tu/45/5, Bevin to Cadogan, 19 November 1945.

19 Roberts and Wilson (eds), *Britain and the United States*, pp. 167–70; S. L. McFarland, 'A peripheral view of the origins of the Cold War: the crisis in Iran, 1941–47', *Diplomatic History*, vol. 4 (1980) pp. 333–52; R. Pfau, 'Containment in Iran, 1946: the shift to an active policy', *Diplomatic History*, vol. 1 (1977), pp. 359–72; E. Mark, 'Allied relations in Iran, 1941–1947: the origins of a cold war crisis', *Wisconsin Magazine of History* vol. 59 (1975), pp. 51–63; G. R. Hess, 'The Iranian crisis of 1945–1946 and the Cold War', *Political Science Quarterly*, vol. 89 (1974), pp. 117–40; B. R. Kuniholm, *The Origins of the Cold War in the Near East: Great Power Conflict and Diplomacy in Iran, Turkey and Greece* (Princeton, N.J. 1980); B. Rubin, *The Great Powers in the Middle East 1941–1947: The Road to the Cold War* (London, 1980); W. R. Louis, *The British Empire in the Middle East 1945–1951. Arab Nationalism, the United States, and Postwar Imperialism* (Oxford,1984), pp. 65–8; R. L. Messer, *The End of an Alliance: James F.Byrnes, Roosevelt, Truman, and the Origins of the Cold War* (Chapel Hill, NC, 1982).

20 FO 800/501, fol. 57, SU/45/35/B, Clark Kerr to Bevin, Telegram no.5088,Top Secret and Personal, 24 November 1945; fos 64-5, SU/45/40, Halifax to Bevin, Telegram no. 7997, Top Secret, 29 November 1945; fos 73-5, SU/45/42, Halifax to Bevin, Telegram no. 8115, Top Secret, 5 December 1945.

21 FO 800/501, fos 127-9, SU/46/6, Clark Kerr to Bevin, Top Secret and Personal, 29 January 1946; fol. 45, SU/45/31, *Daily Worker* cartoon.

22 FO 800/501, fol. 58,SU/45/35/C, Clark Kerr to Bevin, Telegram no. 5091, Top Secret, 24 November 1945; fos 69-71, SU/45/41/B, Clark Kerr to Bevin, Telegram no. 5192, Particular Secrecy, 3 December 1945.

23 FO 800/501, fos 90—1, SU/45/56A, Clark Kerr to Bevin, Telegram no. 5259, Top Secret, 8 December 1945.

24 FO 800/501, fos 111-12, SU/45/74, Note by P. Dixon of conversation with

Bohlen and Harriman on 20 December 1945, 21 December 1945; fos 115–18,SU/45/77, Berlin to Bevin, Secret, 21 December 1945.

25 FO 800/507, fol. 8, Tu/45/7, Bevin to Attlee, Telegram no. 53, Top Secret, 20 December 1945; 489, fol. 3, Per/45/2, Bevin to Attlee, Telegram no. 142, Most Secret, 26 December 1945; FO 371/57089 and CAB 133/82, Proceedings of the Moscow Conference of Foreign Ministers, 16–26 December 1945, printed in part in Ross (ed.),*The Foreign Office and the Kremlin* pp. 267–81.

26 FO 800/501, fos 127–9, SU/46/6, Clark Kerr to Bevin, Top Secret and Personal, 29 January 1946.

27 FO 800/499, fos 2–3, RO/46/1, Clark Kerr to Bevin, Top Secret and Personal, 6 January 1946.

28 See J. Barzun and H. F. Graff, *The Modern Researcher*, rev. edn. (New York, 1970) pp. 157–9 for a discussion of this evidence.

29 G. Kennan, *Memoirs 1925–1950* (London, 1968) pp. 286–7; W. B. Smith, *Moscow Mission 1946–1949* (London 1950), p. 95

30 FO 371/56830, Roberts to Bevin, 31 December 1945; 52327, Roberts to Bevin, no. 797, 16 January 1946; Barker, *The British between the Superpowers* p. 44; Rothwell, *Britain and the Cold War* pp. 247–50.

31 Kennan, *Memoirs*, pp. 292–5; L. J. Halle, *The Cold War as History* (London, 1967), pp. 103–8; the summer 1972 issue of *Foreign Policy* is devoted to a series of articles on Kennan and containment; see also D. S. McLellan, 'Who fathered containment? A discussion', *International Studies Quarterly*, vol. 17 (1973), pp. 205–26; R. J. Powers, 'Who fathered containment? Review and discussion', *International Studies Quarterly*, vol. 15 (1971), pp. 526–43.

32 Halle, *The Cold War as History* pp. 100–2; S. E. Ambrose, *Rise to Globalism* (London, 1971), p. 127; see generally E. F. Goldman, *The Crucial Decade and After* (New York, 1966) pp. 1–91; J. L. Gaddis, *The United States and the Origins of the Cold War* (New York, 1972), pp. 341–2.

33 Public Record Office, London, CAB 128/5, fol. 111, CM23(46)6, Secret, 11 March 1946; Williams, *A Prime Minister Remembers*, pp. 162–3; Yergin, *Shattered Peace*, pp. 174–7.

34 FO 371/56840, Roberts to Warner, no. 3369, 2 March 1946; 56763, N4065/97/38, Roberts to Bevin,no. 4065, 14 March 1946; 56831, Roberts to Bevin, nos. 1090–3, 20 March 1946; Barker, *The British between the Superpowers*, pp. 44–5; Rothwell, *Britain and the Cold War*, pp. 246–52: Morgan, *Labour in Power*, pp. 244–5.

35 British Library of Economic and Political Science, London, Dalton Diaries, 34, fol. 3, 18 February 1946; fol. 12, 22 March 1946; Bodleian, Oxford, Attlee Papers, 5, Liddell Hart to Attlee, 10 May 1946; Memorandum on Africa or the Middle East, Reflections on strategic peace policy by Liddell Hart, 20 March 1946.

36 FO 800/489, fos 14–15, Per/46/4, Bevin toAttlee, 22 February 1946; fol. 16, Per/46/5, Howe to Attlee, 2 March 1946; CAB 128/5, fol. 121, CM26(46)3, Secret, 18 March 1946.

37 Wheeler–Bennett and Nicholls, *The Semblance of Peace*, p. 328; McNeill, *America, Britain and Russia*, pp. 713–14; Williams, *A Prime Minister Remembers*, p. 163; *FRUS* 1946(7), pp. 820–70; J. Knight, 'American statecraft and the 1946 Black Sea Straits controversy', *Political Science Quarterly*, vol. 90 (1975), pp 451–75.

38 Louis, *Imperialism at Bay*. pp. 80–1.

39 See T. G. Paterson, (ed.), *Cold War Critics: Alternatives to American Foreign Policy in the Truman Years* (Chicago, 1971) for a collection of articles on contemporary criticisms of Truman's attitude; Wheeler–Bennett and Nicholls, *The Semblance of Peace*, pp. 436–8; P.D. Ward, *The Threat of Peace: James F. Byrnes and the Council of Foreign Ministers* (Kent, Ohio, 1979); Barker, *The British between the Superpowers*, pp. 61–2.

40 CAB 128/6, fol. 24, CM68(46)1, Secret, 15 July 1946.
41 FO 800/466, fos 99–101, Ger/46/33, Memorandum by Bevin, Top Secret, 3 October 1946: Barker, *The British between the Superpowers* pp. 62–8; Rothwell,- *Britain and the Cold War*, pp. 291–357; Morgan, *Labour in Power*, pp. 256–60: J. Tusa, 'The unsettled peace; landscape with ruins', *The Listener*, 24 October 1974, pp. 523–4; *contra* J. Gimbel,'On the implementation of the Potsdam agreement: an essay on U.S. postwar German policy', *Political Science Quarterly*, vol.87 (1972), pp. 242–69; T. Sharp, *The Wartime Alliance and the Zonal Division of Germany* (Oxford, 1975); R. Morgan, *The United States and West Germany 1945–1973* (London, 1974); J. H. Backer, *The Decision to Divide Germany: American Foreign Policy in Transition* (Durham, NC, 1978); B. Kuklick, *American Policy and the Division of Germany: The Clash with Russia over Reparations* (Ithaca, NY, 1972); G. Warner, 'The division of Germany 1946–1948', *International Affairs*, vol.51 (1972), pp. 60–70; J. Gimbel, *The American Occupation of Germany: Politics and the Military, 1945–1949* (Stanford, Calif., 1968); J. E. Smith (ed.), *The Papers of General Lucius D. Clay: Germany, 1945–49* (Bloomington, Ind., 1974).
42 FO 800/501, fos 195–6, SU/46/42, Note of a conversation between Molotov and Bevin, 6 November 1946; fos 200–2, SU/46/46, Record of a conversation between Molotov and Bevin, Secret, 9 December 1946.
43 FO 800/502, fol. 25, SU/47/4, Minute by Roberts, 13 January 1947.
44 *FRUS* 1947(4), pp. 523–4, Smith to Marshall, 25 January 1947.
45 FO 800/502, fos 50–3, SU/47/14, Memorandum by Bevin on the question of an Anglo–Soviet military alliance, and Anglo–American standardisation, Top Secret, 27 January 1947.
46 *FRUS* 1947(4), p. 528, British Embassy Washington to Department of State, 8 February 1947.
47 W. Knight 'Labourite Britain: America's "Sure Friend"? The Anglo–Soviet treaty issue, 1947', *Diplomatic History*, vol. 7 (1983), pp. 267–82 and pp. 278–81. There has perhaps been undue emphasis on the impact of domestic criticism on Bevin. See M.A. Fitzsimons, *The Foreign Policy of the British Labour Government* (Notre Dame, Ind., 1953); E. J. Meehan, *The British Left Wing and Foreign Policy: A Study of the Influence of Ideology* (New Brunswick, NJ, 1960); B. Jones, *The Russian Complex: The British Labour Party and the Soviet Union* (Manchester,1977).
48 FO 800/451, fol. 44. Def/46/3, Bevin to Attlee,13 February 1946.
49 B. L. Montgomery, *The Memoirs of Field–Marshal the Viscount Montgomery of Alamein* (London, 1958), pp. 440–2; Anderson, *The United States, Great Britain and the Cold War*, pp. 139–40; Barker, *The British between the Superpowers*, p. 55.
50 FO 800/513, US/46/91, Bevin to Attlee, 23 August 1946; US/46/105, Bevin to Attlee, 26 September 1946; US/46/114, Inverchapel to Bevin, 24 October 1946; SU/46/128, Inverchapel to Bevin, 11 December 1946; Bullock, *Ernest Bevin*, p. 315.
51 Anderson, *The United States, Great Britain and the Cold War*, pp. 140–1; Barker, *The British between the Superpowers*, pp. 74–6.
52 FO 800/475, fos 57–60, ME/46/22, Attlee to Bevin, Private and Personal, 1 December 1946.
53 FO 800/475, fos 63–4, ME/46/24, Dixon to Bevin, 9 December 1946.
54 FO 800/468, Gre/46/35, Bevin to Foreign Office, 26 November 1946.
55 Wittner, *American Intervention in Greece*, pp. 64–7; Anderson, *The United States, Great Britain and the Cold War*, pp. 159–65.
56 FO 800/475, fos 65–9, Minutes by J. N. Henderson, 28 December 1946.
57 FO 800/476, ME/47/1, fol. 2, Attlee to Bevin, Top Secret, 5 January 1947; fos 3–9, Memorandum by Attlee on Near East policy.
58 FO 800/476, ME/47/2, Note by Dixon for discussion by certain Foreign Office officials on 8 January 1947, Top Secret, undated.
59 FO 800/476, fol. 12, Note for Dixon based on information from Sir Norman

Brook on 8 January 1947.
60 FO 800/476, fos 13–20, ME/47/4, Bevin to Attlee, Top Secret, 9 January 1947.
61 FO 800/476, fos 21–2, ME/47/5, Minute by P. Dixon, 10 January 1947.
62 CAB 128/11, fos 7–9,CM6(47)3, Confidential Annex, 15 January 1947.
63 Princeton University Library, George Kennan Papers, Box 17, The National War College Strategy, Policy and Planning Course, National Security Problems, 17–28 March 1947, Restricted.
64 Anderson, *The United States, Great Britain, and the Cold War*, pp. 168–9.

3

Marshall Aid and Western Defence

Following Marshall's instructions, the State Department immediately started preparing specific plans for aid to Greece and Turkey. Truman did not like the prospect of a communist Greece. He told his Cabinet on 7 March that he had taken the decision to ask Congress for $250 million for Greece, and to say that that was only the beginning. The President observed: 'It means U.S. going into European politics. It means the greatest selling job ever.'[1] He decided to present the issue in broad terms: 'This was America's answer to the surge of expansion of Communist tyranny. It had to be clear and free of hesitation or double talk.' Dean Acheson maintained that a guerilla victory in Greece would mean that most of Europe would fall to communism. The State, Navy and War Departments drew up proposals for military aid accordingly. Truman, through Arthur Vandenberg, the Republican chairman of the Senate Foreign Relations Committee, tried to lobby support for the new policy. Kennan was alarmed by the final draft of Truman's speech to Congress: the plan was too 'grandiose' and sweeping. Probably he did not appreciate Truman's tactics.[2] On 12 March 1947 Truman outlined what was to become known as the 'Truman doctrine' and 'containment' to both houses of Congress. The reason offered for aid to Turkey and Greece was 'that it must be the policy of the United States to support free peoples who are resisting attempted subjugation by armed minorities or by outside pressures'. Hostile domestic reaction to this speech has been exaggerated. The United Nations was bypassed, a point not lost upon the columnist Walter Lippmann. This marked the end of the Roosevelt policy, discernible even before Pearl Harbor, of managing affairs in the postwar world under the aegis of the United Nations. American leaders realized that such a policy did not match the realities of power on the European continent. Truman's policy was not very different from that enunciated by Churchill during the

Second World War. Congress bickered, but on 15 May it appropriated $400 million for Greece and Turkey. This, though not an open-ended commitment to containment, was the first step.[3] Zionists in the United States tried unsuccessfully to link American relief of Britain's financial position in Greece with forcing Britain to accept the displaced persons in the American zone in Germany into Palestine. Senator Robert Wagner of the American Christian Palestine Committee raised this matter with a fellow member, Vandenberg, in the middle of March.[4] But by then Greece was an issue within the framework of the emerging Anglo-American alliance, and Washington was reluctant to endanger that.

In any case the British message of 21 February announcing a withdrawal from Greece and Turkey was tactical. It was intended, in Bevin's words, 'for the sole purpose of bringing matters to a head'. Marshall persuaded Bevin in March to allow the British mission to stay in Greece; the Secretary of State also wanted to leave military affairs in Turkey to the British. In the middle of 1947 Marshall was irked by a British plan to reduce forces in Italy and the Trieste area to 5,000. Bevin gave the assurance that there was no change in British policy in Germany, Italy and the Middle East, but Britain could not keep troops in Greece and Italy indefinitely. At the end of July the Americans said that they had information that the Russians were intending to get their satellites to move into northern Greece. Averell Harriman, the former American ambassador in London, attributed the British threats to the influence of the extreme left wing of the Labour Party, Hugh Dalton, Harold Laski and John Strachey. Harriman suggested that Britain should be faced with the ultimatum of no more American aid until its people returned to hard work. British nationalization could not be underwritten by the United States.[5] On 26 July Bevin let the Americans know that Britain would be bankrupt by the end of the year, and would have to rely on the United States for the maintenance of its world position. The Under Secretary of State, Robert A. Lovett, regretted that American forces had been withdrawn from Europe before the peace treaties were written.[6] In the United States the newly formed Policy Planning Staff on 31 July estimated that the world crisis would come to a head in a few months. By then Britain, with all its difficulties, would be 'out of the picture as a dominant world force'. The other democratic countries would only be able to play passive roles. The crisis would be between Russia and the United States.[7] In Britain, however, the Chiefs of Staff insisted that military information had to be freely exchanged between the British and the Americans: the effect of a

British withdrawal from Greece by a given date on the Americans would be 'out of all proportion'.[8] A compromise was reached: the withdrawal of the British forces from Greece was delayed, first until the end of 1947, and in the end British troops remained in Greece until 1954.[9]

In March 1947 Bevin had no assurances that the United States would go further than supporting Greece and Turkey. He knew, as he told the Cabinet on 3 February, that Britain would be placed in an impossible position if the United States withdrew from Europe.[10] Britain, however, was not prepared just to rely on the United States. Truman's abrupt cancellation of Lend Lease, an American Palestine policy dictated by domestic pressures[11] and the revocation of the Quebec and Hyde Park agreements convinced a group of British ministers that Britain should build its own atomic bomb. This decision was taken on 10 January 1947. At the end of that year there were hopes of closer co-operation with Washington on nuclear energy. Indeed the Chiefs of Staff were worried about collaborating with Commonwealth countries on this matter lest this 'frighten the Americans off for a long time', but little materialized from the American side.[12]

With an eye on the situation in Europe, and with the hope of reducing the influence of the Communist Party in France and of balancing the attraction of Russia, Bevin at the beginning of 1947 negotiated the Dunkirk treaty with France. From 1944 there had been some sort of contingency plans for an alliance with France, possibly widened into a broader Western group, but these never became official policy, and in any case France's internal position in 1946 put them out of court. The British ambassador in Paris, Duff Cooper, favoured an alliance with France, seemingly even at the expense of one with the United States, but Bevin told him in September 1947 that he would have to go.[13] In December 1946 the acting Assistant Under Secretary in the Foreign Office, Nigel Ronald, observed that Byrnes's offer of a twenty-five year treaty for the demilitarization of Germany implied a less isolationist stance. If the Americans would accept a commitment to European defence 'the need for an Anglo-French alliance would disappear so far as this particular context is concerned'. This distressed Duff Cooper. Without authorization, on 26 December, he raised the question of an Anglo-French alliance with Léon Blum who fronted the caretaker socialist administration. Blum wanted coal for France. In a letter to Attlee he emphasized this, but also mentioned the possibility of a treaty. Britain could not give the coal. Worried that if Blum went back to Paris from his January visit to London with nothing, the socialists in France would be weakened and there could be a subsequent line-up of France and Russia on the German question, on the advice of the Foreign Office Attlee and Bevin offered Blum an alliance. During the negotiations in February Britain was on the one hand worried that the envisaged treaty might lead to similar demands during the negotiations for a revised Anglo-Soviet treaty, and on the other that the Americans might conclude that their help was no longer needed. References to exchange of military information were deleted, and even the account of envisaged commercial and economic developments was weakened. The French wanted common action to meet a German 'menace'. The British would only allow 'attack'. The reason was that 'the isolationist elements in the United States would be able to claim that arrangements to guard against a German menace made any American guarantee superfluous'. Bevin insisted that there be a specific clause stating that the Anglo-French treaty was not to be regarded as a substitute for the Byrnes treaty over Germany. The final treaty signed on 4 March at Dunkirk, as the British admitted, was 'rather bare and does not seem to contain very much'. The British guarantee of support for France against renewed German aggression was compromised by the reference to the anticipated Byrnes treaty: it was thought that Britain would be unlikely to have to act on its own. After all, the Chiefs of Staff opposed the idea of sending a British army to the European continent in the event of war. They argued also that the treaty should 'in no way impair our relations with the US'. The French saw the treaty as purely technical, one that normalized Anglo-French relations. Britain had little confidence in France. The Foreign Office felt that little reliance could be placed in a country dominated by a Communist Party which took its orders from Moscow. As late as November 1947 Bevin resisted Anglo-French military staff conversations: 'we have no confidence in French security'. In negotiating this treaty Britain had Russia rather than Germany in mind. Britain hoped to reduce Russia's influence in France, and also to show that France's foreign policy was more in line with that of the West than the communist bloc. At the time it was not seen as the beginnings of a military alliance with which to face Russia. The idea that the Anglo-French alliance could be extended to include Belgium and the Netherlands was dismissed: 'more harm than good may be caused by trying to go too quickly'.[14]

At the Conference of Foreign Ministers which met in Moscow during March and April 1947 nothing came of Byrnes's envisaged four-power treaty over Germany. On 15 April Marshall told

Stalin that the United States was determined to give assistance to countries threatened with economic collapse and the consequent challenge to democracy. The United States, however, did not want to dominate any country. Within the American administration warnings about Britain's economic plight, France's instability and a growing awareness that other countries could face the same problems as Greece and Turkey led to suggestions for better planning and more co-ordination in the use of American sources to meet the threat. There were fears of another Great Depression, and it was argued that prosperity in the United States depended on suitable export markets. Only a comprehensive aid programme could win the necessary congressional support. In the early stages planning for a European recovery programme was focused on the newly formed Policy Planning Staff under George Kennan, and on a special agency of the State-War-Navy Co-ordinating Committee established on 11 March by Acheson. On 14 April a report from the latter committee said that new forms of aid were needed to protect American security and other national interests. Policy should be guided by considerations like economic stability, political disorder, the need to contain Russian advances, the contribution to a multilateral trading system and the need to keep strategic locations and resources in 'friendly hands'. In May Kennan insisted that it was up to the Europeans to correct the 'economic maladjustment' that made the continent vulnerable to communist domination. The Europeans had to act collectively to draw up recovery programmes, and assume responsibility for them. The Eastern European states could participate in the recovery programme, but only if they agreed to co-operate in a constructive fashion. The American contribution should be to offer 'friendly aid' through drafting a recovery programme, and also to give the finance necessary to implement it. After a visit to Europe the Under Secretary of State for Economic Affairs, William L. Clayton, on 27 May recommended 6 to 7 billion dollars in aid for Europe each year over a three-year period. This was essential to avert economic, social and political chaos in Europe, contain communism, stop the collapse of exports and achieve multilateralism in trade. At a meeting the next day Kennan, Clayton and others spoke to Marshall. There Marshall's special assistant, Charles E. Bohlen, concluded that American aid to Europe should be conditional on 'substantial evidence of a developing over-all plan for economic co-operation by the Europeans themselves, perhaps an economic federation to be worked out over 3 or 4 years'. Russia was not excluded for tactical reasons: there were fears that West Europeans would not be attracted to an anti-communist crusade. The American administration, however, did nothing to encourage Russian participation.[15]

Bohlen drafted the speech Marshall gave at Harvard on 5 June. The Secretary of State spoke of the need for recovery in 'Europe as a whole'. He invited all European countries to co-operate in achieving this. The United States would give financial support and provide 'friendly aid' in drafting a recovery programme. It was up to the Europeans to show initiative and responsibility. Marshall wanted a 'joint' programme 'agreed to by a number, if not all, European nations'.

Marshall had considered giving Bevin advance warning, but had decided not to in case this offended the French. Little effort was made to publicize the Harvard speech in the United States, and the British embassy in Washington did not think it worth the cost of a cable to send an advance copy to London. Acheson, however, warned the BBC correspondent in Washington, Leonard Miall, and it was from the wireless that Bevin first heard the report of Marshall's speech. The French tried to take the initiative: their ambassador in Washington handed over a plan envisaging ad hoc committees to assess Europe's productive assets and aid requirements. But it was Bevin's leadership that mattered. Without any advice from his staff in Washington, he acted on his own initiative. He assured the Americans that there would be a response, and on 9 June suggested joint action with the French. He told the governments of Belgium and the Netherlands that they would be included as well. Bevin went to Paris and agreed to Russian participation in the talks, but insisted that Russia should not be allowed to get away with delaying or obstructive tactics. British officials had talks with Clayton and the new American ambassador, Lew Douglas, between 24 and 26 June. At first Bevin argued that Britain should be treated as a partner in the Marshall programme, rather than being lumped together with the other European countries. Clayton was adamant: that would violate the principle that there would be no piecemeal approach to the European problem; congressional and public opinion would be difficult enough to handle anyway. Bevin went to Paris again with as developed ideas of the American administration's approach as Clayton was able to pass on to him. There Molotov refused to allow any pooling of resources. Bevin felt that the Russians were determined to have American aid on their own terms. He praised the French firmness in the face of

Russian 'intransigence and bullying'. During exchanges in the last meeting of the tripartite conference Bevin whispered to Dixon: 'This really is the birth of the Western bloc.' Molotov left with the warning that rather than a united effort in the reconstruction of Europe, there might be very different results. Bevin told Douglas on 3 July that there should be no weakening on the part of the United States in the face of Russian hostility. If Western Europe was to be saved the United States would have to give effective and speedy help: 'Unless by our joint efforts Western Europe were again put on its feet the Soviet Government would be able to say that their prophesies were well founded, and the ground would be prepared for them to undermine political stability in all Western Democracies.'[16] Bevin had told the Cabinet that it was important that there should be no delay; the proposals should embrace 'as large an area of Europe as possible'.[17]

Sixteen European nations met in Paris between July and September. Initially some of the countries of Eastern Europe showed interest, in particular Poland and Czechoslovakia. But Frank Roberts had warned from the British embassy in Moscow that the Russians were confident and hoped to consolidate their hold on Eastern Europe to the extent that even if Russian troops withdrew the West would not regain influence in the area. He felt that the Russians also wanted to use the Communist Parties, especially those in France and Italy, to unsettle Western Europe. Russia ensured that those East European satellites that were interested rejected the invitation to Paris. It took strong action against what it viewed as opposition forces in Romania, Bulgaria and Hungary. Early in October the Cominform was created, partly with the intention of bringing into line the Communist Parties in Eastern Europe, France and Italy. Russia announced its own recovery plans for its satellites, and the Cominform denounced the United States and Britain. The British Foreign Secretary earned special mention: 'the foreign policy of British imperialism has found in the person of Bevin its most consistent and zealous executor'. At this time the West European countries were drawing up a shopping list. The Americans and some of the French argued for an economic integration of Europe, but this was resisted by Britain. The Labour government did not want to become part of Europe. The British view prevailed: economic co-operation was to be multilateral and functional. Truman presented the European Bill to Congress on 19 December 1947. But there it met with intense opposition. The Republicans disliked steps towards socialism in Europe.

65

The Council of Ministers met again in London on 25 November. There was deadlock on Germany and conflict over the Austrian peace treaty. In private conversations Bevin pressed on the French the importance of organizing the three Western zones of Germany as a unit. He explained that his long-term policy was a closer union between Britain and France, which would include Italy and the Benelux countries at a later stage, leading to the development of an area of Western Europe and Africa that could support itself. By 15 December the Western powers had decided to end the conference. That day Bevin told the Cabinet that there was no purpose in continuing discussions with the Russians, even through the Council of Foreign Ministers.[19]

On the evening of 17 December Bevin outlined the gist of a policy that he was formulating to deal with what Walter Lippmann, the American columnist, a few months earlier had described as the 'Cold War'. Bevin felt that it was important to take a wider view of the situation, and not just regard it as a dispute between Russia and the Western powers. A positive plan was essential for the association of the Western democratic countries – including the United States, Britain, France, Italy and others – and the Dominions. This was not to be a formal alliance, but 'an understanding backed by power, money and resolute action', 'a sort of spiritual federation of the West'. Bevin preferred the British conception of informal and unwritten understandings to the written constitutions. A powerful consolidation of the West would show Russia that it could not advance any further. Marshall commented that it was necessary to distinguish between the material and spiritual aspects and that the two of them should reach an understanding between themselves as soon as possible on immediate objectives: 'They must take events at the flood stream and produce a co-ordinated effect.'[20]

Churchill had proposed an association of the English-speaking peoples in March 1946 at Fulton, Missouri. Louis St Laurent, the Canadian Foreign Minister, addressing the General Assembly on 17 September 1947, had mentioned that nations might 'seek greater safety in an association of democratic and peace-loving states willing to accept more specific international obligations in return for a greater measure of national security'. St Laurent felt, however, that such associations could be formed within the United Nations.[21] But what Bevin seems to have envisaged at this time was something like the alignment Chamberlain had brought about by September 1939. Bevin's association, like that in 1939, was to be informal, and to include the Dominions.

Bevin summarized his policy towards Russia in a Cabinet paper early in the new year. He explained that throughout Eastern Europe the pattern of a Russian-dominated political and economic structure was becoming increasingly obvious. Even Czechoslovakia was threatened. Western and particularly British and American interests and influence were being eliminated everywhere. This undermining was also the keystone of Russian policy in the Middle East. If the Russians secured control of France and French North Africa, of Italy and of Greece, and particularly if they could undermine Britain's position in the Middle East, they could effectively dominate the Mediterranean and could deprive Britain of access to extensive markets and raw materials, especially oil, without which Britain's economic recovery would be difficult or impossible, and the strategic position both of Britain and the United States gravely jeopardized. If Russian political plans for southern and Western Europe were to succeed they would be in a position with their armed forces to place Britain in a hopeless position strategically. Furthermore, without the oil reserves of Iran and the Middle East, neither the British Commonwealth nor the United States could exert their full strength. The Foreign Secretary concluded: 'It is thus evident that the success of Russian expansionist plans would threaten the three main elements of Commonwealth defence, the security of the United Kingdom, the control of sea communications, and the defence of the Middle East.'[22]

To meet this menace Bevin outlined to the Cabinet, on 8 January 1948, a suggestion that Britain should try to form, with the backing of the United States and the Dominions, a Western democratic system comprising Scandinavia, the Low Countries, France, Italy, Greece and possibly Portugal. This might include Spain and Germany at a later stage. This did not have to be a formal alliance, though the Foreign Secretary did concede that Britain had an alliance with France and could conclude alliances with other countries. Bevin thought it important also to mobilize the resources of Africa and the other British and European colonial territories. The Cabinet supported the proposal, and Bevin sent a copy of his memorandum to Marshall.[23]

Bevin also sent a copy to Paris, and on 13 January the British ambassador, Sir Oliver Franks, was asked to impress on Georges Bidault that Britain wanted close co-operation with France. The two countries should make a simultaneous approach to Belgium, Holland and Luxembourg offering treaties like that of Dunkirk signed in March 1947 between Britain and France. At the same time they should think how Italy, other Mediterranean countries and Scandinavia could be included. Bidault liked the idea, and on 22 January Bevin announced to a crowded House of Commons that talks had been proposed to the Benelux countries. The Foreign Secretary spoke to the house of a 'Western Union' to meet the threat of Russia, and stressed that he was not just thinking of Europe as a geographic conception, but of collaboration with the Commonwealth and European territories overseas, initially in Africa and South-East Asia. Sensitive to American opinion he did not mention the United States.[24]

On 19 January Marshall told the British ambassador, Lord Inverchapel (formerly Sir Archibald Clark Kerr), that he was considering what procedure would be the most effective, and at what point he could suggest the participation of the United States in Bevin's plan.[25] Bevin was not worried about the form of the American approach, provided that they were prepared 'to come in'.[26] For a while the Americans hesitated: in the State Department Jack Hickerson, the Chief of the Division of European Affairs, supported by John Foster Dulles, wanted American participation, but they were blocked by Kennan and the counsellor Charles Bohlen. Bohlen argued that the United States should avoid any undertaking involving a direct commitment. The Under Secretary, Robert A. Lovett, was a cautious man. In any case there were difficulties in congress with the European Recovery Programme.[27]

Bevin, too, had his problems: with the Chiefs of Staff and the Prime Minister. Committing British troops to the European continent was anathema to some of the military planners. Attlee thought much the same as he did at the beginning of 1947. On 11 June 1947 Attlee and the Chiefs of Staff had approved a paper, DO(47)44, which outlined Britain's broad strategy in the event of a war with Russia. That paper did recommend that 'every effort should be made to organize an association of Western European Powers, which would at least delay the enemy's advance across Europe'. It went further: Britain should 'encourage the building up of a strong Western Region of Defence with France as its keystone, and ensure that Germany does not become a Russian satellite'. But the priorities decided previously were to stay: the basic requirements of British strategy remained the defence of the United Kingdom and a firm hold on the Middle East – both areas were to be developed as offensive bases – and the control of sea communications. Operations with land forces on the European continent were not contemplated at the outbreak of war. The Chiefs of Staff had estimated that the annual cost of the forces needed to implement DO(47)44 was £1,100 million. Because of this forces had had to be drastically cut. On 30 January 1948 Montgomery, the Chief of the Imperial General Staff, questioned the premiss of DO(47)44. He argued that in any future war the only enemy envisaged was Russia. Prevailing conditions in that country meant that war before 1957 was unlikely, and possibly it would not start before 1960. The struggle could be between two ideologies: communism and democracy. The first objective of the 'East' was the German 'soul' as a necessary step towards world domination. The West wanted to stop this: a united Germany looking westwards rather than eastwards was essential. If a war against Russia was to be successful Britain had to ensure the early entry of the United States, see that there was sufficent strength from Commonwealth resources to hold the position in the Middle East until American aid could become effective, and keep on good terms with the Arab countries. The Chief of the Air Staff, Lord Tedder, and Sir John Cunningham, Admiral of the Fleet, both responded that no details of strategy could be stated, particularly any which committed Britain to a land campaign on the European continent, until there had been an assessment of the effects to be expected from weapons of mass destruction, and before the Americans had said what armed forces they would contribute to a war against Russia. It had already been decided that the British Commonwealth, without the help of the United States, could not expect to defeat Russia and its satellites. Cunningham reminded the Chiefs of Staff Committee on 2 February that it had been traditional British policy in the past to avoid European continental commitments: 'Twice in the past we had given a guarantee to assist a continental nation to the limit of our power by the provision of land forces. On both occasions we had suffered severely, first at Mons and more recently at Dunkirk.' But Montgomery insisted that the Western Union powers alone would not be able to stop the Russians from overrunning Europe. The Western Union had to have the full assistance of Britain and the British Commonwealth. He insisted that a Western Union could only be created and supported if Britain gave 'a guarantee to support those countries to the limit of our power by the provision of land, sea and air forces'. Because of the political implications of this difference of opinion Tedder referred the matter to A. V. Alexander, the Minister of Defence. On the one hand Montgomery insisted that Britain should decide immediately, and tell the Americans, that irrespective of any American plans, it would support the Western powers on the European continent with all its forces. Unless Britain did that Western Union would collapse. Against Montgomery stood Tedder and Cunningham. In the latter's view British policy on operations in Europe would only be decided in collaboration with the Americans, and any policy of engaging in a continental war had first to be related to its effect on Britain's ability to meet its other commitments.

On 4 February Attlee, Bevin and Alexander met the Chiefs of Staff. Tedder and Cunningham argued that it would prove financially and economically impossible to place an army on the continent on the outbreak of war, especially as in any future war Britain would have to be prepared for full-scale operations at the start. Supporting air forces would be needed as well as additional land forces. Furthermore, 'it was open to doubt whether it was militarily sound to attempt to hold an enemy, with such predominant superiority in manpower, on the Continent'. British support of a strong 'Western Region of Defence with France as its keystone' should be limited in Western Europe to naval and air forces. What Britain could afford had to determine its assistance to any Western Union. Attlee reminded the meeting that a previous staff conference had accepted that the whole of Europe might be overrun by the enemy. The Prime Minister was disturbed by this new idea that Britain might send land forces to the continent. He had thought that the British plan was to develop a counter-offensive from the Middle East. This would need considerable land and air forces in the Middle East, and Attlee did not see how Britain could support forces on the European continent as well: 'Previous experience had shown how Continental commitments, initially small, were apt to grow into very large ones.' In any case, the countries of the Western Union would not be much encouraged by a British offer of land forces if it turned out that the British contribution was only one or two divisions. Attlee also disliked Montgomery's suggestion that Germany should be built up again. It was dangerous to think of Russia as the only potential enemy: the Chiefs of Staff might have said that in 1922. The Prime Minister insisted that British defence policy should not be too rigid. A future world war might not start in Europe: Russia and the United States might fight in the Far East. Finally, he did not like 'the conception of holding a specific line on the Continent'. He was opposed to Britain giving any definite assurances as to how it would participate in a future war. Attlee wanted to know what American intentions were.

As in January 1947 Bevin fought his Prime Minister. The Foreign Secretary did not know what the Americans intended: they had not made up their minds. But he intended to tell them that Britain 'could not act as a mercenary army or defensive outpost for them'. Bevin believed that the American military authorities knew that security lay in taking action at once wherever it might be. His approach to Western Union differed from that of any of the Chiefs of Staff. He regarded the forces of Western Union as one force. The Western Union had sufficient manpower to withstand attack; forces should be provided on a budgetary basis. National pride must be overcome and all resources pooled. There was already a close link between the French and British navies; he would like to see the same thing happen with the air forces. An approach along these lines would lead to the result that the European continental countries would provide the bulk of manpower for the land forces. Bevin had envisaged the Rhine as the dividing line between the Western democracies and their opponents. But that was not the way to approach the problem. First it was necessary to see what forces could be provided, and then how best they could be used. If Britain found that it had land forces to spare, Bevin had no fundamental objection to these fighting on the European continent. The Foreign Secretary asked the Chiefs of Staff to consider how the forces of Britain, France, the Benelux countries and possibly Italy should be organized and rationalized so as to form one effective whole. He could then make the Americans realize that they had to join any future war at the outset. Indeed Marshall had already suggested to him the possibility of rationalizing the British and American forces. In any case collaboration in defence was only one facet of Western Union. Bevin was trying to arrange close links between the countries concerned in banking, finance and currency, and for economic links with Africa and with the British Commonwealth. Both East and West were courting Germany. Germany might become a menace again. This was another reason for having a regional defence organization in Western Europe, possibly within the framework of the Charter of the United Nations.

The meeting resolved that the sending of land forces to the European continent needed further study, and in the meantime policy would be along the lines suggested by Bevin.[28] At the time Britain was undertaking commitments under the Brussels treaty and so these fundamental questions of European strategy remained unresolved. On 17 March the Chiefs of Staff outlined a possible new strategy for Britain designed to support Bevin's foreign policy of concluding treaties with the Benelux, Atlantic and Mediterranean powers. On the assumption that the defence resources of these powers were available, and that the Americans would participate both politically and militarily, the Chiefs recommended that the primary aim of Britain's defence policy was to prevent war, but to be ready to act if war were forced upon it. The collective defence policy to be adopted by Britain and its allies should be to build up defensive forces to prevent Russia from crossing a given 'stop' line. It had already been agreed that it was essential for the security of the Commonwealth to defend the United Kingdom, the Middle East and sea communications. Under the prevailing British foreign policy and the collective defence policy envisaged, 'the *desirable* strategic objectives' were: first, the defence of Europe as far to the East as possible; and, secondly, the defence of the Middle East. If American support were promised, the military thought that the next step was to get agreement from Washington and the other allies on these definitions of desirable defence policy and strategic objectives. Planning talks could then proceed to assess the defence resources of Britain's allies; to agree the timing and likely scale of attack, and the forces needed to meet it; and to decide the defence contributions of the individual allies. Only when the last point had been decided would it be possible to assess whether the *desirable* strategic objectives' were attainable, whether modifications had to be made and where and on what scale it was desirable to commit British forces to participate in operations.[29]

While the Chiefs of Staff were evolving a strategic policy to implement the new British foreign policy little progress was being made in Washington. Further advances by Russia, however, changed that. On 25 February there was a coup in Prague, and the Russians took over Czechoslovakia, the country which in 1945 the United States had anticipated would develop free from interference of East or West. The next day Bevin saw the American ambassador, Douglas, and told him that 'we were now in the crucial period of six to eight weeks which I had long foreseen would decide the future of Europe'. By mid April he expected that the Russians would have completed the next stage of their forward march. Within the following three months they might be on the Pyrenees if resolute action were not taken. Talk was no good. Action was needed to stop the further spread of 'dictatorship and totalitarian ideas'. Seeing the issue as a struggle with communism just raised theoretical issues. Rather it was 'a straight issue between dictatorship and liberty'. New heart had to be put into the countries directly menaced such as Italy and even France. Bevin wanted a meeting of the Western governments including the United States. Strong action could entail the risk of war. Bevin thought war less likely if firm action were taken instead of letting matters slide from crisis to crisis as had happened in the 1930s.

Questioned by Douglas, Bevin said that he did not insist on a conference; private consultation would do. As well as Britain and the United States, Bevin wanted to include France, the Benelux countries and Italy. He did not expect the Scandinavian countries to join at that time. Above all he wanted secret talks with the Americans to evolve a sort of joint military and civil strategy.

We should be able to pool our ideas and obtain real solidarity in Western Europe, thus facing the Soviet Union with solid resistance and so preventing them from developing their present technique of absorbing countries one by one. I had no fear of the future provided we got through the next six or eight weeks. But I was really anxious lest the period immediately before us should turn out to have been the last chance for saving the West.[30]

Bevin thought that Italy was the immediate danger-spot. Douglas agreed that the Russians would do everything possible to capture that country. There was the danger that the Italian Communist Party allied with the militant Italian Socialist Party, would win the election in April. On 6 March Bevin suggested to Douglas that they should both study how a coup d'état in Italy, similar to the one in Czechoslovakia, could be prevented. Consideration should be given to British, American and French military support to a legitimate government against any communist attempt to drive it out. After the coup in Prague, Bevin thought that such a policy would be supported in Britain. Recent information suggested that the Russians were relaxing pressure on Greece to concentrate on Italy. Bevin was prepared to suggest that the British and American Chiefs of Staff should consider sending military equipment and troops to Italy if events developed there along the lines of the Prague coup. The idea appealed to Douglas.[31] On 10 February the National Security Council had decided that the United States should use military power if necessary to ensure that Italy remained a friendly and anti-communist state. On 8 March it authorized secret operations by the Central Intelligence Agency. Truman allowed covert arms shipments. American propaganda stressed the importance of Marshall Aid for Italian economic recovery. The Foreign Office arranged for Italian social democratic trade unionists to visit London for a conference on Labour participation in the European Recovery Programme. The Christian Democrats defeated the Popular Front alliance, winning 48·5 per cent of the vote and an absolute majority in the parliament.[32]

Following the coup in Czechoslovakia Bevin presented the Cabinet with a paper entitled 'The Threat to Western Civilisation'. On 5 March he told that body that resolute action had to be taken to counter the Russian threat to Western civilization. In giving general support, the Cabinet laid special emphasis on the need to strengthen the democratic forces in France and Italy, and to prevent the weakening of the Commonwealth through the secession of India and possibly Pakistan. It was thought that resistance to Russian expansion could not be successful unless Britain could 'secure a higher standard of living both at home and in those countries which were ranged on our side; but it would also be necessary to base our campaign on the higher moral and spiritual values of Western civilisation'. A pooling of defence resources between these countries was necessary and the weapon of propaganda should be used to the full. An unnamed member of the Cabinet, however, suggested that 'we should use United States aid to gain time, but our ultimate aim should be to attain a position in which the countries of Western Europe could be independent both of the United States and of the Soviet Union'.[33]

Later that day, after the Cabinet's approval for a policy of a wider conception of Western Union, Frank Roberts, Bevin's new principal private secretary – Dixon had gone as ambassador to Prague – noted down the thoughts of the Foreign Secretary. Bevin hoped for the general co-ordination and defence of the whole world outside the Russian orbit, the United Nations as it should have been had the Russians co-operated. Without eliminating the United Nations machinery, it was necessary to develop a more practical world organization which would gradually be extended from the Western European nations. That alone would be able to provide genuine collective security. South America would be brought in on an economic basis. In another war South America would have to provide food and raw materials on Lend Lease terms since other countries would be bearing the main burden of defence. India and Pakistan should be brought in, and as co-operation developed with those Dominions, and with the whole 'middle zone' stretching to Indonesia and Malaya, Britain's Middle Eastern problems would fall into place in the wider perspective. It was necessary to consult the United States, and make Washington face up to its responsibilities at an early stage, but care had to be taken over the timing of this. The immediate practical steps to implement these objectives included, first, co-operation with the Commonwealth. Bevin wanted consultation between the Commonwealth governments on the new British policy approved by the Cabinet. It was unrealistic consulting with the Commonwealth at long range by telegrams. Secondly, there needed to be a study of defence, looking at the defence problems of the Western Union, the Atlantic approaches which meant close co-operation not only with the United States but with Eire and Iceland – the Scandinavians should also be brought into the scheme on this Atlantic basis and not in the context of the narrower Western Union being worked out with France and the Benelux countries – and collective security, embracing the Americas, Africa and Asia in the wide sense. Thirdly, Bevin thought that the moment had come to harness spiritual forces. The freedom of the individual was so closely bound up with religious freedom and general spiritual values that all the great religious faiths, Christian, Moslem and Buddhist, could be brought together in opposition to communism. Before organizing Islam and Buddhism there needed to be unity among the Christian churches. The Roman Catholic Church was a problem. He intended to see all the leaders of the Christian churches in Britain including the Roman Catholic Cardinal and the Archbishop of Canterbury. Bevin wanted a world congress of Christian churches to be held, possibly in Geneva, later that year. Fourthly, the socialist parties should be strengthened under British leadership with the slogan 'Democratic Socialism' rather than 'Social Democracy' which had Marxist associations.[34]

Shortly afterwards, apparent Russian moves against Norway seemingly led Bevin to conclude that the time was right for a specific approach to the United States. On 8 March Halvard Lange, the Norwegian Foreign Minister, told the British and American ambassadors that Norway might soon be asked to sign a pact with Russia. Lange asked for a judgement on Norway's strategic position, and whether Britain and the United States would come to Norway's aid if Russia went too far.[35] Bevin also feared Russian moves against Finland: at the end of February Stalin had proposed a pact of friendship and military alliance with that country. On 11 March Marshall received a message from

Bevin asking for immediate consultations on the setting up of an Atlantic security system. Bevin mentioned the defence system being negotiated at that time in Brussels, but thought that it would be impractical to ask the Scandinavian countries to join that. Instead 'the most effective steps would be to take very early steps, before Norway goes under, to conclude under Article 51 of the Charter of the U.N. a regional Atlantic Approaches Pact of Mutual Assistance, in which all the countries directly threatened by a Russian move to the Atlantic could participate, for example U.S, U.K., Canada, Eire, Iceland, Norway, Denmark, Portugal, France (and Spain, when it has a democratic regime)'. The Foreign Secretary suggested three defence systems: the first involved Britain, France and the Benelux countries with American backing; the second was a scheme of Atlantic security with which the United States would be even more closely concerned; and the third was a Mediterranean security system which would particularly affect Italy. These proposals also went to the Canadian Department of External Affairs. Mackenzie King and Marshall were both enthusiastic. Marshall consulted Truman, ignored his obstructionist State Department officials and replied on 12 March that Washington was 'prepared to proceed at once in the joint discussion on the establishment of an Atlantic security system'. He wanted British representatives in Washington early the following week.[36]

On 17 March Bevin confided to Bidault that he felt the Americans should underwrite the Brussels treaty. If there were war the United States should be in from the first day. An exchange of views would take place shortly through the Chiefs of Staff with the Americans. Both men agreed that Norway could not be left to face the Russian threat on its own: the Americans would have to face up to their responsibilities.[37] The Treaty of Brussels, signed that same day, set up the Western European Union. It was to last for fifty years. The five signatories, Britain, France Belgium, the Netherlands and Luxembourg, were to come to the aid of any one of their number which was attacked. It was understood that other powers could join.[38]

Opinion was changing in the United States. The day the Brussels treaty was signed Truman asked Congress for selective service to maintain the strength of American armed forces. The coup in Czechoslovakia so shook Congressmen that the bill for Marshall Aid had a relatively easy passage. It was against this background that delegates from Britain, Canada and the United States met in the Pentagon between 22 March and 1 April. The

Americans blocked French participation on the grounds of security. One of the British delegates, however, was Donald Maclean, the Russian spy, and it seems evident from an article in the Polish press of 4 April that the Russians knew what went on. Bevin's envisaged triple system of alliances was abandoned. It was evident that if the United States were to join any defence system it would have to be in association not only with certain selected Western European democracies but if practicable with all of them. If possible, Italy would have to be admitted. Furthermore, a defence organization was eventually envisaged under Article 51 of the United Nations Charter which acknowledged the right of individual and collective self-defence, covering all the Middle Eastern states and Greece. The Americans also wanted further defence agreements under this article covering South-East Asia and eventually the whole of the Far East. In the end the issue focused on whether the Americans should propose a collective defence agreement for the North Atlantic area as a whole, or whether a presidential declaration of support of the Western European democracies would be enough. Bevin thought that the Russians would not be deterred by a presidential declaration, and in any case Britain would be lucky if Truman and the leaders of the Senate pronounced in favour of 'a treaty binding the United States for the first time in her history to accept positive obligations in the way of the defence of her natural associates and friends'. The Pentagon did not want a war with Russia; if there were people in the United States who wanted to force the issue while the Americans still had the monopoly of the atomic bomb, they were elsewhere. Like the British, the Canadian delegates wanted a treaty rather than a presidential declaration. It was hoped that the Americans would summon a conference to discuss the new 'Security Pact for the North Atlantic Area' in May, after the Italian elections. Later in April Lovett saw Senator Vandenberg. As a result of this meeting, helped by a declaration by St Laurent in Canada, the Senate adopted Resolution 239 on 11 June: it recommended the 'association of the United States, by constitutional process, with such regional and other collective arrangements as are based on continuous and effective self-help and mutual aid, and as affect its national security'. In the end the negotiations with all the states concerned did not start until 6 July 1948. By then Kennan's opposition had collapsed, and the other principal opponent of the pact, Bohlen, was sent to Paris as adviser to the American delegation at the General Assembly.[39]. But the British embassy in Washington warned that the Americans were in no hurry: they did not regard themselves as equal partners in the enterprise. 'They still feel that they are in the position of a kind of fairy godmother handing over favours to the less fortunate Western European countries – provided always that the latter can justify their claims for such favours.[40].

Bevin, however, was confident. If the Americans asked him to take the initiative, they did respond appropriately. That had been evidenced with Marshall Aid. When he had taken the lead with Western Union, they had backed him. The Foreign Secretary thought the Atlantic Pact the most important task in front of the new British ambassador in Washington, Oliver Franks. Franks had had great success in negotiating the European Recovery Programme. Advantage had to be taken of 'the present honeymoon period' in Washington to clinch the Atlantic Pact.[41] Bevin trusted the American leaders. He was not shaken by the Russian 'peace offensive' which took the form of exchanges between the American ambassador in Moscow, Walter Bedell Smith, and Molotov during April and May 1948.[42] Whatever misunderstanding there had been, Bevin said that he himself had never had any suspicions about American intentions 'on those matters in which we were moving in full consultation'. Without meaning any offence, the Foreign Secretary explained that 'he realised that America had not so much experience in foreign affairs as we had and that while she was developing a sense of responsibility remarkably well, there must occasionally be setbacks to which he did not attach excessive importance'.[43]

On 28 July Attlee approved a Foreign Office paper, endorsed by Bevin, to be used in preliminary discussions with the Americans. The paper outlined the series of well-timed moves by which Russia had consolidated its hold on Finland, Poland, Czechoslovakia, Hungary, Romania, Bulgaria, Albania and Yugoslavia. Encouragement should not be taken from signs of strain in the Russian system. In Yugoslavia Marshall Tito was a communist unlikely to transfer his allegiance to the West. The dispute was a family one, and there were signs that the Yugoslav leaders were seeking an accommodation. Popular dissatisfaction was likely to be used as an excuse for further repression and for tightening the communist stranglehold. The Russians had established themselves solidly in Eastern Europe, and from that secure entrenchment they were trying to infiltrate into Western and southern Europe. Their tactic was to probe along the Western line in the hope of finding a weak spot, 'and so of effecting a penetration which would cause the whole line to collapse. Measures to consolidate the West in the face of this menace had not deflected Russia from its purpose. The struggle was concentrated in varying degrees upon the principal bastions of the Western line in Europe: Germany, Austria, Trieste, Greece and Turkey. Special attention was given to Germany. Britain wanted a Western Germany forming part of the Western defence system. That would be the most effective barrier against the spread of communism across Europe. By then the Russians had blockaded Berlin:

> To retreat from Berlin, the last democratic island in the Soviet sphere of control, would immensely increase Soviet prestige, win over the doubtful masses in Germany to their side and depress our friends in each of the free countries of Europe. It would also encourage the Russians to hazard adventures in Vienna, Turkey or elsewhere. On the other hand, if we stand fast in Berlin we shall undoubtedly rally German opinion and gain the time which is so necessary to pursue the advantages we possess in the West.

The West had to remain in Berlin.[44]

The Berlin blockade marked the joining of the Cold War. In his conversation with Douglas, on 26 February, Bevin had anticipated 'serious happenings' in Germany within the following two months.[45] Following a collision in the air corridor to Berlin between a British civil aircraft and a Russian fighter, Montgomery visited the city in March. He instigated an emergency plan whereby the West would only withdraw to the Rhine. Russia imposed a partial blockade on the city on 1 April. On 12 May Alexander finally agreed with Montgomery that British forces stationed on the European continent would stay and fight in an emergency. They would, however, not be reinforced apart from administrative backing. By the end of May the Americans had agreed that their forces would stay in Germany. On 24 June Russia severed the rail, road and water routes between the Western zones and Berlin. General Sir Brian Robertson, the British Military Governor, suggested to his American counterpart, General Lucius Clay, that Berlin might be supplied by air. On 27 June Bevin suggested to American officials the need for an Anglo–American force which could lift at least 2,000 tons a day. Marshall, on 30 June, said that the United States would stay in Berlin. Bevin then urged the Americans to take military measures by increasing the airlift, and sending the B–29 bomber to Britain.

The National Security Council on 15 July agreed to dispatch these 'atomic bombers' to Britain from where they could reach Moscow. Sixty bombers were sent to East Anglia, and the first American Strategic Air Command base was established on British soil. At the time it was not known whether these B-29s did carry atomic bombs. But it was a psychological move. The modified B-29s capable of carrying atomic bombs did not arrive in Britain until the summer of 1949. Bevin did not think that the Russians would go to war over Berlin, and he was determined not to give way.[46] American bombers on British soil might have made Britain an obvious target for Russia, but it also probably ensured that the United States would fight at Britain's side. Britain would not have to wait for a Pearl Harbor. The bombers were seen as a 'protection' for Britain. The Cabinet did not accept the principle that there should be a permanent American base in Britain, and the matter was not reported to Parliament. At the end of 1949, in any case, Britain was prepared to formalize the American presence in 'an adequate, proper and agreed arrangement'.[47] At the end of 1948 the Royal Air Force did not know what plans the Americans had for the use of the atomic bomb in war; Tedder asked the American Secretary of Defence, James Forrestal, for technical details so that British bombers could be designed to carry the American atomic bomb. Forrestal thought that these could be supplied, but doubted whether information could be disclosed about atomic energy developments generally.[48] The psychological threat of the B-29s, Western resolution and the technical success of the airlift forced the Russians to give way. At the end of May 1949 they lifted the blockade. On a military level, in mounting the Berlin airlift the Anglo–American alliance had been revived almost on its Second World War footing. With the arrival of the B-29 bombers Bevin had the practical assurance of the American commitment to Europe. The Anglo–American special relationship was working.[49]

The Berlin blockade encouraged Western unity, and was a favourable background for the negotiations leading to the establishment of the North Atlantic Treaty Organization. During these Bevin was irked by unofficial hints, spurred on by speeches from Churchill, that Britain should become part of a united Europe. He told Marshall that Britain was not 'a small country of no account'.[50] On 19 October 1948 Bevin explained to the Commonwealth Prime Ministers meeting in London that he did not favour an immediate attempt to establish a united states of Europe. Within the foreseeable future it was not practicable: 'It was alien to the British inclination to create grandiose paper constitutions.'[51]

At this gathering Bevin also tried to complement the Washington discussions with his earlier scheme to involve the Dominions. The Dominion Prime Ministers, including those from India and Pakistan, were given comprehensive details of the new British defence policy. The British Chiefs of Staff suggested that, in the event of war, five aims should be pursued in co-operation with all the allies: to secure the integrity of the Commonwealth countries; to mount a strategic air offensive; to hold the enemy as far east as possible in Western Europe; to maintain a firm hold on the Middle East; and to control essential sea communications. The two main aspects of defence co-operation were: first, the co-ordination of general issues affecting all allies, for example, the fundamental objectives of defence policy and strategy, and the utilization of resources and dispersal; secondly, the planning of action in the various regions. The Chiefs of Staff also suggested the essential measures required in peace to allow the Commonwealth countries to fight successfully in war. Common strategic objectives had to be prepared and plans co-ordinated. Balanced armed forces had to be ready for immediate use on the outbreak of war, with the necessary resources to support them. Co-operation had to be maintained between all members of the Commonwealth on all aspects of defence. The early support and action of the United States had to be ensured. The Commonwealth had to co-ordinate defence plans with the Western Union. The Allied scientific and technical lead had to be maintained and increased.[52] Tedder told the Commonwealth Prime Ministers that the worldwide Cold War being waged by the Russians was designed to sap the will of the people to resist, and the economic strength of the countries concerned. There was no definite evidence of Russian preparations for war in the immediate future, but British sources of intelligence in Russia were scanty. Because of the national economy Britain could not retain large forces, so its 'deterrent' forces had to be highly organized and equipped on the most modern lines, and trained and ready for action. St Laurent said that Canada did not want to be committed to anything more than regional defence. Herbert Vere Evatt of Australia reflected his own socialist and pacifist views when he said that only through making the United Nations effective could war be averted. The Prime Minister of New Zealand, however, said that all New Zealand wanted was to be told what the Chiefs of Staff required of it. New Zealand would do all in its power to carry that out.The new Afrikaner Nationalist South African Foreign Minister, Eric Louw, said that South Africa would welcome close co-operation in defence. For political reasons South Africa emphasized the regional aspect, but that meant much more than 'local'. South Africa was interested in the whole of the African continent and its approaches. The Middle East was considered a keystone of the international structure, and consequently was of great interest to South Africa. South Africa was also likely to become one of the largest producers of uranium, found in its gold-bearing ores, and important for the nuclear programme. Nehru took up this theme. India had vast quantities of uranium, and he wanted the Commonwealth countries to co-operate with India in the development of atomic energy, for peaceful purposes if possible, but for others if necessary. He favoured a positive policy to avert war, but was not frightened by the communist menace in India. Pakistan's Prime Minister, Liaquat Ali Khan, complained that partition had left Pakistan with responsibilities without a fair share of resources. The north–west and Burmese frontiers had to be defended, and Commonwealth countries should recognize that their defence was for the benefit of the Commonwealth as a whole. Ceylon was prepared to do all in its power to co-operate in the defence of the Commonwealth, but could not make any substantial contribution in the way of manpower or equipment. Montgomery warned that in any grand design or master plan for Commonwealth and Western Union defence it had to be realized that parts of the empire could be temporarily overrun. But provided the United Kingdom, the Mediterranean, Africa and the control of communications on the Atlantic and Indian Oceans were retained, it would be possible to fight back. The retention of the Middle East would protect the land approach to Africa.[53]

Following the Commonwealth Prime Ministers' Conference, bilateral defence discussions and strategic planning were started between Britain, Australia and New Zealand.[54] Talks began with South Africa in 1949. In February of that year the British Chiefs of Staff maintained that the close co-operation between the British Commonwealth and the United States, together with the development of the Western Union and the European Recovery Programme, were most disquieting to Russia's leaders. Given the prevailing balance of strength Russia would pursue a policy of communist penetration aided by economic distress rather than open warfare.[55]

By the end of 1948 the caution of the American delegates negotiating the Atlantic Pact evaporated. In the summer they had been worried about committing Congress, and the likelihood of Truman losing the presidential election. But Truman was returned against all the odds, and opinion in the United States moved strongly in favour of a pact. Lovett spoke to Franks about the need to take the 'present tide of favourable opinion at the flood'. The final round of talks took place in Washington between January and April.[56] Iceland, Norway, Denmark, Ireland and Portugal were invited to join the talks. Truman was persuaded to drop his objections to Italian membership. There were difficulties in the American Senate over Article 5 which in its final form stated: 'The Parties agree that an armed attack against one or more of them in Europe or North America shall be considered an attack against them all; and consequently they agree that, if such armed attack occurs, each of them, in exercise of the right of individual or collective self-defence recognized by Article 51 of the Charter of the United Nations, will assist the Party or Parties so attacked by taking forthwith, individually and in concert with other Parties, such action as it deems necessary, including the use of armed force, to restore and maintain international peace and security.' The North Atlantic Treaty was signed in Washington on 4 April 1949 by twelve governments.[57] Bevin felt that the pact had 'steadied the world'.[58]

It was, at one time, easy and fashionable to dismiss the events of these years as British and American imperialism threatening a peaceful non-expansionist Russia.[59] To do this neglects the real sense of threat felt in Britain and the United States. At one time it appeared that the agitation of the Communist Parties in France and Italy might easily lead to those countries falling under Russian influence, and after that there would not be much of Europe left. British and, by 1946, American statesmen were inclined to think of Europe in terms of what later became known as the domino theory when it was applied to Asia. After its rejection by Russia the Marshall Plan was used to stop the dominoes from falling. It can be said that the emergence of the Cold War marked a transitional period in relations between Britain and the United States, and the Western world and Russia. The United States took over Britain's mantle of world leadership – which British statesmen, in view of the supposed Russian threat, saw as necessary. Even during the Second World War, Churchill had been obsessed with the need to secure a firm American commitment to Europe. Bevin, the Foreign Secretary of a socialist government, continued in the Churchillian tradition and achieved the objective. Although British and American statesmen had, at various times, markedly different views of Russia's intentions, by the beginning of 1946 these were beginning to coincide. Only then was unified action possible, though there were earlier indications of the United States and Britain acting on parallel lines. But in the United States public opinion lagged behind the perceptions of the statesmen. Though it is possible to make too much of 'left–wing' criticism of Truman, he nevertheless had to move carefully to secure congressional support for his programme. Bevin did not have to educate the British public to the same extent. On 17 December 1947 he envisaged an association of the Western democratic countries – including the United States, Britain, France, Italy and others – and the Dominions. By the middle of 1949 the North Atlantic Treaty had been signed, and defence discussions initiated with Australia, New Zealand and South Africa. Bevin saw the Cold War not just in European but in global terms. It was spreading to the Middle East, Asia and Africa.

Notes: Chapter 3

1 Anderson, *The United States, Great Britain, and the Cold War*, p. 169.
2 S. M. Hartmann,*Truman and the 80th Congress* (Columbia, Miss., 1971); T. G. Paterson, 'Presidential foreign policy, public opinion and Congress: the Truman years', *Diplomatic History*, vol. 3 (1979), pp. 1–18; L. S. Wittner, 'The Truman doctrine and the defense of freedom', *Diplomatic History*, vol. 4 (1980), pp. 161–88.
3 *FRUS*, 1947(3), pp. 197–248.
4 Georgetown University Library, Washington DC, Robert F. Wagner Papers, Box 3, File 47, Confidential Memorandum, 13 March 1947; Wagner to Vandenberg, 19 March 1947.
5 Princeton University Library, Forrestal Diaries, Box 4, Vol. 7, fol. 1762, 4 August 1947.
6 Forrestal Diaries, Box 4, Vol. 7, ofl. 1751, 26 July 1947.
7 George C. Marshall Library, Lexington, Va, RG 59, Records of the Policy Planning Staff 1947–53, Box 31, Berry to Kennan, Secret, 31 July 1947.
8 Public Record Office, London, DEFE 4/7, COS (47) 116, Top Secret, 5 September 1947.
9 Wittner, *American Intervention in Greece*, pp. 228–30.
10 CAB 128/9, fol. 63, CM15(47), Secret, 3 February 1947.
11 See R. Ovendale, *The Origins of the Arab–Israeli Wars* (London,1984), pp. 74–119.
12 Bullock, *Ernest Bevin*, pp. 352–3, 481–2; Barker, *The British between the Superpowers*, pp. 76–7.
13 S. Greenwood, 'Ernest Bevin, France and "Western Union": August 1945–February 1946', *European History Quarterly*, vol. 14 (1984), pp. 319–37; 'Return to Dunkirk: the origins of the Anglo–French treaty of March 1947', *Journal of Strategic Studies*, vol. 6 (1983), pp. 49–65; *contra* J. Baylis, 'Britain and the Dunkirk treaty: the origins of NATO', *Journal of Strategic Studies*, vol. 5 (1982), pp. 236–47; 'British wartime thinking about a post–war European security group', *Review of International Studies*, vol. 9 (1983), pp. 265–81; C. Wiebes and B. Zeeman, 'Baylis on

post-war planning', and J. Baylis,'A reply', *Review of International Studies*, vol. 10 (1984), pp. 247–52; D. Cooper, *Old Men Forget* (London, 1953), pp. 369–71; Public Record Office, London, FO 800/465, fol. 28, Cooper to Bevin, 3 September 1947.

14 'Return to Dunkirk', pp.57–62; Bullock, *Ernest Bevin*, pp.357–9; Barker, *The British between the Superpowers*, p. 73; Morgan, *Labour in Power* pp. 268–9.

15 M. J. Hogan, 'The search for a "creative peace": the United States, European unity, and the origins of the Marshall Plan', *Diplomatic History*, vol.6 (1982), pp. 267–85; W. C. Cromwell, 'The Marshall Plan, Britain and the Cold War', *Review of International Studies*, vol. 8 (1982), pp. 233–49 at p. 237.

16 FO 800/460, fos 50–1, Eur/47/14, Bevin to Douglas, Telegram no. 583, Secret, 28 June 1947; fol. 52, Eur/47/15, Bevin to Douglas, Telegram no. 591, Secret, 29 June 1947; fol. 53, Eur/47/16, Bevin to Douglas, Telegram no. 601, Top Secret, 1 July 1947; fos 54–7, Eur/47/17, Note of a discussion between Bevin and Douglas on 3 July 1947, 4 July 1947; Bullock, *Ernest Bevin*, pp. 403–22; Cromwell, 'The Marshall Plan', pp. 238–47.

17 Public Record Office, London, CAB 128/10, fol. 38, CM54(47)2, Secret, 17 June 1947; fos 43–4, CM55(47)5, Secret, 19 June1947; fol. 47, CM56(47)3, Secret, 24 June 1947.

18 Barker, *The British between the Superpowers*, pp. 89–90, 92, 98; Morgan, *Labour in Power*, pp. 271–2; Bullock, *Ernest Bevin*, pp. 433–65; A. Rapport, 'The United States and European integration: the first phase', *Diplomatic History*, vol. 5 (1981), pp. 121–49 at pp. 122–8.

19 Bullock, *Ernest Bevin*, pp. 489–98; CAB 128/10, fol. 234, CM95(47)7, Secret, 15 December 1947.

20 FRUS 1947(2), pp. 815–16, Anglo–US–French conversations, British memorandum of conversation, Top Secret, undated.

21 E. Reid, *Time of Fear and Hope: The Making of the North Atlantic Treaty 1947–1949* (Toronto, 1977), p. 33.

22 Public Record Office, London, CAB 129/23, fos 30–6, CP(48)7, Review of Soviet policy by Bevin, Confidential Annex, 5 January 1948.

23 CAB 128/12, CM2(48), Secret, 8 January 1948: FRUS 1948(3), pp. 4–5, Inverchapel to Marshall, 13 January 1948.

24 Bullock, *Ernest Bevin*, pp. 520–1; Sir Nicholas Henderson, *The Birth of NATO* (London, 1982) pp. 2–5.

25 FO 800/460, fol. 65, Eur/48/1, Inverchapel to Bevin, Top Secret, 19 January 1948.

26 of 800/460, fos 69–70, Eur/48/4, Bevin to Inverchapel, Telegram no. 1032, Top Secret, 26 January 1948.

27 T. P. Ireland, *Creating the Entangling Alliance. The Origins of the North Atlantic Treaty Organization* (London, 1981), pp. 61–9; Henderson, *The Birth of NATO*, pp.7–9.

28 FO 800/452, fos 19–30, Def/48/5, COS (48)26(0), Memorandum by Montgomery on the problem of future war and the strategy of war with Russia, 30 January 1948; fos 32–41, Def/48/5A, COS(48)16, Confidential Annex, 2 February 1948; fos 47–52, Def/48/7, COS(48)16, 4 February 1948.

29 FO 800/452, fos 66–7, Def/48/12, Sargent to Bevin, 10 March 1948; fos 73–4, Def/48/15, COS(48)58(0), Hollis to Alexander, 17 March 1948.

30 FO 800/460, fos 86–95, Eur/48/13, Record of conversation between Bevin and Douglas on 26 February 1948, Top Secret.

31 FO 800/460, fos 86–95, Eur/48/13, Record of conversation between Bevin and Douglas on 28 February 1948, Top Secret; 471, fol. 145, It/48/3, Minute by Roberts of conversation between Bevin and Douglas on 6 March 1948, Top Secret, 6 March 1948.

32 J. E. Miller, 'Taking off the gloves: the United States and the Italian elections of 1948', *Diplomatic History*, vol. 7 (1983), pp. 35–55.

33 CAB 129/25, fos 47–64, CP(48)72, Memorandum by Bevin, Top Secret, 3

March 1948; CAB 128/12, fol. 128, CM19(48), Secret, 5 March 1948; 14 CM19 (48), No Circulation, 5 March 1948.

34 FO 800/460, fos 79–80, Minute by Roberts, approved by Bevin, Top Secret, 5 March 1948.

35 N. Petersen, 'Britain, Scandinavia, and the North Atlantic Treaty 1948–9', *Review of International Studies*, vol. 8 (1982), pp. 251–68 at p. 253.

36 *FRUS* 1948(3), pp. 46–8, British Embassy to Department of State, Top Secret, 11 March 1948; p. 48, Marshall to Inverchapel, Top Secret, 12 March 1948; Bullock, *Ernest Bevin*, pp. 528–31; C. Wiebes and B. Zeeman, 'The Pentagon negotiations March 1984: the launching of the North Atlantic Treaty', *International Affairs*, vol. 59 (1983), pp. 351–63 at pp. 353–4.

37 FO 800/460, fos 130–4, Eur/48/17, Record by Roberts of conversation between Bevin and Bidault on 17 March 1948.

38 Bullock, *Ernest Bevin*, p. 537.

39 FO 800/515, fos 67–79, US/48/32, Bevin to Attlee, Top Secret, 6 April 1948; fos 85–7, Annex B, Minute by Jebb, 5 April 1948; Wiebes and Zeeman, 'The Pentagon negotiations', pp. 351–63.

40 FO 800/453, fos 83–6, Def/48/40, British Embassy Washington to Foreign Office, Top Secret, 13 July 1948.

41 FO 800/454, fol. 59, Def/48/65, Ivone Kirkpatrick to Franks, 29 November 1948.

42 J. S. Walker, "No more Cold War"; American foreign policy and the 1948 Soviet peace offensive', *Diplomatic History*, vol. 5 (1981), pp. 75–91.

43 FO 800/483, fol. 2, NA/48/1, Roberts to Wright and Jebb, 1 June 1948.

44 FO 800/502, fos 157–84, SU/48/8, Bevin to Attlee, 28 July 1948.

45 FO 800/460, fos 86–95, Eur/48/13, Record of conversation between Bevin and Douglas on 28 February 1948, Top Secret.

46 FO 800/465, fol. 110, Fr/48/12, Kirkpatrick to Ashley Clarke, Top Secret, 31 July 1948.

47 FO 800/516, fol. 86, US/49/57, Bevin to Franks, no. 1628, Top Secret, 26 November 1949.

48 FO 800/454, fos 50–5, Def/48/39, Misc/M(48)39, 13 November 1948.

49 A. Shlaim, 'Britain, the Berlin blockade and the Cold War', *International Affairs*, vol. 60 (1984), pp. 1–14; *The United States and the Berlin Blockade, 1948–1949: A Study in Crisis Décision-Making* (Berkeley, Calif., 1983); Barker, *The British between the Superpowers*, pp. 118–27; Bullock, *Ernest Bevin*, pp. 571–80, 588–94.

50 FO 800/460, fos 200–1, Eur/48/48, Extract of a conversation between Bevin and Marshall on 4 October 1948.

51 Australian Archives, Canberra, A5954, Box 1970, PMM(48)9, Secret, 19 October 1948.

52 A5954, Box 1790, Report by the Australian Defence Committee on PMM(48)1, Top Secret.

53 A5954, Box 1790, Notes of discussion on British Commonwealth defence co-operation, 20 October 1948.

54 A5799, 48/15, Attlee to J. B. Chifley, Top Secret, 29 December 1948.

55 A5954, Box 1797, COS(49)49, Chiefs of Staff Committee defence appreciation, 9 February 1949.

56 FO 800/454, fos 98–100, Franks to Bevin, Top Secret, 29 December 1948.

57 Henderson, *The Birth of NATO*, pp. 35–122; Ireland, *Creating the Entangling Alliance*, pp. 100–48; Reid, *Time of Fear and Hope*, pp. 62–233; E. T. Smith, 'The fear of subversion: the United States and the inclusion of Italy in the North Atlantic Treaty', *Diplomatic History*, vol. 7 (1983), pp. 139–55.

58 FO 800/483, fol. 75, NA/49/13, Bevin to Franks and Lady Franks, 14 April 1949.

59 Principal 'revisionist' writings include: W. A. Williams, *The Tragedy of American Diplomacy*, rev. and enl. edn (New York, 1962); D. F. Fleming, *The Cold War and its*

Origins (New York, 1961); D. Horowitz, *The Free World Colossus: A Critique of American Foreign Policy in the Cold War*, rev. edn (New York, 1971); G. Alperowitz, *Atomic Diplomacy* (New York, 1965); G. Kolko, *The Politics of War* (New York, 1968); D. S. Clemens, *Yalta* (New York, 1970); L. C. Gardner, *Architects of Illusion* (Chicago, 1970). Wheeler-Bennett and Nicholls's dismissal of these works in 1972 led to angry protests from reviewers: see, for example, M. Howard, 'Frozen postures', *Sunday Times*, 24 September 1972. In 1973 R. J. Maddox in *The New Left and the Origins of the Cold War* (Princeton, NJ, 1973) exposed methodological aberrations in the revisionist writings. W. F. Kimball, though critical of Maddox in 'The Cold War warmed over', *American Historical Review*, vol. 79 (1974), pp. 1119–36, does concede that most revisionist writings have been eliminated from university reading lists. D. Yergin's *Shattered Peace* has been criticized on lesser grounds: see D. F. Harrington, 'Kennan, Bohlen, and the Riga axioms', *Diplomatic History*, vol. 2 (1978), pp. 423–37; D. C. Watt, 'The British Cold War', *The Listener*, 1 June 1978, pp. 711–12. See also J. L. Gaddis, 'The emerging post-revisionist synthesis on the origins of the Cold War', *Diplomatic History*, vol. 7 (1983), pp. 171–204.

PART THREE

The Cold War in the Middle East

4

British Paramountcy in the Middle East

In 1945 Britain was the paramount power in the Middle East. British influence had been established there in the aftermath of the First World War. At the San Remo Conference, in April 1920, British and French mandates were unceremoniously imposed on reluctant Arab populations, and Palestine was specifically excluded from the principle of self-determination. The Western powers carved up the area in their own domestic and imperial interests. The Arabs had little say. Lawrence of Arabia felt that he discharged his debts to those who had helped him during the desert campaign by establishing Feisal in Iraq and Abdullah in Transjordan. The Russians had no real opportunity to penetrate the area. The French were preoccupied with problems in Syria and did not interfere with the British mandates. In May 1945 the French, determined to crush Arab nationalism, tried to re-establish their influence in the Levant by bombing Damascus. To Britain this move seemed to threaten the security of the whole of the Middle East. The British commander-in-chief forced the French troops to withdraw to their barracks. General Charles de Gaulle complained that this humiliation both insulted the French and betrayed the West. Effectively Britain forced France out of Syria and the Lebanon. Some Americans were worried that Britain was securing too large a share of the world's potential oil resources, and American commercial interests were established in Saudi Arabia, but at that time these did not seriously challenge British predominance. For many public school products the Middle East remained an area in which they could apply Dr Thomas Arnold's principles of discipline and moral leadership. They were able to relate to the Arab leaders who had been chosen. They appreciated their courtesy. The Arab hierarchy responded in return: it sent its sons to Harrow and Sandhurst. A section of the British upper and upper middle classes came to respect and admire the Arabs, and particularly the bedouin.

91

The desert seemed clean. On the whole the British administrative structure established in the Middle East showed at least a façade of equality to the governed. There was a liberal tradition and even an idealism. The social snobberies so prevalent in the Indian subcontinent were largely absent, except in Egypt. Above all, British policy in the Middle East appeared to be flexible, and to respond to local needs.

The principal challenge to British predominance came from the Zionists. To the Arabs it seemed that it was the British government which had issued the Balfour declaration in 1917 favouring the establishment of a Jewish homeland in Palestine, it was Britain that held the Palestine mandate and admitted the Jewish immigrants who took over Arab land. After the increase in Jewish immigration, following the rise of Adolf Hitler in Germany, the Arabs revolted in 1936. The Balfour declaration had specifically stated that 'the civil and religious rights of existing non-Jewish communities in Palestine' should not be prejudiced. In the 1930s, as war seemed likely, Britain abandoned the policy sympathetic to Zionism which had been secured by the Zionist lobby. The Middle East was unlikely to be a secure base in time of rebellion. The British Empire contained many millions of Muslim subjects. They were concerned over Jewish immigration into Palestine, and opposed vehemently the creation of a Jewish state which they regarded as a base for foreign influence in the Arab world. Britain was still the paramount power. In May 1939 it issued a White Paper limiting Jewish immigration into Palestine. The Zionists changed their tactics. Instead of concentrating on the mandatory power, they focused on the United States. The new policy was accepted at the American Zionist Conference meeting at the Biltmore Hotel in New York in 1942. The Zionists threatened electoral punishment through the Zionist vote if the American administration failed to support a Jewish state. It was thought that the United States could force Britain to hand Palestine over to the Zionists. In the mandate itself the Zionists used new methods. A policy of attrition was waged against the administration. Violence and terrorism were aimed at wearing down British morale. Britain, rather than the Arabs, became the principal enemy. Palestine became an area of Anglo-American controversy at the time of the emergence of the Cold War.[1]

At the end of the Second World War the Middle East, to the British military mind, had an importance second only to that of the United Kingdom. The experience of Mons and Dunkirk lingered. British land armies should not again fight on the European continent. That was a job for the Europeans. Air and naval support might be possible, but that was all. Britain could not stop the advance of Russian armies across the continent. Only the United States could do that. The security of the British Commonwealth depended on protecting the United Kingdom, maintaining vital sea communications and securing the Middle East as a defensive and striking base against Russia. The existence of the atomic bomb did not affect this strategy.[2]

As strategic planners began to assess the situation after the devastation of Hiroshima and Nagasaki, the British military presence in the Middle East was considerable. There were over 200,000 troops in the Canal Zone on the Suez base, occupying an area about the size of Wales and equipped with almost every facility needed for war. The Suez base was supported in the front line by the air installations at Lydda, and a British naval presence at Haifa in the Palestine mandate. There were two further air bases at Habbaniyah and Shaiba in Iraq. In Transjordan the Arab Legion was led by a British officer, John Glubb. There were naval bases at Bahrein and Aden, and air and military installations at Khartoum in the Sudan. Britain had oil interests in Iraq, and particularly in Iran where the Abadan refinery was the largest in the world and produced, in 1945, more oil than the other Arab states together. In Iran the Anglo-Iranian Oil Company was staffed by what was virtually an autonomous British community which had vastly increased its oil production by 1950. The pipeline from the oilfields at Kirkup in Iraq ended in Haifa where there was a large British refinery. But none of these areas was under permanent British sovereignty. Alternatives did exist: Cyrenaica, the eastern province of Libya, and Kenya. The island of Cyprus was the only British possession in the Middle East. It had twenty airfields, but only a small harbour, Famagusta, which was not a deep-water port. On 5 September 1945 the Chiefs of Staff recommended that British rule be maintained over Cyprus. 'Enosis', or union with Greece, had to be resisted.[3]

This strategic policy meant that the British Empire in the Middle East, acquired almost accidentally earlier in the century, had to be maintained and consolidated. As the British Commonwealth became the Commonwealth, and the empire was wound up in Asia, and power began to be transferred on the African continent, it was the only large area over which British suzerainty could still be exerted. After 1947 even the United States acknowledged the need to maintain the British presence in the Middle East. With the joining of the Cold War those two countries agreed that the Middle East was to be a British and Commonwealth area of responsibility.[4] Bevin masterminded this British policy. He hoped for a relationship between Britain and the Arab states based on mutual interdependence and trust. British policy in the Middle East had to be broadened to secure the economic welfare of the inhabitants. Aware of the significance of the rise of a new generation of young Arabs, just as disenchanted with their own rulers as with any British presence, Bevin felt that this policy had to be based on peasants and not pashas. Increasingly, Arabism was not just synonymous with the Islamic religion, the Arabic language and the geographic area of Arabia. The inhabitants of North Africa stressed their Arab identity. During the 1930s and 1940s Arab writers and thinkers developed the idea of the *ba'ath* or renaissance of the Arab nation. In 1942 Nuri el Said and Abdullah developed the Greater Syria concept into the Fertile Crescent which would be formed by the union of Transjordan, Palestine, the Lebanon and Syria, and to include in the end Iraq and Saudi Arabia. Britain was disturbed by the likelihood of an adverse reaction to this by Egyptian nationalists and the obvious consequences for the British base in Egypt. The young generation's dislike of Western imperialism was partly fomented by a scorn for the defeat of France and the subsequent division between Gaullist and Vichy officers in the Levant, by the crushing with Anglo-Indian troops in 1941 of the Rashid Ali government in Iraq, and by Sir Miles Lampson's (later Lord Killearn) forcing Farouk – with British tanks in the palace grounds – to appoint Nahas Pasha as leader in Egypt on 4 February 1942.[5]

On 24 August 1945 Bevin let the Foreign Office know that he was anxious that Middle Eastern policy should be such that the Russians should have no opportunity to criticize it.[6] Six days later Bevin suggested to the Cabinet a conference of British representatives in the Middle East to discuss general policy in the area: it was time to consider whether Britain should continue to assert its political predominance in the Middle East and its overriding responsibility for the area's defence, or whether on defence and manpower grounds Britain should ask for the assistance of other powers; an economic and social policy covering the Middle East was also needed.[7] The conference met in London during September. It decided that a British influence in the Middle East which rested on military or political props could not be enduring. Britain should broaden the base on which its influence rested, and develop an economic and social policy that would make for the prosperity and contentment of the area as a whole. But the Middle East was to remain largely a British sphere of influence: Britain 'should not make any concession that would assist American commercial penetration into a region which for generations has been an established British market'.[8]

The Palestine Committee of the Cabinet, however, took a more precise view of Britain's strategic position in the Middle East. It was a region of 'vital consequence' for Britain and the empire. It formed the nodal point in the communication system, by land, sea and air, linking Britain with India, Australia and the Far East. It was the empire's main reserve of oil. Within it lay the Suez Canal, and the principal naval bases in the eastern Mediterranean and at Alexandria. In this important region Cyprus was the only territory under full British sovereignty: Palestine, as a mandated territory, was subject to international agreement; all the other Middle Eastern countries were independent except Transjordan which was likely to achieve that status in the near future. Britain, therefore, depended on co-operation from these independent states. The attitude of the Arabs was of the first importance. British prestige, at that time, was 'immensely high' and relations with the various rulers 'friendly and cordial'. This could be transformed overnight if Britain took any action which the Arabs might construe as injurious to their interests: the Arabs were sensitive about the future of Palestine. The Arab League had been formed in March 1945. That made the situation more difficult: individual Arab states might resist policies they did not like. If Britain enforced a policy in Palestine which the Arabs resented, especially if that policy could be called a breach of faith, that would undermine Britain's position in the Middle East. There would be widespread disturbances in the Arab countries, and the co-operation on which British imperial interests so largely depended would be withdrawn.[9]

The Cabinet discussed these reports on 4 October. Bevin said that he wanted to broaden the basis of British influence in the Middle East 'by developing an economic and social policy which would make for prosperity and contentment in the area as a whole'. Economic development and social reform could make for an easier solution of military and political problems which included a threatening situation in Palestine, an agitation in Egypt for the withdrawal of British forces and difficulties with France in the Levant. The Cabinet was interested in Britain's strategic position. The Chiefs of Staff were considering the feasibility of basing forces needed for the protection of the Middle East on British territory rather than in Egypt. It was hoped that there would be some joint agreement for the defence of that country leaving Britain with responsibility for the Suez Canal. Sir Alan Brooke, the Chief of the

Imperial General Staff, agreed with the proposed policy for Egypt. The Mombasa area was being considered, but while it was suitable as a base, it had difficulties of rail and road communications and port facilities. George Glenville Hall, the Secretary of State for the Colonies, asked for the strategic importance of Cyprus to be considered again. The Cabinet approved the new policy for the Middle East.[10]

In effect British strategic policy for the Middle East was dependent on a British military presence in Palestine. On 24 January 1944 the Chiefs of Staff had pointed to the military disadvantages of dividing Palestine into separate states.[11] At the end of that year the State Department warned that an expansion of Russian influence in the Middle East had to be prevented. That area was of vital strategic importance to the United States. There were obvious difficulties with Britain: that country might capitalize on Arab resentment of the United States to maintain its pre-eminence in the area. At that time Roosevelt viewed the world with a different perspective: referring to difficulties with Britain, the President told his Cabinet on 16 March 1945, in a 'semi-jocular' way, that Britain was prepared for the United States to fight Russia at any time – 'to follow the British programme would be to proceed toward that end'.[12] A meeting of the Commanders-in-Chief and British officials near Cairo on 3 April 1945 was unanimous in insisting that the 'insane' idea of partition for Palestine should be killed. Lord Killearn, the ambassador in Egypt, thought that Britain should stay in Palestine indefinitely.[13] In August 1945 the Chiefs of Staff opposed partition: it would be drastic and irrevocable.[14] If partition had to be enforced they estimated that three additional divisions, including one airborne division, would have to be dispatched to the Middle East, as well as two infantry and one armoured brigade. A British division in India would be needed as an additional reserve. Furthermore, Indian troops should not be used to implement a policy in the Middle East that would arouse agitation in India. If that happened British requirements would be increased by one armoured division and a further two brigades.[15]

At this point Truman intervened. He had sent Earl G. Harrison to investigate the condition of displaced persons in Europe. Harrison recommended that Washington should, under existing laws, allow reasonable numbers of Jewish refugees into the United States. Truman, realizing that Congress would not relax the immigration quotas, chose instead to assign the responsibility to Britain. In doing this he overrode the advice of the State and War Departments. There was an election in New York, and the Jewish vote seemed crucial. Truman wrote to Attlee on 31 August suggesting that the main solution lay in the quick evacuation of Jews to Palestine. Harrison had recommended that 100,000 be admitted. Bevin, who could not accept that Jews could not live in Europe, suggested to the Cabinet an Anglo-American commission to investigate the refugee problem. The American response was hesitant, at a time when British soldiers were being killed by terrorists in Palestine, because of Zionist agitation in the New York election campaign. Bevin wanted to involve the United States. Increasingly worried about Russian advances in the Middle East, Bevin saw the area as essential to Western security at a time of the emergence of the Cold War. To maintain its position, Britain had to negotiate treaties with the new Arab states. This would hardly be possible if Britain were seen as the sponsor of a Zionist state in Palestine, to be achieved through Jewish immigration. After the New York election was over – in which Truman's Democrat won a resounding victory – an Anglo-American commission was appointed, heard evidence in Washington, London, Europe and the Middle East, and reported in April 1946.[16]

In the meantime the Chief of the Imperial General Staff toured the Middle East to assess the chances of implementing the new British policy in the area. In Egypt he saw the Prime Minister, Nokrashi Pasha, King Farouk and the Chef-du-Cabinet, Sir Ahmed Hassanien Pasha. Nokrashi was not impressed with arguments about the need for partnership in defence throughout those countries in the Middle East which had a common interest in its security. He responded that without real freedom and the removal of British forces from Egypt the internal conditions in that country would make it unsuitable for participating in defensive plans. Farouk, however, was worried about Russia: there would be war within a few years. Concerted action in the Middle East was desirable, and the king liked the idea of partnership. But political considerations might make that difficult. He was not antagonistic to Britain, but he was pro-Egyptian before anything else, and after that pro-British. Farouk seemed to believe that in Europe only two great powers were left: Britain and Russia. He appeared to be frightened of the latter, and prepared to co-operate with the former. Hassanien Pasha confirmed this. Abdullah, then the Emir of Transjordan, was ready to fit into any form of defensive confederation. He was apprehensive as to Russian intentions. At a conference in Iraq with the regent, the Prime Minister, the Finance and Defence Ministers, the British ambassador and the Commander-in Chief Middle East, it was clear that Baghdad wanted some form of Middle East defence confederation backed by Britain. It was felt that the partnership could be extended to include economic development. The Chief of the Imperial General Staff thought the conception of a Middle East Defensive Confederation, based on a partnership between those concerned, a promising line of approach, especially if Britain worked mainly through the rulers. This was pashas not peasants.[17]

The new Middle East policy was successfully implemented in Transjordan. Possibly with an eye to his Fertile Crescent scheme, Abdullah early in 1946 was pleased to agree to a mutual defence pact with Britain: he willingly ceded Britain the right to station and train troops, insisted on by the Chiefs of Staff; Britain could develop the port of Aqaba, move troops across Jordan, establish a signal communications system and maintain air bases at Mafrak and Amman. In return Abdullah became king, and the British subsidy of £2 million a year continued. Under the treaty, signed on 22 March 1946, Transjordan was given 'full independence'. In London, Abdullah warned Attlee that Russia was playing a dangerous game: 'Russia is following a forward policy in Iran and Kurdistan, a policy which may well aim at expansion to the Persian Gulf and the Mediterranean. Against this, it is desirable that a defensive front should be built up covering Turkey, Iran and Afghanistan by the "fertile crescent" of Arab countries stretching from Basra to Aqaba.'[18] Abdullah also told Bevin that British divisions in Iraq and Transjordan would have a salutary effect on the Middle East, especially on Egypt.[19]

Transjordan, however, was the only success. On 20 December 1945 Egypt asked for a revision of the Anglo-Egyptian treaty of 1936. That treaty gave Britain the right to station troops in the Suez Canal Zone and Sinai, and the right of reoccupation in the event of war. Early in 1946 Killearn was removed from Cairo, possibly as a result of another altercation with Farouk, possibly because of pressure from sections of the Labour Party to make changes in the staffing of the Foreign Office and diplomatic posts abroad. Killearn, apparently to his annoyance as it meant a considerable loss of salary, was made Special Commissioner for South-East Asia. He was replaced by someone thought to be more amenable to the Egyptians, Sir Ronald Campbell.[20] Attlee argued that the strategic importance of the Middle East needed to be reconsidered. On 18 February he said that it was useless to pretend that Britain could keep the Mediterranean route open in wartime. If this was accepted Britain could withdraw troops from Egypt, the rest of the Middle East and Greece. Britain could not defend

Turkey, Iraq, or Iran against the pressure of the Russian land masses. If India went its own way, as it had to, there would be even less point in thinking of lines of imperial communications through the Suez Canal. Britons should be prepared to travel around the Cape to Australia and New Zealand. American interest in Middle Eastern oil could change the situation. At the end of March Attlee urged the Defence Committee to consider disengagement from areas where there was a risk of clashing with Russia. Britain should withdraw from the Middle East and concentrate on a line of defence across Africa from Lagos to Kenya. A large part of British forces could be stationed in Kenya, while Commonwealth defence would be concentrated in Australia. The Arabs and the desert would form a barrier between the British and the Russians. Bevin, however, thought that the Canal Zone should be the ultimate line of British withdrawal. The Foreign Secretary was attracted by the Lagos-Kenya idea, and spoke of building a road across Africa so that Britain could protect the mineral deposits in the Belgian Congo. He also envisaged a triangular ocean trade between East Africa, including Natal in South Africa, India and Australia. Captain B. H. Liddell Hart, in a memorandum dated 20 March, debated whether British strategic policy should be based on the Middle East or Africa. He questioned the importance of the oilfields of Iraq and Iran: they provided only a small fraction of Britain's national income. Oil could come from the United States, Venezuela and British Guiana. Synthetic oil was possible. Britain should retire from the Middle East with dignity and consolidate its position in Africa. The British disposition there would not be seriously disturbed even if Russia spread its influence to Egypt.[21] The Egyptian ambassador in London warned Bevin about Russian influence in Egypt. On 18 March he told the Foreign Secretary that the Egyptian government's investigations into the prevailing difficulties had revealed that the Wafd Party was responsible for part of the trouble, but a large proportion was due to the Russians. There were eighty staff in the Russian legation in Cairo: they had a cinema and plenty of money; and voluminous literature coming into the country was being sent from Beirut and Palestine.[22]

On 2 April 1946 London announced that it had decided to send a delegation to Cairo. The Chiefs of Staff were prepared to compromise. Fighting troops in the Canal Zone could go. But British fighting squadrons and bomber bases had to stay.[23] Lord Stansgate, the Minister for Air, arrived in Cairo on 15 April, and had discussions with the Prime Minister, Ismail Sidky. Sidky immediately demanded the evacuation of all British forces.

Stansgate advised that Britain give way on this. The Cabinet decided to concede, and the decision was made public. Sir Orme Sargent warned Campbell:

> It is true that as a matter of tactics we have decided to announce our willingness to clear out altogether if asked to do so but unless Egyptian leaders *are* made to realise what this entails, we shall be encouraging them to live in a fool's paradise, for the Alliance is just not going to be a guarantee of Egypt's independence in modern conditions of warfare if the evacuation now promised is to be the beginning and the end of the Treaty.

Sargent did not like the defeatist attitude of the delegation. It was wrong not to tell the Egyptians what were the 'inevitable consequences' of Britain's leaving Egypt to its own devices both in respect of Egypt's defence and the defence of the Middle East.[24] At the end of May Bevin warned the Egyptians that steps had to be taken to defend the Canal Zone. Britain could not leave a vacuum. That would be a 'magnet of attraction' that could lead other countries to start a political and expansive aggression. While the Egyptian government had great nationalist claims on it, it also had international security obligations to meet because, by the mere accident of geography, its territory lay where it did. Britain might have to fall back on the treaty of 1936, and the negotiations would break down. That would be unfortunate. Britain hoped to weave the whole of that strategic area into an international security system.[25] In October Sidky saw Bevin in London, but the arrangement worked out foundered on Cairo's insistence on the unity of the Sudan with Egypt under the Egyptian Crown. At the end of January 1947 Bevin told the Cabinet that the negotiations had broken down: Britain had to ensure that the Sudanese would be able to sever their connection with Egypt on reaching self-government if they chose to do so.[26]

The negotiations with Egypt, and the discussions over Palestine, took place against the background of the conclusions of the Chiefs of Staff on 2 April 1946 that if Britain moved out of certain parts of the world in peacetime, the Russians would move in. This would enable Russia to extend its influence, by all means short of war, to further strategic areas. It was imperative that Britain stay in the Mediterranean: first, to protect British access to Middle Eastern oil; and secondly, to preserve political influence in southern Europe. If the Russians secured control of the Egypt-Palestine area, they would have a ready-made base. It could be quickly built up by the short sea route from Russia. Russia would then be able to extend its influence westwards and southwards into Africa. The British position in both north-west Africa and the Indian Ocean would be prejudiced. It would be the first step in a direct threat to Britain's main support area of Southern Africa.[27] Attlee's scheme for retreating from the Middle East and standing on a line in Africa from Lagos to Kenya was rejected. The Defence Committee of the Cabinet decided on 5 April that Britain's position as a 'World Power' should be maintained. Bevin was determined that Britain should remain as a 'great Power'.[28] He told the Commonwealth Prime Ministers meeting in London in April 1946: ' In my view it is essential that we should maintain our position in the Mediterranean and Red Sea. It is not only a question of preserving this lifeline in time of war, but also the vital importance of acting in peacetime on the soft under-belly of Europe from the Mediterranean.'[29] Backed by arguments from General J. C. Smuts, the South African Prime Minister, Bevin resisted Russian claims for a trusteeship over a former Italian colony in Africa at the Council of Foreign Ministers meeting in Paris in May. With the situations in Egypt and Palestine in mind, Bevin lodged a British claim for Cyrenaica – it could become a British strategic base.[30]

At this time the controversy over Palestine erupted. On 30 April, without consulting London, Truman endorsed the recommendation of the Anglo-American commission that 100,000 certificates be issued for Jewish immigrants to go to Palestine, and two other aspects favourable to Zionism. The British public was outraged: British soldiers had just been murdered by Zionist terrorists. Truman had succumbed again to Zionist pressure, and threats of electoral punishment in the forthcoming November congressional elections. The Chief of the Imperial General Staff, Viscount Alanbrooke (formerly Sir Alan Brooke), told the Dominion Prime Ministers meeting in London that, from the military angle, it was essential to seek the active assistance of the United States.[31] So far as the Chiefs of Staff were concerned the strategic importance of Palestine could not be questioned. On 24 May they concluded that Britain had to be able to place in Palestine any forces it considered necessary; Britain had to retain complete control of the organization of the defence of the area.[32] Their American colleagues agreed. The Joint Chiefs of Staff insisted on 21 June that no American armed forces should be used to implement the recommendations of the Anglo-American commission. There was the danger that the Middle East could 'fall into anarchy and become a breeding ground for world war'. Russia could replace Britain and the United States in influence and power throughout the area:

As to the importance of a stable Middle East, friendly to the Western Powers, it is obvious that this area is the buffer between Russia and the British Mediterranean life line. It the peoples of the Middle East turn to Russia, this would have the same impact in many respects as would military conquest on this area by the Soviets. Under these conditions, even if Turkey maintains her internal political integrity, it is highly questionable that she could continue her stand on the Dardanelles and maintain her position as other than a satellite Russian state. Also, for very serious consideration from a military point of view is control of the oil of the Middle East. This is probably the one large undeveloped reserve in a world which may come to the limits of its oil resources within this generation without having any substitute. A great part of our military strength, as well as our standard of living is based of oil.[33]

Anglo-American differences over Palestine were temporarily resolved when delegates from both countries met in London in July 1946 and suggested a scheme of provincial autonomy. The Chiefs of Staff had reservations: Lord Tedder again insisted that any future government of Palestine should give Britain power to control and co-ordinate the defence of that country, as well as maintaining forces and military facilities. The Chiefs wanted 'a certain airfield' in Arab territory. Above all, Britain should not alienate the Arab states.[34] In Palestine, Menachem Begin and the Irgun, with the co-operation of the Haganah, blew up the King David Hotel, one wing of which was used as British army headquarters: ninety-one were killed. Zionist propaganda throughout the world publicized what was construed as an anti-Semitic statement by the British army commander, and, as a result, turned a terrorist outrage into a Zionist victory. Under the threat of Zionist electoral punishment, Truman withdrew his support from the provincial autonomy scheme.[35]

Britain tried to implement the provincial autonomy scheme on its own. A Palestine Conference met at Lancaster House on 2 October, but was adjourned until 16 December. The Arabs were worried that the Zionists would fill their state with immigrants from Europe, creating conditions which would warrant a demand for more *Lebensraum*.[36] Chaim Weizmann, a Zionist delegate, told Bevin that there was no need for immediate partition: there could be a transitional period of two to three years. The Foreign Secretary warned him that he had never known such strong latent anti-Semitism in Britain: 'The destruction of the King David Hotel had burned deeply into the hearts of the British people.' Britain could not allow its young soldiers in Palestine to be slaughtered. Bevin also said that he had to ensure that the rights and position of the other inhabitants of Palestine were not prejudiced. 'If a person's land and livelihood had to go in order to make room for another, his rights and position were certainly prejudiced.' Bevin was not prepared to force partition on the Arabs at the point of British bayonets. Instead he would hand the problem to the United Nations. Palestine was not the only home for the Jewish people: the Foreign Secretary hoped that they would be a great force in the reconstruction of the European continent. The Zionist leaders agreed to talk to the Colonial Office about administrative procedures and the release of detainees in Jerusalem, and then come back to Bevin. They made participation in the Palestine Conference dependent on the release of the detained members of the Jewish executive in Palestine. They hoped that the Jewish delegates could be brought into the conference even before the return of the Arab delegates.[37]

Truman ruined this hopeful prospect. The Zionists, working with Robert E. Hannegan, the chairman of the Democratic National Committee, with an eye on a forthcoming election in New York and the presidential election of 1948, urged Truman to make an immediate statement in favour of partition. The State Department advised against this, as did the Joint Chiefs of Staff: partition might alienate the Arabs from the West. Attlee asked Truman to delay. But on 4 October, the eve of the Jewish day of atonement, Truman said that a solution along the lines of partition originally proposed by the Jewish Agency on 5 August would 'command the support of public opinion in the United States'.[38]

With British policy towards Palestine in a state of suspension, and the Egyptian negotiations breaking down, in December 1946 it was decided to move a further division from Egypt to Palestine, That would leave only administrative troops in Egypt, and by 1 April 1947 the numbers there would have been reduced to 32,000.[39] In December Attlee again suggested that Britain should withdraw from the Middle East. The Prime Minister wanted to hand over the mandate for Palestine.[40] He argued that Britain had 'either to offend the Arab States and probably Turkey and Persia as well or offend world Jewry with its powerful influence in the U.S.A.'.[41] At this time British public opinion was aroused : in retaliation for the judicial caning of a convicted Zionist terrorist, too young to hang, Begin's Irgun kidnapped and flogged four British army officers. Britain gave way, and stopped using judicial corporal punishment in the mandate.[42] Tedder warned that a solution to the Palestine problem which alienated Arab goodwill would be unacceptable. Britain would be denied freedom of movement through an essential area, and its wider interests in the Middle East would be endangered.[43] The Chiefs of Staff reiterated their insistence that Britain had to be able to station forces in Palestine. Air bases were needed for imperial communications. With Egypt being evacuated, apart from the Canal Zone, Palestine was the only area able to accommodate Britain's Middle East reserve.[44] Tedder told the Cabinet on 15 January that there were three cardinal requirements for the future defence of the British Commonwealth: the defence of the United Kingdom and its development as a base for air offensive; the maintenance of sea communications; and the retention of Britain's existing position and influence in the Middle East. These were the three 'vital props' of Britain's defensive position. They were all interdependent and if any one were lost, 'the whole structure would be imperilled'. These fundamental principles would be unaffected by any change in the nature and use of weapons, or assumptions made about the potential enemy. It was essential for Britain's defence that it could fight from the Middle East in war. This meant that Britain had to maintain a foothold there in peace. Though lightly manned in peace, these bases could be used for the rapid deployment of greater force against a threat of war. India would no longer be available for such bases so the retention of those in the Middle East was essential. Palestine was of special importance. In war Egypt would be Britain's key position in the Middle East. Palestine had to be held as a screen for the defence of Egypt. As Britain had undertaken to withdraw from Egypt, it had to be able to use Palestine as a base for the mobile reserve of troops which had to be kept ready to meet any emergency throughout the Middle East. The facilities in Transjordan were insufficient. If separate states were established in Palestine it would be necessary to secure the full use of ports, airfields and communications, and to obtain military facilities by treaty arrangements with both states. Provided such facilities were obtained, it was immaterial whether Palestine became one or two states. If one of the communities had to be antagonized, it was preferable that a solution be found which did not involve the continuing hostility of the Arabs. Arab hostility would mean difficulties for Britain throughout the Middle East.[45] Tedder was supported by the Minister of Defence, A. V. Alexander: if the Arabs were alienated they would be supported by Russia which intended to undermine the influence of the British Commonwealth and the United States in the Persian Gulf area.

Alexander advised the Cabinet that Britain should look to its own strategic interests, and it was therefore vital to retain the goodwill of the Arab world.[46] Bevin and the new Colonial Secretary, Arthur Creech Jones, who had been sympathetic towards Zionism, submitted a plan early in February which envisaged self-government in Palestine leading to independence after a transitional period of five years under trusteeship, and 100,000 Jewish immigrants over the following two years. The Chiefs of Staff did not like the suggestion that if neither the Arabs nor the Zionists would accede to the plan, Britain would have to submit the problem to the United Nations without making any positive recommendations. The Chiefs felt that such a step would almost certainly entail the loss of practically all British military rights in Palestine. It was essential that Britain, during the interim period of trusteeship, retain these rights, and ensure that they could be acquired when that ended. Five years was too short a time for trusteeship. It would not be long enough to establish a stable state with which Britain could negotiate a favourable treaty. The period should be left indefinite.[47]

Despite these warnings, on 14 February the Cabinet decided to submit the Palestine problem to the United Nations without any recommendation for a solution. On 3 April 1947 it agreed, solely for 'political considerations' (demands from the left wing of the Labour Party), to reduce the period of national service from eighteen to twelve months. The Chief of the Imperial General Staff, Montgomery, felt that this was acceptable provided overseas commitments such as Palestine and India were liquidated by 1949 or 1950.[48] On 15 May the United Nations Special Committee on Palestine (UNSCOP) was established with broad powers of investigation. Russia insisted that the membership be increased from seven to eleven. In the Foreign Office, Harold Beeley surmised that Russia hoped to be associated with a joint trusteeship over Palestine. During the UNSCOP inquiry British morale in Palestine was eroded. The *President Warfield*, renamed *Exodus*, arrived in Palestine with 4,493 illegal immigrants. These were returned to their French port of embarkation. In retaliation for the execution of Zionist terrorists, the Irgun hanged two British sergeants and booby-trapped their bodies. These were found on 31 July. The American consul in Jerusalem argued that the terrorist thinking was based on the premiss, proclaimed by both the Irgun and Stern gang, that all of Palestine and Transjordan belonged to the Jewish people: the British were merely there to bring about the unchallenged Jewish occupation of those two states. The consul concluded: 'During the time of the Nazis it was a commonplace to hear the opinion that Hitler and his followers were deluded to the point where their sanity was questionable. If such generalisations are permissable, it may be well to question whether the Zionists, in their present emotional state, can be dealt with as rational human beings.'[49] There were outbreaks of anti-semitism in Britain. As Bevin explained, Britain had no alternative other than to ship the refugees on the *President Warfield* back to Germany. This gave the Zionists the most notable propaganda success of the time. The British authorities in Hamburg complained of the attitude of the American press correspondents who witnessed the landing: they were 'unfriendly' towards the British and their reports were coloured and exaggerated.[50]

UNSCOP, in a majority report, recommended in effect the partition of Palestine and the creation of a separate Zionist state. In a memorandum of 18 September the Chiefs of Staff emphasized again that Britain's strategic position made it essential that the goodwill of the Arab states, and the Muslim world as a whole, was retained. If Palestine were handed to an authority containing a considerable Russian element, Britain's interests would not be served. An American-dominated body would be comparatively acceptable. Control should pass to a 'national or international authority friendly to us, and both willing and able to resist Russian encroachment'. Even American control would only afford temporary security.[51] Bevin told the Cabinet on 20 September that the UNSCOP proposals were unacceptable. The Minister of Defence merely explained that Britain would have to choose between ceasing to administer Palestine immediately, and maintaining such order as was necessary to ensure the withdrawal of British forces and civilians, or attempting to maintain law and order throughout the whole of Palestine until the date announced for the end of the British administration. The Prime Minister did not think it reasonable to ask the British administration to continue in the prevailing conditions. The Cabinet accepted the policy of withdrawal.[52] Hugh Dalton noted that this was a historic decision. Britain was withdrawing to the eastern Mediterranean.[53]

The original assessment by the British Directors of Plans and the Service Directors of Intelligence estimated that withdrawal from Palestine would lead to the total collapse of Britain's position in the Middle East. The final report of the Joint Planning Staff, dated 19 September, argued that Britain's position in the Middle East and the possibility of recovering some of the military requirements would depend on the extent to which the British withdrawal from

Palestine could be made acceptable to the Arab world. If the Arabs were convinced that British withdrawal was dictated by a refusal to implement a solution unjust to the Arabs, Britain might regain Arab friendship and a part of its strategic requirements in the Middle East. If the Arabs could not be persuaded, British influence in Iraq would be undermined, and hopes of renewing the treaty with that country on a friendly basis would disappear. All the other Arab states might be alienated. The situation could arise where Britain had no footing in the Middle East, apart from Cyprus, since the attainment of British requirements in Egypt was doubtful, and the future of Cyrenaica undecided. Britain would lose oil interests not only in Palestine but possibly also in the oilfields themselves, and at the gulf terminals. All this could lead to Russian infiltration, and the eventual establishment of Russian domination in the area.[54] Early in October the Joint Administrative Planning Staff said that withdrawal from Palestine could not be efficiently mounted without deploying troops to Cyrenaica and the Sudan.[55] The Foreign Office raised the future strategic position of Transjordan. Abdullah would want the Arab part of Palestine. The Mufti of Jerusalem, backed by Syria and Egypt, would not accept that. Transjordan would then be surrounded by three unfriendly states. The Foreign Office thought a friendly Transjordan of considerable strategic importance. Abdullah might want to use the Arab Legion to fight in Palestine. That would be awkward: Britain helped to pay for, and staff, the Legion.[56] Similarly, the Joint Planning Staff pointed to the strategic importance of Transjordan. That state was traversed by all the direct communications connecting Iran and Iraq with the vital central area, namely Egypt and Palestine. Transjordan lay either on, or adjacent to, the two main strategic lines of approach to Palestine and Egypt from the Near East. Transjordan was also the only remaining Arab state in which Britain, by treaty, enjoyed extensive freedom of movement. It was definitely pro-British. If Britain were forced to evacuate Egypt and Palestine, it would still need to re-enter those countries in an emergency: without this facility Britain's Middle East strategy would collapse. Provided Britain could re-enter Palestine, the importance attached to Transjordan would not be affected. The Joint Planning Staff envisaged the eventual development and unification of the military facilities Britain enjoyed in Transjordan, but inadequate communications made that impossible in the immediate future. Transjordan, without extensive development, could do little to ease the wider military problems consequent on British withdrawal from Palestine. The most serious threat to Transjordan's independence would be the spread of communist influence if Russia were allowed to participate in the administration of Palestine after the British withdrawal. Indeed, Bevin thought that Russia hoped for the establishment of a communist state in Palestine, or at least in the Zionist areas organized by indoctrinated illegal immigrants from Eastern Europe.[57]

Britain tried to secure its position in the Middle East through alliances with Arab states. On 9 October the Cabinet agreed to informal and secret talks with the regent and the government of Iraq about the revision of the Anglo-Iraqi treaty of alliance of 1930.[58] To avoid demands for the evacuation of the two British air bases in Iraq, Britain negotiated on the principle of sharing the bases, and a Joint Defence Board to co-ordinate defence plans.[59] This seemed agreeable to an elite group of Iraqis at the end of the year, and on 15 January 1948 an Iraqi delegation signed the Treaty of Portsmouth. The regent's strong men were in Britain. With the news of the treaty there was a political outburst in Iraq, and the regent had to repudiate the document within a week of its being signed. Against the background of the withdrawal from Palestine, Britain had difficulty in negotiating alliances with Arab states[60] – except Jordan. Neither country was dissatisfied with the treaty of 1946, but a new one was negotiated in January and February 1948 to give the appearance of an arrangement between equals. A joint defence board was established responsible for external and strategic planning. Before the Jordanian delegate, Tawfig, left London he saw Bevin. Glubb recorded that Bevin said that Transjordan's intention of occupying the west bank in Palestine was 'the obvious thing to do'.[61]

At this point the Americans began to acknowledge to Britain the importance, for the West, of Britain's strategic position in the Middle East. Informal political and strategic talks were held in Washington between 16 October and 7 November between British and American officials. The reason for these meetings was the American fear of the repercussions of the withdrawal of British troops from Greece. Bevin did not want a combined Anglo-American policy for the Middle East: the Foreign Secretary still saw this as an area primarily of strategic and economic interest to Britain. Both Truman and the British Cabinet endorsed the recommendations of the officials, though there was no formal agreement. The American participants recommended that their government strengthen the British strategic, political and economic position throughout the Middle East. This would include American diplomatic support for Britain, and also at the United Nations, over the retention of facilities in Egypt, Cyrenaica and Iraq. The United States also favoured the retention of Britain's strategic position in the Sudan, Gibraltar, Aden and Cyprus.[62]

On 26 September Creech Jones told the United Nations that if the General Assembly recommended a policy not acceptable to the Arabs and Jews, Britain would not be able to implement it. Russia, on 13 October, 'mystified' Britain and the United States by announcing its support for the partition of Palestine. Bevin thought that the Russians hoped to pour enough indoctrinated communist Jews into Palestine to turn it into a communist state in a short time. He observed: 'The New York Jews have been doing their work for them.'[63] The Chiefs of Staff became worried that a communist regime could be set up in Palestine after the British withdrawal on 15 May 1948, but Bevin insisted on a British attitude of neutrality in the United Nations. The calculation probably was that partition would not secure the necessary two-thirds majority. On 24 November Bevin dined with Marshall and told him that Britain would abstain in the United Nations vote. 'This great issue' had been handled by the United States more with 'the electoral situation in New York City in mind than the large issues of foreign policy which were involved'. Before the murder of the two British sergeants Bevin had felt that the situation in Palestine could be held. He told Marshall that Britain could not be committed to a position which might involve military action against the Arabs.[64]

On 29 November the General Assembly voted for partition. Prior to the vote, and particularly during the immediately preceding three days, the American Zionists exerted unprecedented pressure on the American administration, and both delegations to the United Nations and their governments, to secure the necessary majority. Senators belonging to the American Christian Palestine Committee petitioned wavering United Nations delegations: Haiti, Greece, Luxembourg, Argentina, Columbia, China, El Salvador, Ethiopia, Honduras, Mexico, the Philippines and Paraguay. The senators called attention to the 'gravest consequences' of those countries' relations with the United States if the partition resolution was not adopted.[65] Emmanuel Celler campaigned actively for partition at Lake Success. Some of this correspondence suggests that Truman himself might have intervened at the last minute.[66] Sol Bloom acknowledged his role on changing the votes of the delegations of Liberia, the Philippines and Haiti.[67] Loy W. Henderson recalled that David Niles, Truman's minority rights adviser, had telephoned Hershel Johnson and said that Truman had instructed him to say that 'by God, he wanted us to get busy and get all the votes that we possibly could, that there would be hell if the voting went the wrong way'. Johnson, apparently in tears, told Henderson that the delegation was working under terrific strain to carry out the President's orders. Henderson refused to believe that the President had authorized Niles to give such a strong order.[68] Zafar Khan, the Pakistan delegate to the United Nations, claimed that had the partition vote been taken on Wednesday 26 November, it would have been 26 to 16 and thus defeated. Knowing this the Zionist leaders went directly to Truman and told him that the vote had to be delayed. The President is alleged to have then instructed Johnson to secure a delay of the vote at all costs – which was done.[69] Edward Stettinius, a former Secretary of State, instigated pressure from the Firestone Tire and Rubber Company on Liberia.[70] The State Department thought that the votes of Haiti and the Philippines, at least, had been secured by the unauthorized intervention of American citizens. It felt that the danger to the interests of the United States and the United Nations could only be averted by a presidential statement admitting the undue pressure and saying that in future offenders would be prosecuted and existing legislation would immediately be reviewed with that in mind.[71]

The situation in Palestine deteriorated. The Arab reaction was worse than Bevin had expected. On 17 December he warned Marshall that the Middle East could 'blow up'. There would be serious consequences, even for the United States. Russia might profit when the Zionists and Arabs started fighting. The Foreign Secretary thought, however, when Russia intervened it would be in Iraq and not Palestine.[72]

Early in 1948 the American Joint Chiefs of Staff warned that partition would lead to Arab hatred, the loss of oil, Russian penetration in the area in the guise of enforcing the United Nations plan, and a call for American troops for Palestine. On 29 January Kennan explained that British relations with the Arabs and the remaining British strategic positions in the Middle East were among the few 'real assets' the United States still had in the area. Forrestal said that without Middle Eastern oil the Marshall Plan could not succeed. The United States began to move away from partition. In Britain the Chiefs of Staff were instructed to investigate accelerating the British withdrawal. Zionists working through Clark Clifford, Truman's electoral adviser, George M. Elsey, Clifford's assistant, and Max Lowenthal, a White House consultant with Jewish Agency connections, secured a reversal of American policy. Truman, concerned about the significance of the Zionist vote in the forthcoming presidential election, recognized

Israel on 14 May. At midnight HMS *Euryalus* left Palestinian waters with Sir Alan Gordon Cunningham, the High Commissioner, on board. Britain was no longer the paramount power over the Zionists. David Ben-Gurion proclaimed the State of Israel at 4 p.m. the same day. On 15 May various Arab armies entered Palestine. On 21 May the Policy Planning Staff advised that American policy threatened 'not only to place in jeopardy some of our most vital national interests in the Middle East and the Mediterranean but also to disrupt the Unity of the western world and to undermine our entire policy towards the Soviet Union'.[73]

During the First Arab-Israeli War the Foreign Office was worried that the Russians might benefit from an Anglo-American rift. The Arabs could become desperate, and Russia consequently might be able to get control of their oil. The Arabs were divided. On 1 December 1948, to the fury of Egypt and other Arab states, Abdullah organized a ceremonial conference at Jericho where Palestinian and Transjordanian delegates favoured the joining of Palestine and Transjordan as an indivisible Hashemite Kingdom of Jordan. When the Israelis invaded Egypt, and on 7 January 1949 shot down five Royal Air Force planes, Britain sent troops to Aqaba and alerted its Mediterranean ships. London reminded Washington of the Middle East talks of November 1947, and the implied support offered by the United States to maintain Britain's position in the Middle East. Lovett warned that the position might arise whereby Britain would be arming one side in the dispute and the United States the other, with Russia the permanent beneficiary. Ben-Gurion withdrew his offending troops. On 24 February an armistice was signed at Rhodes between the Egyptians and the Israelis. Agreements with other Arab states followed. Israel increased its territory by 21 per cent, but acquired insecure frontiers. In 1949 the legally certified number of Palestinian Arab refugees was almost one million.[74]

Britain's overall position in the Middle East was assessed by the newly formed Permanent Under Secretary's Committee under Sir William Strang in April 1949. This committee was the equivalent of the American Policy Planning Staff. Like Bevin's Middle East Conference of September 1945 it stressed the economic aspect. The Middle East, and particularly the oil-poducing countries, and Egypt with its cotton, was seen as an area of cardinal importance in the economic recovery of Britain and Western Europe. It was hoped that by 1951 82 per cent of Britain's oil supplies would come from there; in 1938 the figure had been 23 per cent. This would present the largest single factor in balancing Britain's overseas payments. If

Britain failed to maintain its position in the Middle East the plans for Britain's economic recovery and future prosperity would fail.

The Middle East was strategically as crucial to Britain as it had been in 1945. Strang's committee pointed out that it shielded Africa, it was a key centre of land and sea communications and contained large supplies of oil. Above all, however, in the event of attack on the United Kingdom, it was one of the principal areas from which offensive air action could be taken against the aggressor. The strategic key to the area was Egypt; no alternative existed as a main base. If the Middle East was to be denied to an enemy in wartime, at least two conditions were necessary: certain peacetime facilities which included the maintenance of airfields and stores; and the goodwill of the inhabitants. It was also desirable that Britain should have the right of entry or reinforcement in case of apprehended emergency. Otherwise Britain might be obliged to enter or reinforce certain countries either 'without right' or too late. The security of the Middle East was vital to the security of the United Kingdom.

The committee recognized, however, that it would be impossible for the British government to hold the Middle East in a major war without the assistance of the United States. Britain and the United States could not be rivals in the area. The two countries should have a common policy. And apart from Palestine, American policy had for some time been crystallizing on lines similar to those of Britain. There was a common approach to the problems of Greece, Turkey and Persia, to defence and to the promotion of social and economic advancement. Washington had undertaken to help London maintain its position in the Middle East.

Policy towards the Middle East had to be viewed in the light of the extension of communism in various parts of the world. China was largely communist. South-East Asia was in danger. If the Middle East were also to fall to the communists the cause of the democratic countries would suffer a crippling blow. The economic recovery of Britain and Western Europe would be seriously affected. The way would be open for the spread of communism into Africa. Turkey, Greece and Italy would be largely undermined. Russia's ability to wage a successful war against the West would be greatly enhanced. The defence of the United Kingdom in the event of war would be compromised. Many of the conditions which favoured the extension of communism in China existed in the Middle East. Britain had overseen the emergence of most of the Middle Eastern countries to independence and self-government. But the transition from centuries of Turkish misrule to self-government under modern world conditions was difficult. Corruption, inefficiency and poverty were endemic. The standard of living of the mass of the people was appallingly low, and the contrast with the wealth of the small and selfish ruling classes glaring. In spite of the contradiction between the principles of the Muslim religion and of communism, there were almost classic opportunities for communist agitation by the exploitation of hardship, chaos and discontent. To prevent the Middle East falling behind the iron curtain had to be a major objective of British policy and therefore merited a high priority in effort and contribution.

Strang's committee noted that Britain had treaties of alliance with Egypt (expiring in 1956), Iraq (expiring in 1957 with right of review in 1952) and Transjordan (expiring in 1968). These treaties provided for the stationing of certain minimum forces in peacetime, the right of entry in an apprehended emergency and the provision of facilities in wartime. The treaties were not permanent, and the treaties with Egypt and Iraq expired at dates which were particularly awkward in terms of Russian preparedness. In the event of war, Britain had no alternative but to use Egypt as the main base. Cyrenaica and Transjordan 'can afford adjuncts but not a substitute'. Airfields in Iraq were important and desirable elsewhere, particularly in Saudi Arabia (there was an American airfield in Dhahran) and in Cyprus. Air warning facilities, and possibly airfield and port facilities, were desirable in Syria and the Lebanon. The Americans wanted a fighter base in Tripolitania or Cyrenaica. A Middle East pact, along the lines of the Atlantic pact, or alternatively new treaties or agreements, would help to prevent the Middle East falling under communist domination.

Israel was a new factor. The Arab countries were united in their dislike and fear of Israel. The Arabs considered the creation of an independent state of Israel against the wishes of the majority of the former inhabitants as a major injustice and as an example of Western imperial colonization on a grand scale. The creation of Israel was tending to promote Arab unity. Although Britain was criticized as being largely responsible for the creation of Israel, the Arab states were, for the moment, turning towards Britain as being the only country likely to oppose indefinite Israeli expansion. Israel would have considerable strategic importance in the event of war. It should also be prevented from becoming communist. It was hoped that Israel would turn towards the West and not Russia, and have friendly relations with Britain and the United States. The committee wanted all of the Middle East, Greece, Turkey, the Arab countries, Iran, the Persian Gulf, Egypt and Cyrenaica, and Israel to be friendly towards Britain. But it stressed that if Britain were to secure the friendship of Israel at the expense of the Arab countries, Britain would lose economically and strategically more than it gained. Britain had to be friendly to Israel, but not at the cost of losing the friendship of the Arab world. Strategically facilities in Israel would be no substitute for facilities in Egypt and the other Arab states.

In conclusion, the committee suggested that Britain needed to explore the possibility of a Near East and African pact. Dr D.F. Malan, the new Afrikaner Nationalist Prime Minister of South Africa, had mentioned that South Africa would join the Atlantic pact if invited. Alternatively Malan had ideas of an African pact including Britain, the United States, South Africa and the European countries with possessions in Africa. Strang's people, however, felt that the Middle East was the shield of Africa. Any African pact had to be accompanied or followed by a Middle East pact. South Africa could join a Middle East and African pact. It could be extended to include other African countries. This suggestion formed the basis of British policy in the Middle East, designed to deal with the Cold War, until the fall of Attlee's second Labour administration in October 1951.[75]

Notes: Chapter 4

1 Ovendale, *The Origins of the Arab-Israeli Wars*, pp. 15–91.
2 Public Record Office, London, FO 800/452, fol. 46, Def/6, Tedder to Alexander giving details of DO(47)44, 2 February 1948.
3 Public Record Office, London, CAB 79/39, COS (45)215, 5 September 1945; Ovendale, *The Origins of the Arab-Israeli Wars*, pp. 130–2, 136–7; Louis, *The British Empire in the Middle East*, pp. 8–12, 205–25, 265–306, 307–44, 689.
4 R. Ovendale, 'From British Commonwealth to Commonwealth: the English speaking Holy Roman Empire', *Interstate* (1978–9), pp. 12–15; 'The South African policy of the British Labour government, 1947–51', *International Affairs*, vol. 59 (1983), pp. 41–58 at pp. 44–50.
5 Ovendale, *The Origins of the Arab-Israeli Wars*, p. 130.
6 FO 800/475, fos 17–19, Dixon to Sargent, 24 August 1945.
7 Public Record Office, London, CAB 128/3, fol. 34, CM26(45)2, Secret, 30 August 1945.
8 Public Record Office, London, CAB 129/2, fol. 91, CP(45)174, Memorandum on Middle East policy by Bevin, Secret, 17 September 1945.
9 CAB 129/2, fol. 20, CP(45)156, Great Britain's position in the Middle East, Secret, 8 September 1945.
10 CAB 128/1, fol. 81, CM28(45)6, Secret, 4 October 1945.
11 L. Woodward, *British Foreign Policy in the Second World War*, Vol. 4 (London, 1975), pp. 366–8.
12 Princeton University Library, Forrestal Diaries, Box 1, Vol. 2, fol. 230, 16 March 1945.
13 Public Record Office, London, FO 954/19A, fol. 80, Killearn to Eden, Telegram

no. 813, Top Secret and Personal, 6 April 1945; T. E. Evans (ed.), *The Killearn Diaries 1934-46* (London, 1972), pp. 336-8, diary, 2 April 1945; 3 April 1945.

14 Public Record Office, London, FO 371/45379, E6405/15/31G, COS(45)543(0), Top Secret, 22 August 1945; G. H. Gater to Secretary, Chiefs of Staff, 21 August 1945.

15 FO 371/45379, E6622/15/31G, Minutes by Baxter, 23 August 1945, Howe, 24 August 1945; 1 September 1945; Beeley, 4 September 1945; Memorandum by Hall on future policy for Palestine, August 1945(draft); Memorandum by Hall on summary for Palestine Committee, Top Secret; E6744/15/G, P(M)(45)10, Memorandum by Hall for Palestine Committee, Top Secret, 1 September 1945.

16 Ovendale, *The Origins of the Arab-Israeli Wars*, pp. 82-94.

17 FO 800/457, fos 5-6, Eg/45/4, Brook to Bevin, Top Secret, 5 November 1945.

18 Public Record Office, London, CO 537/1847, Memorandum by Kirkbride, 14 March 1946. Quoted by Louis, *The British Empire in the Middle East*, p. 357.

19 ibid., pp.354-8.

20 FO 800/463, fol.32, FO/46/3, Unsigned minute, 11 February 1946.

21 British Library of Economic and Political Science, London, Dalton Diaries, 34, fol. 3, 18 February 1946; fol. 12, 22 March 1946; Bodleian, Oxford, Attlee Papers, 5, Liddel Hart to Attlee, 10 May 1946; Memorandum on Africa or the Middle East, Reflections on strategic and peace policy by Liddell Hart, 20 March 1946.

22 FO 800/457, Eg/46/14, Bevin to Bowker, no. 213, 18 March 1946.

23 CAB 131/2, DO(46), 15 April 1946.

24 FO 800/457, fol. 37, Eg/46/17/A, Sargent to Campbell, Telegram no. 821, Secret, 30 April 1946.

25 FO 800/457, fol. 44, Eg/46/22, Bevin to Campbell, Telegram no. 393, 23 May 1946.

26 F. S. Northedge, 'Britain and the Middle East', in Ovendale (ed.), *The Foreign Policy of the British Labour Governments*, pp. 166-9.

27 Public Record Office, London, CAB 131/2, DO(46)47, Strategic position of the British Commonwealth, 2 April 1946.

28 CAB 131/1, DO(46)10, 5 April 1946.

29 CAB 129/9, CP(46)165, Memorandum by Bevin, 18 April 1946.

30 Louis, *The British Empire in the Middle East*, pp. 277-8.

31 Public Record Office, London, PREM 8/627, Pt 2, PMM(46)8, Top Secret, 30 April 1946.

32 FO 371, 52527, E5065/4/31G, Minute by Howe, 25 May 1946; DO(46)67, Chiefs of Staff Conclusions, Top Secret, 24 May 1946.

33 *FRUS* 1946(7), pp. 631-3, Memorandum by McFarland, 21 June 1946; Truman Library, Independence, Missouri, Truman Papers, Box 184, PSF, McFarland to State-War-Navy Co-ordinating Committee, Top Secret, 21 June 1946.

34 CAB 128/6, fol. 37, CM71(46), Secret, 22 July 1946; FO 371/52548, E7448/4/31G, COS (46)203(0), Chiefs of Staff Committee, Top Secret, 24 July 1946.

35 Ovendale, *The Origins of the Arab-Israeli Wars*, pp. 94-6.

36 CAB 129/13, fos 26-7, CP(46)358, Secret, 5 October 1946.

37 FO 371/52560, E10030/4/31, Minutes of meeting at Foreign Office, 1 October 1946; PREM 8/627, Pt 5, Note by G. H. Gater of interview between Bevin and Weizmann on 26 September 1946, 27 September 1946; *FRUS* 1946 (7), pp. 700-1, Attlee to British Embassy Washington, 2 October 1946; CAB 129/13, fos 26-7, CP(46)358, Secret, 5 October 1946.

38 Ovendale, *The Origins of the Arab-Israeli Wars*, pp. 96-7.

39 CAB 128/6, fol. 193, CM105(46)4, Secret, 12 December 1946.

40 FO 800/475, fos 65-9, ME/46/25, Minutes by J. N. Henderson, 28 December 1946.

41 FO 800/476, fos 2–9, ME/47/1, Attlee to Bevin, Top Secret, 5 January 1947; Memorandum by Attlee on Near East policy.
42 Ovendale, *The Origins of the Arab-Israeli Wars*, p. 98.
43 FO 371/61763, E463/46/G, COS(47)4, JP(47)1, 6 January 1947.
44 PREM 8/627, Pt 6, COS161/7, Top Secret, 6 February 1947.
45 CAB 128/11, fos 7–9, CM6(47)3, Confidential Annex, 15 January 1947.
46 CAB 128/11, fos 11–18, CM6(47)4, Confidential Annex, 15 January 1947.
47 PREM 8/627, Pt 6, COS161/7, Top Secret, 6 February 1947.
48 CAB 128/9, fol. 159, CM35(47)5, Secret, 3 April 1947.
49 National Archives, Washington, DC, RG 59, Decimal Files 1945–9, Box 6760, 867N.01/8-447, Robert B. Macatee to Merriam, Top Secret, 4 August 1947; enclosing memorandum, Secret, 3 August 1947.
50 National Archives, Washington, DC, RG 59, Decimal Files 1945–9, Box 6760, 867N.01/9-1347, R. S. Huestis, Consul Hamburg, to Marshall, no. 647, Confidential, 13 September 1947.
51 CAB 129/21, fos 120–9, CP(47)262, Memorandum by Alexander on military and strategic requirements, Top Secret, 18 September 1947.
52 CAB 128/10, fos 148–50, CM76(47)6, Secret, 20 September 1947.
53 British Library of Economic and Political Science, London, Dalton Diaries, 35, fol. 91, 20 September 1947.
54 FO 371/61789, E8913/46/G, Hayter to Warner, 20 September 1947; JP(47)131 (Final), Report by the Joint Planning Staff on the implications of withdrawal from Palestine, Top Secret, 19 September 1947.
55 FO 371/61791, E9562/46/G, JAP/P(47)39 Revised Draft, Top Secret, 8 October 1947.
56 FO 371/61790, E9411/9373/31, B. A. B. Burrows to D. C. Stapleton, 11 October 1947.
57 FO 371/61790, E10133/9373/G, JP(47)136, Report by the Joint Planning Staff, 24 October 1947; Minute by P. Garran, 5 November 1947.
58 CAB 128/10, fol. 165, CM79(47)3, Secret, 9 October 1947.
59 FO 800/476, fol. 233, E12234/3/G, Bevin to Busk, no. 414, 23 December 1947.
60 Louis, *The British Empire in the Middle East*, pp.331–44.
61 Bullock, *Ernest Bevin*, pp. 508–9; Louis, *The British Empire in the Middle East*, pp. 366–72; J. B. Glubb, *A Soldier with the Arabs* (London, 1957), pp. 63–6.
62 *FRUS* 1947(5), pp. 488–96, Department of State memorandum on exchanges of views leading up to the discussions with the British on the Middle East, Top Secret, undated; FO 371/61114, AN4017/3997/45/G, COS(47)144, Top Secret, 21 November 1947; AN3997/3997/45/G, Record of informal political and strategic talks in Washington on Middle East held from 16 October to 7 November 1947, Top Secret; AN4080/3997/45/G, Bevin to Inverchapel, 13 December 1947.
63 FO 800/509, Bevin to Hector McNeill, Confidential and Personal, 15 October 1947.
64 Ovendale, *The Origins of the Arab-Israeli Wars*, pp. 104–5.
65 Georgetown University Library, Washington, DC, Robert F. Wagner Papers, Palestine Files, Box 3, File 47, Senators to United Nations Delegations of Haiti, Greece, Luxembourg, Argentina, Columbia, China, El Salvador, Ethiopia, Honduras, Mexico, the Philippines, and Paraguay, Telegram, 25 November 1947.
66 Truman Library, Independence, Missouri, Truman Papers, Box 773, OF 204-Misc., Celler to Truman, Telegram, 26 November 1947; Celler to Truman, 3 December 1947; Celler to Matthew Connelly, 3 December 1947.
67 Forrestal Diaries, Box 4, Vol. 10, fos 2094–5, 22 February 1948.
68 Truman Library, Oral History Interview with Loy W. Henderson, fol. 138.
69 RG 59, Decimal Files 1945–9, Box 2183, 501.BB Palestine/12–547, Robert B.

Memminger, Chargé d'Affaires Damascus to Marshall, no. 859, 5 December 1947.
70 Forrestal Diaries, Box 4, Vol. 9, fol. 1956, Cabinet, 1 December 1947.
71 RG 59, Office of Near Eastern Affairs Palestine, Box 1, Merriam to Henderson, Top Secret, 11 December 1947.
72 *FRUS* 1947(5), pp. 815–16, Anglo-US-French conversations, British memorandum of conversation, Top Secret, 17 December 1947.
73 Ovendale, *The Origins of the Arab-Israeli Wars*, pp. 112–19.
74 ibid., pp. 119–25; Louis, *The British Empire in the Middle East*, pp. 113, 532–71.
75 FO 800/455, fos 191–6, PUSC(19)Final, Near East, Top Secret, 30 April 1949.

5

The Middle East Command

Bevin, when speaking to Marshall on 17 December 1947 about his global plans for coping with a world locked in a Cold War, envisaged a positive plan for the association of the Western democratic countries – including the United States, Britain, Italy, France and others – and the Dominions. Like Neville Chamberlain in the 1930s, Bevin thought that the Dominions were a significant factor. What Bevin outlined in December 1947 was not very different from the situation that Chamberlain had helped to bring about in September 1939. Bevin hoped that the English-speaking world, and the European democracies, would stand together in a loose association. It did not have to be a formal alliance. In 1939 the Dominions, though not committed to do so, had gone to war alongside the mother country. What counted in the end, to many people, were the kith and kin relationship and a common idealism. The Commonwealth's participation in defence was of vital importance for Britain. This was shown in 1934 with Hankey's visit to the Dominions, and again at the 1937 Imperial Conference. In 1946 when the issue was again raised at the Commonwealth Prime Ministers' Meeting in London, Mackenzie King of Canada said that although there might be military and financial advantages to a Commonwealth defence policy, there were also 'political' considerations: Britain should trust the Dominions to accept obligations which they believed to be 'natural and right'.[1] At a time when the North Atlantic Treaty was being negotiated in Washington, Bevin raised the matter of defence co-operation again at the Commonwealth Prime Ministers' Meeting in 1948. At that time, with the addition of the Asian Dominions, the British Commonwealth was being transformed into the Commonwealth. With the emergence of the Cold War in Asia the former concept of the old boys' club gave way to that of a loosely knit association. The communist advances in Asia convinced the king and the Cabinet that it was essential to keep India within the body, even if it meant changing its nature.[2] At the meeting of Commonwealth Prime Ministers in 1949 the British Commonwealth became the Commonwealth:[3] the common bond of the British monarch being the titular head of each state was abolished. General J. C. Smuts had warned that this could mean that the Commonwealth would become like the Holy Roman Empire, merely a matter of language with nothing behind it.[4]

In October 1948 Britain again raised the issue of defence with the Commonwealth Prime Ministers. Rather than attempting to achieve a common Commonwealth defence policy, it was decided that Britain should enter into bilateral defence discussions with individual dominions. A distinction developed between the old 'white' Dominions and the new Asian members. Sir Frederick G. Shedden, the Secretary of the Australian Department of Defence, discerned this on a visit to London in 1949. He attributed the reluctance of people in higher defence circles to talk about policy on Commonwealth defence as it affected the Dominions primarily to the 'recent constitutional developments'.[5] With the outbreak of the Korean War, Britain, fearing the reliability of certain of the Asian Dominions, distinguished between the full information it sent to Australia, New Zealand, Canada and South Africa, and that going to India, Pakistan and Ceylon. At the Commonwealth Prime Ministers' Conference in January 1951 special meetings were arranged to discuss defence matters from which the Asian members were excluded.[6]

The Middle East remained one of the three cardinal pillars of British strategic policy. It became increasingly evident that the Americans regarded the defence of the Middle East as an area of British and Commonwealth responsibility. Given its financial and manpower commitments elsewhere, Britain felt that it could not undertake this on its own. It needed the support of the Dominions to defend an area considered essential for the security of the United Kingdom. Britain hoped that defence planning could be carried out between the Australian and New Zealand Chiefs of Staff, together with the British planners, for the protection of the Middle East. It was also encouraged by South African interest in the area. But throughout the last years of the Labour governments Australia was prepared to talk, but not commit itself. This was the time, particularly under the premiership of Sir Robert Menzies, that Australia became convinced that the principal threat to its security lay in Asia and not the Middle East. It could not accept the British order of priority: the Middle East and then Asia. In September 1949 Shedden warned that Britain was strained in providing for its defence commitments in Europe, the Middle East and Asia. In the event of war, Britain wanted immediate Australian assistance in the front extending from Iceland to the Middle East. Attlee said that Britain could do nothing to help in the Pacific if it were committed elsewhere. As a result Shedden suggested that, while pressing on with strategic planning with Britain and New Zealand, it was imperative that Australia establish a close link with the United States, even if it fell short of American co-operation in a regional arrangement.[7]

At the end of December 1948 Australia was informed it was the view of the British Chiefs of Staff that the most immediate and dangerous Russian threat would be in Western Europe and the Middle East. American naval and air strength could handle any threat to the Pacific area. In Western Europe the plan was to build up the strength of the Western Union, and to depend on American support. The successful defence of the Middle East, however, depended on the rapid build up of Commonwealth and American forces. Britain would be hard put to deploy adequate forces to the Middle East in time. The British Chiefs of Staff, therefore, suggested that any forces Australia did not need for those areas vital for its home defence should go to the Middle East. Any campaign in the Far East would be primarily an American one and fought from bases on the Japanese islands. The British Chiefs of Staff thought that Russia could mount simultaneous attacks in Europe and the Middle East. Russia wanted to establish communism directed from Moscow throughout the world. Its leaders were trying to achieve this by methods short of open war, but if they thought that they could not achieve this except by war, they would provoke a war as soon as they considered themselves ready. The Russian regime was committed to the Marxist belief that ultimately communism would triumph throughout the world, and that in the meantime the communist and capitalist powers could not live together except in a state of constant friction and unrest. The need for economic and military rehabilitation meant that Russia was unlikely to fight before 1957. But Russia's strength was such that victory could only be achieved if all the allies made the maximum possible contribution to implement the allied plan, and to meet the threat as soon as, and wherever, it developed. The British concept of allied strategy was that the general allied offensive would be in the air. To do this essential air bases would have to be held. These were in the United Kingdom, the Middle East, and the Japanese islands. It would, further, be necessary to defend territories essential to the allies. These were: the air base areas; the main support areas; other areas essential for the defence of the air bases, support areas and communications. The essential sea communications between operational and support areas would also have to be controlled. To achieve this the allies would have to pool their resources.[8]

The Australian Defence Committee recognized the importance of Egypt in this British strategy, but questioned whether the Egyptian government would give adequate and timely co-operation. It suggested that the prospects of holding and using Egypt as a base should be assessed.[9] At this time the British Chiefs of Staff also hoped for wider South African responsibilities over Egypt. South Africa should be convinced that its frontier was the Middle East.[10]

The Australian and New Zealand Chiefs of Staff met with British planners in Melbourne between 22 and 26 August 1949. The view of the British Chiefs of Staff was endorsed that it was not possible to limit the allied war aim to the narrow one of restoring the situation to that immediately preceding the outbreak of war, or even that of driving the Russians out of territories over which they had acquired control. The allied war aims were: first, to ensure the abandonment by Russia of further military and ideological aggression; secondly, to create conditions conducive to world peace. Russia's geographical characteristics, and its superior numbers of land forces, meant that a strategic air offensive was the only means of initial offensive action. Air bases had to be selected so that all the important targets in Russia were within range. Nearly all the major targets could be reached from bases in Western Europe, the Middle East, Pakistan and the Japanese islands. There was no defence arrangement with Pakistan. There was general agreement that certain military measures were essential to implement allied strategy. First, the strategic air offensive had to be delivered from the outbreak of war; secondly, it was necessary to hold the air bases and sea areas essential for the air offensive; thirdly, it would also be desirable to hold as bases for air offensive the sea areas for possible carrier offensives and Pakistan. The main support areas had to be defended: the United States and Canada; Australia and New Zealand; South Africa and certain other parts of the African continent; Argentina and certain other parts of South America. It was also essential to ensure the internal security and local defence of support areas of less importance, and to hold those areas necessary to give defence in depth to allied air bases and support areas. Finally, there had to be firm control of the essential sea and air communications, and of land areas necessary to limit this control. Because of the strategic importance of Europe and the Middle East, Russia's main armed effort would be in those areas. The Australian Chiefs of Staffs conceded that, provided there was an adequate superiority of allied naval and air forces in the Pacific, and a secure hold was maintained on the Philippines and Malaya, there was no threat of invasion for Australia, and the scale of air attack would be negligible.[11]

Following further bilateral conversations with individual Dominions, often with the defence of the Middle East as a priority, the Chiefs of Staff nine months later on 7 June 1950 submitted a paper, Defence Policy and Global Strategy, DO(50)45. This was slightly revised in 1951 as MDM(51)2, but substantially what it outlined remained British policy into 1952 when it was changed by the new Conservative administration. Defence Policy and Global Strategy had considerable ramifications for British policy in the Middle East. The Chiefs of Staff considered, first, defence policy and global strategy from the allied rather than from the British standpoint. They considered the Cold War strategy which should be adopted, and its effect on a hot war should one develop:

> Allied defence policy cannot be divided into watertight compartments of 'cold' and 'hot' strategy. The former is largely conditioned by our ability, in the last resort, to defend our interests against armed aggression; which our readiness to fight defensively is inevitably affected by the demands of the cold war. Our aim must be to reduce to the minimum the extent to which it is so affected, but not to the fatal compromise of our ability to win the cold war which is rightly our first defence priority.

It made no sense to think of British or Western European strategy as something individual and independent. Full collaboration with the United States in policy and method was vital. That truth was recognized 'in the most important area of conflict' by the North Atlantic Treaty. But the Cold War against Russian communism was a global war, as a hot war would 'inevitably' be. After stabilization of the European front, the next most important objective should be to secure an agreed allied military strategy in the Middle East and East Asia theatres, and also the machinery to implement it. It was also necessary to obtain the fullest possible political, economic and military collaboration in the British Commonwealth as a whole – if possible including the countries of the Indian subcontinent, but if necessary without them.

The British Chiefs of Staff pointed out that Britain, itself, could not afford all the forces required for the Middle East, in addition to those required to defend itself and Western Europe. Additional forces had, therefore, to be found from other parts of the Commonwealth and the United States. In the event of a hot war, in the short term, it was not the American intention to send any forces initially to the Middle East, although the American Chiefs of Staff were understood to attach great strategic importance to that region, and might revise their existing policy when resources were available. Britain did not intend to send bomber reinforcements to the Middle East in the early stages of a war to conduct an offensive from that region. The Middle East, however, was viewed as 'a potentially important base for air action against Southern Russia'. It was British policy to send reinforcements of bomber aircraft to the Middle East as soon as it had the necessary resources. The primary burden for the defence of the Middle East would fall on the army, which should be in a position as soon as possible to have at its disposal a reserve for cold war emergencies. Second priorities in the Middle East were a share in the defence of the Egyptian base, and 'control of the Mediterranean sea-route for as long as possible in conjunction with the United States Navy and its denial to the enemy'.

There was no co-ordinated or agreed allied cold war strategy in relation to Asia. Furthermore, agreement had not been reached on allied military hot war strategy in the Middle East and east Asia. Agreement on these matters would be necessary before firm military arrangements could be made for the defence of these regions.[12]

The British Chiefs of Staff, in May 1950, were convinced that in any war Egypt would be singled out by Russia for an early attack.[13] The Chief of the Imperial General Staff, Sir William Slim, emphasized this in talks with Farouk in June.[14] When Menzies visited Egypt in July, after the outbreak of the Korean War, he had a long talk with Dr Salah el Din Bey, the Foreign Minister. Menzies concluded that the Egypt slogan of the time was: 'The British must evacuate. The presence of their troops is an affront to our sovereignty.' He felt that Egypt had a virulent inferiority complex, and had suddenly 'discovered' that the weakness of its defences was due to British neglect over the previous fifty years. Britain had created Israel in order to threaten and weaken Egypt. Menzies noted that the Egyptians said that they would defend the Canal Zone, but that they had not the first idea of the military preparations and equipment necessary. The Foreign Minister told Menzies that in the event of a war Australian, New Zealand and

South African troops could arrive quickly, and 'all would be ready for them!' Menzies concluded that although, politically, it might be necessary to go through the motions of withdrawing troops, the retention of some of the bases for equipment, air force personnel and some technical personnel was vital. Menzies told the Egyptian Foreign Minister that the integrity of the Canal Zone and the Middle East was vital to Australian security. Australian policy was to co-operate to the fullest extent with Britain and other Commonwealth countries in defence planning, and to regard the defence of the Canal Zone as a practical military problem which could not be solved by political arguments. Menzies was disgusted by the logic of 'these wretched creatures'. In reply to his assertion that it was 'most unlikely' that Australia would ever be neutral in a British war, the Egyptian Foreign Minister replied: 'Well then, you will come to the rescue in the event of war; therefore all British forces can safely be evacuated now.' The Australian Prime Minister confided to his diary: 'These Gyppos are a dangerous lot of backward adolescents, mouthing their slogans of democracy, full of self importance and basic ignorance. Two bombs dropped on Cairo, and their only grievance would be that the British troops didn't come back fast enough.'[15]

While abroad Menzies met American leaders. They all said that while they attached considerable importance to Australia providing a small force for Korea as a contribution to winning the Cold War, it would be undesirable to allow this to interfere with the basic objectives of British Commonwealth strategy, particularly strategic planning for Australian participation in the Middle East in the event of global war. The United States appreciated the vital nature of the Middle East in global strategy. In war, quick action was needed there. Heavy American commitments in Europe and responsibilities in the Pacific meant that the United States would not be able to help in the Middle East in the early stages of a war. Washington thought of the Middle East as a British Commonwealth commitment in which Australia would be expected to help.[16]

In discussions with their British counterparts in Washington between 23 and 26 October, the American Chiefs of Staff reiterated that they saw the Middle East as a British and Commonwealth responsibility: the United States could make no commitment of forces for the area, in the event of war, but its Strategic Air Command would strike targets to assist in the defence of the area. The American fleet in the Mediterranean was there primarily to cover action in Italy and southern Europe. Operations in the eastern Mediterranean would be a secondary task. The

Americans thought that, in defending the Middle East, every effort should be made to hold a ring to include Turkey and to cover Middle East oil. Britain had probably underestimated the value of a properly equipped and trained Iranian army. There was to be a combined study of the position between the Commander-in-Chief, Middle East, with the Commander of the American Mediterranean Fleet and the heads of the missions in Turkey and Iran. The Americans thought Middle Eastern oil essential to the war effort. There had to be a new review of the role of Middle East oil in allied strategic plans. The Americans also agreed that Egypt was indispensable as a wartime base for forces defending the Middle East. There was also to be a study of the association of Greece and Turkey with NATO planning.[17]

Britain, initially with some reluctance,[18] was thus left with 'primary responsibility' for the defence of the Middle East. An offer of assistance however, came from South Africa, related to the defence of Africa against the spread of communism. By October 1950 Pretoria had indicated that in the event of war it would provide for service outside South Africa, together with those forces of other powers interested in the area, one armoured division, one fighter group of nine squadrons, personnel for one air transport squadron and such naval forces as could be spared from their primary task of defending South African waters. These forces would be available to serve in the Middle East if required.[19] Canberra, in contrast, was beginning to shift from giving the Middle East priority. In a discussion of the British Chiefs of Staff's Defence Policy and Global Strategy, the Joint Planning Committee, on 6 November, argued that while from the aspect of allied global strategy in a hot war the retention of Malaya was considered desirable, but not vital, from the Australian viewpoint it would be essential to hold Malaya to give defence in depth to Australia. If the prevailing situation in Indochina and Malaya deteriorated, it was possible that the Australian effort in Malaya would need to be increased during the cold war period. In the event of a hot war a much larger force would be needed in Malaya. In those circumstances it was probable that an early contribution of Australian ground and air forces would not be available for the Middle East as hoped for by the British Chiefs of Staff. If the non-availability of Australian forces for the Middle East would prejudice the holding of that region, it would be necessary to decide the relative priority of Malaya and the Middle East, in the light of the prevailing situation. On global strategic grounds the Middle East should have first priority, but until more was known about British and allied plans in the Middle East and Malaya, and the forces available, it would not be possible for planning to proceed on a firm basis.[20]

At the time of the Commonwealth Prime Ministers' Conference in London in January 1951, the Assistant Under Secretary for Middle Eastern Affairs in the Foreign Office, R. J. Bowker, offered the assessment of the Foreign Office and the views of the Chiefs of Staff on this area of British Commonwealth responsibility. British defence plans for the Middle East aimed to defend as much of the Middle East as possible. Egypt was the only base from which this could be done. It was also 'a platform' from which an attack could be launched against Russia's most vulnerable area, the oil fields in the Caucasus. The Middle East also had to be held as a barrier to Africa to deny that continent's rich resources to the Russians. Egypt was the best base for doing that as well. The Suez Canal was not of vital importance in wartime. But 'Suez remains of vast importance as the back door to Egypt and will no doubt be of great importance in the next war in servicing the vital Australian and New Zealand, and also South African, contributions to Middle East defence'.[21]

Britain decided that at the meeting of Commonwealth Prime Ministers in London not all the countries 'would wish to participate' in certain discussions. Talks on the defence of the Middle East and Africa were confined to Britain, Canada, Australia, New Zealand, South Africa and Southern Rhodesia. Those on military liaison arrangements between Commonwealth countries in peace and war, including the question of the association of Commonwealth countries with the higher military direction of a future global war, were to include the same countries, with the exception of Southern Rhodesia.[22] In the end Southern Rhodesia did attend the meeting on higher military direction in war, at which the Minister of Defence, Emmanuel Shinwell, explained that the three main essentials were: first, the smallest possible body for the conduct of war; secondly, as much consultation as possible on strategic planning before war started; and thirdly, in war, adequate liaison arrangements to ensure that all allied countries were kept fully informed of the reasons underlying the decisions taken. In particular Shinwell welcomed co-operation with Commonwealth countries, and thought that periodic meetings of Commonwealth Defence Ministers would be valuable.[23]

On 6 January 1951 Sir William Slim, the Chief of the Imperial General Staff, opened the special meeting on the Middle East and the defence of Africa with the observation that the allies could almost certainly lose a hot war by losing the Middle East, and could not win the war without regaining the Middle East. Besides its vital strategic importance for the allies, the Middle East remained one of the three basic pillars of strategy for the Commonwealth, the others being the security of the United Kingdom, as an essential base, and the maintenance of sea communications. The Americans had said that they could not contribute to the defence of the area for the first two years of a major war. The defence of the Middle East remained a Commonwealth responsibility, while that of the Pacific was mainly up to the Americans. In outlining possible lines of defence of the Middle East, Slim used ideas promulgated by the American Chiefs of Staff in October. The only satisfactory line from a military point of view was an 'outer ring'. That included a large part of Turkey, likely to be the soundest ally, and the oil-producing territories. It would keep the Russians a long way from Egypt, and was a sound military line resting on mountain ranges with only a few passes.But it was a long line, would need a lot of troops and was a long way away from the position of allied troops in peacetime. The second alternative was an 'inner line'. This would mean abandoning the oil-producing territories and most of Turkey. It was a compromise. The third position, 'the Lebanon-Jordan line', would merely hold a position of the Mediterranean covering part of Jordan, as well as Israel and Egypt. The extent of the threat to the position in the Middle East depended on whether the Russian attack started from the existing Russian border, or whether the Russians would first advance their position by an operation in part of Iran. Such an action could reduce by almost two months the time at which the Russians were in position. Assuming that the Russians started from the existing borders, it was estimated that they would reach the Iranian passes on the 'outer ring' in about fourteen days, and after eighty days would have six divisions on the east bank of the Euphrates. Three or four months after the operation started, the Russians would have three or four divisions advancing over the desert towards 'Northern Palestine' and the 'inner ring', and in four to five months after the beginning of operations they would have eight divisions through Turkey moving southwards from Alexandretta. They would then have twelve divisions in position after about four months.

All that Britain could provide to meet this threat on the basis of existing planning was one and one-third divisions already in the Middle East, another two divisions three months after operations started and another three and one-third divisions six months after operations started. To these could be added the Arab League which was a first-class force and suitable for operations in the Middle East, but amounting only to the strength of a single division. The total opposing the Russians after four months would thus be between five and six divisions. According to the medium-term plan which would come into operation in 1954, there would be a little acceleration, and six divisions could be in the field rather more quickly.

Military conversations with various Commonwealth countries had indicated that one division could be expected from Australia, one division, eventually, from New Zealand and one armoured division from South Africa. If those Commonwealth forces arrived in the Middle East in time, they would greatly affect the position, leaving the allied force not greatly inferior to the Russians in size, while superior in equipment and fighting capacity.

The British Chiefs of Staff were satisfied that the objective should be to hold the 'outer line'. That would ensure close contact with Turkey who could produce nineteen divisions which, together with air support, would be 'a source of great strength'. There was the possibility of two not very reliable divisions from Iraq which were 'weakly officered'. The Americans were training an army in Iran, but the Chiefs of Staff in London thought that the Americans overestimated the value of these troops. If Israel fought on the allied side, it could contribute one further division of 'real fighting value'. The Americans and British were due to start talks about holding the 'outer ring', or failing that, the 'inner ring'. The problem was the Egyptian base. From the beginning of a war it was essential that the allies should be able to use Egypt. Sir Arthur Sanders, the Chief of Staff for Air, warned that the air force would not be able to protect even the 'inner ring' or the Lebanon-Jordan line.

Britain wanted a larger Commonwealth contribution. Shinwell pointed to the great moral and psychological advantages of Commonwealth countries keeping small token forces in the Middle East in peacetime, on which they could build their larger contribution in war. He suggested that Commonwealth battalions could be placed with British forces to train with them in peacetime. Shinwell was worried about the danger of potential disorder in Iran. That would make the defence of the whole area more difficult, and might mean that the allies could not rely on Iranian oil. Furthermore, the envisaged Commonwealth build up could not match Russian developments. The Australian contribution was not to be expected until D-day plus twelve months, though after 1955 that date was to be advanced to D-day plus ninety days. The New Zealand brigade group could arrive in D-day plus six months. South Africa's armoured division depended on the provision of equipment.

Southern Rhodesia had not specified when its field artillery regiment would arrive.

Bevin, at that time ill and with only a few months to live, offered what was virtually his swansong on an area which he saw as crucial for Britain's very existence. Initially determined to work with peasants and not pashas, Bevin had been left in the position where Britain's only hope of maintaining suzerainty over the Arabs lay in working with the old ruling houses. During his period of office, Bevin had successfully resisted moves from his Prime Minister to withdraw the British presence from the Middle East. Probably more than any other British statesman at the time, Bevin was identified with the Middle East. The Foreign Secretary told the conference that the main difficulty in arranging a comprehensive plan for the defence of the Middle East was the reality that Britain had to deal with a number of small countries which were politically and economically unstable. Turkey was the most stable country in the area. Geographically, however, it was in the wrong place. A defence plan could not be centred on it. There were only a few places where British forces could be placed in the Middle East in peacetime, and begin to plan an offensive defence in war. Even in Cyprus, Greece, from time to time, 'provoked activities for independence'. In the United Nations, Britain's friends had not been co-operative in the attempt to secure the necessary strategic facilities in Cyrenaica. Britain had been faced with impossible obstacles in handling the former Italian colonies: a plan proposed for the partition of Eritrea which was sound both politically and ethnically had been rejected. Egypt, however, was still the principal problem. For sixty-seven years Britain had been promising to leave the Canal Zone, but Britain was still there, and still trying to make arrangements by which it might stay. There was also the trouble with Egypt over the condominium of the Sudan. Britain's legal position on both these matters in the United Nations was weak. Egypt did not seem to realize that geography made it a magnet for attack in war. In 1947 Stalin had hinted to him that he would not promote subversive agitation in Egypt while Britain remained, but would do this if the British tried to bring the Americans into Egypt. Britain had to look for military facilities elsewhere in the Middle East. Whatever accommodation might be reached with Egypt, Britain would have to leave in 1956. Because of this Bevin was working with the Chiefs of Staff on a scheme by which the Egyptians would be left with the responsibility for looking after the stores, workshops and communications in the Canal Zone on Britain's behalf. Egypt would look after the Suez base in peacetime;

but in war Egypt should allow Britain all the facilities it might require. These included base facilities, as well as the necessary immunities for British and allied forces. Bevin hoped that the Egyptians would allow Britain to decide when there was an emergency likely to lead to war. The Chiefs of Staff, however, had to find an alternative peacetime base for troops in the Middle East. Facilities were also necessary in Israel and Libya. Egypt and Israel would not co-operate. It was British policy to make the Middle Eastern countries feel that they were equal partners in efforts to defend their territories. The Sudan problem would solve itself as the Sudanese achieved more self-government, but it might be necessary to have some loose connection between the Sudan and the Egyptian Crown.

Discussion suggested that, with the exception of Israel where it might be difficult to get facilities, there was no base like Egypt. It had a front door on the Mediterranean, and a back door to the Red Sea. This was particularly important for the Commonwealth forces from Australia and New Zealand. The Chiefs of Staff, however, thought that at least for the first few months of the war it would be possible to keep open a sea line of communication through the Mediterranean. There were doubts about the Egyptians' ability to maintain valuable equipment. The Prime Minister of New Zealand, Sidney George Holland, thought that the Egyptians could provide manual labour and be supervised by British civilians.

The Commonwealth Prime Ministers would not make firm commitments. Menzies pointed out that Australian conscripts could not serve outside the ANZAM area, an area mainly located in the Pacific seen as crucial for Australia's own protection which did not include the Middle East. Defence of the Middle East would be more effective if Pakistan would co-operate. He could not make firm commitments as to the destination of Australian forces in war. That would depend on the wishes of the Australian government in power at the time. Menzies had sent Australian forces to the Middle East immediately in 1939. But he could not guarantee that the present planning agreed between Britain and Australia would 'bear practical fruit' in the event of war. Australia could not look at the defence of the Middle East in isolation. There were 'urgent dangers' in Malaya, Dutch New Guinea and Indochina. Australia might become more attached to the idea of sending forces to the Middle East if it knew American strategic intentions in the whole Pacific area. Holland said that there were no domestic difficulties in New Zealand where defence was a bipartisan issue. The only problem was that a recent plebiscite had resulted in training for 18-year-olds, but New Zealanders could not be sent to serve overseas until they were 21. The South African representative, Dr T. E. Dönges, said that his government agreed with the estimate of the vital importance of the Middle East for global strategy. Africa as a whole had to remain in the Western orbit. While Western Europe and Britain might be described as the 'soul of the defensive system, Africa was the body, with its immense resources'. The Middle East was the vital entry into Africa. Facilities had to be developed in Africa for the maintenance of forces sent to the Middle East. 'It was the policy of his Government to ensure that South Africa remained a white man's country, strong and reliable, and ready to co-operate with other African powers for the development of the Continent.' The commitment to the Middle East was dependent upon a satisfactory condition of internal security in South Africa itself. It was the first priority of South Africa's defence policy to ensure internal security against communist subversive activities. Sir Godfrey Huggins said that Southern Rhodesia would try to make its contribution available as soon as was possible. Canada refused to be involved. St Laurent presumed that the Americans had not included Canada in assigning the Middle East to the Commonwealth: the Americans would rather expect Canada to make its contribution in the same area as the American.[24]

The Dominions were not committed to the defence of the Middle East after the Commonwealth Prime Ministers' Conference in January 1951. Their position was analogous to that on the outbreak of the Second World War. In 1939, however, even after the outbreak of war, there had been time for defence preparations. The British Chiefs of Staff did not anticipate any such interval in 1951. Planning had to be based on the assumption of the immediate preparedness of forces in certain areas. The Middle East, seen as one of the vital props of Commonwealth security, posed particular problems. During the first six months of 1951 Britain's position in the Middle East deteriorated. Egypt remained obdurate. In Iran, British oil interests were challenged by Mohammed Mussaddiq when he nationalized the Anglo-Iranian Oil Company. Hints of assistance, however, did come from the Prime Minister of Israel, David Ben-Gurion. But these were politely turned aside lest Arab opinion be alienated. Friendship with the Arab world, however fragile, could not be endangered by an alliance with Israel. At the time of the next Commonwealth gathering to discuss the defence of the Middle East in London in June 1951, Britain's position in the area was being rapidly undermined.

Bevin, just before his death, was succeeded by his enemy,

Herbert Morrison, as Foreign Secretary. Morrison, assisted by Shinwell, shifted the basis of British policy towards Egypt. Bevin had accepted that the British would have to leave Egypt on Egyptian terms, but had hoped that the Egyptians might have been persuaded to accept a gradual British withdrawal and the right of British re-entry in the event of an emergency. Shinwell and Morrison fought for a firm British stand. The Cabinet agreed. New demands were made of the Egyptians: Britain would make a 'phased' withdrawal, but only after the conclusion of a new treaty. The Egyptian position on the Sudan was rejected. The Egyptians thought that what they received on 11 April 1951 looked like an ultimatum. Within two weeks they turned down the British proposals.[25]

On 1 May Mussaddiq secured the passage through the Iranian parliament (Majlis) of a bill nationalizing the Anglo-Iranian Oil Company. The British Cabinet considered military action, but Washington approved of nationalization, urged restraint and sent a mediator to Tehran, Averell Harriman, who, en route, assured Hugh Gaitskell in Paris that he would do his best to sustain the British position. Just before handing over to Churchill, Attlee told his colleagues that Britain could not afford to break with the United States on an issue like this.[26]

Israel, however, made friendly overtures. On 19 and 21 February 1951 Ben-Gurion and the British Commander-in-Chief Middle East Land Forces, General Brian Robertson, spoke cordially to one another. Ben-Gurion wanted Israel to survive. There was a 'great danger to civilisation'. The situation called for the 'closest possible collaboration' between Israel and Britain. Ben-Gurion meant by this that 'in an emergency Israel should act "as if" she were part of the British Commonwealth and should be regarded by Great Britain in exactly the same way'. Ben-Gurion was not proposing that Israel should join the Commonwealth. He did, however, want Israel to play an active rather than a merely passive role in resisting the common enemy. Israel could play a useful role by placing its industrial capacity at Britain's disposal. If Britain were interested, it could help to develop it. Israel was worried that in a general war the Arab states would try to destroy it. Ben-Gurion, therefore, wanted peaceful relations with the Arab states, and particularly Egypt: Morrison replied on 24 April that the development of a relationship between Israel and Britain should be a gradual process, 'taking account of the realities of the existing situation and our respective world interests'. The process had to come about naturally, as a result of continued contacts, exchanges of views and individual acts of co-operation. The best way to start could be practical co-operation in the military field, co-operation that would contribute to Israel's security and the safeguarding of Britain's vital interests in the Middle East.[27] Israel, however, was not invited to join the envisaged Middle East defence organization. It was not thought possible for both sides on the Palestine dispute to belong to the same defence body. Any inclusion of Israel would prejudice Arab participation. And the Arabs were more important.[28]

By the end of June Britain was having difficulties with the United States over the selection of the NATO commander for the Mediterranean. This, combined with the realization that Britain might be forced out of Egypt and that a solution acceptable to the Egyptians could be internationalization of the occupation force, led to the concept of a Middle East Command.[29] This was broached at the meeting of Commonwealth defence delegates in London.

Over the previous six months, particularly with the situation in Malaya and Indochina, British defence planners had placed increasing emphasis on South-East Asia. More forces were needed to stop the communist threat. More money had to be spent on defence. On 25 January the British Cabinet accepted a huge increase in Britain's defence budget: £ 4,700 million was to be spent over the years 1951-4.[30] As in 1934, Britain hoped that the Dominions would follow. When surveying defence policy and global strategy in 1951 the Chiefs of Staff remained convinced that the three pillars of British Commonwealth strategy remained the defence of the United Kingdom and its development as an offensive base; the control of vital sea communications; and a firm hold in the Middle East and the development of Egypt as an offensive base. The Australian Defence Committee, however, had evolved a dual approach to the Middle East question: the situation might arise where Australia would be confronted with the choice of sending forces either to Malaya or the Middle East.[31] In the paper on defence policy and global strategy prepared for the Dominion defence delegates, MDM(51)2, the Chiefs of Staff pointed to the 'one very serious gap' in the worldwide cold war front – Asia, but concluded that South-East Asia in a hot as well as in cold war was 'a secondary but none the less immensely important front'. The Australian Defence Committee thought that MDM(51)2 was basically similar to DO(50)45.[32]

MDM(51)2 stated that the aim in the Cold War, which was to be achieved if possible without real hostilities, involved, first, a stabilization of the anti-communist front in the free world and then, as the Western military powers became militarily less weak, the intensification of 'cold' offensive measures aimed at weakening the Russian grip on the satellite states and ultimately achieving their complete independence from Russian control. If total war was forced on the Western allies the aim would remain broadly the same. The first preoccupation had to be to ensure survival in the face of the initial onslaught. The ultimate military aim was to bring the war to the speediest possible conclusion, without Western Europe being overrun, by bringing about the destruction of Russian military power and the collapse of its existing regime. The British Chiefs of Staff saw a close interrelationship between cold war policy and military preparedness. Failure to make progress in the Cold War increased military difficulties and commitments. Recent developments in the Far East had shown that. The allies had to continue to adopt a more offensive policy, backed by necessary force. A policy on these lines offered the best hope of preventing a total war. History supported that view. The Chiefs of Staff did not regard a total war as inevitable, and considered it unlikely that Russia would start one deliberately, provided the Western allies combined resolution and restraint while they built up their military strength. But they did not exclude the possibility that Russia might provoke a total war before Western rearmament became effective, or that total war might result from some situation that obliged the Western powers to take military action which might involve them in hostilities with Russian forces. The moment of greatest danger within the following few years would probably be about the latter half of 1952. Indeed Slim told the Commonwealth defence delegates that the one factor which could provoke Russia to go to war was German rearmament: 'The Russians were probably more afraid of the German bayonet than of the American atomic bomb.' German rearmament would not be practicable until 1952. That was the most dangerous period. Before that Russia might continue to provoke industrial and economic unrest, and could even attempt further political offensives in Italy or France. Russian policy would also include taking advantage of all the nationalist movements in the Middle East and the Far East, and, Slim thought, Russia could try to encourage another war by proxy on the lines of the Korean conflict.

The defence of the United Kingdom, and its development as an offensive base, required holding the enemy on a line as far east in Europe as was possible. European civilization could not survive a Russian occupation of all Western Europe. It would only be with the utmost difficulty and sacrifice that Britain could survive an enemy occupation of the Channel and Atlantic coasts. In the long run the rest of the free world could not survive if Britain and Europe were 'submerged'. The defence of Western Europe, initially at least as far east as the Rhine, was vital. This meant that, militarily, the defence of Europe, including the United Kingdom, had to have top priority. The primary offensive weapon in total war had to remain the atomic bomb, but Western Europe could not be held without conventional forces far stronger than those then in existence. Britain had undertaken to make its due contribution to the land defence of Western Europe, but it had to insist that the land and air defence of the European continent had to be, in the main, the responsibility of the European powers.

The security of sea communications vital to the allies remained another pillar of allied strategy. Britain on its own could no longer protect all the important allied sea communications. The United States and Commonwealth countries would have to defend some. Some would have to be left unguarded. One area was really vital: the north Atlantic and the home waters of the allied powers through which run what were literally their lifelines. If the north Atlantic were not secured, the allies would lose the war.

The third pillar was a firm hold on the Middle East, and the development of Egypt as an offensive base. In the Cold War the defence of the Middle East had always been one of the three pillars of British defence policy, and it was of equally 'critical importance' in allied strategy. It formed the land bridge between Europe, Asia and Africa, and was a most important link in the Commonwealth system of sea and air communications. Its oil supplies were of great importance, and if it fell under Russian influence, the repercussions on the whole Muslim world from French North Africa through Pakistan to South-East Asia would be 'critically serious'. To retain control of the Middle East within the Western orbit was a vital cold war measure, and military sacrifices had to be made to secure this. In total war the Middle East remained critically important. The retention of some of the oil fields could well be essential. It was also a potentially important base for offensive air action against southern Russia. The loss of the Middle East would be a catastrophe not only to the British Commonwealth but also to Western Europe. The extension of Russian communist influence throughout Africa would follow. The North African ports would be lost, and when Russia reached Dakar it would pose a direct threat to the United States. The Chiefs of Staff did not like to contemplate the problems the loss of this vast area would present after the war. While the loss of the Middle East would not necessarily lose the allies the war, it would vastly increase allied difficulties in winning it. If the Middle

East fell to the Russians, the allies could not be considered to have won the war so long as the Russians remained there. The allied plans, therefore, had to include provision for the minimum forces required to hold a sufficient area of the Middle East to ensure the security of the Egyptian base and the south-west Persian gulf oil fields. Britain could not provide all the forces required to defend the United Kingdom and Western Europe. Additional forces for the Middle East would therefore have to be found from other parts of the Commonwealth and from the United States. Provided these forces arrived early enough, the British Chiefs of Staff thought the defence of the Middle East 'practicable'. All these arguments applied with equal force to the Mediterranean line of communications.

A substantial threat would exist against Turkey, Iran and Iraq at the outbreak of war. Because of restrictions due only to logistic factors, a reduced threat could be expected to develop against the Levant in from two to three months. There also existed the overall air threat to the Middle East. A proportion of the Russian tactical aircraft was expected to be of the light bomber type, and these aircraft would be available for the whole Middle Eastern campaign, and could be used in an independent role. There was also the Russian long-range air force which could be used from existing Russian bases. But it was thought unlikely that the Russians would use their long-range air force against the Middle East. An examination of strategic and tactical factors showed that the allied aim should be to try to hold the line called the 'inner ring' which covered part of Turkey, Syria, the Lebanon, Israel and Transjordan, thus protecting the Egyptian base. It was also proposed to hold the Bahrein oil area in isolation.

Provided that the Russians had not gained control of Iran, the requirement to meet the Russian threat would be one division and 482 aircraft at D-day plus thirty, building up to seven divisions and 1,062 aircraft at D-day plus six months. This latter figure included two divisions and 250 aircraft for the support of Turkish forces in the northern sector. If Russia had occupied Iran for a year or two before the outbreak of war, the requirement would not vary greatly, except that a larger and more rapid build up would be required during the first two months of war. For the defence in isolation of the Ras Tanura, Bahrein, Qatar and Dhahran oil areas, a force of approximately one division, including anti-aircraft artillery, and a small fighter force would be required. The availability of Commonwealth forces, in the view of the British Chiefs of Staff, to meet the threat to the Middle East varied slightly from year to year as the peacetime garrisons were strengthened. In 1951 the

136

equivalent of two divisions, which included two brigade groups of the Arab Legion and one armoured regiment, and 176 aircraft on D-day plus thirty, building up to nearly six divisions and 365 aircraft by D-day plus six months, were expected to be available. There would be an appreciable deficiency in air forces. In 1954, however, that deficiency would be less serious, as the available forces would have increased to three divisions of 288 aircraft on D-day plus thirty, building up to nearly eight divisions and 530 aircraft by D-day plus six months.

The Americans still did not intend to send any forces, in the short term, to the Middle East in war, but the British Chiefs of Staff understood that their American counterparts attached great strategic importance to that area, and could revise their existing policy when they had the resources available. It was important that the United States should participate, at least with air forces and a carrier task group, in the defence of the Middle East, although it was understood that the United States might be unable to contribute land or air forces for the first two years of war. It would not be in the wider allied interests for the United States to reinforce the Middle East at the expense of their ability to make their due contribution to the defence of Western Europe, but a small American contribution to the Middle East would pay a disproportionately large dividend.[33]

At the meeting in London between 21 and 26 June the Commonwealth representatives were told that an increase in their air contribution to the defence of the Middle East would be appreciated. That would be particularly important over the following three or four years. Shinwell again urged the Commonwealth countries to send token forces to the Middle East in peacetime. Britain suggested substantially greater target figures for the Commonwealth forces in the Middle East than had been mentioned in January. But it was appreciated that governments could not be committed in advance. It was agreed that Britain, New Zealand, South Africa and Southern Rhodesia, subject to constitutional procedures, had entered into a commitment to dispatch forces to the Middle East as early as possible after the outbreak of a war. Australia authorized planning on a service level for concurrent alternatives of deployment in the Middle East of the first army contingent and air task force raised, with the proviso for later forces to be allotted to Malaya should a possible threat develop there. The conference was told that discussions with the United States were continuing, and that certain proposals might have to go before the North Atlantic Treaty council. The idea of a Middle East

Command was taking shape. It was agreed that in any comprehensive command structure to be established in the Middle East, the contributing countries of the Commonwealth would be adequately represented. The principal was also accepted of associating the non-NATO members of the Commonwealth with the higher direction of global war, both political and strategic.[34]

Britain pursued the idea of the Middle East Command. If Egypt were invited to join that could solve the problem of an allied presence on Egyptian soil considered essential by the Chiefs of Staff to hold the Middle East and Africa against the Russians in the event of war. Britain resisted French pressure to be included in talks on the Middle East: France, after all, was making no contribution to the defence of the area.[35] About a month after the meeting of Commonwealth defence representatives in London, Britain submitted a paper on the subject to the Standing Group of NATO. Britain authorized its new ambassador in Cairo, Sir Ralph Stevenson, to announce to Egypt details of a Middle East defence scheme in which it was proposed that Egypt would share as an equal partner with Britain and other nations. This would be a Middle East Command, and although at first naturally a British commander would be in charge, later on any other competent commander of the new allied Middle East command could take over. Stevenson was told to put this proposition to the Egyptians just before the proposed date of the announcement in the Egyptian parliament of the abrogation of the Anglo-Egyptian treaty of 1936.[36] In a letter of 27 September, Shinwell urged Australia to give priority to the Middle East over Malaya. He reminded Canberra of the conclusions of the British Chiefs of Staff in Defence Policy and Global Strategy, MDM(51)2, approved by London, that the loss of Western Europe and the Middle East would result in effects more disastrous for the whole world than the loss of Malaya. Shinwell concluded that, in his mind, there was no doubt that it was in the Middle Eastern theatre that 'the greater danger to both our countries lies'.[37]

Canberra proved difficult to convince. On 25 September the Cabinet decided only to accept the British invitation to take part in discussions about the establishment of an allied Middle East Military Command. The British government was informed accordingly on 29 September. Canberra had reservations in principle about participating in the command. New Zealand did not like the idea of Egyptian participation. Holland was uneasy about any suggestion that an Egyptian might be given control of 'the British base'. When told that the Egyptians would probably not accept anything but 'evacuation and unity of the Nile Valley under

King Farouk' Holland doubted whether a Middle East Command would solve any of Britain's problems. New Zealand, however, indicated that it was prepared to participate in the setting up of a command. Canberra felt that that was all right: New Zealand had a commitment at that time in the Middle East whereas Australia did not.[38] Pretoria was prepared to participate subject to the 'clear understanding' that South Africa would not dispatch troops to the Middle East 'until called upon to do so in interest Union's obligations in event war (sic).'[39]

On 9 October Egypt denounced the Anglo-Egyptian treaty although it knew that the Middle East Command proposals were about to be presented. Cairo formally rejected the proposals on 16 October. When it assumed office the new Conservative government in Britain continued to pursue the idea with variations.

In September 1945 the conference of British officials in the Middle East, chaired by Bevin, concluded that that area was to remain largely a British sphere of influence. In September 1951 Britain, effectively left with responsibility for the area in the agreed allied planning to cope with the cold war situation and a potential hot war, was desperate to involve other countries. The Egyptian base was seen as crucial, and Egypt was determined that Britain should evacuate. Britain had to go in 1956 anyway if Egypt did not want it to stay. Bevin, in his global scheme to cope with the Cold War, had envisaged an association with the Dominions something like that in 1939. But the strategic situation was different in 1951. In a future war it was anticipated that forces would have to be ready immediately. The Middle East was regarded as a Commonwealth responsibility. The Americans would not be able to participate effectively for two years after war broke out. Britain had neither the money, the manpower, nor the weaponry to cope on its own. It hoped for commitments from the old 'white' Dominions. In 1939 the Dominions had not been prepared to give formal commitments, and in May of that year the British War Book plans had had to make provision for the contingency that it was possible that some would not fight at Britain's side. But it had all been all right on the day. In 1951 the Dominions were once again reluctant to undertake formal commitments. South Africa and New Zealand were committed in a way to the Middle East, but made certain reservations. Australia, with the Cold War in Asia on its doorstep, had difficulty in accepting the view of the British Chiefs of Staff that Malaya, though important, was expendable, and not as vital as the United Kingdom and Western Europe, and the Middle East. Australia saw Malaya as crucial for its own security. Increasingly Australia thought of itself as part of the Pacific. The Middle East was a long way away.Throughout the period of the Attlee administrations, however, the Middle East remained an area of cardinal importance for Britain. This was not something that the Prime Minister believed. But Bevin did, and so did the Chiefs of Staff. In 1945 Britain was the paramount power in the area. At the time of the joining of the Cold War its position was undermined by Zionist terrorism, and a nationalism among the Arabs often directed just as much at their hierarchical leadership as at Britain. Bevin had hoped to work with the peasants rather than the pashas. In the end what position Britain had depended on the support of the ruling houses. At the time of the fall of Attlee's second administration Britain, perhaps reluctantly, still had the major commitment for the defence of the area.

Notes: Chapter 5

1 Public Record Office, London, CAB 133/86, PMM(46) 18th Mtg, Confidential Annex, 22 May 1946.
2 R. Ovendale, 'Britain, the United States and the Cold War in South-East Asia, 1949 –1950', *International Affairs*, vol. 58 (1982), pp. 447–64 at p. 454; Public Record Office, London, CAB 128/15, fos 61–2, CM17(49)2, Secret, 3 March 1949.
3 Australian Archives, Canberra, A5954, Box 1685, PMM(49)3rd Mtg, Secret, 25 April 1949.
4 R. Ovendale, 'From British Commonwealth to Commonwealth: the English speaking Holy Roman Empire', *Interstate* (1978–9), pp. 12–15 at p. 13.
5 A5954, Box 1681, Some general impressions of a visit abroad in 1949 by Shedden, Secret, September 1949.
6 A5954, Box 1813, Shedden to P. A. McBride, Top Secret and Personal, 23 January 1951.
7 A5954, Box 1681, Some general impressions of a visit abroad in 1949 by Shedden, Secret, September 1949.
8 A5799, 49/15, Attlee to J. B. Chifley, Top Secret, 29 December 1948; Chifley to Attlee, Top Secret, 16 February 1949.
9 A2031/29, no. 42/1949, Report by Australian Defence Committee on COS(49)49, 5 May 1949.
10 Public Record Office, London, DO 35/2752, F2077/1, Note of a meeting at the Commonwealth Relations Office, Secret, 21 April 1949.
11 A5799, 49/68, Strategic planning in relation to British Commonwealth defence, 15 September 1949; Appendix C, The basic objectives of British Commonwealth defence policy and general strategy (revised 26 August following discussions between the Defence Committee and the New Zealand Chiefs of Staff).
12 A5799, 50/108, Defence policy and global strategy, Report by the British Chiefs of Staff, Top Secret, 17 August 1950; Report by Joint Planning Committee, Top Secret, 6 November 1950; *FRUS* 1950(3), p. 1687 n. 5.

13 CAB 131/9, DO(50)40, Report by Chiefs of Staff, 19 May 1950.
14 Louis, *The British Empire in the Middle East*, p. 715.
15 National Library of Australia, Canberra, MS 4936, Series 13, Folder 5, Diary, 12 June 1950.
16 A426, 439/1/10 Pt 1, Extract from top secret inward cable no. 11504 received from the Australian Embassy, Washington, on 1 August 1950.
17 *FRUS* 1950(3), pp. 1686-9, Approved summary of conclusions and agreements reached at a meeting of the Chiefs of Staff of the United States and the United Kingdom, Top Secret, 23 October 1950; A5799, James Marjoribanks to Secretary Prime Minister's Department, Top Secret and Personal, 4 December 1950.
18 *FRUS* 1950(3), pp. 1657-60, Jessup to Acheson, Top Secret, 25 July 1950.
19 A426, 439/1/17, E. J. Williams to Menzies, Top Secret, 23 October 1950.
20 A5799, 50/108, Report by Joint Planning Committee, Top Secret, 6 November 1950.
21 Public Record Office, London, FO 371/91219, E1192, Minute by Bowker, 10 January 1951.
22 A426, 439/1/10 Pt 1, Commonwealth Relations Office Memorandum, Top Secret, 3 January 1951.
23 A426, 845/20, 9/85/8 - 2nd Mtg, Higher military direction in war, Top Secret, 8 January 1951.
24 A426, 845/20, 9/85/8 - 1st Mtg, The Middle East and the defence of Africa, Top Secret, 6 January 1951; Public Record Office, London, FO 800/457, fol. 155, Eg/47/3, Bevin to Foreign Office, no. 344, Top Secret, 25 March 1947.
25 Louis, *The British Empire in the Middle East*, pp. 720-3.
26 CAB 128/19, CM28(51)3, 16 April 1951; CM30(51)3, 23 April 1951; CM33(51)7, 10 May 1951; CM37(51)2, 28 May 1951; CM44(51)5, 21 June 1951; CM50(51)2, 9 July 1951; 20, CM60(51)6, 27 September 1951; Louis, *The British Empire in the Middle East*, pp. 666-89; F. S. Northedge, 'Britain and the Middle East', in Ovendale (ed.). *The Foreign Policy of the British Labour Governments*, pp. 149-80 at pp. 173-6.
27 A426, 439/1/10 Pt 1, Marjoribanks to A. S. Brown, Top Secret, 21 May 1951; enclosed text of message from Morrison to Ben-Gurion delivered 24 April 1951.
28 A426, 439/1/10 Pt 2, MD 14 on Israel reaction to proposed Middle East Command, 29 October 1951; 439/1/10 Pt 3, C. J. Beaumont to Mr McKnight on British proposals for Middle East defence organisation, 1 September 1952.
29 A426, 439/1/10 Pt 2, P. C. Spender to External Affairs Canberra, Secret, 2 November 1951.
30 Morgan, *Labour in Power*, p. 433.
31 A2031/34, no. 70/1951, Minute by Defence Committee, Top Secret, 22 March 1951.
32 A2031/36, no. 366/1951, Minute by Defence Committee, Top Secret, 25 October 1951.
33 A5954, Box 1799, Draft for Cabinet on meeting of Commonwealth Defence Ministers in London between 21 and 26 June 1951 by Shedden, Top Secret.
34 A426, 845/36, McBride to Menzies, Telegram no. 3469, Top Secret, 27 June 1951; BcBride to Menzies, Telegram no. 3470, Top Secret, 27 June 1951; A. S. Brown to Menzies, Top Secret, 27 June 1951; 439/1/10 Pt 1, History of Middle East Command prepared by Alan Watt, Top Secret, 5 September 1951.
35 A426, 439/1/10 Pt 1, Marjoribanks to Secretary Prime Minister's Department, Top Secret, 30 May 1951.
36 A426, 439/1/10 Pt 1, History of Middle East Command prepared by Alan Watt, Top Secret, 5 September 1951.
37 A5954, Box 1799, Report by Joint Planning Committee at meetings held on 9 and 12 November 1951, Top Secret.

38 A426,439/1/10 Pt 1, G. Davey to Prime Minister's Department, Top Secret, 29 September 1951; E. J. Bunting to McKnight, 28 September 1951; Middle East Command: Views of Minister for External Affairs, 24 September 1951; Minute left by Garnett with Menzies on Middle East Command, 16 September 1951; 439/1/10 Pt 2, Narration of Middle East Command, unsigned, Top Secret, undated.

39 *FRUS* 1951(5), p. 189 n. 2.

PART FOUR

The Cold War in Asia

6

The Cold War in South-East Asia

With the signing of the North Atlantic Treaty on 4 April 1949 Britain secured an American commitment to Europe. At the conversations in Washington at the end of 1947 between American and British officials on the Middle East, the Americans acknowledged that they should uphold the British position in that area. The Middle East remained largely a British preserve. At the time that was what Britain wanted. But as the Cold War was joined with the Berlin blockade, there was an obvious weakness in the line drawn to stop the advance of communism: Asia. Only the Americans could do anything there, and in 1949 the fall of China disillusioned them about the prospects of helping Asians. South-East Asia was an area of British, French and Dutch influence; the Americans had few interests in the region. During the years immediately following the end of the Second World War, London had persuaded Washington to see the dangers in parts of the globe through British spectacles. Or at least that was how it appeared to some officials in the Foreign Office. At the beginning of 1949 the immediate problem seemed to be, how could the same vision be achieved over South-East Asia? That area, in the view of the British Chiefs of Staff, on 7 June 1950, was 'critically important', even if, as had been proved between 1939 and 1945, it was not 'vital to our survival in war'.[1]

In 1946 Lord Killearn was moved from Egypt and sent as Special Commissioner to South-East Asia. Instructed to investigate Russia's activities in the area, he reported on 4 December 1946 that there was very little to tell about Russian, as distinct from local communist tactics. There was a small Russian military mission in Indochina, apparently there to repatriate non-existent Russian citizens, and a Russian legation was going to be set up in Bangkok. Surveying communism as a whole, he pointed to Chinese and indigenous communist parties in the Philippines, in Indochina, Malaya, Burma, Thailand and in the Netherlands East Indies. These

144

parties were in contact with each other, and their influence extended to Sydney. But it was hard to find reliable evidence that they were in touch with Moscow, or that Russia influenced or prescribed their policies. The British chargé d'affaires in Moscow, Frank Roberts, had observed, in a dispatch of 30 August 1946, that while South-East Asia was outside the scope of Russian expansion, it offered excellent opportunities for disruptive activities which could seriously affect West European countries. He added: 'In South-East Asia the restoration of war-shattered economies, the radical improvement of social conditions among the coolie populations ... and the rapid evolution of political life to something consonant with local aspirations would go far to eliminate the condition in which Soviet influence can thrive, for it is a germ that requires unhealthy tissue.' Killearn agreed. Britain's task in South-East Asia at that time was not so much to counter Russian activities, for these had not developed, but to encourage a growth that would prevent them from doing so.[2] Eighteen months later Killearn still saw no sign of Russian control, but he suggested a further antidote for the dependent territories in the area: the speedy development of self-government on truly democratic lines. A reason for the great strength of communism was that in South-East Asia the communist parties were the only well-organized political groups. He concluded:

> The awakening political consciousness of S. E. Asia, therefore presents an opportunity no less to ourselves than to the instruments of the Soviet Union. Our opponents prosper from the fact that this awakening has taken the form, in most of the countries of the area, of opposition to the control of the Western democracies. The task of reorientating this opposition into the establishment of a truly democratic tradition is going to be one of the most important functions of the British Commonwealth in this part of the world.[3]

Two years later, with the fall of China imminent, London assessed communist strategy in South-East Asia. After the defeat of Japan that area was a classic example of a potentially revolutionary situation: politically dislocated; ravaged by war in places; dominated by a nationalist struggle against Western colonial governments which was often also a social revolt against foreign economic exploitation. There was no integrated economic society in most of South-East Asia. The peasants were largely outside the political system. There was hardly any indigenous middle class.

Industry, commerce and banking were mainly in foreign hands. The governments themselves seemed alien. The Kremlin was not fully prepared for these opportunities, but it soon exploited the situation. The international communist movement prepared the ground in South-East Asia for over a quarter of a century. Mr Manuilsky interested himself in the area even before 1917, and M. André Malraux described Comintern activities in Indochina in the early 1920s. During the interwar years a few picked communist leaders from the various colonial territories received communist indoctrination either in China or in Russia. There appeared to have been a small concealed network of cells. In the early stages the communists preferred to work with loose nationalist coalitions, with inexperienced leaders and an emotional following. These would be likely to take over when the colonial powers left. The international Kremlin-controlled communist movement did not favour open communist revolt if its aims could be achieved by other means. Communists were taught that they should only resort to insurrection when the enemy was paralyzed, for example by strikes, and success was certain.

After the defeat of Germany, Moscow concentrated on eliminating colonial influence, and South-East Asia seemed promising. Dimitri Manuilsky launched the world communist campaign for the independence of Indonesia at the first meeting of the Security Council. South-East Asia, and particularly Vietnam, the Burmese Anti-Fascist Peoples' Freedom League and the Filipino Hukbalahap were extensively covered in the Russian press. The major increase in communist activity, however, started with Marshall's Harvard speech of 21 June 1947. The communists thought that if the Marshall Plan were implemented the economic collapse in Europe which had been thought of as the prelude to the inevitable proletarian revolution would be postponed. Russia had to start new offensives, offensives that could deprive the West European countries, particularly Britain, of the great material resources of South-East Asia. Economic recovery in Europe would be hindered. If the areas fell within the Russian orbit, Moscow would gain important commodities then lacking in its economic system. The war potential of the Russians would be strengthened, and that of the democracies weakened.

The spirit of this new offensive was indicated at the conference of the Nine Communist Parties held in Poland in September 1947. There Zhdanov spoke of the division of the world into two camps with Russia being at the head of the anti-imperialist camp. In Europe this conference was followed by strikes in Italy and France.

Shortly afterwards there were notable developments in Asia. The last weeks of 1947 saw a general tightening of communist discipline. The Communist Party of India and the Burma Communist Party decided on a reorientation of policy in December 1947: they decided to abandon their previous tactics of collaboration with and penetration of the nationalist movements in their countries, and to develop offensive tactics instead. That month Mao Tse-tung, in his report to the Central Committee of the Communist Party of China, declared that all the anti-imperialist forces of the East must unite against imperialism. In February 1948 in Calcutta, under the guise of attending a youth conference, communists from Britain, Yugoslavia, France, China, Czechoslovakia, Pakistan, Ceylon, Vietnam, Indonesia, Australia, Burma and Russia probably discussed forming a South-East Asia communist bloc. The British paper, probably drafted by the Russian spy, Guy Burgess, put forward the view that it was important not to overestimate the strength of armed communists in the field in South-East Asia, or the extent to which communism was controlled and co-ordinated by Moscow. Such controls were often 'tenuous or remote, the advice often inappropriate, and the picture complicated by local rivalries'. Organized communism there was not then in a position to do more than exploit the national, social and economic unrest in the area. The ultimate aim of communism, however, was not just subversion but control.[4]

The Joint Intelligence Committee offered a slightly different diagnosis in October 1948. Looking at the East as a whole, it argued that the spread of communism was encouraged by increasing nationalist feeling after the end of the Second World War. This was later encouraged by the granting of independence to India, Pakistan, Burma and Ceylon. Russia's prestige, in Asian eyes, was enhanced by the war, while that of the European powers after their defeat by the Japanese suffered. Furthermore communist-operated guerillas had in many Asian countries provided the core of the anti-Japanese resistance movements. Consequently the communists now had a reserve of arms of allied origin which made them more formidable. The large overseas Chinese communities in territories throughout the Far East were also influenced by the success of the Chinese communists against the Nationalist government. This had assisted the spread of communist doctrine. It seemed that communist tactics in Burma, the Federation of Malaya and Indonesia were broadly based on the Chinese communist example involving guerilla warfare, the destruction of capitalist economy and the establishment of communist-controlled areas as bases for expansion. In detail, tactics were dictated by expediency.[5]

In South-East Asia, French Indochina was the key area. The British Chiefs of Staff, in drawing up their global strategy in June 1950, concluded that 'The front line of the cold war in Asia lies in Indo-China. If that front gives way it is only a matter of time before Siam and Burma fall under Communist influence. In that event our difficulties in Malaya would become almost insuperable and ultimately communism would probably prevail throughout Malaya and the Archipelago.'[6] French Indochina consisted of four territories: the Kingdom of Laos, located in the valley of the upper Mekong with a population of over 1 million; the Kingdom of Cambodia, lying between the lower Mekong and the Thai border, with a population of over 3 million; the Republic (formerly the Colony) of Cochin-China, lying at the mouth of the Mekong and having a population of nearly 5 million; and the Republic of Vietnam, made up of the old territories of the Kingdom of Annam and the Protectorate of Tonkin, respectively occupying the east coast and the valley of the Red River, with populations of 6 million and 9 million. French policy was to federate the four territories and then to link the Federation to the French Union, embracing metropolitan France and the French territories overseas. The Vietminh Party, led by Ho-Chi-Minh, was a federation of a number of proletarian and nationalist movements. On 19 August 1945 it seized power and established the Republic of Vietnam, with Peoples' Committees serving as regional governments in Tonkin, Annam and Cochin-China. The King of Annam abdicated. A convention signed at Hanoi on 6 March 1946 gave French recognition to the free state of Vietnam as a republic forming part of the Indochina federation within the French Union. A modus vivendi was achieved at Fontainbleau in September 1946, but in November 1946 hostilities started again between the French forces and Vietnam.[7]

When the Vietminh League was founded in China in 1941, it was theoretically an all-party organization. In November 1945 the Communist Party of Indochina was dissolved 'in the interests of national unity'. The disguise was thin. The British Consul General in Saigon, D. C. Hopson, reported in November 1948 that an examination of the internal organization of the Vietminh League showed that it followed the communist pattern closely. The cells and affiliated organizations conformed to the traditional pattern. The communist nature of many of the league's political activities was blatant. Ho-Chi-Minh had several other colleagues and collaborators who had been trained in Moscow. Other Communist

Party members held key positions. The government itself preserved a semblance of being nationalist by retaining ministers who were either ex-mandarins or, nominally at least, members of other nationalist organizations. An analysis of the administrative services in the provinces, however, showed the reality of communist control. While most of the supporters of the Vietminh League were not communist, it was ruled and directed by Communist Party members. The same could be said of the army. The Commander-in-Chief, Vo Ngutin Giap, was a well-known communist, and had the reputation of being the strong man of the league. The rest of the army appeared to be firmly in the communist grip. Recently captured documents showed that out of the one Cochin-Chinese battalion of 700 officers, NCOs and other ranks, 150 were communists, though it was true that ninety-five of these had enrolled before 1945, and only ten were known to have belonged to the Communist Party before 1941. Most of the key posts were reserved for communists, and each unit down to company level had its political commissar. Purges had been organized, particularly in the south, to get rid of 'the less reliable elements'. A French officer who had been a prisoner of the Vietminh had recently been released, and had said how surprised he was at the number of French communists serving with the rebels. The Vietminh League maintained close contact with the Communist Party abroad. They had organized what were virtually military training camps just the other side of the Thai border, and certainly received arms from Thailand and South China. It was not definitely known whether Ho-Chi-Minh had direct contact with Moscow, but he had a permanent representative in Bangkok who was presumably in contact with the Russian legation there. The Vietminh League maintained information offices in Bangkok, Rangoon, Hong Kong, Singapore and even in Paris, presumably financed by Russia. There was no evidence, however, that the policy of the Vietminh League was directed from external sources. But their deliberate efforts to ruin the economy of the country, and in particular to reduce the exportable surplus of rice, was in line with communist policy elsewhere in South-East Asia. The communist rebels in Burma were reported to have said that Ho-Chi-Minh was their chief. The Vietminh League had its internal difficulties, but its hold on the country was unimpaired.

Hopson speculated, in November 1948, as to what would happen if Bao Dai returned. There were many waverers, including the important Catholic Party under Ngo Dinh Diem. They would almost certainly support the emperor, Bao Dai. Ho-Chi-Minh could continue the fight, or he could disappear with his 'more obnoxious colleagues', and try instead to infiltrate Bao Dai's government by allowing his more respectable ministers to take part in it. He would certainly watch what was happening in China, and perhaps wait for the chance presented by a complete communist victory there. But, like most Annamites, Ho-Chi-Minh was 'probably not blind to the dangers of allowing his country to fall under the influence of the Chinese, Communist or otherwise'.[8]

In Indonesia, however, communist activity of a violent sort did not start until September 1948. Until then the communists had, on the whole, supported a republican government. In any case they were divided between the followers of Tan Malakka and those of the more orthodox leader, Alimin. The revolt of 1948 broke out with the return of Moeso, an old Indonesian communist who had spent twenty years in exile mainly in Russia. Moeso arrived in the guise of being secretary to Soeripno, the Indonesian Republicans' representative in Prague. Soeripno was recalled because of his embarrassing action in negotiating an agreement with Russia for an exchange of consular representatives. Moeso arrived in Java in August 1948, and immediately started an energetic campaign against the republican leaders. Armed revolt followed in the middle of September, but was soon crushed by the republican government. Russia probably sent Moeso with orders to counter Tan Malakka's influence, and to start a communist revolt. Plans were probably made before his arrival. The Communist Party and the Tan Malakka factions remained disorganized, but in September 1949 the Joint Intelligence Committe thought that the influence of the Tan Malakka group was increasing and that it was managing to infiltrate the republican army. The period of the final transfer of power from the Dutch would give 'these factions unrivalled opportunities for increasing their hold in the country by widespread subversive activity'.[9]

There was no parallel development in Thailand. There the communist movement was almost exclusively Chinese. It seemed absorbed in Chinese affairs and there was no apparent effort to subvert the regime in Thailand. In any case the Chinese in Thailand were a minority group. There was no evidence that the Russian legation in Bangkok had materially affected the situation.

The communists in Burma, it seemed, were working with their Chinese counterparts after 1948. Mao Tse-tung's writings appeared there, and the leader of the Burmese Communist Party, Than Tun, started to advocate co-operation with the Chinese.

There were rumours, by 1949, of a treaty of alliance between the Burmese and Chinese communists.[10]

Indeed, by March 1949 the Joint Intelligence Committee, though it did not have proof, felt that Russia had delegated to the Chinese Communist Party at least some responsibility for building what Mao Tse -tung called 'a bulwark of world Communism in Asia'. The difficulty for the Russians was to ensure that they retained the ultimate control of the movement in Asia. The Chinese, on the other hand, had to overcome the suspicions of many Asian races about Chinese motives. Six months later the Joint Intelligence Committee was more certain: 'Russia has made clear to Communists throughout the world that she has confidence in the loyalty of the C.C.P. and is prepared to back it to the hilt.'[11]

It could be argued that the Cold War in Asia was joined when Britain and the United States failed to inform Russia about the ultimatum to Japan, and the proposed use of the aomic bomb.[12] But for Britain it effectively began with the communist insurgency in Malaya, and the subsequent declaration of the Emergency on 18 June 1948.[13] This was an area of imperial responsibility and, in effect, British conscript troops were fighting the communist terrorists to enable Malaya to become independent and help itself, rather than to sustain an indefinite British presence.

The communists in Malaya rose after the anti-imperialist directive of the Belgrade Cominform in September 1947. Britain's withdrawal from India and Burma apparently led the Malayan Communist Party to believe that provided sufficient strife was fomented and a state of economic chaos created, the British would be forced to withdraw from Malaya. The postwar economic conditions were ideal for this. Nearly 1 million people in Malaya could be classed as underprivileged and depressed labourers. The Communist Party claimed 100,000 supporters, of which 10,000 were staunch communists. In January 1948 the Chinese were in complete control of the Communist Party which was consolidating its position in the trade unions. There was a continuous movement into Malaya of Chinese communists, instructed less in local politics than in weakening the overseas organizations of the Chinese Nationalist government. The central executive committee of the Malayan Communist Party decided in March 1948 to launch a campaign of violence. Plans could have been made earlier: an arrested bandit said that as early as March 1947 some thirty Chinese Communists were sent from Malaya to Indochina for training in guerilla warfare. Malcolm MacDonald, the British

Commissioner General for South-East Asia, thought that the Malayan communists, as they had failed to capture the leadership of the trade unions, and to infiltrate the political parties, were losing ground, 'so these desperate men decided to make a bid for power by violence'. The Malayan communist plan provided for an all-out campaign of burning and looting of villages and properties, the assassination of property-owners and capitalists and the defiance of law and order. It was hoped that this would lead to the disruption of economic life with consequent unemployment, labour agitation and general chaos. It seems that it was on the advice of the Chinese Communist Party that the terrorist campaign was started in June 1948, but not in full force. That month a member of the central committee of the Malayan Communist Party, Cheng Chieh, issued 'The Present Situation and Direction of Struggle' in which, like his counterparts in India and Burma, he denounced the 'opportunist line' formerly pursued by his party. The following three months saw increased communist attacks in what became a battle for morale. Then the security forces started to get control. The introduction of a national registration system helped contain terrorist activity. The monsoon, starting in October, hindered the terrorists. They also squabbled amongst themselves and murdered one another. With the success of the security forces' counter-offensive in October and November, the terrorist tactics changed. Instead of direct attacks, the Communist Liberation Army started sabotage activities such as the slashing of rubber trees and the destruction of hydro-electric plants. The success of the communists in China, and the influx of more efficient leaders from that country, led to a renewal of violence early in 1949 and a further reorganization of the terrorist forces.[14]

It was against this background, at the beginning of 1949, that Britain started to evolve an overall policy to cope with the Cold War in South-East Asia. Crucial to British thinking about this was the importance of the Anglo-American special relationship. After all, only the United States could really do anything in the area. The significance of the United States was emphasized by the Permanent Under-Secretary's Committee under William Strang, a group which had a function similar to that of George Kennan's Policy Planning Staff in the United States. In November 1949 Bevin refused to circulate to the Cabinet their conclusions, evolved over the previous six months. These stated that following the victorious wartime alliance, collaboration between Britain and the United States had been closer than ever before; the United States maintained closer relations with Britain than with any other country. In the military field the partnership had been maintained by the combined Chiefs of Staff organization. For the United States, Britain remained the principal military partner and ally, and the United States wanted that partnership to endure. British interests were likely to be best served by the maintenance and consolidation of the existing relations between the two countries. Any British attempt at self-sufficiency, even with the support of some Commonwealth countries, would entail 'a sharp contraction of political influence and material prosperity'. If it failed, Britain would be forced to beg once more for the benefits of association with the United States, not as an independent partner, but instead as 'a client existing on permanent doles from the American tax payer'. Strang's committee concluded that Britain had to continue to shoulder the political, economic and military burden of playing a leading role in world affairs, in close association with the United States, but not necessarily dominated by its policies. The Anglo-American partnership would for some time be an unequal one, and might eventually need a more formal expression. The inherent inequality could be ameliorated by Britain and the United States working closely in conjunction with other friendly states, such as the members of the Commonwealth, particularly in Asia and the Far East. Indeed it was in this region that Britain thought the alliance would be least effective. Here American naïvety and selfishness seemed particularly evident. Inexperience could account for the narrowly conceived American policy towards China. The treatment of Japan, however, was an instance of the 'somewhat unimaginative tendency of the Americans to graft their own way of life on to rather improbable stock', and the insistence on restoring the low-cost Japenese economy on multilateral principles took little account of British economic interests. But an American 'stake' in the area was of great importance for the consolidation of Western influence. Although the United States was likely to maintain a line of strategic defence in the Pacific, the degree to which it would extend this westwards was dependent on the extent to which Britain and the other members of the Commonwealth would contribute. American sources were not unlimited, and the United States appeared unwilling to contemplate any major effort in south Asia. Therefore, Western resistance to the spread of Russian influence in the region depended largely on Britain.[15]

Mao Tse-tung's successes in China led the Foreign Office to conclude, late in 1948, that communist movements would be stimulated throughout Asia; the agitation was likely to be serious in Indochina, Thailand and Burma. Indochina, where the communists

153

worked in alliance with the nationalists, was of particular concern: the Foreign Office felt that the strengthening of the communist position there would have repercussions on South-East Asia generally. The United States was not prepared to accept any responsibility for South-East Asia. It therefore fell to the powers geographically situated in the region to meet the communist menace by their own measures. Britain felt that the countries concerned should alert their police and intelligence services; and ensure that the legal powers were adequate to deal with any growth of communist activity. The Foreign Office decided to try to elicit support for these measures from France, the Commonwealth, the Netherlands, Burma and Thailand, and even to approach the United States.[16] Political differences prevented a conference on the containment of communism in South-East Asia.[17] Burma would find it difficult to associate with French Indochina and Dutch Indonesia. Those colonial powers would reciprocate the feeling. The Commonwealth countries principally concerned – Australia, New Zealand, India and Pakistan – would be unwilling to do anything that could support the French and Dutch governments in the area. Britain was probably in the best position to act as co-ordinator.[18]

France responded warmly to the British initiative, and suggested that the small Asiatic countries would be encouraged to take positive action against communism if the United States showed an interest. But, as Peter Scarlett of the Far East desk observed, there were signs that the State Department was already 'shying at just this thought'. J. O. Lloyd offered the assessment of the South-East Asia department. There was the seed of a wide regional organisation for South-East Asia: Pandit Nehru, the Indian Prime Minister, had held a conference of nineteen countries in New Delhi which had endorsed the idea of a regional organization within the framework of the United Nations for joint consultation on common problems. One of those was likely to be the spread of communism; but any participation of Western countries presupposed a satisfactory settlement in Indonesia.[19]

In contrast to Paris, Washington was cautious. On 23 February H. A. Graves, the counsellor to the British embassy, discussed the issue with State Department officials. Basing his case on a memorandum provided by M. Esler Dening of the Foreign Office, Graves tried to allay the fears of W. Walton Butterworth, the director of the Far Eastern division, that the 'financial appetites' of the South-East Asian countries might be 'whetted' for increased assistance from Britain, and especially from the United States.

Graves offered the assurance that Britain did not envisage an anti-communist movement in terms of American dollars. Instead he hoped that the United States would offer moral support for the British thesis that 'the Asiatic countries must set their houses in order and must evolve a policy of their own in the struggle against communism'. Butterworth was interested, but in his survey did not mention the continental territories in Asia in the line of the communist march. The drive was southwards, according to Graves, and so particular attention needed to be given to South-East Asia. Butterworth, however, appeared lukewarm to any suggestion of the communist danger in the region: the United States was apparently not prepared to accept any responsibility for the area, or to take any action to maintain the position of friendly powers there.

Charles S. Reed, the head of the South-East Asia division, was more co-operative, After Butterworth had left he suggested that Britain and the United States should consider 'remedial measures'. But that evening Butterworth telephoned Graves and told him to forget that any such proposal had even been hinted at. Graves consequently advised the Foreign Office that the American approach to the area was likely to be cautious. Dean Acheson, the Secretary of State, was preoccupied with the Atlantic Pact.[20]

With the communist expansion, British and American officials in Asia offered a joint solution. J. Leighton Stuart, the American ambassador in China, urged a 'new approach' directed primarily at the 'mind and heart': Britain, France and the Netherlands should be asked to join with the United States in forming a federation to assist in the restoration of complete independence to the peoples of Eastern and South-Eastern Asia, and through this to protect them from the highly organized minorities of their own people linked to international communism.[21] This was later modified by a scheme drafted by the Indian ambassador to China in consultation with his British, Australian and American counterparts. In the short term a permanent Consultative Council of the states of the area was necessary to work out common policies, and to provide for an integrated economy capable of resisting communist economic doctrines. Before this could be established, however, Indochina and Indonesia needed 'political freedom' and Malaya the constitutional power to enable it to participate in the economic activities. The Western powers could assist by providing a specialist advisory committee.[22]

MacDonald offered a diagnosis at the end of March 1949 similar to the one that had emanated earlier in the month from the ambassadors in China. He insisted that South-East Asia should be regarded as a whole: the communists saw the region that way and planned their campaign on a theatre-wide basis. Frustration in the West had probably forced the planners of international communist strategy to give more attention to the East. MacDonald saw the area in terms of what later became known as the domino theory: unless the West's counteraction were firm it would quickly lose important areas like Burma and Indonesia, and that could be a prelude to the loss of a large part of the rest of South-East Asia, and hence the power of the Western democracies to avoid defeat in a war against the communists would be 'gravely imperilled'. Taking the analogy of Western Europe, MacDonald suggested an Asian equivalent of the Marshall Plan and the Atlantic Pact. Though differing from the arrangements in Europe the scheme should offer the Asian governments and peoples economic, political and, if necessary, military aid to resist communism. The governments involved in the region could devise it with the help of the United States, Australia and New Zealand. American assistance was crucial: without it no adequate economic or military plan would be possible. Indeed American reluctance to participate could mean that, in the very near future, such a scheme would not be realistic: MacDonald therefore suggested a preliminary conference of Commonwealth countries interested in the region.[23]

In Washington, George F. Kennan, the director of the Policy Planning Staff, noted similarities between a paper drawn up by his department at the end of March and the ideas offered by the ambassadors in China.[24] The paper advocated that the United States should adopt 'multilateral collaboration', primarily with certain Commonwealth countries and the Philippines, and approach South-East Asia as a whole. That region, however, was to be seen as an integral part of the great crescent formed by the Indian peninsula, Australia and Japan. The objective was to contain and reduce Russian influence in the area. Any urging of an area organization was to be avoided at the outset. Instead the initial effort should be directed towards 'collaboration on joint or parallel action and then, only as a pragmatic and desirable basis for more intimate association appears, should we encourage the area to move step by step toward formal organisation'.[25]

The Policy Planning Staff paper was, however, only projected policy. It formed the basis of a report finally issued as National Security Council Paper 48/1 of 23 December 1949.[26] Indeed, as R. C. Blackham of the Foreign Office observed, the United States would be unlikely to support any proposal which offered effective Anglo-American military assistance to the French in Indochina.

Such a scheme could only be put to the Americans in the context of a general attempt to combat communist penetration in South-East Asia, and there was no sign that the United States was prepared to do anything about that.[27]

The Foreign Office became increasingly aware of the need to secure an American commitment to South-East Asia.[28] During his visit to Washington in April 1949, to sign the North Atlantic Treaty, Bevin hoped to discuss the matter with Acheson. Dening accordingly prepared a brief. A year previously Dening had sounded the Americans about the possibility of secret talks on the Far East. Washington had indicated that it could not treat the other members of the Commonwealth in the same way as it did Britain and Canada. That also made any talks on the Far East impossible. But the Foreign Office was concerned about 'disquieting' indications: not only was the United States without a clear policy for the Far East and South-East Asia, but also the Americans were inclined to decrease rather than to extend their commitments in the area. Earlier British attempts to alert the United States to the dangers inherent in the situation had only resulted in desultory interchanges. The least Britain hoped for was that in the event of Asian countries showing a disposition to form a united front against Russian expansion, the United States would offer material help.

The Foreign Office saw the primary Russian threat being against Europe, and then the Middle East. In the Far East, China would fall to communist domination; in Korea the resistance of Rhee's south to the communist north was uncertain, though the United Nations had a continuing obligation to sustain the position there; but there did not seem to be any immediate Russian threat to the Pacific. Nevertheless, the Foreign Office saw a distinct danger in South-East Asia. As measures developed for the security of Europe and the Middle East, it was felt that Russian pressure on the area would increase, although the threat, for some time, was unlikely to be military. The conditions in South-East Asia, however, were favourable for the spread of communism. If the impression prevailed in the area that the Western powers were unwilling and unable to resist Russian pressure, the psychological effect could be the weakening of local resistance. With that, the governments in the region could be undermined to the extent that eventually the whole of South-East Asia would fall to the communist advance, and come under Russian domination without any military effort on the part of Moscow. It was therefore necessary, simultaneously with the efforts to strengthen the defensive position of Europe and the Middle East, to stiffen the South-East Asian territories' 'will to resist'. This need not involve vast resources: in the initial stages the question would be one of 'political and economic effort rather than of large scale outright aid'. A purely Western approach was unlikely to succeed – the Asian governments needed to build up the resistance themselves and to assume the principal burden. Provided this was done the Western powers, including the United States, could contribute through technical assistance and advice, capital goods and the small-scale provision of armaments. Before there could be a common front against Russian expansion there were major difficulties to be overcome in the area: there was the friction between Afghanistan and Pakistan over the North West Frontier Province; the Kashmir dispute between India and Pakistan; the conflict between the Burmese government and the Karens; the uneasy political situation in Thailand; and the situation in Indonesia. A realization of the significance of the communist menace could, however, encourage the settlement of local disputes. Britain had a special relationship with the area through its Commonwealth connections, the treaty with Burma, close links with Thailand, contacts with the French and Dutch, and the British presence in Malaya, Borneo and Hong Kong. The post-1945 surge of nationalism, however, meant that these Asiatic countries were suspicious of anything savouring of imperialism, or of either dictation or domination by the West. Furthermore, the states of South-East Asia were not likely to be attracted by the possibility that a closer relationship with the West would involve them in hostilities with Russia on a European issue. The territories of South-East Asia would only unite in a common front against Russia if they saw it as being in their own interests. Indeed self-interest should provide the inspiration for the unity necessary to resist Russian pressure. This could create a pan-Asiatic union hostile to the West. But so long as the countries of South-East Asia realized that co-operation with the West was on a basis of equality and self-interest that danger should not arise. Although it was essential that the sovereign states of South-East Asia took the initiative themselves, Britain and the United States could hope to prompt it. Provided that a common front could be built up from Afghanistan to Indochina, it should be possible to contain the Russian advance southwards, to rehabilitate and stabilize the area, and to preserve Western communications across the middle of the world. A stable South-East Asia could also possibly influence the situation in China, and make it possible to redress the position there. Although the strategic necessities of Europe and the Middle East should still have priority, the requirements of South-East Asia were of vital importance.[29]

The British Chiefs of Staff, when consulted about the situation, advised that the spread of communism into southern China would mean unrest, and consequently an increased security commitment throughout South-East Asia. If the Russians established bases in southern China, the threat to South-East Asia and to British sea communications could become serious. And if communism spread successfully into the Indian subcontinent the whole position in South-East Asia would become untenable. Until all the countries interested had agreed on a policy for the area, the only effective military co-operation was likely to be the exchange of intelligence and police information on communist activities.[30]

The Foreign Office brief was left with Acheson.[31] The Americans were told, however, that this represented only the personal views of Bevin and had not been discussed by the Cabinet. The issue would involve Britain in talks not only with the United States but also with the Commonwealth.[32] On 2 April Bevin expounded to the Secretary of State his concept of world geographical-political factors and how South-East Asia fitted into this. Bevin envisaged a Western Europe that would develop a multilateral system. In the Middle East there were 100 million Muslims, potentially one of the biggest forces in the world, and Britain was the 'best window' towards this area. Rather than forming joint military pacts in this area, Bevin thought that Britain and the United States should adopt 'a common line' for the development of the great potential resources, particularly oil, needed for their defence. The Foreign Secretary then developed his Muslim theme for South-East Asia: there 60 percent of the population were Muslims, and Russia had an obvious opening. Britain could exercise influence through Pakistan, but hoped for American help. He wanted a conference arrangement set up for South-East Asia in which Britain, the United States, Australia and New Zealand could co-operate for economic and political purposes, as distinct from a military pact or understanding. Britain intended to stand in Hong Kong and, if necessary, make it a 'Berlin of the East'.

But despite Bevin's exhortations the American participants ignored his suggestions about South-East Asia.[33] Indeed what little official American policy there was for the area was outlined in a reply to the earlier British memorandum on the Far East. At the end of April, Hibbert of the Foreign Office observed that this contributed little to the thinking about South-East Asia, 'but the fact that its contribution is so little has an important significance'. If the United States chose to stand back from the attempt to create a cordon against communism in South-East Asia, it would be difficult for other nations to press forward.[34] As Graves observed, it would be a difficult task to bring in the Americans: 'they have burnt their fingers so badly in China that they are at present in a very cautious mood'.[35]

For Britain, however, the threat of communist encroachment into South-East Asia seemed so real that it was prepared to modify the nature of the Commonwealth in the hope that India would remain within that body.[36] With the rapid advance of the communists in China, the British Defence Co-Ordination Committee in the Far East suggested the urgent need for diplomatic, economic and military action 'to form a containing ring against further Communist penetration', including India, Burma, Thailand, Indochina and the Dutch East Indies.[37] On 24 May MacDonald and Lieutenant General Sir Archibald Nye met Foreign and Colonial Office officials to discuss the issue. Dening explained that India was the key to regional co-operation in South-East Asia. MacDonald, however, directed his comments to the communist menace represented by China and enunciated a 'domino theory'. He urged the formulation of an overall policy that could be discussed with the United States, the Commonwealth and later with the foreign countries in South-East Asia. But Dening warned that the Americans were 'holding aloof' from the problems of South-East Asia. Britain would have to take the lead discreetly. Nye foresaw difficulties: the Indian leaders thought that the Chinese communists would be Chinese first and communists second. India might only agree to some economic scheme.[38] For Britain the first test was Hong Kong. Attlee told the Cabinet on 26 May that the whole common front against communism would crumble in the Far East and South-East Asia unless those peoples were convinced of the British determination and ability to resist the threat to Hong Kong.[39]

The Far Eastern committee advised that positive steps should be taken to counter communism in the Far East and South-East Asia.[40] In June a preliminary report by the working party on economic and social development in the area outlined the objectives of any British assistance as being the establishment of healthy economic and social conditions enabling South-East Asia to resist the spread of communism[41]

But, as MacDonald warned from Singapore early in September, the time factor pressed with increasing urgency. The commissioner general advised that unless Britain and the United States showed a constructive interest in South-East Asia, Indochina and Thailand would fall to the communists. Britain was not amiss; rather the problem was to persuade the Americans. If this was not done reasonably soon the communists would take over in Burma and the front line would then be the borders of Malaya. Lloyd, however, minuted that MacDonald's desires for the United States were unlikely to be realized: conditions for private investment by American capital in South-East Asia were unsound, and American government loans would be opposed in Congress.[42]

Lloyd's fears were confirmed with the Anglo-American conversations in Washington in September. On the question of South-East Asia the State Department warned that Congress was unlikely to vote fresh funds for aid anywhere. The Americans thought that the Asians should get together on their own initiative.[43] In any case the Americans believed that Britain was reluctant to 'have a rival to the Empire' in that part of the world, and considered 'the Empire' the 'proper instrument of pressure'.[44]

Britain certainly did see for itself a special role in South-East Asia. This was evident in the papers drawn up on long-term policy by the Permanent Under Secretary's Committee, to serve as general guidance on the policy to be adopted. Bevin approved the general approach before leaving for the September talks in Washington.[45] The Cabinet endorsed the policy in November.[46]

Strang's committee argued that there was a real danger that the whole of Asia would become the servant of the Kremlin unless Britain exploited its special position in Asia to bring about a close collaboration between East and West. Britain was dependent on the area for rubber, tea and jute. Earnings from Malaya helped the sterling area's dollar pool. A combination of Western technology and Eastern manpower could be welded into a formidable partnership – but Asian nationalism was sensitive to anything which savoured of domination by the West. Dictation by Russia, however, had little meaning or reality to Asians, and this was to Moscow's advantage. Political immaturity and economic distress make their countries particularly susceptible to communist tactics. Although communist China was unlikely to extend control over the area, the existence of large Chinese communities within the countries of South-East Asia heightened the possibility of internal disruption. It was possible, however, that the unpopularity of the Chinese settlers with the local inhabitants could encourage resistance to the spread of communist doctrines propagated from China. Alternatively, India could try to dominate the area, but India was unpopular and its expansionist aims were feared, so the countries of South-East Asia were unlikely to accept its lead. From the Persian Gulf to the China Sea no single power could dominate the region. Nor could any combination of powers resist Russian expansion. And no Asian power could bring about unity and co-operation. As Britain had come to terms with the new nationalist spirit in Asia it could use its political and economic influence to weld the area into some degree of regional co-operation. Most of Britain's former territories in the area were friendly independent members of the Commonwealth, and had been built upon a British foundation. Britain also had a peculiarly close relationship with those countries in South-East Asia within the sterling area. The United States did not enjoy the same degree of prestige as did Britain, partly because it lacked the historical connections, partly because of the failure of its policy in China and partly because of its reluctance to play a leading part in South-East Asia. Laissez-faire American economic philosophy had little special appeal in Asia where practically all progressive thought was socialist. Asian nationalists tended to see the choice between democratic socialism and communism, in effect between the British and Russian ways of life. Full development of the area, however, was only possible through American assistance, and the United States was reluctant to risk further losses after its experience in China.

Britain's commitments and interests in Asia were possibly in excess of its postwar strength, but the economic ties could not be severed without serious consequences. Britain, however, could not make any military commitment which would offer resistance against a full-scale attack in war. The most it could do in peace was to maintain internal security within its own territories, encourage 'confidence in the adolescent nations of the region, and local efforts to form sound defence establishments'. With proper guidance the Asian nations could resist Russian aggression, particularly as Moscow's major commitments would probably be in the West and Middle East. Britain still had to cope with Asian suspicions that it was trying to re-establish its domination, and the memory of Britain's ignominious defeat by the Japanese lingered. The original draft of the paper drawn up by Strang's committee suggested that the absence of hostility towards Britain was partly because Britain was 'no longer regarded as a force to be reckoned with'.

The Permanent Under Secretary's Committee thought that Britain was in the best position to build up a regional association in South-East Asia in partnership with the West. Not only could Britain interest the United States, but it had means of influencing and co-ordinating the policies of the Asian Dominions, and Australia and New Zealand. The immediate intention was to prevent the spread of communism and to resist Russian expansion. The long-term objective was to create a friendly system of partnership between East and West, and to improve economic and social conditions in South-East Asia and the Far East.[47] Working on the premiss that the Far East comprised principally Japan, Korea and China – the first two being primarily an American commitment and the third a potentially hostile power – it was in South-East Asia that Britain had to start promoting greater regional collaboration. Only later could the Far East be attached to any system that might emerge. Strang's committee argued that there were advantages in using a Commonwealth rather than just a British approach to achieve these aims, though the racial policies followed by South Africa and the resentment Asian countries felt over the 'White Australia' policy might endanger this. Furthermore, it was unrealistic to expect democracy to develop on the British pattern in the area: corruption and inefficiency would not vanish overnight. The masses of the peoples of Asia for many years would have little voice in government; universal suffrage was only likely to be exploited by the governing classes. The paper suggested that Britain should attempt to establish the nucleus of strategic co-operation between itself, Australia, New Zealand and the Commonwealth countries of Asia. This was essential before any wider regional defence system could be contemplated. And then the co-operation could only be in the field of planning and exchange of views. Britain would have to supply the arms, and other commitments made any increase impossible. As so little could be done in the military field the most profitable line seemed to be the economic one. A draft of the paper, amended at the request of the Colonial Office, referred to the problem of how to 'reconcile the insatiable appetite of India and the Colonial Empire' for economic assistance with Britain's slender resources and the need to develop South-East Asia as a whole. Indeed, economic collaboration seemed to be 'the only form of greater unity' the countries of the area were likely to accept. It was hoped that this could lead to greater political and military cohesion. American participation was, however, essential and Britain's main objective should be to secure this.[48]

The Russians presumably received a copy of these documents. It was decided to send them as a Foreign Office dispatch to Nanking. That was passed to Guy Burgess of the Far Eastern Department. The dispatch went missing. G. A. Carey Foster of the Security Department noted that several top secret papers had gone astray.

Burgess, after trying a suggestion that the paper might have become attached to another document, insisted that he had returned it to the South-East Asia department. There Blackham, on an impending transfer to La Paz, thought that it might have been consigned to confidential waste, though Lloyd could not remember the act of tearing up. Security accepted that explanation. It is probable that Burgess passed on the information, if not the documents, to his Russian masters.[49]

The policy outlined by Strang's committee was endorsed by the Cabinet on 27 October. The Chancellor of the Exchequer, Stafford Cripps, was hesitant about Britain's continuing its existing level of aid to South-East Asia, and his colleagues hoped for American participation on the basis of Britain providing the experience and the United States the finance.[50] These reservations were passed on to the conference of His Majesty's Representatives in the Far East and South-East Asia which met at Bukit Serene, Johore Bahru, between 2 and 4 November in preparation for the forthcoming Commonwealth Prime Ministers' Conference at Colombo.[51] At Bukit Serene the representatives warned that the danger from communism in South-East Asia was so great that energetic short-term action was required irrespective of any steps to secure the long-term objective. Although the Chinese communists were unlikely to fight beyond their frontiers, they would stimulate conspiracy and subversion through the strong communist elements among the Chinese and other populations in Indochina, Thailand and Burma. Domination of these great rice-growing countries could give the communists a stranglehold on the whole of Asia. South-East Asia should be regarded as an area where an emergency existed. The conference endorsed the long-term aim of a regional pact including the North Atlantic Treaty countries, Australia and New Zealand, but as this was unlikely in the near future an initial approach should be made to stimulate economic co-operation in the region.[52]

Following the conference at Bukit Serene, Dening sounded Australian and New Zealand opinion. On 11 November at a meeting in Canberra Dr John Wear Burton of Australia pointed to his country's dilemma: on the one hand there was the view that Australia had a vital interest in what happened in Asia and should play an increasingly active role there; on the other hand there was the feeling, stimulated by the recent awareness of the internal menace of communism, that Australia should recede from Asian affairs and attend to its own security. Mr McIntosch of New Zealand pointed out that his country was leaning more and more towards a policy of complete isolationism from the area: New Zealanders regarded themselves as belonging to Western Europe. Dening suggested that perhaps, in an increasingly smaller world, the Pacific Dominions would not have a choice, and would find themselves involved in Asia whether they liked it or not.[53] It was thought that New Zealand hoped that Australia and the United States would assume sufficient defence responsibilities in the Pacific to enable New Zealand, in the event of another war, to send troops further afield where they would be of maximum assistance to Britain. New Zealand remained the 'Peter Pan' Dominion: it did not want to grow up; it did not want to be strengthened by large-scale immigration. New Zealand wanted Britain to be as strong as possible, and enjoyed its sense of dependence on Britain. It hated to think of Britain being dependent on the United States and concealed its own dependence on the United States. New Zealand was irritated when other members of the Commonwealth took steps which it regarded as weakening the bonds of the empire. The British High Commissioner in Wellington warned: 'closer alliance with Western Europe will bring us some undoubted gains, but if it leaves New Zealand with a belief that we have forsaken her it will also bring undoubted and by no means insignificant losses'.[54]

Although the attitude of the Pacific Dominions appeared rather negative, by December 1949 that of the United States was moving closer to Britain.[55] In November the Foreign Office and the American Policy Planning Staff exchanged information on South-East Asia. J. O. Lloyd found Kennan's paper of March, endorsed by Truman, 'very stimulating'. Kennan and his staff were allowed to read an edited version of the British papers drawn up by Strang's committee – the editing removing unfavourable references to the United States – and they commented that there was 'a remarkable similarity of view' in the British and American studies. The Americans felt that there was no reason why the envisaged multilateral collaboration, preceded by joint Anglo-American action, should not be successful. R. H. Scott of the Foreign Office minuted that the British and American papers were complementary rather than conflicting; though reached by different routes the conclusions were much the same. The American approach, however, was ideological whereas the British one was 'severely practical'. He was worried that the Americans glossed over 'the fissiparous trends' in South-East Asia.[56] In the middle of December Acheson dined with the British ambassador in Washington, Sir Oliver Franks, and explained that the world across the Pacific would be the principal preoccupation of the State Department in 1950.

The Secretary of State and his advisers had changed their minds: the communists in China were likely to expand beyond their borders, 'early', to the south and east. This would be especially dangerous in the areas with considerable Chinese settlements. With this in mind Acheson had 'scratched together' about 75 million dollars to use in Indonesia, Indochina, and possibly Thailand to help bolster the regimes in those countries. He interpolated a 'paeon of praise' about French achievement in Indochina: the American view had changed, and he was anxious to recognize and help Indochina. The Colombo Conference now appeared as a 'most important event'. Acheson was thinking in terms of 'some rough geographical division of responsibilities': the United States would look after Indonesia, the Philippines, Indochina and spare a little for Thailand; the Commonwealth could help the countries in the Indian Ocean and particularly Burma. Franks, to the subsequent relief of the Foreign Office, hastily discouraged thoughts about any sharp divisions or functions.[57] As H. B. C. Keeble minuted, the Americans seemed prepared to 'take a fairly helpful line' in South-East Asia.[58]

Indeed the final Policy Planning Staff paper, NSC 48/2, endorsed by Truman on 30 December 1949, reflected many of the ideas of the papers drawn up by Strang's committee. The basic security objective was the gradual reduction and the eventual elimination of the preponderant power and influence of Russia in Asia. Non-communist regional associations were to be encouraged, but the United States was not to take an obvious lead. The United States was, however, on its own initiative to 'scrutinize closely the development of threats from Communist aggresssion, direct or indirect, and be prepared to help within our means to meet such threats by providing political, economic, and military assistance and advice where clearly needed to supplement the resistance of the other governments in and out of the area which are more directly concerned.' The Commonwealth was to be induced, in collaboration with the United States, to play a more active role in Asia. As a matter of urgency 75 million dollars was to be 'programmed' for the area.[59]

Bevin explained British policy to the Commonwealth ministers in Colombo in January 1950. When it became clear that Russia's policy was one of 'nineteenth century expansionism' it had been necessary to develop Western consolidation. Thwarted in the West, Russia was turning East where special circumstances made the equivalent of an Atlantic Pact inappropriate. Like-minded countries with interests in the East should be ready to help one another resist any attempt to hinder peaceful development on democratic lines. There could be financial help without domination. With remarkable unanimity the representatives viewed communism as a menace, and agreed on the need to improve the standard of life and the social welfare of the peoples of South and South-East Asia to combat this. Nehru rejected the idea of a Pacific Pact, and recommended reliance on mutual consultation and co-operation between like-minded countries as the occasion arose. Mr Paul Sauer of South Africa thought that the best defence against communism was the improvement of economic conditions, but was concerned how best to meet the short-term problem of Russian infiltration. Percy Spender from Australia emphasized the need for a concrete plan for economic assistance to the countries of South and South-East Asia to help resist the spread of communism. The Ceylonese delegate introduced a plan to support the underdeveloped areas of the Commonwealth. The New Minister of External Affairs in New Zealand, F. W. Doidge, was thought to have 'ultra conservative' personal views of the relationships within the Commonwealth, and to have been unaware of all the changes within that body over the previous thirty years. But New Zealand also supported the idea of economic development. The Colombo Conference adopted a joint Australian-Ceylon-New Zealand resolution on the need for the economic development of the area, and examined the practical economic steps that could be taken to help the threatened areas of Asia resist communist encroachments.[60]

Foreign Office officials, however, remained aware of the need to secure American encouragement and support for this. They were warned by Franks that although there was a genuine acceptance by the American people of the position of the United States as a world power and a willingness to shoulder the responsibility that accompanied that position, there was a budget deficit of 5 billion dollars and the American people associated that with the money spent by their government.[61]

At the end of January 1950 the Joint Chiefs of Staff advised that if the communist penetration of South-East Asia continued allied military requirements would increase, and these would have to be underwritten, if not directly furnished, by the United States.[62] Ambassador at Large Philip C. Jessup, after a fact-finding tour of fourteen nations in Asia, including a talk with MacDonald at Bukit Serene, advised that South-East Asia was vitally important to the United States. Jessup agreed with the British representatives he had consulted that all measures should be taken to prevent communist expansion there. Indochina was the key to the situation and the fate of South-East Asia was in the balance.[63]

167

When British, American and French officials met for talks on the area in May, the Foreign Office observed that there was 'a close identity of outlook' between the British and American adminstrations.[64] The American delegate explained that although Britain and France had a primary responsibility in the area, the United States wanted to continue its practice of assistance in stemming further communist advances.[65] The United States felt that a regional pact in the Pacific would only succeed if it arose spontaneously and was not forced on Asia by the West. The emphasis should be on cultural and economic matters. This coincided with the British view: it was hoped that fuller economic co-operation would arise out of the Sydney Conference following up the suggestions made at Colombo.[66] The Commonwealth economic programme was orchestrated by the Australian Minister for External Affairs, Percy C. Spender: Bevin had arranged this as he thought it best that the proposal came from a country other than Britain.[67] The United States sent a mission under Robert Allen Griffin to develop a programme of economic assistance on an emergency basis to remove impediments to economic development in South-East Asia. Its recommendations were accepted and implemented.[68] As John Foster Dulles, Consultant to the Secretary of State, observed: 'what is going on in Asia is little more than a resurgence in a new guise of the aggressive ambitions of the Czars'.[69]

For Britain, American participation remained essential. As Bevin told the Cabinet on 8 May 1950, Western Europe, even with the support of the Commonwealth, was not strong enough to contend with the military dangers confronting it from the east: 'To withstand the great concentration of power now stretching from China to the Oder, the UK and Western Europe must be able to rely on the full support of the English speaking democracies of the Western Hemisphere; for the original conception of Western Union we must now begin to substitute the wider conception of the Atlantic Community.'[70]

With this in mind the British government became alarmed by the effects of American policy on Asian opinion during the early stages of the Korean War. Bevin acknowledged that from 1945 the United States had regarded South and South-East Asia as primarily a British interest. It was only with the communist threat late in 1949 that the United States took a closer interest in the developments of South-East Asia to the extent of giving military and economic aid to certain countries. But the United States still expected Britain to take the lead, and showed a 'welcome disposition' to consult before taking any action; this was 'satisfactory and should be encouraged'.

The American declaration neutralizing the straits of Formosa, however, had alarmed Asian countries, and aroused suspicions, particularly in India, of American imperialism. It was feared that unless American policy towards China, Japan and Korea took more account of Asian opinion and Asian susceptibilities, Asia would be alienated from the West to the benefit of Russia.[71] But the American administration was also conscious that much of Asia was unconvinced of its devotion to peace, its lack of imperialist ambitions and its interest in Asian freedom and progress.[72]

The Foreign Office brief for the ministerial talks between France, Britain and the United States, held in New York between 12 and 14 September, pointed out that although communist aggression in Korea had produced a certain hardening of opinion against communism amongst the free Asian peoples, it was essential for the Western powers to show that they were strong enough to contain China and its communist protégés in Indochina and Malaya, and that the free countries of Asia would receive help from the West in making themselves strong and independent. Indochina was singled out as the principal problem. There an American military mission was already arranging the urgent delivery of considerable supplies to the forces of France and the Associated States. The British Chiefs of Staff warned that if the French, even with American aid, could not contain the Vietminh, there would be the gravest repercussions on the British position in South-East Asia.[73] The preliminary talks between the three countries' representatives on 1 September pointed to Indochina as the principal problem. On 15 September Acheson told his British and French colleagues that the American government attached the greatest importance to the development of military power in Indochina; military aid to Indochina had been given the highest priority and the amount of American help would be increased. He hoped for talks in the Far East on a high military level.[74] On 9 October Dean Rusk, the Assistant Secretary of State for Far Eastern Affairs, suggested that the United States form a closer relationship with Australia and New Zealand of a military and political character. This was seen as implementing NSC 48/2. It marked the beginning of the assumption by the United States of Britain's traditional role in the area.

While securing the American 'commitment' to South-East Asia, the British government gave particular attention to two areas in the region: Indochina and Malaya. British thinking was dominated by what became known later as the 'domino theory'. MacDonald, the Chiefs of Staff and the Foreign Office were all convinced that Indochina was crucial. If it fell, Thailand and Burma would follow, and it would not be possible to hold Malaya. As early as 23 May 1949, the Joint Intelligence Committee in the Far East warned that the effects on British interests in the event of a complete withdrawal of the French from Indochina 'would be most serious'. The strategic bulwark separating China from South-East Asia would go. There would be a loss of Western prestige, and the moral effect on anti-government movements in South-East Asia would assist the communists' domination of Burma, might provoke a militant outbreak in Thailand and would seriously increase the pace of communist activities in Malaya. A renewed outbreak of anti-government action in South-East Asian countries would add to the food problem of British territories in the area by disrupting the flow of rice from Burma and Thailand. Furthermore, the strategic effect of a complete withdrawal in the event of a war with Russia could be considerable. Besides gaining military facilities for air operations and possibly naval bases, Russia would have a place from which to conduct subversive warfare against the allies. The communications from South-East Asia to Hong Kong would become more difficult, and Singapore with its sea communications would be exposed to air and submarine attack.[76] The fate of Indochina was inextricably linked with that of Malaya. Britain hoped for Commonwealth assistance in this region. Given its resources it could not manage on its own. Australia and New Zealand, because of their geographical positions, were obvious allies. But Australia, in particular, was worried about the Pacific; it wanted to know whether it could rely on the United States. Through the British Chiefs of Staff a meeting was arranged at Pearl Harbor between 26 February and 2 March between Admiral William Radford, the American Commander-in-Chief for the Pacific, and the Australian Chief of the Naval Staff, Vice Admiral Sir John Collins, and naval representatives of Britain and New Zealand to discuss the co-ordination of the defence and sea communications in the Pacific theatre and the ANZAM region, that area stretching roughly from Thailand, and including Malaya, Australia, New Zealand and through to the Gilbert and Ellice Islands.[77] By the end of 1951, however, Australia was satisfied that it had the assurance of the American Chiefs of Staff that the American navy would be sufficiently strong in the Pacific to deal with any seaborne threat to Australia and New Zealand. By the middle of 1950 it was agreed that Australia had primary responsibility for the planning of defence in the ANZAM region, but Britain insisted on maintaining control in Malaya. Australia's 'White immigration' policy was anathema in Malaya, so, for reasons of internal security, Britain could not allow too great an Australian involvement.

For Britain, South-East Asia was essentially an area where, in Bevin's words, 'the full support of the English speaking democracies' was essential. Basic to British policy, however, was the assumption of the Chiefs of Staff in their papers on Defence Policy and Global Strategy in 1950 and 1951 that South-East Asia, though 'critically important', was 'not vital to our survival in war'. In total war the Chiefs of Staff wished to reinforce the area, 'but must set our faces against any diversion of resources required from vital areas'.[78] This view presented a dilemma for Australia with its geographical position, and its perceived need to defend its home waters. There was an obvious conflict with the British view that Australia should be prepared to send forces to the Middle East at the expense of Malaya.[79]

Despite the importance of the Pacific Dominions, Britain felt throughout the period that only the United States could stop communist expansion in Asia. And serious as the situation was in Malaya, Britain considered Indochina the key. MacDonald enunciated this clearly in December 1949: if Indochina were lost, Thailand and Burma would follow shortly, and international communism would be on the borders of Malaya. The Commissioner General felt that Britain could hold Malaya militarily, but the fall of Thailand and Burma would mean the loss of essential rice supplies. Indochina was crucial.[80] It was the view of the Foreign Office that the Americans had sown some of the seeds of the trouble when, towards the end of the Second World War, officers of the Office of Strategic Services had trained and armed the left-wing Vietminh, taken up the Annamite cause and become unnecessarily biased against the French. The Vietminh's espousal of 'simple nationalism' in November 1945 was merely a camouflage to secure public support, and the Vietminh League was a communist organization.[81] British military intelligence described the Vietminh leader, Ho-Chi-Minh, as a Moscow-trained communist who in 1948 was backed by an effective military strength of 82,500 men, and a large number of sympathizers. On 23 December 1947 the French stopped dealing with Ho-Chi-Minh, and tried to persuade Bao Dai, the former Emperor of Annam, to head a new government. But initially Bao Dai would not leave the comfort and security of Hong Kong, and after being enticed to France, being of a sybaritic nature he enjoyed the fleshpots of Paris and Cannes, and seemed reluctant to return to 'a more precarious and less comfortable' existence in the Far East. Bevin, in one of his rare minutes, noted: 'They deserve to lose the throne.'[82] On 14 January 1949 M. Robert Schuman told the Foreign Secretary that Bao Dai's reluctance to take on responsibility could be attributed to 'Asiatic temperament and characteristics'. Schuman insisted that Ho-Chi-Minh was a communist: 'there was plenty of proof of that'.[83] The Americans, however, did not agree.[84]

It appeared to the Foreign Office that the Americans considered they had no direct interest in or responsibility for counteracting communist influence in South-East Asia. R. C. Blackham noted further that if the Bao Dai solution did not work, Britain might consider giving the French covert military support to bring the campaign to an early conclusion, but thought that the Americans would be unlikely to offer similar aid.[85] The minister in Paris, Henry Ashley Clarke, saw 'modest grounds for hope' that Bao Dai might succeed.[86] Guy Burgess, however, noted that nothing the Far Eastern department knew justified anything but depression and foreboding about the failure of the French to put their Indochina house of cards in order.[87] In September 1949 Bevin told the Americans, and also the Commonwealth representatives in Washington, that as there was sufficient evidence of Ho-Chi-Minh's communist affiliations with Moscow, Bao Dai seemed to offer the only alternative.[88] Indeed the British representatives in Saigon reported that there were signs that support for Bao Dai was gradually increasing,[89] but Attlee rated the chances of the continuation of French rule and influence in Indochina very low: he thought the French had 'missed the bus'.[90] As early as June 1949 British and American officials had agreed that they should 'keep in step' over the recognition of Bao Dai, but Britain warned of possible difficulties with the Commonwealth as Nehru thought Ho-Chi-Minh a 'nationalist' rather than a Kremlin communist.[91] Nehru, with his 'sentimental regard' for the new China of Mao Tse-tung, sympathized with Marxist doctrine and had personal connections with Ho.[92] It proved difficult to disabuse Nehru, though his Foreign Minister, K. P. S. Menon, understood the vital importance of Indochina.[93]

Indeed Britain was so anxious to persuade India of the need to support Bao Dai that there were hesitations over meeting a French request for a Royal Air Force survey to help the French war effort in the north of Indochina.[94] The Chiefs of Staff were in favour of the survey,[95] and the War Office wanted discussions with the French because of the significance of Indochina for Malaya and Singapore. The British and French commanders in the area were also old friends. But the planning staff were worried that such wide-scale talks would imply the eventual use of British forces to assist the French in Indochina, and there was concern on the South-East Asia desk in December 1949 over a French inquiry about British military support in Indochina in the event of an attack by Chinese communist armies. Ministers, however, decided on 16 December that Britain could not get involved in Indochina. The Foreign Office explained to the Ministry of Defence that the best way to preserve Indochina as a bastion against the spread of communism in South-East Asia was to assist the development of Vietnam, Laos and Cambodia as stable independent states under non-communist leaders. Frank talks with the French on mutual defence problems in South-East Asia would be welcome, provided they did not envisage Britain taking military action if the Chinese attacked Indochina. The essential prerequisite that the United States be associated with the talks was eliminated from the version sent to the Ministry of Defence.[96]

The conference of British representatives in the Far East which met at Bukit Serene between 2 and 4 November recommended support for the French attempt to consolidate the Vietnamese national movement around Bao Dai: specifically, Britain should grant *de facto* recognition to Bao Dai immediately after the French transfer of power on 1 January 1950, and *de jure* recognition following ratification of the agreement by France and Bao Dai.[97] MacDonald endorsed this. The Commissioner General met Bao Dai later that month and found him 'intelligent and charming', possessing 'physical courage, patriotism, and independence from subservience to the French', and having a sound grasp of political problems and good judgement. Bao Dai was not a genius, but had the makings of an adequate national leader, and was a 'proper and good man to back'.[98] MacDonald estimated that the Bao Dai experiment had rather more than a 50 per cent chance of success; military victories would not be enough to strengthen Bao Dai's position: the solution had to be a political one. Bao Dai particularly wanted British and American diplomatic recognition, and Mac-Donald endorsed this request.[99] Bao Dai offered the only chance of saving Indochina from the communists,[100] and the Commissioner General complained of the inadequate appreciation in Washington of the importance and urgency of the situation in Indochina. His information, however, was out of date. By the end of 1949 the United States no longer stood aside from the affairs of South-East Asia. Truman had endorsed NSC 48/2. American recognition of Bao Dai followed, together with military support for the French position in Indochina. The United States took over the responsibilities of the old colonial and imperial powers.

Malaya, however, was another matter. By the middle of 1949 it was evident to British defence planners that in any major war Britain, with the limited defence forces it could afford, could not discharge unaided its responsibilities to dependencies outside certain vital strategic zones, and that it was almost certain that the Malaya-Borneo area would be in a non-British theatre of war with an American supreme commander. Consequently it was decided to encourage other members of the Commonwealth to participate in strategic planning, and to assume some responsibility for the defence of the Commonwealth in war. Particular attention was given to the Far East. Talks with Australia led to a provisional agreement from that Dominion to initiate defence planning, as distinct from operational responsibility in war, in an area which could include Mayala and Borneo. MacDonald had earlier objected to any Australian involvement in Malaya: not only would it suggest that Britain was abandoning some of its responsibilities and involve a further loss of prestige and have a bad effect on morale, but there was no nation more unpopular with both the Malays and the Chinese than Australia. This was because of the Australian 'white immigration' policy, and the 'flat-footed' way it was administered. Accordingly Britain secured from Canberra an undertaking that the special obligations Britain had assumed with the Malayan rulers were recognized, and that the local command in Malaya in war had to remain in British hands.[101] New Zealand leaned towards a policy of increasing isolationism from Asia: it regarded itself as belonging to Western Europe. That Dominion remained unquestioningly loyal: it hoped in any future war that Australia and the United States would defend the Pacific, and enable New Zealand to send troops where they could be of most use to Britain. Towards the end of 1949 the New Zealand Prime Minister wrote to Attlee that unless there were a major change in the strategic situation forecast, New Zealand forces would be used in accordance with the proposals recommended by the British Chiefs of Staff.[102] At this time, after American complaints that Commonwealth defence planning was not in a sufficient state of readiness, Air Marshal Sir Walter Elliot proposed a mission to Australia, New Zealand and South Africa to form a common front against Russia in the Cold War. By the end of 1949 London distinguished between the four older Dominions who had 'spontaneously' gone to war alongside Britain in 1939, and the Commonwealth's new members. Even so it was thought unwise to deal collectively with the four as their interests were bilateral ones with Britain rather than with each other. Consequently, instead of a mission, Bevin, at the Colombo Conference in January 1950, approached Australia, New Zealand and South Africa about combined defence planning. The immediate result of this for Asia was a reaffirmation by the New Zealand Prime Minister, Holland, that he would place his country's troops in war in an area designated by the British Chiefs of Staff. Then, on 21 June 1950, the Australian Defence Council agreed to collaborate with Britain in South-East Asia according to the requirements of the situation, and to send a squadron of Lincoln bombers to Malaya.[103]

Despite this aid from its Commonwealth partner, late in 1951, at the time of the fall of the Labour government, the British Defence Co-ordination Committee for the Far East advised that the communist hold on Malaya was as strong, if not stronger than it had ever been. According to the Colonial Office assessment the enemy was the Malayan Communist Party, which was almost exclusively Chinese. The main enemy force operated in the jungle and was highly elusive. Though only a few thousand strong, it was assisted by numerous insidious underground operations which existed wherever there was a Chinese element in the general population. The underground intimidated the 500,000 Chinese squatters who had been without police protection, and were the main source of communist supplies. In October 1950 Sir Harold Briggs had been appointed Director of Operations in Malaya. He instituted a plan to resettle the squatters and to isolate the regular bandit forces from the Chinese civilian population, to cut the enemy lines of communication, to break the underground lines and to force the enemy to fight for its existence on ground of Britain's choosing. But it proved difficult to attract the Chinese to Britain's side, and after three-and-a-half years of war there was no prospect of a definite break in the communist ranks. So far as the Malays were concerned, a communist victory would mean Chinese hegemony: they came forward in their thousands to fight the enemy. The Chinese, however, were reluctant: this could be attributed to their character but also to events inside as well as outside Malaya. Tension between the Malay and Chinese communities was dangerous. The Malays in particular were exasperated by the apparent inability of the Chinese to assist in countering the terrorists. In 1950 Malay's American dollar earnings were $350 million out of total sterling area earnings of $1,285 million. But in 1951 terrorist activity made some estates unworkable and rubber production fell substantially. Terrorism also prevented the prosperity necessary to sustain the production of tin. The operation was expensive: the estimated cost for 1951 was £56,900,000, £900,000 of which was borne by Australia.[104]

Throughout the period Britain saw the Cold War in Asia in a global perspective. Though critically important, it was not vital to Britain's survival. In defence planning it had a lower priority than

Western Europe and the Middle East. The Chiefs of Staff emphasized this in their paper on Defence Policy and Global Strategy, MDM(51)2, of 11 June 1951. That paper defined the 'First Things, the really Vital Things – in which if they fail, the Allies cannot survive in the opening stages of a total war, or hold their position in the cold war' as being: primarily, a secure base which included the defence of the United Kingdom against air attack; the defence of the really vital lifelines, those between North America and Europe, and the home waters of the allied powers; and the defence of the front in Europe. There also had to be adequate strategic striking power, including provision for the time when the manned bomber was no longer usable, and the bases from which that striking power could achieve its objective. Thirdly, it was essential to have the bare minimum land, air and sea strength to hold positions in the Cold War. That included the necessary occupation forces and garrisons in Europe, the Middle East, South-East Asia and the Far East, and the forces 'necessary to sustain outbreaks of active hostilities on the Korean model'. Lastly, there had to be the minimum forces to ensure the security of the Egyptian base and the south-west Persian Gulf oil fields. All 'other things' had to be 'put into a lower order of priority and the resources allocated to them must not be allowed to compromise those really vital commitments'. South-East Asia was a lower priority. There efforts had to be directed to building up the local security forces and civil administrations to a point at which, with the minimum of external assistance, they could regain control of the internal situation. Hong Kong, like Korea, was an important outpost of the cold war front, and its loss to Communist China would have grave repercussions throughout the world: 'Our policy should be to show a bold front there and, if this should fail to discourage attack, to defend it vigorously.' Such a defence had some chance of success against Communist China alone, provided that substantial reinforcements were available. It was thought that Hong Kong would be indefensible against serious attacks in a global war by Russia in full alliance with Communist China, and in such circumstances Britain should not reinforce the colony, but accept its loss. Australia and New Zealand had accepted responsibility for certain aspects of defence in the ANZAM region. The Chiefs of Staff hoped that Australia and New Zealand would 'not allocate more than the minimum essential strength to that commitment, and will make available any surplus to reinforce the Middle East'. It was important to link the defence of the ANZAM region closely with the American system of defence of the Pacific. Shinwell defined British strategic policy more specifically in a letter to Canberra on 27 September 1951: if local war started in South-East Asia with the rest of the world at peace, and if the Chinese communist forces attacked Malaya, Britain would fight to hold Malaya 'with all available resources'. If Chinese communist forces attacked Malaya while a total war was being fought, as Field Marshal Sir William Slim had told the Commonwealth Defence Ministers in London on 21 June 1951, Britain's intention was to hold Malaya, but if there was 'a question of Chinese Communist land forces actually threatening Malaya, we shall of course have to reconsider the problem and decide whether forces can be spared from other theatres as reinforcements'. On 14 February 1952 the Australian Defence Committee, in reply to an inquiry from A. S. Watt, the Secretary of the Department of External Affairs, as to whether strategic planning matched the political realities, recommended the adoption of the relevant sections of MDM(51)2 for the 'Strategic Concept for the Defence of the ANZAM Region'.[105]

Australia became Britain's principal Commonwealth partner in the attempt to halt the spread of communism in South-East Asia. But Britain was not able to abdicate its responsibilities, and had to retain control of the situation in Malaya because of the resentment of Australia's 'white immigration' policy. One Australian minister refused the hospitality and comfort of Bukit Serene because MacDonald had the reputation of arranging for visiting Australians to be beseiged by protesters about the white immigration policy. The minister stayed instead in the 'austere' Raffles Hotel in Singapore. In January 1953 a memorandum was drawn up in the Department of External Affairs suggesting what Australian spokesmen abroad should say. The author conceded that 60 per cent of Australians probably still thought and spoke in terms of 'nationalism and racialism of the 1890 variety – sound enough perhaps for those days but unsuitable for the modern world in which we live surrounded by newly independent neighbours, all varying slightly from us in the colour of their skins'. Attacks on Australian 'racial prejudices', particularly in Asian countries, should be countered both by Australia's official representatives and by private citizens with the argument that the individual concerned did not like the policy of 'White Australia'. It would be impossible to defend the policy, because to Asians it was indefensible. The Australian should say that the idea of 'White Australia' dated back to the early years of a young nation. The term had never been used in the stated policy of any government, though it was the motto of one well-known journal. It had to be admitted that Australia

177

THE ENGLISH-SPEAKING ALLIANCE

wanted to develop a homogeneous community of assimilable people, and only to have as immigrants peoples of the same or similar cultures to its own. There were numerous instances in history which showed that peoples whose cultures were very different did not easily become assimilated with each other. There were many examples of minority troubles throughout the world. Australia could not offer the solution to the problems of the overpopulation of Asia; Australia's resources were not limitless.[106]

For Britain the Cold War became a reality in South-East Asia with the communist insurgency in Malaya in 1948. At the beginning of 1949 the United States appeared uninterested and was not prepared to accept any responsibility for halting the communist advance there. The United States regarded the area as being primarily a British interest. The American experience in China made the administration wary of considering economic support for the region. But Britain realized that even with Commonwealth assistance it could do nothing to counter communist moves without American participation. In the same way as it had prepared Western Europe for the American commitment, the British government did its best to organize the countries of South-East Asia. At first the British task seemed almost impossible, but by the end of 1949 there was a considerable amount of congruence between the British plan drawn up by Strang's committee and that developed by Kennan's staff. Conversations, and the exchange of views between British and American officials, helped. In the end the key American document, NSC 48/2, reflected many of the same ideas as those propounded by Strang's committee. It took less than a year to convince the Americans of the need to make a firm commitment to South-East Asia. That took the immediate form of military aid to the French in Indochina. With the outbreak of the Korean conflict, however, the American commitment evolved rapidly. With the moves towards the formation of a defence agreement with Australia and New Zealand the United States was increasingly assuming Britain's responsibilities and role in South-East Asia.

Notes: Chapter 6

1   Australian Archives, Canberra, A2031/34, no. 46/1951, Minute by Defence Committee quoting paragraph 56 of DO150)45, Top Secret, 1 March 1951.
2   A1838, 463/6/3, F18057/87/61, Killearn to Attlee, no. 87, Secret, 4 December 1946.
3   A1838, 383/5/1 Pt 1, F9979/90/61, Killearn to Bevin, Secret, 15 July 1947.
4   A1838, 383/5/1 Pt 2, Copy of British paper 'Outline of communist strategy in South-East Asia', Secret, August 1949.

5   A1838, 383/5/1 Pt 1, JIC(48)12(Final), Communism in the Far East, Secret, 7
    October 1948.
6   A5799, 51/16, Report by Joint Planning Committee at meetings on 12 and 13
    February 1951, Top Secret, quoting paragraph 38 of DO(50)45.
7   A1838, 461/3/1/1, Paper prepared for Australian Prime Minister's guidance,
    13 October 1947
8   A1838, 463/6/3, XIII/1/1/48, Hopson to Paul Grey South-East Asia Depart-
    ment Foreign Office, 16 November 1948.
9   A1838, 383/5/1 Pt 2, Copy of British paper 'Outline of communist strategy in
    South-East Asia', Secret, August 1949; JIC(FE)(49)42 (Final), Report by Joint
    Intelligence Committee Far East for period 1 April to 30 September 1949,
    Secret, 3 December 1949.
10 A1838, 383/5/1 Pt 2, Copy of British paper 'Outline of communist strategy in
    South-East Asia', Secret, August 1949.
11 A1838, 383/5/1 Pt 1, JIC(FE)(49)9(Final), Communism in the Far East covering
    the period 1 October 1948 to 31 March 1949; 383/5/1 Pt 1, JIC(FE)(49)42
    (Final), Report by Joint Intelligence Committee Far East for period 1 April to 30
    September 1949, Secret, 3 December 1949.
12 N. Mineo, 'The Sino-Soviet confrontation in historical perspective', in Y.
    Nagai and A. Iriye (eds), *The Origins of the Cold War in Asia* (New York, 1977), pp.
    203–23 at p. 207.
13 D. C. Watt, 'Britain and the Cold War in the Far East, 1945–48', in ibid., pp.
    89–122 at p. 89.
14 A1838, 463/6/3, Extract from A.M.F. Intelligence Review Vol. II no. 1,
    February 1949; 383/5/1 Pt 2, Copy of British paper 'Outline of communist
    strategy in South-East Asia', Secret, August 1949.
15 Public Record Office, London, FO 371/76386, E5573/3/500G, Makins to
    Bevin, 9 November 1949; Foreign Office minute, 23 November 1949; PUSC
    51(Final) Second Revise, Anglo-American relations: present and future, Top
    Secret; E5573/3/500G, PUSC 22(Final), A Third World power or Western
    consolidation? Top Secret.
16 FO 371/75735, F424/1015/10G, Memorandum on the possible effects of the
    war in China on the general situation in the Far East and South East Asia, 29
    December 1948.
17 *FRUS* 1949(7), p. 1115, Circular airgram, Lovett to certain American missions,
    Confidential, 4 January 1949; for the assessment Britain sent to the United
    States of the effects in South-East Asia of the spread of communism, see *FRUS*
    1949(9), pp. 6–11, British Embassy to Department of State, 10 January 1949.
18 *FRUS* 1949(9), pp. 821–2, British Embassy to Department of State, 10 January
    1949.
19 FO 371/75740, F2277/1015/10, Viscount Hood (Paris) to Dening, 102/10/6/49,
    Secret, 10 February 1949; Minutes by P. W. S. Y. Scarlett, 15 February 1949; R.
    H. Scott, 16 February 1949.
20 FO 371/75743, F3299/1015/10, Graves to Scarlett, G47/14/49, 25 February
    1949; *FRUS* 1949(7), pp. 1118–19, Memorandum by Reed, Secret, 23 February
    1949.
21 *FRUS* 1949(7), pp. 1117–18, Stuart to Acheson, Telegram, 15 February 1949.
22 FO 371/75745, F3790/1015/10, Stevenson to Bevin, no. 141, Confidential, 4
    March 1949 received 12 March 1949; *FRUS* 1949(7), pp. 119–23, Stuart to
    Acheson, no. 59, Secret, 8 March 1949 received 29 March 1949, and Enclosure,
    Secret, undated.
23 FO 371/76033, F4545/1073/61G, MacDonald to Bevin, no. 16, Top Secret, 23
    March 1949 received 28 March 1949.
24 *FRUS* 1949(7), p. 1123.

25 *FRUS* 1949(7), pp. 1128–33, United States policy toward Southeast Asia, PPS 51, Secret, 29 March 1949.
26 *FRUS* 1949(7), pp. 128–9.
27 FO 371/75961, F3519/1015/86, Memorandum by Blackham, undated, received in registry 9 March 1949.
28 FO 371/75744, F3729/1015/109, Commonwealth Relations Office to British High Commissioners, Telegram Y no. 69, Secret, 2 March 1949; F2180/39, Commonwealth Relations Office to British High Commissioners, Telegram Y no. 25, Secret, undated.
29 FO 371/76023, F4486/1023/61G, Dening to Sir Cecil Syers (Commonwealth Relations Office), 18 March 1949; Dening to J. J. Paskin (Colonial Office), 18 March 1949; Draft brief on South-East Asia and the Far East, Top Secret, undated.
30 FO 371/75743, F3507/1015/10G, Scarlett to Sir Oliver Franks (Washington) for attention of Bevin, Secret, 23 March 1949.
31 FO 371/76023, F5743/1023/61G, Graves to Dening, G47/37/49, Top Secret, 16 April 1949; *FRUS* 1949(7), pp. 1135–7, Bevin to Acheson, Top Secret, 2 April 1949.
32 FO 371/76023, F4486/1023/61G, Dening to Graves, Top Secret, 25 March 1949.
33 *FRUS* 1949(7), pp. 1138–41, Memorandum by Beam, Top Secret, 4 April 1949.
34 FO 371/75747, F4595/1015/10, Franks to Bevin, no. 224, 22 March 1949, received 26 March 1949; Minutes by Hibbert, 27 April 1949; Lloyd, 28 April 1949; Scott, 29 April 1949; Scarlett, 30 April 1949.
35 FO 371/76023, F5743/1023/61G, Graves to Dening, G47/37/49, Top Secret, 16 April 1949.
36 Public Record Office, London, CAB 128/15, fos 61–2, CM17(49)2, Secret, 3 March 1949.
37 CAB 128/15, fos 127–8, CM33(49)2, Secret, 9 May 1949; FO 371/76034, F6670/1075/61G, British Defence Coordination Committee to Chiefs of Staff, Telegram no. SEACOS 900, Top Secret, 5 May 1949.
38 FO 371/76034, F8338/1075/61G, Record of a meeting held at the Foreign Office on 24 May 1949.
39 CAB 128/15, fol. 248, CM38(49)3, Secret, 26 May 1949.
40 FO 371/76041, F7438/1103/61, Memorandum of the first meeting of the Far Eastern (Official) Committee Working Party, Secret, 19 May 1949.
41 FO 371/76041, F8883/1103/61, Memorandum by Lloyd of the Preliminary Report by Working Party on Economic and Social Development in the Far East and South East Asia, received in registry 20 June 1949.
42 FO 371/76023, F13136/1024/61, MacDonald to Dening, Telegram no. 665, Particular Secrecy, 2 September 1949; Minute by Lloyd, 10 September 1949.
43 FO 371/76023, F14149/1024/61, Dening to Strang, G33/3/49, Secret, 15 September 1949; F15735/1024/61, Dening to Bevin, 12 September 1949; F15775/1024/61, Dening to Bevin, 12 September 1949.
44 *FRUS* 1949(7), pp. 1204–8, Report by Yost of discussions of Far Eastern affairs in preparation for conversations with Bevin on 13 September 1949, Top Secret, 16 September 1949.
45 FO 371/76385, W4639/3/500G, Strang to Bevin, 10 August 1949; Minute by Bevin, undated.
46 FO 371/76030, F17397/1055/61G, Minute by W. G. Hayter, 3 November 1949. Circulated to Cabinet as CP(49)207. All reference to this document has been deleted from the Cabinet papers. It is evident, however, from cross-referencing that the Cabinet endorsed the document.
47 FO 371/76386, W5572/3/500G, PUSC(32)Final, The United Kingdom in South East Asia and the Far East, Top Secret.

48   FO 371/76386, W5572/3/500G, PUSC(53)Final, Regional co-operation in South East Asia and the Far East, Top Secret; Strang to Bevin, Top Secret, 16 October 1949; Minute by Bevin, undated; PUSC(72), Amendments to committee papers on South East Asia and the Far East in the light of comments received, Top Secret, 11 October 1949.

49   FO 371/76030, F17397/1055/61G, Green Division to Tucker, 27 January 1950; Minutes by W. C. Tucker, 27 January 1950; R. Molland, 30 January 1950; G. A. Carey Foster, 31 January 1950; J. E. Puleston, 1 February 1950; G. Burgess, 1 February 1950; J. O. Lloyd, 4 February 1950; G. A. Carey Foster, 8 and 10 February 1950; W. C. Tucker, 8 February 1950.

50   CAB 128/16, fol. 85, CM62(49)8, Secret, 27 October 1949.

51   FO 371/76022, F6056/1022/61G, Scrivener to Dening, 3 March 1949; Strang to MacDonald, Telegram no. 429, Particular Secrecy, 26 March 1949; 76010, F16233/10110/61, Bevin to Rees Williams and Dening, Telegram no. 1431, Particular Secrecy, 31 October 1949.

52   Public Record Office, London, CAB 129/37 Pt 3, fos 381–4, Memorandum by Bevin on conference at Bukit Serene, Secret, circulated 1 December 1949; FO 371/76010, F16631/10110/61, MacDonald to Bevin, Telegram no. 928, Particular Secrecy, 6 November 1949.

53   FO 371/76010, F17568/10110/61, Minutes by Dening of meeting in Canberra on 11 November 1949, 12 November 1949.

54   FO 371/76386, W5772/3/5008, A. W. Snelling to Sir Percival Liesching, 12 October 1949.

55   FO 371/76983, F19106/1055/86, MacDonald to Bevin, Telegram no. 1098, Particular Secrecy, 19 December 1949 received 20 December 1949.

56   FO 371/76025, F17668/10345/61G, Hoyer-Millar to Sir Roger Makins, Top Secret and Personal, 16 November 1949; Minutes by Lloyd, 24 November 1949; Scott, 24 November 1949; 76386, W5665/3/500G, Minute by R. M. Hadow, Top Secret, 18 October 1949; Makins to Hoyer-Millar, Top Secret and Personal, 19 October 1949.

57   FO 371/76025, Franks to Bevin, Telegram no. 5855, Particular Secrecy, 17 December 1949 received 18 December 1949; Minute by R. H. Scott, 22 December 1949.

58   FO 371/75983, F19106/1055/86, MacDonald to Bevin, Telegram no. 1098, Particular Secrecy, 19 December 1949 received 20 December 1949; Minute by H. B. C. Keeble, undated.

59   FRUS 1949(7), pp. 1215–20, Executive Secretariat Files, Souers to National Security Council, Top Secret, 30 December 1949; NSC 48/2, The position of the United States with respect to Asia, Top Secret, 30 December 1949; United States–Vietnam Relations, 1945–1967, Bk 8, pp. 225–64, NSC 48/1, The position of the United States with respect to Asia, Top Secret, 23 December 1949.

60   CAB 129/38, fos 66–70, CP(50)18, Memorandum by Bevin on the Colombo Conference, Secret, 22 February 1950; A1838, 540/1, Annexure 4, Memorandum by the Australian Delegation on Economic Policy in South and South East Asia; 532/7 Pt 1, B. Kuskie, Official Secretary of the Office of the High Commissioner for Australia in New Zealand to Secretary of Department of External Affairs, Australia, Memorandum no. 421, 9 December 1949; 540/2 Pt 1, Memorandum by Spender for Cabinet on Colombo Conference, Secret, 6 February 1950.

61   FO 371/84528, FZ10345/3, Note of a discussion with Sir O. Franks held in Strang's room on 8 February 1950.

62   FRUS 1950(6), pp. 5–8, Johnson to Acheson, Top Secret, 1 February 1950; Memorandum by Joint Chiefs of Staff to Johnson, Top Secret, 20 January 1950.

63   FRUS 1950(6), pp. 11–18, Memorandum by Jessup of conversation with

MacDonald, Secret, 6 February 1950; pp. 29–30, Stanton to Acheson, Telegram, Top Secret, 27 February 1950; pp. 68–76, Memorandum by Ogburn of oral report by Jessup upon his return from the East, Top Secret, 3 April 1950.

64 FO 371/84517, FZ1025/1, British brief for London Conference in May 1950, South East Asia general, Secret, 29 April 1950.

65 FO 371/84517, FZ1025/3G, British record of a meeting of a tripartite official subcommittee held in the Foreign Office on 1 May 1950, Top Secret.

66 FO 371/84517, FZ1025/3G, British record of a meeting of a tripartite subcommittee in the Foreign Office on 2 May 1950, Top Secret; FRUS 1950(3), pp. 935–48; pp. 1082–5, Agreed tripartite minutes on South East Asia, Top Secret, 22 May 1950.

67 FRUS 1950(6), p. 146, Memorandum by Battle of conversation between Bevin and Acheson, Secret, 26 September 1950.

68 FRUS 1950(6), pp. 87–92, Record of interdepartmental meeting on Far East on 11 May 1950, Confidential; pp. 93–4, Acting Secretary of State to the legation at Saigon, Secret, 15 May 1950.

69 FRUS 1950(6), pp. 128–9, Dulles to Acheson, Confidential, 7 August 1950; Memorandum by Dulles, Confidential, 4 August 1950.

70 CAB 128/17, fos 94–6, CM29(50)3, Secret, 8 May 1950.

71 CAB 129/39, fos 242–3, Memorandum by Bevin of a review of the international situation in Asia in the light of the Korean conflict, Secret, 30 August 1950.

72 FRUS 1950(6), pp. 136–9, McGhee to Matthews, Top Secret, 30 August 1950; Policy paper 'A new approach in Asia' by McGhee, Top Secret, 30 August 1950.

73 FO 371/84536, FZ1073/1/G, Foreign Office memorandum for tripartite ministerial talks in New York. Briefs on South East Asia and Indochina, Secret; Current developments in Indochina, Secret; Secretary of Chiefs of Staff Committee to J. D. Murray, 24 August 1950; FRUS 1950(3), pp. 1146–53, United States delegation minutes, preliminary conversations on communist threat to South East Asia and developments in Indochina, Top Secret, 30 August 1950; pp. 1172–5, Paper prepared by tripartite drafting group on South-East Asia, Top Secret, 1 September 1950.

74 FO 371/84536, FZ1073/2/G, Document on South East Asia prepared in preliminary tripartite talks, Secret, submitted to ministers, 1 September 1950; British Delegation United Nations to Jebb, Telegram no. 1017, Particular Secrecy, 15 September 1950.

75 FRUS 1950(6), pp. 147–8, Rusk to Matthews, Top Secret, 9 October 1950.

76 A1838, 462/8/1/2, JIC3FE(49)6 Third Draft, The likelihood and probable effects of a French withdrawal from part, or the whole, of Indochina, Secret, 23 May 1949.

77 A5799, 51/48, Report by Joint Planning Committee at meetings held on 12 February and 19 March 1951.

78 A2031/37, no. 38/1952, Minute by Defence Committee on strategic concept for the defence of the ANZAM region, Top Secret, 14 February 1952; Appendix A quoting paragraph 60 of MDM(51)2.

79 A2031/36, no. 408/1951, Minute by Defence Committee on defence policy and global strategy South-East Asia, Top Secret, 15 November 1951; see also Chapter 5 above.

80 FO 371/75983, F19106/1055/86, MacDonald to Foreign Office, Telegram no. 1098, Particular Secrecy, 19 December 1949.

81 FO 371/75963, F6720/1015/86, Memorandum on historical background of French Indochina 1939–1948, Confidential, July 1949.

82 FO 371/75960, F1539/1015/86, Appreciation of situation in French Indochina

by M12, 3 December 1948; F720/1015/86, Ashley Clarke to Dening, 7 January 1949, Minute by Bevin, undated.

83 FO 371/75960, F1315/1015/869, Conversation between Bevin and Schuman at Foreign Office on 14 January 1949.

84 N. Sheehan *et al., The Pentagon Papers* (New York, 1971), p. 8.

85 FO 371/75961, F3519/1015/86, Memorandum by Blackham, received in registry 9 March 1949.

86 FO 371/75961, F3519/1015/86, Ashley Clarke to Attlee, Confidential, 28 March 1949.

87 FO 371/75991, F7231/1201/86, Minute by Burgess, 26 May 1949.

88 FO 371/76023, F14305/1024/61G, Notes of meeting between Bevin and ambassadors from Canada, Australia, New Zealand, South Africa, Pakistan, India and Ceylon in British Embassy in Washington, 16 September 1949.

89 FO 371/75969, F15300/1015/86, Hopson to Roberts, 1 October 1949.

90 FO 317/76030, F15857/1055/61G, Attlee to Bevin, 22 October 1949.

91 FO 371/75964, F9051/1015/86, Minute by J. O. Lloyd, 15 June 1949.

92 FO 371/75996, F11459/1015/86, Minute by R. C. Blackham, 9 August 1949.

93 FO 371/75976, F14198/1025/86G, Conversation between Dening and Butterworth on 14 September 1949; 76010, F16889/10110/61, Roberts to Noel-Baker, Telegram no. X1917, Secret, 8 November 1949.

94 FO 371/75977, F16255/1026/86, MacDonald to Foreign Office, Telegram no. 888, Particular Secrecy, 28 October 1949; Minute by H. B. C. Keeble, 31 October 1949.

95 FO 371/75977, F16999/1026/86, Foreign Office to Paris, Telegram no. 3074, Particular Secrecy, 12 November 1949.

96 FO 371/75977, F17921/1028/86, Hopson to Paris, Telegram no. 222, Particular Secrecy, 30 November 1949; Minute by J. O. Lloyd, 17 December 1949; 75978, F19127/1027/86, Minute by H. B. C. Keeble, 19 December 1949; 75990, F16901/1195/86G, Secret meeting between Chief Imperial General Staff and General Carpenter at Saigon, 30 October 1949; Minute by Keeble, 11 November 1949; F18573/1195/86G, British Co-ordination Committee Far East to Chiefs of Staff, Telegram no. SEACOS 3, Top Secret, 9 December 1949 and Foreign Office minutes; R. H. Scott to C. R. Price MOD, 23 December 1949.

97 CAB 129/37 Pt 3, fol. 383, CP(49)244, Memorandum by Bevin on conference at Bukit Serene, Secret, circulated 1 December 1949.

98 FO 371/75977, F17779/1026/86, MacDonald to Foreign Office, Telegram no. 1018, Particular Secrecy, 28 November 1949.

99 FO 371/75977, F17833/1026/86, MacDonald to Foreign Office, Telegram no. 1017, Particular Secrecy, 28 November 1949.

100 FO 371/75983, F19106/1055/86, MacDonald to Foreign Office, Telegram no. 1098, Particular Secrecy, 19 December 1949.

101 Public Record Office, London, DO 35/2273, D2060/84, Garner to James, 16 June 1949; 94001/26/49, Draft memorandum by Colonial Office on defence responsibilities of Australia in the Far East, Top Secret, August 1949; 1101/21/7/9, C. R. Price (COS) to Trafford Smith (CO), 21 July 1949.

102 FO 371/76010, F17568/10110/61, Minutes by Dening of meeting in Canberra on 11 November 1949, 12 November 1949; 76386, W5772/3/5008, A. W. Snelling to Sir Percival Liesching, 12 October 1949; DO 35/2277, D2000/99, Note of talk with P. T. Hayman (MOD) on 28 October 1949 on the stage reached in defence planning with Australia, New Zealand and South Africa, Top Secret, 2 November 1949.

103 DO 35/2277, D2000/99, Note of talk with Hayman, 2 November 1949; fol. 4, Notes on defence burden of Commonwealth for meeting on 30 November 1949; fol. 19, Note for ministers, Top Secret, received 26 July 1950.

104   CAB 129/48, fos 105–11, C(51)26, Memorandum on situation in Malaya by Lyttleton and Ismay, Secret, 20 November 1951; see also A. Short, *The Communist Insurrection in Malaya 1948–1960* (London, 1975), pp. 19–344; R. Clutterbuck, *The Long War. The Emergency in Malaya 1948–1960* (London, 1967), pp. 13–64; *Riot and Revolution in Singapore and Malaya, 1945–1963* (London, 1973), pp. 174–94; perhaps the most incisive account is A. Burgess, *The Malayan Trilogy* (London, 1972).

105   A2031/37, no. 38/1952, Minute by Defence Committee on strategic concept for the defence of the ANZAM region, Top Secret, 14 February 1952; no. 91/1952, Minute by Defence Committee on Report of ad hoc committee on South-East Asia, Top Secret, 10 April 1952.

106   A1838, 532/3/1 Pt 3, Memorandum for the Acting Secretary on 'Anti-colonialism – radicalism', 14 January 1953.

7

The Recognition of Communist China

The Permanent Under Secretary's Committee under William Strang considered, in 1949, the Anglo-American special relationship as the pivot of British foreign policy. There was, however, an inequality inherent in the association, and Britain thought that the alliance would be least effective in Asia and the Far East. In that area American naïvety and selfishness were particularly evident.[1] The spread of Mao Tse-tung's communists across the Chinese mainland emphasized Britain's predicament, especially as, initially, the Chinese were regarded as orthodox communists.

A Foreign Office research department memorandum of February 1949 pointed to the 'essential orthodoxy' of the Chinese communists. It argued that until the end of 1947 the Chinese communist propaganda programme had maintained that they were peaceful tillers of the soil and had no connections with Moscow. But this was just a 'simple picture', the creation of which was part of communist policy. A study of the origin, growth and methods of the Chinese Communist Party, however, showed that even if the leaders were not pure Marxists, they were governed by orthodox communist principles under the guidance of Russian influence.[2] If the Chinese communists were directed from Moscow it was likely that Russia, thwarted in the West, would turn East and use its pupils to subvert local governments and spread Marxist-Leninism. For Britain the question was essentially how best to safeguard British interests in the area. Only the United States could stop the spread of communism in China, and it was not prepared to do so. If Britain were to pursue a pragmatic rather than an ideological policy, it was possible that the obvious step would be to recognize the new Chinese communist government, and hope for a normalization of at least trading relations.

Much, however, depended on the analysis of the nature of the

185

communism in China. Foreign Office officials like P. W. S. Y. Scarlett regarded the Chinese communists as orthodox. In February 1949 France felt that in the international field Communist China would align itself with Russia. Scarlett thought this 'good straight thinking'.[3] He was conscious, however, that there was little evidence of direct Russian intervention in Chinese affairs.[4] On the Far Eastern desk Guy Burgess analysed the nature of communism. Many of his minutes read like undergraduate lecture notes. Possibly this was a reflection of the inadequate knowledge in the Foreign Office of Marxist-Leninism, and the consequent need to pass on seemingly basic information. It did mean that the British had as adviser not only a specialist, but a Russian convert and agent. Burgess, in May 1949, singled out a report from the acting consul general in Tientsin, Franklin, as being particularly significant. According to Franklin the communists in China were 'real', power was in their grasp, they had come to stay and intended to revolutionize the social, political and economic structure of China. Burgess endorsed the observation of his Foreign Office colleague, P. D. Coates, that 'we are in the presence of a real revolution'. And, according to Burgess, the Foreign Office knew nothing about this apart from the 'interested, romantic or wishful utterances of old China hands'. This real revolution was 'in the hands of a very highly trained, confident and efficient Communist Party'. He warned that the absence of overt Russian assistance was not a sign of 'potential Titoism'. Efficiency and incorruptibility of the party organization extended over both the military and civil fields. The shortage of technical personnel had never been 'an insuperable obstacle to minority rule when the minority is fanatical'. Burgess diagnosed the links between the Chinese communist treatment of foreigners and economics in a way that was particularly significant for later British policy towards the Chinese People's Republic. He pointed to the lack of xenophobia as a propaganda weapon in internal matters, and the 'complete protection' of foreign lives and property. This was obviously a high level policy decision. It implied that the party would grasp political power, and control the key elements in the economic system such as heavy industry and foreign trade, but that much of the restoration and development of production would be left to private capital, foreign as well as Chinese.[5]

The feeling in the Far Eastern Department, endorsed by Burgess at the end of June 1949, was that neither Mao nor the Chinese Communist Party were fellow Titos. To substantiate this view Burgess pointed out that the Chinese Communist Party was one of the first to support the Cominform resolution against Tito. Even more important than the Foreign Office view that the Chinese Communist Party did not deviate, and that its opinion was Moscow opinion, was that the Russian press had several times specifically endorsed the Chinese Party's orthodoxy.[6] Burgess insisted on Mao's orthodoxy, and threatened a 'theological' dispute when contradicted.[7] But, as P. D. Coates pointed out, London knew nothing about Mao's personality and personal views. He could only be judged by his actions.[8] According to Burgess these suggested Russian connections: Mao himself had served on the executive committee of the Third International.[9] At the end of September 1949 Burgess argued that the indications were that the economic policy the Chinese communists intended to follow was modelled on the one the Bolsheviks had been forced to adopt: 'The Russian-Chinese parallel has been consistently stressed by Stalin and the Chinese Communist Party long before either decided or was instructed to follow suit. Probably both.' The views of people like the first Lord Lindsay, his son Michael, Edgar Snow and Sir John Pratt did suggest that Mao's communism had sources other than Marxist-Leninism, but these were dismissed by the Foreign Office, and the Lindsays were regarded as eccentric nuisances.[10]

Early in January 1949 London approached Washington about the threat a communist China would pose to Western interests. Working on the basis that Mao Tse-tung appeared to be a Marxist-Leninist, Britain still hoped to pursue its interests in China for some time expecting that economic weaknesses in that country might mean reasonable treatment of Western interests.[11] On the question of the recognition of any successor government in China, the State Department hoped that Britain and the United States would keep 'in step'.[12]

Dean Acheson, the Secretary of State, gave 'the best clue' as to American policy towards China when, on 24 February, he said that the State Department intended to 'wait until the dust had settled'. As W. Walton Butterworth of the China division explained to the British Counsellor in Washington, H. A. Graves, the United States would test any successor administration in China to see whether it gave signs of good faith, and future moves would be decided in the light of Chinese reactions.[13] The Foreign Office also advised caution: at the end of February it pointed out that the communist administration in north China was provisional, and so even *de facto* recognition would be premature. In any case Britain would have to consult friendly governments before considering recognition, and there had been little response to earlier inquiries about the threat posed by the Chinese communists. Apart from the general agreement of the French government, the only significant response had been from India: the Chinese communists could prove to be different from the Russian brand.[14] Bevin did not agree, and the Foreign Secretary told the Cabinet on 8 March that there were no indications that the Chinese communists would pursue policies different from those followed by the communists elsewhere.[15] Washington was told accordingly that Britain did not want to appear 'unduly precipitate' in recognizing the communist regime, and was anxious to proceed only on the basis of full consultation with the other powers concerned.[16]

British policy was to be cautious. A Cabinet paper advocated that there should be no economic pressure on the Chinese communists, and that friendly powers should be dissuaded from any such action. Consequently, when it appeared that the State Department intended to close down the American consulates in Communist China and introduce sanctions, the Foreign Office became concerned. But as Coates observed: American business interests were so vastly smaller than the British that the American government had 'far less urgent reasons than us for acting slowly and with caution'.[17] The irony was that it was the United States that had paid to bolster the Chinese nationalists: from 1937 to V-J Day the American government had spent $1·5 billion. In 1945 the nationalists controlled the major part of China. The quantity and quality of their arms were vastly superior to the communists. But this, and a further £2 billion from the United States, had not helped. The Americans were convinced that external aid was no substitute for self-help in the fight against communism.[18]

Consequently the Foreign Office urged the Americans to avoid exerting economic pressure on the Chinese communists. It argued that Western interests could be maintained in China for some time if, as anticipated, the communists continued to need public utilities, insurance, banking, commercial and shipping agencies, and industrial enterprises. Economic pressure would only expedite the second phase of the revolution in which the communists were likely to attempt some form of expropriation. In 1941 the value of British commercial property in China was assessed at £300 million, without invisible earnings. Despite war damage, the total in 1949 was considerable. On political grounds the Cabinet had decided that British interests should be supported in 'their desire to keep their foot in the door in China as long as possible'. For economic reasons it was thought it would be regrettable if Britain were to cut itself off from a potentially vast market for British goods, and a potentially soft currency source of supply of essential imports. In normal conditions potential trade between Britain and China could double its prewar level.[19] British officials, however, were concerned about the absence of any considered American policy on China. Coates feared that the State Department would conceive ill-advised and hasty *ad hoc* measures to deal with certain aspects of the China situation instead of 'taking the problem as a whole'.[20] Scarlett was more scathing: he feared that Britain had to accept the position that the United States was waiting 'for the dust to settle' with 'an open – or vacant – mind' and had no thoughts to offer in the political field. As the American officials had no framework or policy within which to talk and act they were particularly 'vulnerable to criticism at the hands of the sentimentalists in Congress' who wanted to restore Chiang Kai-shek, or the 'anti-reds' who would 'cry havoc at the first sign of a positive policy towards the new regime'. On China it would be hard to jockey the Americans along the British road.[21] When, at the end of April, the Americans asked for a united front over trade sanctions against the Chinese communists, the British ambassador in China, Sir Ralph Stevenson, warned that he saw sanctions as a two-edged weapon. The predominantly British investment in China could be prejudiced by premature threats against a new communist regime suspicious of foreigners. British merchants should have a chance to revive their long-established Chinese trade connections. Stevenson did not think that Britain would support the American aspirations.[22]

During May Britain sounded its allies on the advisability of extending *de facto* recognition to a communist government in China as soon as it was properly established.[23] The American ambassador in China, John Leighton Stuart, argued that the communists had to earn recognition by showing that they would maintain international obligations. Recognition was the only lever the United States had, and that bargaining counter should not be discarded lightly.[24] Britain and the United States agreed to maintain a reserved attitude and preserve a common front: the question of formal recognition would only arise, in any case, after the formation of a government claiming to be of national character.[25]

The British position was also complicated by Hong Kong. At the end of April the military acknowledged that Hong Kong could not be defended against a major power in occupation of the Chinese mainland. The Chiefs of Staff were determined that until it was clear how communism in China would develop, Britain should plan to hold Hong Kong, and to let this be known.[26] It would be merely aiding the spread of communism to represent Hong Kong as an outpost of Western democracy in the Far East: that could arouse Asian nationalism which was particularly dangerous when aligned with communism. Early in May the Cabinet decided to consider a suggestion that it would be impossible to preserve Hong Kong as a British colony, and that serious consideration should be given to the possibility of making it an international port.[27] Indeed, for Britain, Hong Kong became the Berlin of Asia, in the words of the Foreign Secretary. Following consultations with the relevant Far Eastern British officials, the Prime Minister told the Cabinet on 26 May that failure to meet the threat to the security of Hong Kong would damage very seriously British prestige throughout the Far East and South-East Asia. Any common front against communism in that area would probably crumble if the free Asian peoples were not convinced of Britain's determination and ability to resist the threat to Hong Kong. Attlee insisted that the aim of British policy should be to find a basis on which a communist government of China could acquiesce in Britain remaining in Hong Kong. It was necessary to give practical evidence of the British determination to defend Hong Kong. Even more important than Britain's trading position in Hong Kong was the need to make a stand against communist encroachment in the Far East. If that stand were not made in Hong Kong it would be harder to take it elsewhere in South-East Asia. Australia and New Zealand would be likely to support Britain over this, but the attitude of other Commonwealth governments, and particularly that of India under Nehru, was uncertain. It would also be unwise to count on the support of public opinion in the United States.[28] Bevin was concerned that unless Britain stayed in Hong Kong the growth of communism in Asia would be encouraged through the Chinese communities and the communist parties. The Foreign Secretary, however, thought it might be difficult to convince the Asian members of the Commonwealth of Britain's justification for maintaining Hong Kong indefinitely as a British colony. But it would be unthinkable for Britain to discuss the future of Hong Kong except with a stable, unified, democratic and friendly China.[29] Apart from New Zealand and South Africa, the Commonwealth countries had misgivings about Britain's long-term prospects in Hong Kong and were reluctant to commit themselves. Australia in particular was not prepared to assume any share of responsibility for withstanding the communist encroachment. Despite this the British Cabinet decided, at the end of June, that a positive policy should be formulated to safeguard British interests in Hong Kong.[30] On 27 June, however, Burgess advised that there was no evidence to justify the conclusion that the Chinese communists claimed, or were prepared to claim, that British rule in Hong Kong was an invasion of Chinese sovereignty.[31]

London's attitude towards the Chinese communists was not significantly affected, at this time, by the *Amethyst* incident. In April HMS *Amethyst*, while carrying supplies up the Yangtse River to the British embassy and community in Nanking, was fired upon by the communists. The British authorities decided that this was 'non-political' and 'on the spot unpremeditated firing'. Their version was that a small battery opened fire. The *Amethyst* put out more flags and the firing stopped. The *Amethyst* then moved along the stream, was fired on by another battery and as a result ran aground, and it was only then that the *Amethyst* started firing. Three other British naval vessels which tried to go to its rescue were also fired on. Thirty-two members of the British crew were killed; about eight times that number of Chinese died in retaliatory fire. The Chinese communist commanders said that the *Amethyst* was trying to prevent their forces from crossing the Yangtse, and blocked the ship's exit. In the end the *Amethyst* made a dramatic and heroic escape to Hong Kong. The Joint Intelligence Committee in the Far East thought that the incident was unlikely to alter 'fundamentally' the Chinese communist policy towards British interests. It would raise the prestige of the communist armies, but its effect on the Asian view of British prestige was more difficult to assess. There could be misgivings, particularly in Hong Kong, about Britain's ability to protect peoples in British territories in the Far East.[32]

In July Britain and the United States resorted to exchanges in a 'matey sort of way' on Far Eastern issues and, in particular, on Hong Kong.[33] These revealed similar views, except on the issue of trade with the communists: Britain was reluctant to restrict established commercial interests in China.[34] A Foreign Office memorandum on China, sent to the Americans, argued that the Chinese leaders were orthodox Marxist-Leninists. Their pro-Russian policy constituted a threat to Western interests in China and South-East Asia. The Foreign Office suggested that this could be lessened by convincing the Chinese communists that Western help was necessary to overcome economic difficulties, and also of 'the natural incompatibility of Soviet imperialism with

Chinese national interests'. Every opportunity should be taken to show that Moscow's designs were incompatible with a strong and independent China. And the longer British missionaries and merchants remained in China the more hope there was of maintaining British political and economic interests. It was too early to discuss the recognition question other than in general terms. There was the possibility, however, that the pattern of the relationship could develop in the same way as that with Yugoslavia. Western powers should, therefore, not prejudice future possibilities by developing, at the outset, an openly hostile attitude towards a communist regime. To withhold recognition from a government in effective control of a large part of China was legally objectionable, and could make the protection of Western interests difficult. It was unlikely that any conditions could be exacted from China in return for recognition, as the Chinese communists were unlikely to be inconvenienced by its being withheld. The communists would probably refuse to have diplomatic relations with any power recognizing the nationalists. Continued recognition of the nationalists should be considered on a basis of practical convenience rather than sentiment.[35] This memorandum reflected the argument of the British ambassador in China who insisted that early recognition of the Chinese communists would give Britain more advantages than it would the communists. Burgess was more circumspect: taken in isolation this might be so, but the attitude of the United States and other countries would have to be clearer before he were convinced.[36]

Bevin discussed the differences that emerged between British and American policy with the American ambassador in London, Lewis W. Douglas, towards the end of August. Most of these focused on the issue of trade. Bevin insisted that the British attitude was influenced by past history: it was felt that it had been a mistake to continue the recognition of the Manchu dynasty at the time of the Sun Yat-sen revolution in 1912. London also believed that the Chinese communists were 'first and foremost Chinese, and that they were not capable of becoming Russians overnight'. The State Department, however, was opposed to early recognition, and influenced by the worry that that could increase the communist representation on the Security Council. Bevin insisted that Britain wanted to stay where it was in China to avoid having to withdraw or being pushed out. It was prepared to breach the Nationalist Chinese blockade.[37] Britain, as Bevin told the Cabinet on 29 August, intended to stay in Hong Kong, and was anxious that public pronouncements did not exacerbate the Chinese communists.[38] It did seem to Stevenson that the American decision to reduce drastically the number of its nationals in China suggested the possibility that the United States intended to withhold recognition indefinitely, and to prevent, on strategic grounds, Formosa from falling to the communists.[39]

From Nanking Stevenson reinforced the Foreign Office position. Trade should determine British policy. That would bring Britain solid advantages, and enable non-communist influences to maintain a foothold. Britain owed nothing to the Kuomintang: the organization had been consistently hostile to Britain. Furthermore, support of it would not help stem the tide of communism in Asia. The recognition question should be decided on practical and not ideological grounds, and that decision should be taken without undue delay. Britain should not decide in advance that the new Chinese regime was going to be subservient to Moscow, and should employ its usual empirical methods to deal with it. The ambassador felt that Britain was just as anxious as the United States to stop the spread of communism in Asia, but the abandonment of Britain's great stake in China, and the adoption of a hostile attitude towards the new regime, would not help to attain that end. Britain should judge the new regime by what it did and not by what it said. In the end Britain could only hold Hong Kong with Chinese acquiescence: continued possession of Hong Kong had therefore to be as profitable for China as it was for Britain. Stevenson hoped that, despite American objections, Britain could pursue a policy in China that suited both its short- and long-term interests. He feared that American policy towards China could both prevent Britain from carrying out its own policy in that country and weaken its position, and that of Europe generally, in Asia.[40]

Official discussions took place between Britain and the United States in Washington. On 9 September Sir Esler Dening, the assistant under secretary in charge of the Far East, assured Butterworth that although there was internal pressure in Britain for early recognition of the communist Chinese, Bevin was not part of the group; British policy was that outlined in the memorandum of 15 August which the Cabinet had subsequently endorsed.[41] A few days later the Foreign Secretary himself was more explicit in talks with Acheson: Britain was in no hurry to recognize, but it had commercial and trading interests with China that the United States did not share. Bevin felt that if the West were too obdurate China could be driven to Russia; alternatively, with care, Russia's grip could be weakened. Acheson replied that the Americans doubted 'if recognition is a strong card in keeping China out of Russian hands and they will be there anyway'. There was agreement on the need for continued close consultation, but Bevin foresaw difficulties in that Britain and the United States would be following different courses.[42] As he said at a further meeting on 17 September, with French officials present, Britain was holding on as long as it could and the United States was withdrawing.[43] The State Department was left with the impression that Britain was less disposed to delay recognition than was the United States.[44] Burgess minuted that the emerging American policy of severing trading links and non-recognition had been irresponsibly adopted by the State Department 'for reasons of internal self defence and muddled thinking'.[45] Despite the agreement on close consultation, early in October, Britain in effect gave *de facto* recognition to the Chinese communists. Truman told Acheson that he thought that the British had not 'played very squarely' with the Americans over this.[46] Indeed Dening was lectured by Arthur R. Ringwalt, the First Secretary of the American embassy, that this incident was indicative of a 'distressing lack of coordination' on a working level between the British and American governments. Ringwalt hoped that they could do better in future. Dening had to plead that no 'skulduggery' had been intended, but that his overworked and undermanned staff had committed two stupid errors: the Far Eastern department had 'blundered outrageously' in not checking with its legal adviser whether the note sent to the Chinese communists about establishing 'informal relations' amounted to *de facto* recognition; and the text of this note to be conveyed to the Americans had been sent by airmail instead of being telegraphed. The Foreign Secretary admitted to Douglas that the delivery of the note was a violation of the Bevin-Acheson agreement on consultation.[47]

American anger over apparent 'deliberate' failures on the part of the Foreign Office[48] was misplaced: this was a genuine mistake. On 1 October Stevenson had suggested that a note be sent to the Chinese communists asking for informal relations between British consular officials, and the appropriate authorities in the territory under the control of the Central People's Government. This would be both convenient and promote trade between the two countries. On 3 October Strang discussed the matter with Attlee. The Prime Minister agreed. It was decided to inform the Commonwealth and other governments concerned.[49] Stevenson passed the note to the Chinese Ministry of Foreign Affairs, and the question arose as to whether this move should be publicized. Coates was worried about the reaction of unfriendly elements in the United States and elsewhere who would see this as evidence of a British desire to deal with the Chinese communists. But the debate was forestalled: to the consternation of Foreign Office officials the French reaction was that the British note amounted to *de facto* recognition. W. E. Beckett of the legal branch confirmed the French view: Britain had acknowledged that there was a Central People's Government, and that it had territory under its control. This was the same as saying that it was recognized as the *de facto* government of that territory. He suggested that the only excuse to offer the Americans was that Bevin, in making the agreement to consult, had understood that recognition was interpreted as 'recognition as the *de jure* government of China'. This was the explanation offered to the French.[50] Scarlett tried making the same excuse to the Americans, but Dening later complained 'with asperity' that if any British official in Washington or London had offered such an explanation, he had done so without authority.[51]

Towards the end of October a Cabinet paper, signed by Bevin, argued that since the British interest in China was much greater than that of other powers, Britain should not feel bound by their views on recognition. Agreement with Commonwealth countries was, however, desirable. In time friction could develop between the Russians and the Chinese; Britain could only take advantage of this if it had relations with Communist China. Furthermore, the policy of 'keeping a foot in the door' with trading interests could only work if full and early recognition were accorded. Britain, on political and practical grounds, should recognize the new regime. As resistance from the Nationalist government was hopeless, and its control of the mainland hardly more than nominal, the legal advisers considered *de jure* recognition legally justifiable. Bevin thought that opposition by the State Department to early recognition was influenced by attacks in Congress on its China policy. The publication of the White Paper on China had merely provided the critics with further ammunition. The State Department was more influenced by internal American politics than by the realities of the situation in China. The French High Commissioner in Indochina argued that *de jure* recognition would endanger Bao Dai's position. Accordingly, the French government was deferring *de jure* recognition.[52] The Cabinet decided to delay any firm decision on *de jure* recognition until

195

Commonwealth and other governments, including the United States, had been consulted, and until a meeting of British representatives at Bukit Serene, Johore Bahru, had considered the implications of recognition for British interests in the Far East. Asking Acheson for the State Department's observations, Bevin suggested that the advantage of the supporting vote of the Nationalist Chinese in the United Nations could hardly be maintained indefinitely. The Foreign Secretary admitted that it was not clear how long the Chinese communists would last, or the extent of the orthodoxy of their Marxist-Leninism. But for trading reasons and on political and practical grounds Britain favoured *de jure* recognition.[53] Probably as a result of the fracas over the unexpected *de facto* recognition, Bevin minuted that the Foreign Office should not do anything without his knowledge and approval about an American request for information about apparent British soundings of the Chinese communists.[54]

From New York the British delegate to the United Nations, Sir Alexander Cadogan, advised against recognition during that session of the General Assembly. Such a step could mean that the question of substituting the Chinese Communist government for the Chinese Nationalists on the Security Council would be raised. Bevin minuted on 5 November that recognition should be held up; he did not anticipate action while the assembly was sitting, or even before the meeting of Commonwealth Prime Ministers at Colombo in January 1950.[55]

The meeting of British representatives in the Far East, held at Bukit Serene between 2 and 4 November, reached a conclusion which Coates found 'most satisfactory'. The conference urged that from the point of view of the situation in South-East Asia and the Far East *de jure* recognition of the Chinese communists was 'desirable as early as possible and in any case by the end of the year'. No formal conditions should be attached to this recognition, although the British government should state that it assumed the acceptance by the communists of China's existing international obligations. Recognition should entail the strengthening rather than a weakening of resistance to the spread of communism in Asia. Every effort should also be made to minimize the adverse effects of any disagreement with the United States.[56] It was felt that the presence of Chinese communists in Malaya had to be approached realistically, and dealt with on an *ad hoc* basis. That could not justify delaying recognition. In Singapore it was thought that the dangers were outweighed by the advantages of recognition, and the effects in North Borneo and Sarawak would not be marked. In Indochina, however, Bao Dai would be discouraged. Siam would accept the move as an act of political realism. India, though seeing early recognition as necessary, wanted to safeguard the *status quo* in Tibet.[57] In August, however, the British Commissioner General in Asia, Malcolm MacDonald, had warned that Malaya, Singapore and the three territories in British Borneo had large local Chinese populations. Diplomatic recognition would give the Chinese communist authorities the right to appoint consular representatives in these five countries. These could stimulate anti-British Chinese nationalism amongst the local Chinese. The Governor of Singapore, Sir Franklin Gimson, was worried that if Britain recognized the Chinese communists, the Chinese in Singapore would think that the communists could not be such bad people after all.[58] At Bukit Serene these considerations were outweighed. The Americans were informed about the conclusions reached at Bukit Serene, but were assured that as certain Commonwealth and Western European countries had not replied to British inquiries about the recognition of Chinese communists, the British government had not reached a final decision.[59]

At this time the Americans were considering the significance of the possible development of 'great strains' between Peking and Moscow. A meeting between Acheson and the consultants on the Far East on 26 and 27 October recommended the pursuit of the aims of encouraging 'Chinese Communist deviation from the Moscow line'. But American recognition of the Chinese communists was not 'to be regarded as a major instrument for sowing our interest in the Chinese people or for winning concessions from the Communist regime'. The American attitude should 'not be an eager one, but should be realistic'.[60] The Office of Chinese Affairs, however, advised that hasty recognition by any Western power would have serious repercussions in South-East Asia: that could indicate a break in democratic ranks, and aid and comfort local communist movements. There was, however, the British position in Hong Kong. Should American pressure result in Britain's not recognizing the Chinese communists, complications over the colony could lead to a Chinese communist attack. In those circumstances the Joint Chiefs of Staff had concluded that the British military position in Hong Kong would be untenable, and recommended to the President that the United States should not provide any military support. A communist victory there would mean a serious loss of Western prestige in Asia.[61] An American official in China noted acidly that British feeling could

197

be tinged with pleasant irresponsibility, as the white man's burden fell on American shoulders, leaving Britain free to extract any political or economic profit from the situation.[62] In Japan, General Douglas MacArthur was hostile to any recognition being accorded to those 'barbarians'.[63]

Reaction from Commonwealth governments, and a meeting of High Commissioners in London, left Strang with the impression that there would be some difficulty if Britain announced recognition in advance of the Colombo meeting. General elections were in the offing in Australia and New Zealand, and so these countries wanted to postpone any decision. Canada had considerable interests in nationalist China, and did not want to differ from the United States on the recognition issue. The Netherlands wanted to delay recognition until Indonesian independence, not later than 30 December. Scarlett was not impressed with the French case that recognition would weaken the nationalist Chinese will to resist: there was no such will.[64] But the War Office thought that the most serious consequences of recognition were likely to be felt in Indochina. It would, as the French suggested, mean the collapse of the nationalist Chinese on the Indochina border. The Vietminh would be strengthened, and Bao Dai weakened. If the French were not able to prevent the spread of communism into Indochina, there would be a grave military threat posed to the British position in South-East Asia. On the other hand, recognition would reduce the threat to Hong Kong, and though in Malaya it might stimulate the bandits, the effects there could be minimized by judicious propaganda.[65] After the conference at Bukit Serene, Dening had further conversations in Canberra, New Delhi and Karachi. These led him to suggest that the Chinese communists should be recognized around 31 December. The Cabinet could take its decision around the middle of that month, after the Far Eastern Official Committee had finished its deliberations. India might be persuaded to delay recognition until then, and the Australian and New Zealand elections would be over. Bevin approved.[66]

In the Foreign Office, however, Sir Gladwyn Jebb still had to be convinced. He was puzzled: it did not appear to him that the situation in South-East Asia would benefit from early recognition. Dening explained that the arguments advanced at Bukit Serene about Malaya and Singapore, though not Hong Kong, were unexpected. Sixty per cent of the population of Singapore, and 40 per cent of that of Malaya, was Chinese. There were also 2 million Chinese in Hong Kong. These populations had strong national ties with China, and, elated by recent events, they thought that China had been placed 'on the map' once more. Their loyalties would be divided if Britain remained hostile to the Chinese communist government and refused to recognize it. They feared that Britain might prevent them from maintaining their ties with the motherland. Considerations such as these might make them less co-operative with the colonial governments, and so there was a need for early recognition. British officials thought that there would be no difficulty in reconciling in the local Chinese mind recognition of the Chinese communist government in China, and the suppression of communist terrorists in Malaya. Indeed, the pressure for recognition 'as early as possible' had come from the Governors of Singapore and Hong Kong and the High Commissioner for Malaya. Jebb remained querulous: in view of the French arguments about the position of Bao Dai recognition should be delayed until 15 January 1950. Dening had to explain that the French reasons were not considered valid and, against this, the morale of the British communities in China was low, and non-recognition was creating difficulties for Hong Kong. But Jebb still thought that recognition should be delayed until after 1 January 1950. Strang had to warn him to be careful: Bevin wanted to recognize a day or two earlier, and the views of the Brussels powers were not the most important aspect. Jebb agreed to fall into line. The legal department also saw complications in the Cabinet paper on recognition: Britain could not assume a neutral attitude to Chinese representation on the Security Council, and would have to adopt an attitude corresponding to the recognition it had given. Roger Allen suggested that Britain, if the question of Chinese representation were raised, should maintain that, as it had recognized the Chinese communists, their government should represent China in the United Nations. If this view was not accepted, then recognition of the communists as representatives of China should be accorded as soon as the majority of the members of the United Nations had individually recognized the Chinese communist government. This was agreed.[67]

The Americans continued to be against early recognition. Acheson hoped, at least, that the Commonwealth would not aim at concerted action on this, and that he be given advance notice to minimize possible Anglo-American misunderstanding.[68]

In the end the Foreign Office suggested 29 December as the date. That would not affect the transfer of power in Indonesia: it was close to the dates mentioned by India; it would not affect particularly the newly elected Australian and New Zealand governments; it gave other governments ample time to decide their own policy; and finally it would both obviate undue pressure from the Chinese communists, and meet the recommendations of the conference held at Bukit Serene.[69] On 15 December Bevin told the Cabinet that he had hoped to delay the decision until the matter had been discussed between the Commonwealth governments at Colombo. But India wanted to accord recognition before the end of the year, and so he felt it wise that Britain should also choose a date towards the end of the month.[70] The Foreign Secretary sent Acheson a personal message explaining that he anticipated 2 January 1950 as a possible date. Britain could not delay recognition any further as that could result in trouble in its Asian territories.[71] From Singapore, MacDonald urged that Siam should delay recognition: there was concern about the effect in Malaya of a Chinese communist consul near the border. But the Foreign Office felt that it would be inconsistent for Britain to take official action on this.[72] Bevin finally decided on 23 December to delay recognition until 6 January 1950. He was influenced more by the situation in Indochina than possible internal political repercussions in the United States.[73] He let Acheson know that Britain had done all it could to synchronize its policy with that of the United States, and assured him of Britain's agreement with his views about the need to stimulate the free peoples of Asia to resist the spread of communism.[74]

On 6 January 1950 Britain recognized the Central People's Government as the *de jure* government of China, and said that it was willing to enter into diplomatic relations. As the ambassador had been withdrawn, the former Ministerial Counsellor, J. C. Hutchinson, was nominated chargé d'affaires *ad interim*. The ambassador of Nationalist China in London was told on the evening of 5 January that Britain had withdrawn recognition from his government. The Central People's Government, on 9 January, indicated that it was prepared to establish diplomatic relations, and accepted Hutchinson as the representative to carry on negotiations on this question. This showed that the Chinese communists wanted to test Britain's friendship, and in effect to see whether Britain had severed relations with the nationalists.[75] Immediately after the recognition, the American administration went out of its way to be helpful. Indeed Sir Oliver Franks, the British ambassador in Washington, thought that, judging from the press, American recognition would follow in around three months. Then the communists seized American property in the Peking barracks incident. The reaction in the United States meant that domestic political considerations determined an important foreign policy decision. It seemed unlikely that the United States would return representatives to China until American public opinion had settled down, and that would not happen quickly. The ambassador thought that the State Department would not evolve a new policy towards China unless Britain suggested one. Strang, however, noted that although the recognition question 'had proceeded smoothly from the point of view of U.S. public opinion' there were serious Anglo-American difficulties over China in the offing. The United States was continuing to help the nationalists in Formosa. The nationalists were attacking British interests with bombs, and with a blockade which had American support and possibly encouragement.[76]

Recognition of the communists did not benefit Britain immediately. On 2 March 1950 the Chinese communists suggested that, before diplomatic relations could be established, Britain had first to sever intercourse with the Kuomintang. On 13 January Britain had abstained on a Russian resolution to unseat the nationalist representative to the Security Council, and had taken similar action over seating in other organizations of the United Nations. The communists took this to mean that Britain continued to recognize the legality of the nationalist delegates.[77] Indeed Kenneth G. Younger, the Minister of State, told the British Cabinet on 24 April 1950 that the Chinese communists continued to be unfriendly, and the prospects for British commercial interests were deteriorating. But there was no evidence that this was a consequence of recognition, and Bevin wanted the existing policy to continue. In forthcoming talks with the Secretary of State he hoped to stop Acheson from doing anything that might harm the Anglo-American aim of preventing the permanent alienation of China from the West. The Foreign Secretary wanted to persuade the United States to allow the Chinese communists to occupy the seat on the Security Council, even if they did not feel able to vote for such a change. Ministers felt, however, that the American government would find it difficult 'to go very far in this direction and that it would be inexpedient to press them to do so'. The administration would not be able to modify China policy ahead of American public opinion, and it would be unwise to risk antagonizing the United States merely for the prospect – never bright and then even less promising – of establishing friendly relations with the Chinese communists. The Cabinet finally agreed that British firms could not expect financial assistance to maintain their establishments in China, and that nothing should be done to risk alienating the United States.[78]

On 8 May, just before the meeting with Acheson in London, the Chinese communists complained again about Britain's position over voting in the United Nations, and obstruction in Hong Kong over the right claimed to 'Chinese' property there, including grounded aircraft.[79] Bevin, on 11 May, told Acheson that he thought the Chinese communists had a good case over the seating question: it was difficult for him to acknowledge that Chiang Kai-shek could claim to represent China in the United Nations. Acheson replied that that was a major question of foreign policy, and the United States had no intention of taking the positive action necessary to secure the requisite majority in the United Nations for this change.[80] Following the outbreak of the Korean conflict, the United States maintained that nothing could be done about Chinese representation at the United Nations until after the whole Korean situation had been cleared up. Then it would be treated on its merits. Younger advised Bevin that Britain, despite this, should continue its former policy of supporting the Peking candidature, but unless there was a chance of securing a majority vote, to abstain. The United States claimed that it did not want Russia to leave the United Nations. Younger thought such a move inevitable if Britain and other members followed the American lead. He feared that the United Nations could become merely an anti-communist alliance, with the Asian countries going to the communists. But it was over Formosa that American policy seemed most dangerous. At the end of June Truman sent the Seventh Fleet to neutralize the Formosa Straits. The Chinese communists claimed that this move was designed to prevent them from 'liberating' Formosa, and insisted that it constituted 'armed aggression against Chinese territory'. India, Burma and possibly other Asian states would refuse to support American policy there. That would transform the Far Eastern operations from a measure of collective security into 'an act of imperialism by white troops'.[81]

On 15 July 1950 Bevin accordingly informed the British representative in Peking that the United States could not submit to Russian blackmail in the form of extorting concessions either over Formosa, or over Chinese representation in the United Nations, as the price of halting the war in Korea. Indeed Acheson thought it unlikely that British and American policy on the seating of China could be harmonized. The United States had not recognized the Peking government because, first, Peking apparently did not want to establish normal relations with other countries. Secondly, Peking singled out American citizens and interests for specifically hostile treatment. Then Peking made no pretence of accepting or carrying out the international obligations of China, and it had also recognized Ho Chi Minh, and was actively interfering in Indochina. Peking was supporting communist insurgents in the Philippines, Malaya, Burma and elsewhere. It was also co-operating with a degree of Russian penetration of China which could 'only lead to de facto dismemberment in violation of the territorial integrity and political independence of the country'. The Chinese communists did not enjoy complete support in China or control over the country. Finally, Peking was openly defying the United Nations over Korea and mobilizing political support for the aggressors, and was apparently furnishing more help for aggression in Asia.

Bevin advised, however, that the British approach should ensure that Peking was not irrevocably alienated from the West. There was Anglo-American agreement on this. But the prevailing situation could push Communist China towards Russia. That affected Britain because of its position in Hong Kong and Malaya. The Chinese communists had reacted violently over the American declaration on Formosa that communist occupation of the island would be a direct threat to the security of the Pacific and the United States forces, but neither Communist China nor Russia had committed themselves over Korea, and Bevin doubted whether Peking wanted to become involved in that conflict, or to move further than Formosa.[82] British and American representatives meeting in Washington between 20 and 24 July discussed these issues, and a difference of emphasis emerged. Britain wanted to avoid any further major involvement of Western forces on the Asiatic mainland. It hoped conflicts could be localized to avoid general war, either with Russia or Communist China. Britain was particularly anxious that a 'possible gradual drift of the Chinese communist regime away from Moscow might not be interrupted', and thought Chinese communist intervention in Korea unlikely as Peking would not act at Russian direction without material advantage. The Americans argued that Peking was under strong Kremlin influence, and the Kremlin might wish Peking to fight the West. Chinese communist intervention in Korea was not unlikely. Britain underestimated the closeness of the Moscow–Peking axis.[83]

The Americans were particularly anxious to reach a common understanding with Britain over Formosa. At the end of July Acheson tried to convince Bevin that the action to neutralize Formosa had been taken to safeguard the strategically located island from communist occupation. By doing this the United Nations had not wanted to force an answer to the political questions connected with Formosa. It was hoped that the issues on which governments had divergent views could be frozen until the security situation was clarified. The State Department hoped for at least Anglo-American agreement on the immediate security and United Nations aspects without commitment to the long-range questions.[84] But Bevin, in deteriorating health and seemingly 'mentally quite sluggish', argued that Formosa could not be dissociated from the general question of Far Eastern policy.[85] The Cabinet, on 1 August, discussed the question of Chinese representation on the Security Council. On Attlee's suggestion the Cabinet decided that Britain should not agree to any deal by which a settlement of the Korean situation would be conditional on a change in China's representation on the council. The Prime Minister reminded the Cabinet of the danger of offending sections of American opinion. Already Britain had accepted positive sacrifices to align its policies with those of the United States in Korea: it had sent troops; and stopped British oil and other strategic exports to China. It would be unrealistic to alienate American opinion by registering an ineffective vote in favour of the representation of Peking. The Cabinet decided that if this question were raised in the Security Council the British representative should ask for an adjournment and ask for instructions as to how to cast his vote. The Foreign Secretary should decide this, but would probably find the Cabinet's guidance on the matter useful.[86]

At the end of August the Foreign Secretary outlined Britain's overall position in the Far East for the benefit of the Cabinet. It had been weakened as a result of the Second World War. The United States, on the other hand, having played the principal part in the defeat of Japan, was now in the predominant position. Britain's postwar policy in the area had been comparatively negative: this was both because of weakness and commitments elsewhere. But it did mean that Britain was 'less immediately involved in the debacle in China and Korea', and was thus freer than the United States to determine its policy for the future in the Far East. Since 1945 the United States had been a law unto itself in the Far East, with results which had been 'far from happy'. In China, Roosevelt's policy of cultivating friendship had failed because the United States had supported a regime which, through its failure to reform, had lost the confidence of the overwhelming majority of the Chinese people. But the American government, at the same time as denouncing its hostility to this regime in its White Paper, had proclaimed hostility to the communist government even before it had been established. Then the United States had continued to support Chiang Kai-shek. The Americans lacked all direction in their policy towards China. The Formosa situation showed that this was dangerous. Asian countries, though initially endorsing the American intervention in Korea, were wavering after the declaration on Formosa. They were worried about the possibility of a war between the Chinese communists and the United States. India, always suspicious of American 'imperialism', was worried that American action could endanger the friendly relations India wanted to establish with the Chinese communists. And India could influence Asian opinion. Unless the United States considered Asian opinion more, Asia could be alienated from the West, and that could benefit Russia. Unfortunately, American Far Eastern policy was bedevilled by internal politics: American elections were due in November and this complicated the situation at a time when China and Korea would be in the forefront of the United Nations discussions. American public opinion was highly emotional, likely to be irrational and unreasonable towards Britain where that country's policy diverged from the United States. The situation, however, was not completely hopeless. For the first time since 1945 the United States wanted to consult Britain on Far Eastern affairs.[87] When speaking to the Cabinet on this matter Bevin emphasized the need for a steadying influence on American public opinion to reduce the risk of a conflict between the United States and the Chinese communists over Formosa. Such a conflict could endanger the Commonwealth: the Chinese communities in Malaya and elsewhere in South-East Asia had been exhorted to regard themselves as Chinese citizens rather than as citizens of the countries in which they resided. Bevin opposed a prolonged American occupation of Formosa. In view of the Cairo declaration of 1943 that Formosa should be retroceded to China, independence for the island would not be practicable. The Foreign Secretary hoped for American agreement to a General Assembly resolution that Formosa should in time revert to China, but only after the pacification of the Pacific area, and in the meantime a commission should be established to recommend when, and under what conditions, this should take place. It was the view of the British Chiefs of Staff that the continued occupation of Formosa was not strategically as important as was assumed in certain quarters in the United States. The Cabinet recognized the political difficulties in the way of the Americans following the Foreign Secretary's suggestions, but still felt that the effort should be made, otherwise Britain would be in a difficult position if there were war between the Chinese communists and the United States. Indeed Bevin explained that he had already informed Acheson that if admission of the People's Government of China to either the General Assembly or the Security Council came up in a form not directly connected with the Korean conflict, Britain would support that admission. The Cabinet agreed that as Britain had recognized the People's Government of China it was not practicable to argue that the Chiang Kai-shek administration in Formosa should continue to represent China in the United Nations.[88]

But Bevin's hopes foundered. The Chinese communists entered the Korean conflict, and the American elections in November reflected the significance of the domestic factor. Dening told the American ambassador in New Delhi, Loy W. Henderson, that he feared these elections would mean that 'internal political exigencies would prevent the Americans from following a sensible course'. There was hysteria in the United States, and emotion rather than reason seemed to be dominating American foreign policy. Britain thought the United States 'had made a great error in not recognising communist China and favouring its admission into the United Nations'. Dening said that he had been assured in September by high American officials that, after the November elections, the United States would recognize the People's Government of China, and allow it to take over Formosa. In December the situation was changed.[89] Attlee, however, did claim that he managed to convince Truman and his advisers that a limited war against China was not a good idea; instead of drifting towards a world war the Western alliance should work for a cease-fire in Korea. Britain remained convinced that the People's Government of China was not a puppet of Moscow: if Peking was not forced into a closer alliance with Russia 'her deep-rooted xenophobia and consciousness of her ancient civilisation' would make her reluctant to accept Russian domination.[90]

Although the United States spent over $3·5 billion to sustain the Chinese nationalists, it was Britain that had the major Western economic interest in China. This economic interest, together with the position of Hong Kong and the attitude of some Common-wealth countries, led to the British recognition of Communist China. Officials anticipated that friction could develop between the

Russians and the Chinese, and that Britain should keep 'a foot in the door'. Some State Department experts agreed with this diagnosis but, in the end, American policy was determined by domestic political factors, particularly following the public outrage over the seizure of American property in the Peking barracks incident. For Britain, the importance of the Anglo–American special relationship was such that policy towards the Chinese communists had to take into account American sensibility. The Cold War had been joined. The United States was the only country that could hold the communist advance in Asia. The Anglo–American alliance in Europe could not be endangered by serious disagreement in the Far East.

Notes: Chapter 7

1 Public Record Office, London, FO 371/76386, E5573/3/500G, PUSC(51) Final Second Revise, Anglo–American relations, undated.
2 FO 371/75745, F4062/1015/10, Research Department memorandum on the essential orthodoxy of Chinese communism, 3 February 1949.
3 FO 371/75740, F2277/1015/10, Hood to Dening, 102/10/6/49, Secret, 10 February 1949; Minute by Scarlett, 15 February 1949.
4 FO 371/75746, F4396/1015/10, Record of meeting at Foreign Office between Baron Baeyens of France, Dening, and Scarlett, Secret, 4 March 1949.
5 FO 371/75754, F7101/1015/10, Minute by Burgess, 26 May 1949.
6 FO 371/75760, F8093/1015/10, Minute by Burgess, undated (June 1949).
7 FO 371/75761, F9742/1015/10, Minute by Burgess, 8 July 1949.
8 FO 371/75768, F13044/1015/10, Minute by P.D. Coates, 2 September 1949.
9 FO 371/75763, F10400/1015/10, Minute by Burgess, 19 July 1949.
10 FO 371/75771, F14604/1015/10, Minute by Burgess, 29 September 1949; see also B.E. Porter, *Britain and the Rise of Communist China; A Study of British Attitudes 1945-1954* (London, 1967), pp. 14-20; D.E.T. Luard, *Britain and China* (London, 1962), pp. 64-6.
11 *FRUS* 1949(9), pp. 2-5, Franks to Lovett, 5 January 1949.
12 FO 371/75810, F415/1023/10, Graves to Scarlett, Secret, 5 January 1949 received in registry 10 January 1949.
13 FO 371/75743, F3288/1015/10, Graves to Scarlett, G47/14/49, 25 February 1949.
14 FO 371/75742, F2891/1015/10, Foreign Office minute on situation in China: draft Cabinet paper prepared for Cabinet meeting on 3 March, 24 February 1949.
15 Public Record Office, London, CAB 128/15, fol. 65, CM18(49)2, Secret, 8 March, 1949.
16 FO 371/75810, F3305/1023/10, Foreign Office to Washington, Telegram no. 3068, Particular Secrecy, 18 March 1949.
17 FO 371/75810, F4314/1023/10, Minute by P.D. Coates, 25 March 1949.
18 FO 371/74746, F4229/1015/10, Franks to Bevin, Telegram no. 114, Secret, 18 March 1949; Minute by Coates, 26 March 1949.
19 FO 371/75749, F5523/1015/10, British Embassy to State Department, Memorandum on measures in defence of British economic interests in China, Secret, 5 April 1949.
20 FO 371/75747, F4595/1015/10, Franks to Bevin, G47/20/49, Secret, 22 March 1949 received 26 March 1949; Minute by Coates, 2 April 1949.

21 FO 371/75747, F4804/1015/10, Minute by Scarlett, 5 April 1949.
22 FO 371/75810, F5708/1023/10, Stevenson to Bevin, Telegram no. 467, Particular Secrecy, 22 April 1949 received 23 April 1949.
23 FRUS 1949(9), pp.14–32.
24 FRUS 1949(9), pp. 24–5, Stuart to Acheson, Telegram, 17 May 1949.
25 FO 371/75811, F6875/1023/10, United States Embassy to Foreign Office, Secret, 10 May 1949; Foreign Office to United States Embassy, Secret, 19 May 1949.
26 FO 371/75750, F6218/1015/10G, Aide mémoire summarising the views of the Minister of Defence, Chiefs of Staff, the Commander-in-Chief Far East Station on policy for Shanghai and Hong Kong, Secret, 25 April 1949.
27 CAB 128/15, fos 127–8, CM33(49)2, Secret, 9 May 1949.
28 CAB 128/15, fol. 148, CM38(49)3, Secret, 3 May 1949.
29 FO 371/75755, F7278/1015/10G, Note by Bevin on Hong Kong, 18 May 1949.
30 CAB 128/15, fol. 166, CM42(49)5, Secret, 23 June 1949.
31 FO 371/75760, F9104/1015/10, Stevenson to Bevin, Telegram no. 877, Secret, 22 June 1949; Minute by Burgess, 27 June 1949.
32 Australian Archives, Canberra, A1838, 494/30/3, JIC(FE) (49) 20(Final),The likely effects of the Amethyst incident, Secret, 5 May 1949; Australian High Commissioner's Office London to Department of External Affairs,Telegram no. 1833, Secret, 6 May 1949.
33 FRUS 1949(9), pp. 50–2, Acheson to Douglas, Telegram, 20 July 1949.
34 FRUS 1949(9), pp. 54–5, Douglas to Acheson, Telegram, 29 July 1949.
35 FRUS 1949(9), pp. 56–61, Douglas to Acheson, 17 August 1949 received 22 August 1949; Enclosure British Foreign Office memorandum on China, 15 August 1949.
36 FO 317/75764, F10919/1015/10, Stevenson to Bevin, Telegram no. 1070 Confidential, 20 July 1949; Minute by Burgess, 25 July 1949.
37 FO 371/75814, F12843/1023/10, Bevin to Franks, no. 1243, Secret, 26 August 1949; FRUS 1949(9), pp. 68–9, Douglas to Acheson, Telegram, 26 August 1949.
38 CAB 128/16, fol. 47, CM54/49/2, Secret, 29 August 1949.
39 FO 371/75814, F12884/1023/10G, Stevenson to Bevin, Telegram no. 1366, Particular Secrecy, 29 August 1949.
40 FO 371/75814, F13102/1023/10, Stevenson to Bevin, Telegram no. 1391, Particular Secrecy, 1 September, 1949.
41 FRUS 1949(9), pp. 76–8, Memorandum by Butterworth of conversation with British officials, 9 September 1949.
42 FRUS 1949(9), pp. 81–5, Memorandum of conversation by Acheson, 13 September 1949.
43 FRUS 1949(9), pp. 88–91, Memorandum of conversation by Acheson, 17 September 1949.
44 FRUS 1949(9), p. 91, Acting Secretary of State to Jarman, Telegram, 21 September 1949.
45 FO 371/75771, F14604/1015/10, Minute by Burgess, 29 September 1949.
46 FRUS 1949(9), p. 132, Memorandum by Acheson of conversation with Truman, 17 October 1949.
47 FRUS 1949(9), pp. 134–5, Douglas to Acheson,Telegram 18 October 1949; pp. 138–9, Memorandum of conversation by Ringwalt, 21 October 1949.
48 FRUS 1949(9), pp. 118–19, Holmes to Acheson, Telegram, 10 October 1949.
49 FO 371/75816, F14782/1023/10, Stevenson to Bevin, Telegram no. 1629, Immediate and Confidential, 1 October 1949; Strang to Scarlett, 3 October 1949.
50 FO 371/75816, F14878/1023/10, Foreign Office to British Representatives Abroad, Telegram no. 371, Confidential, 7 October 1949; Minutes by P.D. Coates, 5 October 1949; W. Strang, 6 October 1949; W.E. Beckett, 6 October

1949; Foreign Office to Paris, Telegram no. 2700, Immediate and Confidential, 10 October 1949.

51. *FRUS* 1949(9), pp. 118–19, Holmes to Acheson, 10 October 1949; pp. 138–9, Memorandum of conversation by Ringwalt, 21 October 1949.

52 CAB 129/37 Pt 2, fos 228–9, Memorandum by Bevin on the recognition of the Chinese communist government, Secret, 24 October 1949.

53 FO 371/75818, F16370/1023/10, Foreign Office to Washington, Telegram no. 10266, Particular Secrecy, 28 October 1949; *FRUS* 1949(9), pp. 151–4, British Embassy to Department of State, 1 November 1949.

54 FO 371/75818, F16417/1023/10, Franks to Bevin, Telegram no.5158, Particular Secrecy, 1 November 1949 received 2 November 1949.

55 FO 371/75819, F16531/1023/10, Cadogan to Bevin, Telegram no, 2423, Particular Secrecy, 2 November 1949 received 3 November 1949.

56 FO 371/75819, F16589/1023/10, MacDonald to Bevin, Telegram no. 919, Particular Secrecy, 4 November 1949; Minute by P.D. Coates, 8 November 1949.

57 FO 371/75819, F16590/1023/10, MacDonald to Bevin, Telegram no. 921, Particular Secrecy, 4 November 1949.

58 FO 371/75814, F13405/1023/10G, MacDonald to Strang, 19 August 1949; MacDonald to Strang, Secret, 22 August 1949 enclosing F. C. Gimson to MacDonald, Secret, 15 August 1949.

59 *FRUS* 1949(9), pp. 184–6, Memorandum of conversation by Sprouse, 8 November 1949.

60 *FRUS* 1949(9), pp. 160–2, Memorandum by Ogburn on decisions reached by consensus at the meetings with Acheson and the consultants on the Far East, 2 November 1949.

61 *FRUS* 1949(9), pp. 168–72, Memorandum by Perkins on recognition of the Chinese communist regime, 5 November 1949.

62 *FRUS* 1949(9), pp. 181–2, Bacon to Acheson, Telegram, 8 November 1949.

63 FO 371/75826, F18369/1023/10, Gascoigne to Scarlett, Secret and Personal, 26 November 1949 received 7 December 1949.

64 FO 371/75821, F17052/1023/10, Minute by Franklin, 16 November 1949; 75824/1023/10, East to Tomkins, 16 November 1949; Metcalf to Scarlett, 18 November 1949; F17999/1023/10G, Strang to Bevin, 24 November 1949; 75823, F17467/1023/10, Minutes by Franklin, 30 November 1949; Scarlett, 30 November 1949; *FRUS* 1949(9), p. 193, Douglas to Acheson,Telegram, 16 November 1949; pp. 200–1, British Embassy to Department of State, 28 November 1949.

65 FO 371/75825, F18073/1023/10, Lt Col. A.M. Field (MO2) to Scarlett, Top Secret, 18 November 1949.

66 FO 371/75824, F17999/1023/10G, Strang to Bevin, 25 November 1949; Minute by Bevin, 25 November 1949.

67 FO 371/75826, F18695/1023/10, Jebb to Dening, 3 December 1949; Dening to Jebb, 3 December 1949; Minutes by Jebb, 5 December 1949; Dening, 6 December 1949; Jebb, 8 (?) December 1949; Strang to Jebb, 6 December 1949; Minutes by Jebb, 7 December 1949; Beckett, 5 December 1949; Scarlett, 6 December 1949; Allen, 6 December 1949; Scarlett, 7 December 1949.

68 FO 371/75826, F18481/1023/10, Franks to Bevin, Telegram no. 5726, Particular Secrecy, 8 December received 9 December 1949; *FRUS* 1949(9), pp. 219–20, Memorandum of conversation by Acheson, 8 December 1949.

69 FO 371/75839, F19416/1023/10G, Dening to Bevin, 14 December 1949.

70 CAB 128/16, fol. 131, CM72(49)2, Secret, 15 December 1949.

71 FO 371/75828, F19057/1023/10, Bevin to Franks, Telegram no. 11571, Particular Secrecy, 16 December 1949.

72 FO 371/75827, F18766/1023/10, MacDonald to Bevin, Telegram no. 1082,

Particular Secrecy, 15 December 1949; Minute by Franklin, 17 December 1949; Bevin to Bangkok, Telegram no. 640, Particular Secrecy, 20 December 1949.

73 FO 371/75829, F19350/1023/10G, Minute by Scarlett, 22 December 1949; 75830, F19460/1023/10, Bevin to Attlee, 23 December 1949; Minute by K. M. Wilford noting Attlee's approval, 24 December 1949.
74 FRUS 1949(9),pp. 257–8, Holmes to Acheson, 30 December 1949.
75 FO 371/75827, F18896/1023/10, Research Department Memorandum on Sino-British exchanges on the question of establishing full diplomatic representation, Confidential, 18 June 1970.
76 FO 371/84528, FZ10345/3, Note of a discussion with Franks held in Strang's room on 8 February 1950.
77 FO 371/75827, F188896/1023/10, Research Department memorandum on Sino-British exchanges on the question of establishing full diplomatic representation, Confidential, 18 June 1970.
78 CAB 128/17, CM24(50)5, Secret, 24 April 1950.
79 FO 371/75827, F18896/1023/10, Research Department on Sino-British exchanges on the question of establishing full diplomatic representation, Confidential, 18 June 1970.
80 FRUS 1950(3), pp. 1033-44, The United States Delegation at the Tripartite Foreign Ministers Meeting to the Acting Secretary of State, Secret, 11 May 1950.
81 FO 371/84091, FK1022/215G, Younger to Bevin, Top Secret, 11 May 1950.
82 FO 371/84086, FK1022/111G, Bevin to Hutchinson Telegram no. 1027, Particular Secrecy, 15 July 1950 dispatched 16 July 1950.
83 FRUS 1950(3), pp. 1657-69, Jessup to Acheson, Top Secret, 25 July 1950.
84 FRUS 1950(6),pp. 396-8, Acheson to Douglas, Telegram, Top Secret, 28 July 1950.
85 FRUS 1950(6),pp. 398-9, Douglas to Acheson, Top Secret, 29 July 1950.
86 CAB 128/18, fol. 44, CM52(50)1, Secret, 1 August 1950.
87 CAB 129/39, fos 242-3, Memorandum by Bevin on the international situation in Asia in the light of the Korean conflict, Secret, 30 August 1950.
88 CAB 128/18, fol. 167, CM85(50)3, Secret, 12 December 1950.
89 FRUS 1950(6),pp. 613-16, Henderson to Weil, Secret and Personal, 30 December 1950.
90 CAB 128/18, fol. 167, CM85(50)3, 12 December 1950.

8

Korea and the Pacific

With the signing of the North Atlantic Treaty the United States was committed to the defence of Western Europe. Some, however, thought that there was a distinction between being committed to defend Western Europe, and being part of the defence of Western Europe. In 1948 the British Chiefs of Staff, remembering Mons and Dunkirk, had reservations about Britain's being part of the defence of Western Europe. On 23 March 1950, however, they told the Defence Committee that they wanted a promise that Britain would send a corps of two infantry divisions to the European continent if there were a war with Russia. Emmanuel Shinwell, the Minister of Defence, argued that the Russians had to be held as far east as was possible. The French army had to be revived to do this. The sending of two divisions, as Sir William Slim, the Chief of the Imperial General Staff, pointed out, would not make much practical difference. It was, however, the 'firm intention' of the American Joint Chiefs of Staff to send limited land formations to 'reinforce any line in west or south-west Europe that showed a reasonable prospect of holding'. The French had to hold that line. The British divisions would not arrive until about three months after the war had started, and then only if the line was still holding. But it was thought that the promise would encourage the French, and the Defence Committee agreed to send two infantry divisions in case of war. The Americans, in any case, had to persuade Congress to vote money for the rearming of the European allies. With this in mind Britain had to increase its defence expenditure considerably, and make this known. Shinwell felt that if the Americans doubted Britain's sincerity the alliance's integrated defence scheme could fail.[1] For Britain, the American attitude was crucial. The previous three years had seen the American commitment to Europe, an acknowledgement of the need to uphold Britain's position in the Middle East and, with Truman's acceptance of NSC 48/2, a decision to stop the communist advance in South-East Asia. British policy over the recognition of Communist China had had to allow for American sensibilities as in this area domestic considerations could determine crucial foreign policy decisions. London and Washington differed increasingly on the question of whether Peking could be divorced from Moscow. The test of the American commitment to a global strategy designed to stop the communist advance came on 27 June when troops from North Korea invaded South Korea.

The Foreign Office did not expect the invasion. The cry of 'wolf wolf' had been heard too frequently in Korea; it had 'lost its power to impress UK ears'. The failure of the Supreme Commander for the Allied Powers in Japan to obtain advance information on the troop concentrations on the 38th parallel suggested a deficiency in American intelligence. The Far Eastern department was pleased with the American decision to take a firm stand: it felt that action might stop the gradual crumbling away of the Western position vis-à-vis the communists. Initially the Chiefs of Staff did not think that there would be major hostilities, but that view did not take into account all the international implications of the Korean affair.[2]

Though it might have been felt that Russia was the instigator, care was taken in the United States, Britain and Australia to avoid any public statement charging Russia with this. It was hoped that this would localize the fighting, and make it easier for Russia to stop without losing international prestige. New Zealand was apprised of the policy after a naval officer had made jocular references to 'Uncle Joe' when sending off frigates bound for the Far East.[3]

The British Cabinet, on 27 June, showed concern over a proposed American reference to 'centrally-directed Communist imperialism'. Discussion suggested that it had not been proved that the North Koreans were acting under Moscow's instructions. If the attack were considered an act of aggression committed by North Koreans on their own initiative, Russia would withdraw, without loss of prestige, any support it might have given the North Koreans. By linking Korea with other communist threats in Asia, the Americans could present a major challenge to Russia. An American reference to Formosa might also embarrass Britain in its relations with Communist China and provoke an attack on Hong Kong. But then it was argued that the Americans were doubtless influenced by the events preceding the Second World War, and that it would be easier to make a stand 'in the earlier, rather than the later, stages of imperialist expansion by a totalitarian State'.[4] Indeed Foreign Office opinion compared the American resolution to Britain's actions in Greece and Berlin. Washington accepted London's modifications.[5]

The naval support given immediately by Britain for the Korean operation was seen by the Foreign Office as a useful demonstration of Britain's 'capacity to act as a world power with the support of the Commonwealth, and of its quickness to move when action rather than words are necessary'.[6]

From Washington the British ambassador, Sir Oliver Franks, pointed to the 'steady and unquestioning assumption' that Britain was 'the only dependable ally and partner'.[7] In Korea the American government and people had 'instinctively followed their high destiny in the world'. That was 'a very great thing for all of us'. But Americans felt lonely: Britain should offer to send land forces to reassure them. The Chiefs of Staff did not want to do this,[8] and the Defence Committee was worried lest the Korean conflict diverted attention from other danger-spots in Asia, and blinded Britain to the risks to which it was exposed in Europe.[9] But by the end of July the need for Anglo-American solidarity outweighed the military disadvantages, and the Cabinet agreed to the formation of a brigade group to operate in Korea under American command.[10] In the Foreign Office Pierson Dixon had had reservations: there was the 'nasty possibility' that the Americans might contemplate using atomic weapons, and he urged that Britain should obtain an assurance that these would not be used without prior consultation.[11] Bevin was also worried that China might be irrevocably alienated from the West, and pushed in the direction of Russia.[12] The Minister of State, Kenneth Younger, however, warned that American policy was 'most dangerous' over the neutralization of the Straits of Formosa. As military minds seemed to have the upper hand in the United States it was important to use military arguments, and to stress that India, Burma and possibly other Asian states would refuse to support American policy there, and the 'effect of this on Asian minds would be to transform the Far Eastern operation from a measure of collective security into an act of imperialism by white troops'. This would assist the communist forces in South-East Asia.[13] But, as Attlee explained to the Cabinet on 1 August, Britain had to accept positive sacrifices to align its policy with that of the United States: British oil and strategic exports were being denied to Communist China, and it might be unrealistic to alienate the Americans over the issue of the seating of Peking at the United Nations.[14]

British troops went to Korea. Bevin was worried that the American troops there were inadequately trained. These had to face well-trained and well-equipped forces 'of a type which the communists appear to be able to organise in Asia'. That had consequences for Britain's own military position.[15] Australia also contributed to to the United Nations force,[16] but Canberra's motive was just as much to preserve the good opinion of its emerging American ally as anything else. Australia realized that it depended on the American navy in the Pacific for its security. Despite the hopes expressed in 1949 that it would fight in Europe rather than the Pacific, New Zealand sent troops as well. And so did South Africa. On 20 July the Prime Minister, Dr D. F. Malan, announced that it was 'impracticable and unrealistic' for South Africa to send military aid to Korea. But on 3 August the Cabinet decided to send a fighter squadron of the South African Permanent Force to the Far East. The Australian High Commissioner observed: 'The tortuous manoevrings of the Government Press in its attempts to explain South Africa is not really helping the UN but is taking its stand on the side of the UK, bears witness to the discomfort which the whole incident has caused the Government.' South Africa's 'yearning for isolation' had to be offset against the anti-communist agitation of the previous two years, during which 'one Nationalist after another has called the heavens to witness the party's determination to fight Communism'. The High Commissioner thought the decision 'at least consistent with the Nationalist Party's hysterical attitude to Communism'.[17]

The measures Britain took during the first six weeks of the Korean crisis, in the view of Franks, prevented a crisis in the Anglo-American relationship. The ambassador pointed to the dichotomy between the American view of the Britain it had helped during the previous five years and the Britain it had known in the world wars. With the aggression in Korea, American opinion swung back from its postwar views about the economic weakness of Britain and the efforts that Britain was making to recover, to the older view of a Britain from which more should be expected and demanded. British troops in Korea prevented this split mind from fomenting trouble. On the administrative level, however, the Americans were showing that they thought that 'the effectiveness of the Anglo-American partnership' was reviving. They had agreed to general conversations between General Omar Bradley and Lord Tedder. They also wanted informal conversations with Britain to guide the more general discussions within the NATO framework.[18]

At the time of the initial military successes of the United Nations forces in Korea, Bevin presented to the Cabinet an evaluation of long-term policy for Asia. Since 1945 Britain had encouraged the legitimate aspirations of the peoples of South and South-East Asia for independence. Even the Netherlands had finally been wise enough to recognize Indonesia as a sovereign state, a country in which British efforts had been directed towards the attainment of nationalist aims by legitimate means and non-violence. In Indochina Britain had recognized Vietnam, Laos and Cambodia as associated states of the French Union, and tried to persuade France to allow them more independence. This support of nationalism provided the best possible counter to communist subversion and penetration. There was a strong fund of goodwill towards Britain in this area. In the Far East, however, the Second World War had weakened Britain's position and given predominance to the United States. Britain had tried to re-establish its commercial position in China and Japan, and through the Far Eastern Commission to influence the post-surrender policies for Japan. Korea, however, had been a matter for the United States and Russia; Britain had only a 'watching brief'. Until 1949 the United States had regarded South and South-East Asia as a British interest, but the communist threat had resulted in American economic and military aid to certain countries. The United States still expected Britain to take the lead, however, and showed 'a welcome disposition to consult' before taking action. But in the Far East the Americans had been 'a law unto themselves', and with far from happy results. Bevin even thought that had South Korea fallen like the satellites in Eastern Europe the Americans would have accepted the *fait accompli*. Having supported a regime in China that had lost the support of its peoples, American policy there now lacked 'all direction'. The same was true of Japan, and consultation with other powers was non-existent, even though the United States was not entitled to settle the Japanese problem on its own. The treatment of Japan would determine whether an Asian country of more than 80 million Asians was 'with us or against us'. The declaration on Formosa had led to a feeling in Asia that the Americans were trying to determine the future of that continent to the detriment of its peoples. Bevin suggested that there was a distinct possibility that unless American policy towards China, Japan and Korea took more account of Asian susceptibilities, Asia would be gradually alienated from the West to the benefit of Russia. Unfortunately American Far Eastern policy was bedevilled by internal politics. Congressional elections were due in November. Debates in the United Nations over China and Korea, and the clash between Truman and the field commander in Korea, General Douglas MacArthur, over the latter's support of Chiang Kai-shek were likely to increase party political tension. American political opinion was in a highly emotional state, partly attributable to the Korean conflict, partly to the sense of frustration

215

that in fighting the North Koreans, Americans were not coming to grips with the real enemy. The American public was likely to be irrational in its outlook, and unreasonable towards Britain where its policy diverged from that of the United States. With the elections impending, Britain could not expect the American administration to pursue policies that could lead to its downfall,[19] and so the American administration should never appear to have given way to British pressure. Bevin hoped to secure American support for the adoption by the General Assembly of a resolution that Formosa would revert to China. He had told Acheson that if the issue of the admission of the People's Government of China to the United Nations arose in a form not connected with Korea, Britain would be bound to support its admission.[20] It was difficult, however, to be optimistic about the future of Korea. The domination of the whole Korean peninsula had been an objective of Russian policy since tsarist days. Russia would therefore oppose the establishment of a democratic and independent government of a unified Korea. But the United Nations could not abandon that declared objective. Bevin suggested that as soon as the military situation allowed, the General Assembly should pass a resolution for the holding of elections in Korea on a national basis with a view to establishing a unified, independent and democratic Korean government.[21]

Indeed, for London, from the beginning of September the original intention of the Korean operation began to change from merely repelling the 'aggressor' north of the 38th parallel, to the original United Nations objective of establishing a unified and democratic Korea. On 6 September Air Vice-Marshal C. A. Bouchier reported the 'feeling' that with the defeat of the North Korean army the United Nations forces would cross the 38th parallel; this was necessary to stop Communist Chinese and Russian troops advancing from Manchuria unopposed to the 38th parallel and restoring the stalemate. With all Korea occupied, Bouchier anticipated a general election, and a government representative of Korea as a whole.[22] Following MacArthur's victories Attlee, on 21 September, informed Bevin, then in New York, that he favoured a declaration from the United Nations that it would take responsibility for the rehabilitation of the whole country. The Prime Minister felt the Chinese would not be sorry if Russian influence were eliminated from Korea.[23] The Chiefs of Staff, however, warned against any lasting British military responsibility in Korea, and suggested that forces sent north of the 38th parallel should be kept to a minimum.[24] Bevin agreed with Attlee about the need to forestall the Russians, and took the initiative in drafting a resolution for the General Assembly authorizing the crossing of the 38th parallel with a view to establishing a unified, independent and democratic government of all Korea.[25] The Americans revealed in conversation with the British that they appreciated that a certain amount of risk was unavoidable in crossing the 38th parallel, but the dangers had to be accepted, and there was no evidence of any move by Chinese or Russian forces.[26] Attlee told the Cabinet on 26 September about these developments and secured approval for the policy of a united Korea, though it was emphasized that British commitments in Malaya and elsewhere should prevent it from playing a substantial part in a prolonged pacification.[27] He also agreed to Bevin's suggestion of trying to get Nehru to allay Communist Chinese suspicions that the crossing of the parallel might be a challenge to their security.[28]

As it was evident that the Americans had given little thought to its specific terms, the drafting was left to British who incorporated amendments suggested by the Americans, and then sent the document to nine allies. The United States preferred not to be a co-sponsor.[29] Bevin wanted Australia to be one of the sponsoring states.[30] Australia knew from its embassy in Moscow the opinion of the Indian ambassador, Kavalam Madhava Pannikar, that a crossing by the United Nations forces of the 38th parallel would almost certainly lead to direct Chinese intervention. Pannikar wanted the forces to halt when the parallel was reached, a truce declared and a United Nations commission of the big five – including Communist China and not Nationalist China – and several middle powers of Asia appointed to ensure free elections for all Korea.[31] When Esler Dening discussed the matter with Keith Officer of the Australian delegation to the United Nations, Dening said that Pannikar was apt to exaggerate, but there were usually grounds for his reports and this one had to be treated 'with some seriousness'. The Americans were in a hurry for a resolution: the campaign was going fast and they were worried about a possibly embarrassing Russian manoeuvre in the committee. According to Dening the Americans did not want to provoke Russia or China, and did not want to send American troops north of the 38th parallel but to leave it to the South Koreans. They did not want to move north of the 40th parallel so as to avoid any risk of coming up to the frontier. American escort teams, however, would have to accompany the South Koreans. The phrasing of the proposed resolution which read 'Appropriate steps to ensure peace and stability throughout...' had been drawn up by the British law officer and he was rather 'wedded' to it.[32]

On 28 September the British Cabinet was informed of a report from the Indian ambassador in Peking that the Communist Chinese government had become more hostile to the United States because of the American attitude to Chinese complaints about alleged bombing of places in Manchuria, to Chinese representation in the United Nations and that Chinese intervention in Korea could not be excluded. The Cabinet, however, agreed that British policy would stand, though the Americans should be pressed to improve relationships with the Communist Chinese.[33] Sir Alvary Gascoigne reported from Tokyo on 3 October that MacArthur remained unimpressed by threats from Chou En-lai: he had adequate troops to deal with the Chinese and even the Russians. MacArthur went on to divulge his military plans, and said that if the Chinese came in he would immediately unleash his air force against towns in Manchuria and north China including Peking.[34]

The British Chiefs of Staff became disturbed at the implications of further fighting in Korea, and possible extensions beyond that country. On 6 October the immediate objectives of Foreign Office policy became first to restrain Peking, and then to localize the fighting. London did not want the heavy responsibility of pressing the Americans to abandon any operations contemplated north of the parallel, but felt justified in pressing the need to confine fighting to Korea itself, and to see that there was as wide a gap as possible between the General Assembly resolution and such operations. The Chiefs of Staff feared that direct action against the Chinese, for example in Manchuria, would lead to general hostilities between Communist China and the United States. The Americans would then be involved in an indefinite conflict which would drain the strength of the Western powers, and reduce their ability to deal with crises elsewhere. There was also the danger of a split in the United Nations between the Asiatic and European countries. Britain wanted an assurance that MacArthur should need 'express sanction' to attack targets outside Korea.[35] The Americans gave a satisfactory reply,[36] and the General Assembly passed the resolution endorsing the crossing of the 38th parallel and the objective of a united Korea by a massive majority. Bevin told the Cabinet on 9 October that there was 'insufficient foundation' for the apprehension that China and Russia might be provoked into active intervention. United Nations forces had not yet crossed the parallel in strength.[37]

Just over a week later Bevin gave a survey of British foreign policy to the Commonwealth High Commissioners in London. The Foreign Secretary said that he did not take seriously the Chinese threat about crossing the 38th parallel: had China really intended to take that action it would have given notice of it. Britain, however, could not treat the Korean crisis in isolation. Britain's main concern was possible Russian moves in Europe. The American administration seemed willing enough to bolster European defences. By the middle of October Washington had taken the decision to increase its troops in Europe in peacetime. At the NATO council meetings it seemed evident that the Americans, like the British after March 1950, were prepared to commit troops of a sort to Europe in war. During the previous year American thinking about Western defence had advanced considerably. As Bevin said, the Americans could perhaps be regarded not so much as 'aiding the defence of Europe as becoming part of it'. But there was the difficulty of Congress and money. Europe had to show that it would play its part. When in the United States in August, Bevin had told the Americans that Britain was increasing the period of national service from eighteen months to two years. The Foreign Secretary had insisted that 'Great Britain was not a part of Europe; she was not simply a Luxembourg'. Britain was undertaking a huge defence programme over the following three years and orders were already being placed for the first £100 million. The programme depended on American assistance. Bevin, however, said that there was a wider consideration:

> The people in this country were pinning their faith on a policy of defence built on a Commonwealth-U.S.A. basis – an English-speaking basis. People here were frankly doubtful of Europe. How could he go down to his constituency – Woolwich – which had been bombed by Germans in the war, and tell his constituents that the Germans would help them in a war against Russia? Londoners would not rely on the Germans; if the Germans come in to help, so much the better. But reliance must be placed on America and the Commonwealth. Similarly in regard to France, the man in the street, coming back from a holiday there, was almost invariably struck by the defeatist attitude of the French.[38]

Bevin distrusted the Europeans. He did not want Britain as part of Europe. As Foreign Secretary he consistently resisted pressure from the Americans for Britain to take part in European integration. France, in particular, gave trouble over European defence. When asked by Bevin whether he believed in the reality of the Russian threat and the danger of war, the French socialist Guy

Mollet replied 'No'. Bevin decided that Mollet was no friend of Britain, and that Bevin would have nothing more to do with him.[39]

In the middle of October Bevin told the Commonwealth High Commissioners that the only means of meeting the challenge thrown out by the Russians was to build up sufficient power to check them. Negotiations could only have a satisfactory settlement from a basis of power. The danger of a third world war had receded. The West had been threatened with *faits accomplis* not only in Korea, but also in Vietnam and Iran. The policy followed in Korea had produced the right result, and should have a useful deterrent effect on Russian ambitions at other points. There remained the question of Germany and the setting up of a European defence force. The American view was that past conflicts should be forgotten, and that Germany should be allowed to make its full share in providing an integrated force. Of course the French objected. Britain's continued commitments for defence expenditure, however, amounted to over £36,000 million.[40]

At the end of October Britain advised its consuls in China, purely as a precautionary measure, that in the event of conclusive evidence of organized Chinese armed intervention in North Korea, they should advise all non-essential British nationals to leave.[41] By 4 November British officials thought the presence of Chinese fighting men in North Korea, and the physical contact of Chinese soldiers with United Nations forces, 'beyond doubt'.[42] The British wanted to avoid a major conflict in the Far East.[43] Bevin considered the situation 'ugly', especially as the Republican victories in the congressional elections could harden the attitude of the American government.[44] The Chiefs of Staff advised that the objective of placing the whole of Korea under a United Nations regime was no longer practicable without the risk of a major war. Korea was of no strategic importance to the democratic powers, and further operations there should be conducted to prevent an extension of the conflict and to avoid any major commitment in the area[45] On the recommendations of the Chief of Staff Britain did make recommendations for the establishment of a demilitarized area, but these came to nothing.[46] When it was evident that the Communist Chinese had mounted a major offensive Attlee and Bevin became worried that the war in Korea might draw military resources away from Europe and the Middle East, and provide 'opportunities for those who were anxious to make trouble in Austria and Berlin'. Public opinion in Britain was 'distrustful of General MacArthur's intentions'. But it was pointed out in the Cabinet that MacArthur's great credit had not necessarily been dissipated by the recent setbacks, and governments could not intervene in the day-to-day conduct of military operations. It might be suggested in Parliament that the United States was handling the Korean operation as though it were an American rather than a United Nations matter. The Cabinet was told, however, that this was not the case: the United States had consulted Britain on issues of major policy, and as it was the United States that was providing the greater part of the forces in Korea, Britain could not expect any larger voice in the conduct of the military operation. It was also unreasonable to blame the United States for the situation that had arisen in Korea. Britain had fully supported the crossing of the 38th parallel, despite Indian warnings that it would provoke Chinese intervention. Both Washington and London had taken the risk of Chinese intervention. Furthermore, a strong divergence of policy between Britain and the United States in the Far East would involve a risk of losing American support in Europe. The ultimate threat to Britain's security came from Russia, and, the Cabinet was told, Britain could not afford to break the united front with the Americans against the main potential enemy.

Washington wanted to brand Communist China as an aggressor in the United Nations. It was argued that British policy should continue to be based on the principle that it had no hostile intentions against China. But if Britain withdrew its support from American strategy in the Far East, Washington could be less willing to defend Western Europe, and Britain would then have little chance of withstanding a Russian aggression there. London would be playing into Moscow's hands if it allowed the events in Korea to be a cause of ill-feeling between Britain and the United States; Britain had to be prepared, if necessary, to accept American leadership in the Far East.[47] While Europe remained exposed to grave dangers, Bevin doubted whether Britain would be justified in undertaking any further commitments in the Far East.[48] On 30 November there was grave public anxiety in Britain over Truman's confused statements on the possible use of nuclear weapons in Korea. The same day Attlee told the Cabinet that the consequences of a possible war with Communist China had to be faced, and he proposed to consult Truman directly.[49] Attlee and Bevin met their French counterparts on 2 December. Attlee mentioned the strong feeling in Britain that atomic weapons could not be regarded on a level with other weapons. Their use would bring about a new era in warfare the consequences of which no one could appreciate. The question could not be decided on purely military grounds: 'Short-sighted decisions designed to meet an immediate situation might be fatal, and the matter must be decided at the highest political level and not by one Power alone.' The European countries would get the retaliation. Bevin pointed out that during the Berlin blockade the atomic question had been handled with great skill: then the Russians had really believed that had they had gone too far they could be attacked. It was unfortunate that Truman's press statement had resulted in such a revulsion in allied public feeling that the President had had to retract it, 'and thus weakened the deterrent effect of our possession of the atomic weapon'. Public opinion could recognize the occasions on which atomic weapons might be justified: a conflict in which a power like the United States confronted North Korea was not one. Attlee was worried that it was in Russia's interests to get the Western powers heavily committed in Asia, and to encourage disagreements between European countries. The United States should be satisfied that there were no serious disagreements between its European allies. He thought that the appointment of a Supreme Commander-in-Chief in the West would have a good effect.[50]

Attlee flew to Washington, and the Foreign Secretary sent him a personal message urging a general settlement with Communist China, while the United Nations forces could still create difficulties for the Chinese in Korea. Bevin envisaged the settlement acknowledging China's position as a great power in the Far East; American agreement to considering recognizing the Central People's Government and to stand by the Cairo and Potsdam declarations to return Formosa to China; agreement on a cease-fire in Korea leading to the restoration of the *status quo* before 25 June with the 38th parallel as the dividing line between the Chinese and United Nations forces. He acknowledged the political difficulties this would create for the American government, but felt this was the only policy open to it 'in the interest of us all'.[51] Attlee found the Americans inclining to the belief that Communist Chinese policy was dictated by Moscow. Washington was considering a limited war against China through an economic blockade. Attlee felt that he had aroused doubts about this proposal by pointing to the possible consequences for South-East Asia, and emphasizing that China's 'deep-rooted xenophobia' would make it reluctant to accept Russian domination. Truman agreed that the primary aim should be to secure a cease-fire in Korea. On the issue of MacArthur, Attlee put forward the view of the Foreign Office and British military intelligence that he was an able commander, but stressed the need to distinguish between politico-military decisions on which it was necessary to consult the United Nations, and the purely military questions which could be left to the commander. Truman reassured Attlee about the 'atomic bomb': the President regarded it as the joint possession of Britain, the United States and Canada. Except for an extreme emergency, such as an atomic attack on the United States, he would consult the other countries before using the bomb.[52]

On the question of Nationalist China, Formosa, however, the two leaders diverged. Before the recent developments in Korea, the American Joint Chiefs of Staff had agreed with their British counterparts that while the island would be of no great intrinsic value to the Western powers in a general war, it should be denied, if possible, to a potential enemy. But when the possibility of a limited war with China, including naval blockade, economic sanctions and the encouragement of subversive activity on the mainland was raised, the American military authorities assessed Formosa as being of major significance as a base in the more restricted context. Britain had strongly opposed the concept of limited war which received its most intensive consideration by the Americans at the time when it looked as if the whole of Korea might have to be abandoned. Britain felt that its experience of naval blockades had shown that they were difficult to enforce, and led to quarrels with other countries not involved. Furthermore, a limited war might not remain limited. And Russia could fight. It was the view of the Foreign Office that the essential precondition for negotiations was representation of Communist China in the United Nations, irrespective of whether that country was recognized by the United States. Bevin, however, argued that the admission of Communist China should be treated on its merits, and not as the price of any gesture on the part of the Peking authorities. The Foreign Office was just concerned to get the Chinese in. It took the line that if the Chinese wanted to 'make mischief', nothing could stop them. But if they wanted a settlement there was a chance that the Communist Chinese would move off at a tangent from the Russians. The Russians did not seem to want a settlement. While it would be going too far to speak of driving a wedge between China and Russia, it was worth exploiting the differences. If Communist China's neutrality could be achieved in a general war, that would release large allied forces for other theatres and could even lessen China's pressure southwards.[53] A Foreign Office study of the vulnerability of China suggested that it was a country hard to hit effectively. This exercise supported the conviction that apart from slipping into a general war with Communist China, the American idea of limited war was not a practical proposition.[54]

Peking, on 22 December, rejected cease-fire proposals and demanded a settlement on its terms. Bevin thought that everything possible should be done to avoid a war with China. But China might want to force the issue, and extend hostilities elsewhere in Asia. If this were the case no amount of concessions would deter the Chinese. The only real deterrent would be effective and complete solidarity of free nations in the face of aggression. Bevin, however, thought that it was still an open question whether the Chinese, and their Russian backers, were prepared to 'push matters to the point where war might become inevitable'. He doubted whether the Chinese wanted to precipitate matters immediately, though they could be prepared, if their own terms were not accepted, to try to drive the United Nations forces out of Korea. The allied aim should be to pursue a course of 'realism, patience and maximum solidarity' in dealings with the Peking government. 'We should on the one hand continue to lose no opportunity to impress on them that we are prepared to reach a settlement of the outstanding issues by peaceful means and on the other that we are in no circumstances prepared to make concessions when faced with aggression or threat of aggression.' Bevin hoped that the meeting of Commonwealth Prime Ministers in London in January would consider this.[55] Bevin told the Commonwealth delegates on 5 January that he did not think of China as a satellite of Russia in the same sense as, for example, Poland or Hungary. But he thought that Russia and China were acting in partnership, and he was impressed by the joint strength of China's manpower and Russia's industrial potential. In the Far East the idea was to use Chinese manpower to contain large numbers of the troops of the democracies, and in Europe to neutralize Germany and then to frustrate the plan of the democracies for the defence of Western Europe. Western Europe could not be satisfactorily defended without fighting on German soil.[56]

During the Commonwealth Prime Ministers' Conference Bevin had to counter a challenge – one which in the end even Attlee put to him – to the corner-stone of his foreign policy: the Anglo-American alliance. A memorandum was circulated by John Strachey, a Marxist ideologue and hater of the United States, but a former Labour Cabinet minister, to Younger, Shinwell and Gaitskell and possibly others. Strachey argued that the United States had started to pursue policies both in Asia and Europe which threatened to involve Britain in an early and general war. The Chiefs of Staff had been authorized to work on the hypothesis that war was 'possible in 1951 and probable in 1952'. Strachey argued that general war either in 1951 or 1952 would be fatal for Britain. Rearmament could not alter that fundamental situation. For the United States, on the other hand, all that was at stake was a loss of prestige weighed against the risk of an immediate war which it believed it could survive and would ultimately win. It might soon be necessary, for example, to make a public avowal of an independent British policy in Asia. Bevin could not understand what was being done that justified that sort of memorandum. In the Foreign Office Dixon commented that the danger of a Russian attack would be great if Britain, the United States and the Commonwealth were seriously divided. 'The worst condition of all would be an Anglo-American quarrel, followed by America pursuing a policy of war against China by herself, + leaving us + the Europeans without American help.' Dixon thought that some might advocate a policy of neutrality: 'a compounding with the S.U.'. That surely was unthinkable. Britain had no choice in the long run but to rely on the friendship and support of the United States. It could not press its views on the Far East to the point where it might be abandoned by the United States. Roger Makins agreed: Strachey's paper was highly selective and did not present a balanced picture. Strang thought that Britain should try to deter the Americans from dangerous courses 'without provoking a public row or a break in our relations of confidence'. That might be difficult to do, but that was what Foreign Offices and Foreign Ministers were for. Attlee saw Bevin on 10 January. The Prime Minister had been talking to a number of military and other personalities, including Lord Mountbatten, who were alarmed over the American attitude towards world affairs, and thought that the Americans would drag Britain into war. It had been put to the Prime Minister that if the Americans turned over a great part of their industrial capacity to war production it would be difficult for them to change over to civilian production without causing economic chaos. There would be a strong temptation for the United States to resort to a preventive war. The Americans had announced that they were to spend enormous sums on tanks, aeroplanes, air raid precautions and so on, and it was suggested that this could be interpreted as meaning that they intended to fight China or Russia or both. Bevin's reaction was that it was to Britain's advantage that the United States should be strong, and he did not think that their great production effort would necessarily lead to war. The United States could be prevented from taking any rash action if 'handled wisely'.[57]

Bevin instructed Strang to draft a minute for the Prime Minister. The Foreign Secretary sent it under his signature on 12 January.

Attlee saw and noted the contents. Bevin said that it was not, he thought, 'in the character of the American people to provoke a war, or to commit an act of aggression, nor does their constitution lend itself to action of this nature'. He could not accept the 'economic chaos' argument. The American economy had shown considerable flexibility. There was a risk, particularly in the Far East, that the United States might drift into hostilities. That could be mitigated by wise diplomacy. Britain was in a dangerous situation and risks had to be taken:

> There is no ground for changing the view which we formed after long deliberation that neither the Commonwealth alone, nor Western Europe alone, nor even the Commonwealth plus Western Europe (if such a coalition could ever be held together) were strong enough, either economically or militarily, to hold our own against the forces actively opposing them. The full participation of the United States is essential to sustain the free world which Soviet Russia is trying to undermine.

It was therefore the least of all risks that the United States should be strong, resolute and actively co-operating with the other 'free nations'. That offered the best chance of avoiding a war. There was a risk, that could not be underrated, that if the United States met with strong opposition from its associates, especially on a matter over which the Americans felt that there was a moral issue involved such as condoning aggression, the United States would become disillusioned with collective security and the United Nations, and 'retire into a kind of armed isolation'. Bevin thought the effects would be disastrous for Britain. What would it be like to live in a world with a hostile communist bloc, an uncooperative United States, a Commonwealth pulled in two directions and a disillusioned Europe deprived of the support of American troops and involvement in European defence? Britain was faced with a problem which tested its diplomacy and statesmanship. It had to build up the strength of the free world, morally, economically and militarily with the United States, and at the same time 'exert sufficient control over the policy of the well-intentioned but inexperienced colossus on whose co-operation our safety depends'. This was particularly difficult in the Far East where, at the outbreak of the Korean conflict, Britain and the United States had agreed to differ in their policies. Policy was hard to align in a period of emotional tension. That could only be done by influencing the American government and people, not by opposing or destroying them.[58]

But as Herbert Morrison, the Lord President, told the Cabinet on 15 January 1951, the British public remained apprehensive that another world war could be precipitated by the provocative policies of the American government. He insisted, however, that Britain had to accelerate its defence preparations, even at the cost of social policies, not because of the situation in the Far East, but owing to the Russian threat to Britain's 'more vital interests' in Europe.[59] London was in a delicate position. As Bevin warned the Cabinet three days later, American public opinion was in a crucial mood, and nothing should be said which could jeopardize the retention of the full military support of the United States for the defence of Western Europe.[60]

Washington wanted to brand Communist China as an aggressor in the United Nations. Bevin and the Commonwealth Prime Ministers advocated caution and restraint: widespread sanctions against Communist China would increase the risk of general war in the Far East.[61] The Americans modified their original proposal, and although the British Cabinet remained unhappy, it was argued that Britain could not disassociate itself from the older members of the Commonwealth, and from the United States and France. In particular there could be lasting damage to Anglo-American relations, and thus a major success for Russian diplomacy.[62] At that particular meeting of the Cabinet on 25 January Younger, without any Foreign Office officials present, argued against voting in favour of the resolution in the United Nations. Bevin was seriously ill and not present. The majority agreed. Only Hector McNeil opposed this challenge to the foundation of British foreign policy. Gaitskell suggested that Britain should abstain. The Cabinet decided to vote against. Gaitskell was unhappy and wanted to tell Bevin, but the Foreign Secretary was 'incoherent'. On 26 January Gaitskell saw Christopher Addison, the Leader of the House of Lords. Gaitskell argued that the Cabinet decision would have fatal consequences for Anglo-American relations and would strengthen the anti-European bloc in the United States. The United States might abandon Europe, and that would be the end for Britain. It would be dangerous to vote against all the 'white' Dominions. In any case the Americans seemed to be giving way on some of the clauses. When Gaitskell saw Strang, Younger and Attlee later that day they all agreed that the American concessions had created a new situation. The Cabinet would have to meet immediately. Gaitskell made Strang explain the actual situation to Attlee, and pointed out that the situation was rather different from the account Younger had given to the Cabinet the previous day. Afterwards Gaitskell and Attlee discussed the matter on their own. The Prime Minister was

227

worried that so many senior ministers had wanted to oppose the Americans. Attlee appeared to sympathize with them. He argued with Gaitskell about the Americans. At the Cabinet meeting on 26 January, however, Attlee was firm and overruled the opposition from the anti-Americans: Dalton, Aneurin Bevan, Chuter Ede and Jim Griffiths. If the Americans agreed to the amendments Britain would vote in favour of the United Nations resolution; if not, it would be left to Attlee to decide.[63] Through 'patience and firmness' Britain secured further American concessions, and voted for the resolution.[64]

Britain retreated from the lead it had taken to secure a united Korea. The Chiefs of Staff argued that it was necessary to hold a position up to the 38th parallel, and suggested a military line along the southern waist roughly following that parallel. Franks was told to put this to the State Department, and to argue that every effort should be made to bring the Chinese to negotiations: Asian and Arab susceptibilities should not be offended; furthermore, a drive into North Korea, however successful, would not destroy the enemy. Younger suggested to the Cabinet that there should be a halt at the 38th parallel to stop the spread of hostilities, and to encourage the Chinese to negotiate. Dean Rusk said that the Americans were not prepared to build up their forces to the extent necessary to expel the Chinese communists from Korea. MacArthur had no directive to cross the 38th parallel, and the United States would consult interested governments before issuing such a directive. But the United States could not contemplate a situation in which the communists could build up their strength beyond the 38th parallel as they had done previously, and it was impossible to rule out all action beyond the parallel. The Americans were interested in a genuine cease-fire, and not one that came about through unilateral action.[65]

MacArthur, however, defied the American constitution and against the background of a favourable public opinion in the United States, made unauthorized statements which implied the extension of the war to mainland China. The civilian control of the military, a basic principle of the American way of life, seemed to be at stake. The British Cabinet was concerned about the general's view that the Korean campaign was one to free Asia.[66] They told the Americans again that they did not want United Nations forces north of the 38th parallel. The British Chiefs of Staff thought that there should be no major offensive across the 38th parallel, and no attempt to occupy large areas north of it. Not only would an offensive lessen the chance of negotiations with the Chinese, but it would be militarily unsound. The Chinese line of communications would be shortened, and their length was one of the main factors in the allies' favour. There could be a repetition of what had happened when the United Nations forces had crossed the parallel six months previously.[67]

Truman dismissed MacArthur. The President could not allow his authority to be challenged. Allied concern was only one factor. Rusk told Franks that MacArthur's statement of 24 March had not been authorized. No one in Washington had known that it was going to be made. The American government was in 'grave difficulty': on the one hand MacArthur's statement was at variance with the government's policy, while on the other hand the political situation in the United States was such that the administration could not explicitly disown him. Franks understood this. Washington needed time.[68] Truman handled the situation astutely. MacArthur did not die, he simply faded away like an old soldier.

After Truman's dismissal of MacArthur, Herbert Morrison, who had succeeded Bevin as Foreign Secretary, approached the Americans about an initiative for a political settlement in Korea: there should be a fresh declaration of policy from the governments whose forces were fighting under United Nations command, combined with specific proposals for a settlement, followed by approaches to Peking and Moscow.[69] In May London agreed with Washington, in principle, that there should be retaliatory bombing if there were a major enemy air attack in Korea. London did ask for American consultation before such attacks took place, and before actual directions were issued. Arrangements were made to deal with such a request as 'a matter of the greatest urgency'. There would be no time to consult with the 'white' Commonwealth, but Britain undertook to inform those governments of its decision at the same time as it replied to the United States.[70]

London and Washington did disagree on the matter of sanctions against China. But this was 'a difference of views', and was a matter of 'timing and not substance'. Britain opposed political sanctions against China, but did its best to ensure that those economic sanctions that were feasible were imposed. In May 1951 Britain felt that no goods that could assist the Chinese war effort in Korea were getting through, with the exception of rubber from Malaya and Singapore. That needed the co-operation of other producers and purchasers. But Britain did ask the colonial governments to see that no further rubber was exported to China in 1951. The matter of Hong Kong, however, was difficult. In the wrong hands, that colony with its fine harbour could be a menace to the South China

Seas. Hong Kong could not be cut off from China without creating internal problems. With unemployment, starvation and unrest, communism would flourish in that colony. Britain tried, unobtrusively, to see that exports from Hong Kong did not contribute to the Chinese war effort. In May Britain was prepared for a resolution to go from the Additional Measures Committee of the United Nations to the General Assembly recommending the imposition of a selective embargo on the supply of war materials to China.[71]

In June Britain responded to overtures from Yakov A. Malik, the Russian representative at the United Nations, for a cease-fire and withdrawal of forces from the 38th parallel.[72] Gladwyn Jebb argued that the Malik offer was more than just propaganda. He thought that the Russians had deliberately left out the Chinese and the usual conditions for settlement in the hope of reaching general agreement on a cease-fire. Then the Russians might suggest that the Chinese be brought in as a principal party. Jebb argued that articles in the *Peking Daily* showed that the Chinese were working with the Russians on this.[73] The British Cabinet, in September, considered the possibility of future moves in Korea if the truce talks failed. It accepted the argument of the Chiefs of Staff that no major advance beyond the existing line was desirable. Besides the possible political considerations such an advance could destroy the tactical advantage in the air that the United Nations forces enjoyed.[74] The Foreign Office, in October 1951, outlined British policy in Korea as being an armistice settlement on the existing military dispositions. The final line would be a matter for political negotiations at a later stage.[75]

Outside the Korean conflict, the year 1951 marked a significant British retreat from Asia. This was evidenced both with the formation of the ANZUS military pact, and the signing of the Japanese peace treaty. It meant that British responsibility for containing the communist advance in Asia was limited to specific areas, and was in accord with the reality of Britain's declining resources outlined by the Permanent Under Secretary's Committee in 1949. Part of the problem was to reconcile a Japanese peace treaty which would allow Japan to become a prosperous nation again, and eventually a first-class power outside the communist camp, with the requirements of Australia and New Zealand for assurances of protection against a resurgence of Japanese aggression.

Lord Killearn, the Special Commissioner in South-East Asia, 1946–8, had suggested some form of regional organization between the Pacific countries. After the signing of the Atlantic Pact in April

1949 President Quirino of the Philippines spoke of the need to establish a Pacific Pact. The Nationalist Chinese and South Koreans supported this idea, but the United States and other Pacific countries were not prepared to undertake military commitments to support Chiang Kai-shek or Syngman Rhee. General recommendations for a regional Pacific organization were made at the Baguio Conference organized by General Romulo of the Philippines. The Korean conflict gave fresh impetus to the idea. At the end of June 1950 the State Department let Canberra know that some regional agreement, or even prior consultation between Australia and the United States, might have been helpful in meeting the sudden crisis. Instead, the United States had had to act on its own, and hope for subsequent support from other countries.[76] In September 1949 Frederick Shedden, the Secretary of the Australian Department of Defence, had warned that Britain's attitude to Australia's planning made the Americans in the Pacific of supreme importance to Australia's future defence. While pressing on with strategic planning with Britain and New Zealand, it was imperative to establish a close link with the United States, even if it fell short of American co-operation in a regional arrangement.[77] The Pacific division of the Department of External Affairs suggested in October 1950 that the envisaged bilateral defence pact between the United States and Japan, under the Japanese peace settlement, could be balanced by a pact signed by the United States, Australia, Britain, New Zealand and the Philippines.[78] Shedden told the British Chiefs of Staff on 31 January 1951 that there were domestic political problems in Australia that could affect the defence programme: the Senate had not, as then, passed the National Service Bill; there were problems combating communism, and expanding Australia's industrial potential; public opinion was particularly sensitive about the deteriorating situation in South-East Asia. The development of closer co-operation on an official level with American planning could provide a reassurance to the Australian people that they could make a contribution to the defence of the Middle East without risk to their own local defence.[79]

Truman's ambassador, John Foster Dulles, initially suggested in January 1951 a Pacific Defence Council of an offshore chain of islands including Australia, New Zealand, Indonesia, the Philippines and the United States. Britain was to be excluded. British participation would mean that France, the Netherlands and Portugal would have to be invited as well, and that would give the impression of the council as a bulwark of colonialism. This proposal was rejected by the British Chiefs of Staff: it could be interpreted as

231

a renunciation of British responsibilities; the exclusion of the Asian mainland countries would encourage communist aggression in South-East Asia; Australia and New Zealand could be diverted from vital theatres in war. Canberra and Wellington were advised that this 'white man's pact' would endanger efforts to secure co-operation from India, Pakistan and Ceylon.[80]

In February the Americans said they would prefer a tripartite pact by which the United States, Australia and New Zealand would each undertake to go to the aid of the other in the event of hostilities affecting the interests of any one of them in the Pacific. The First Sea Lord, Lord Fraser of North Cape, supported this proposal: in the discussions on global strategy between the British and American Chiefs of Staff it had been decided that the Far East was an American responsibility, and the Middle East a Commonwealth one. Australia and New Zealand had been reluctant to commit themselves fully to co-operation in the Middle East until they had more definite information about intentions in the Pacific. A tripartite pact like this might allay their anxieties.[81] Indeed the British Chiefs of Staff found this new proposal acceptable: an American guarantee of Australian and New Zealand security was an undoubted strategic advantage and could be the only way Australia and New Zealand could be persuaded to agree to a measure of Japanese rearmament which the Chiefs of Staff considered desirable. They admitted that Britain had major strategic interests in the area, but thought in war the British view could be represented by Australia and New Zealand. Provided it were not extended to other countries like the Philippines, Britain did not need to be a party to the treaty. Attlee put the case that Britain's exclusion might appear to diminish its stature as a world power, but against this Congress might reject the treaty if Britain were a party, and it was in line with the evolution of the modern Commonwealth that individual Commonwealth countries should take the lead on behalf of the whole Commonwealth in areas where they themselves were especially concerned. Britain had acknow-ledged that Australia was in the lead over the occupation of Japan, and it would be appropriate to accept Australian and New Zealand leadership in the Pacific, and to expect them to represent British interests.[82] On 1 March the Prime Minister told the Cabinet that the Australian Prime Minister was anxious for British support and the advantages of concluding the treaty outweighed the political disadvantage of Britain's exclusion. The Cabinet, however, was divided.[83] Attlee chaired a special meeting of the ministers concerned. The Secretary of State for Commonwealth Relations,

Patrick Gordon Walker, warned that any attempt to dissuade Australia and New Zealand would fail. Some ministers were worried that Australia and New Zealand had made no definite commitment to contribute to the defence of the Middle East in war, and Australia could limit its liabilities to the Pacific. The treaty would also upset India, Pakistan and Ceylon. But Attlee's arguments were persuasive, and the Cabinet decided that it was not practicable for Britain to oppose the treaty, or to claim to be associated with it. Even so the Minister of Defence, Emmanuel Shinwell, and Viscount Alexander were worried that it could be represented as implying that Britain had repudiated its interests in the Pacific area.[84]

In Australia, Shedden hoped to establish, on the official as well as on the political level, the same close relationship with the American defence authorities as Australia enjoyed with the British military.[85] He appreciated that there could be 'a delicate problem of balance between the UK and the US in regard to pressure that will be applied from both quarters in respect of commitments which we will be asked to undertake'.[86] Sir Percy Spender, who had been involved in the Australian negotiations for the Tripartite Security Treaty, ANZUS, and had then gone to Washington as Australian ambassador, wrote to the Australian Prime Minister, Menzies, after its signature, that it had been 'amazingly well received here'. Spender thought that Australia was, in many ways, able to exercise influence upon the Americans 'while other nations fail to do so'. He gave a state banquet to celebrate the signing of the pact, and the British ambassador, Oliver Franks, attended. At the banquet Spender made appropriate remarks about the special ties which bound Australia to the Crown, and the support which Britain had given to the treaty. The following day Franks called on Spender to thank him, and to say that 'he thought a very good thing had been done in the interests of Commonwealth unity'.[87]

At this time Britain was negotiating with the United States about the conclusion of the Japanese peace treaty. In December 1948 Sir Alvary Gascoigne, the head of the British mission in Tokyo, reported to Bevin that in general the Japanese mentality had not changed fundamentally since 1941. The impact of democracy upon the Japanese mind had been 'almost nil'. Great play was, of course, made by the Japanese of going through the 'forms' of democratic practice, 'because they know that during the occupation they can but obey the dictates of the Supreme Commander, and that the more they please him (and through him the US), the greater will be the bounties which will flow from Washington'. Gascoigne thought that it would be folly to expect a nation 'fundamentally and permanently' to accept democracy overnight, especially a democracy which had been imposed upon it by the victors during a period of occupation. General Douglas MacArthur, the Supreme Commander Allied Powers, Japan, however, thought that the Japanese would act after the peace in the manner which would 'benefit them best regardless of ethics or morals'. He told Gascoigne that the Japanese would elect to follow the course that he had chartered for them: democracy. MacArthur did not say 'Western democracy'. The supreme commander considered the Japanese fundamentally conservative in outlook: they would lean much more heavily towards 'the Anglo-Saxon way of life' than towards that of Russia. Most Japanese were genuine admirers of the United States and Britain – in that order. They hated Russia, not only because Russia was Japan's traditional enemy, but because the ethics of communism were repugnant to them. They loathed the 'cruelty, the selfishness and the meanness of the Soviet system'. Japan would depend for its livelihood not on Russia, but on the United States and the other Anglo-Saxon countries. Gascoigne observed:

> Such is General MacArthur's fervent belief in the lasting effects of his admittedly great work (the drawing up of a democratic 'Blue Print' for Japan), that it would perhaps be too much to expect him to take a sceptical view of the future of this country immediately after peace. I do not agree with him ... but I can understand the spirit which emanates his work – it is that of a 'crusader' – and this naturally influences his thoughts on the final outcome.

The head of the British mission felt that the distant future of Japan would depend not wholly upon the reaction of the Japanese themselves but upon all 'manner of extraneous events which will take place in the "two worlds" which have been formed since the close of the recent war'.[88]

Between the end of 1947 and the middle of 1950 the Americans showed little inclination to be involved in a Japanese peace settlement. The Korean conflict changed that. At a meeting in May 1950, in London, the Commonwealth nations recognized that a treaty would have to provide both for Japanese security against communist aggression, and the security of the democratic countries against the resurgence of a militaristic Japan.[89] When the United Nations forces in Korea suffered reverses, Gascoigne argued that MacArthur used assiduous propaganda to ensure that most

Japanese felt that these were due to the overwhelmingly numerically superior Chinese. Gascoigne felt that the corollary of this was, in Japanese minds, that American equipment had to be combined with Japanese manpower if Korea and the Far East were to be secured. This stirred sections of Japanese opinion in favour of immediate rearmament. The American military reverses had also given the Japanese the feeling that they were more on a basis of equality with the Americans. The peace treaty and the issue of rearmament, the Japanese felt, should be decided on their terms.[90]

At the Commonwealth Prime Ministers' Conference in London in January 1951 Bevin emphasized Britain's wish to conclude a peace treaty with Japan. It would be difficult if treaties with Japan and Germany had to be negotiated at the same time. The Resident Minister in London for Australia, E. J. Harrison, did not like this. Australia feared the military resurgence of Japan in the same way and for the same reasons as France feared the military resurgence of Germany. Australia doubted whether Japan would be a reliable ally.[91] Many Australians probably shared Spender's attitude to the Japanese. After all, their relatives had suffered in what Australians considered barbarous Japanese prisoner of war camps. Not only should the Japanese be kept weak so they could not attack Australia, but Australia should remain 'white'. There should be no Japanese immigration into their country. In San Francisco in September, at the time of discussions leading to the conclusion of the Japanese peace treaty, Spender invited the pressmen to have a few drinks with him at his residence. Spender then heard that there was a squad of Japanese correspondents who planned to come. It 'was a little bit more than I could stomach to have my good whiskey consumed by them', so he let it be known that the invitation was to the local and Australian press only. He saw the Japanese pressmen at the Australian consulate the following day. They asked him what observations he had as to how the Japanese population problem could be solved. Spender replied that he had 'none'. Another was whether there was any likelihood of immigration restrictions being lifted to allow Japanese into Australia. The Japanese were told: 'none whatsoever'.[92]

London did not like the American draft of a Japanese peace treaty made in March 1951. Morrison told the Cabinet that he felt that Communist China should be a party to the treaty, and that Japan should cede Formosa to 'China' without prejudicing what Chinese authority was entitled to exercise sovereignty there.[93] The Foreign Secretary argued that the accession of Japan to the cause of democracy would be of great value, and could best be secured by the conclusion of the treaty on fairly liberal lines. An unfriendly Japan, allied to Russia, would 'constitute a grave peril to our interests in the Far East and to the peace of the world'. [94] The Chiefs of Staff wanted some Japanese rearmament so that Japan could help to stop communist encroachment in the Far East, but Australia urged adequate safeguards against the resurgence of Japanese military power.[95] Talks with American officials in Washington between 25 April and 4 May convinced the Americans that, on this issue, it was possible for their two countries to work together as a team.[96] Younger handled the detailed discussions, but Dulles also saw Attlee and Morrison in London. The Foreign Secretary reported to the Cabinet on 7 June that Dulles was adopting a 'reasonable attitude', and if the United States went ahead without Britain, British prestige in the Far East would be damaged. [97] Dulles would not agree to the participation of Communist China because of fears of Congress. Some members of the Cabinet were worried that the United States could force Japan to recognize the Nationalist government of China. But it was argued that a Japan under American tutelage was preferable to one under Russian influence.[98] Dulles agreed not to insist on Nationalist Chinese participation, a decision, given the state of American politics, Morrison described as 'courageous'.[99] Indeed the agreed draft treaty contained substantial American concessions to the British point of view: roughly half was contributed by Britain. Comparing this with the previous attitude of MacArthur, Morrison observed that Britain's being able to frame the peace settlement 'on terms of friendly equality with the United States must be regarded as a very favourable development both in Anglo-American relations and as regards our whole position in the Far East and the Pacific'. This was possible largely because of the 'constructive and open minded attitude of Mr Dulles himself and in particular to his realisation of the importance of our connections with the Commonwealth'. Britain had made concessions but this was 'in view of the broader benefits to be secured from full Anglo-American agreement on Treaty problems'.[100]

Dulles told Canberra, in June, that the Australians would have to take the United States 'on trust' over the scale of Japanese rearmament, but Australia need 'have no fears'.[101] At the beginning of August the Australian Defence Committee, though it had misgivings about the absence in the proposed treaty of any limitation on Japanese rearmament, felt it had to endorse the conclusions of the Joint Planning Committee that there was no alternative but to agree to the draft. The Americans had to be taken 'on trust'.[102]

At the end of September 1951 Morrison reported that the conference at San Francisco for the signature of the peace treaty with Japan had proceeded very satisfactorily. He had even managed to impress on the Japanese Premier that he should not be hasty about treaty negotiations with either Chinese government.[103]

With the American reaction to the invasion of South Korea the *pax Britannica*, as Franks implied in a despatch from Washington, was effectively replaced by the *pax Americana*. This happened at a time when the issue of German rearmament was being discussed, and there was opposition from sections of the British Cabinet to the proposed 'European Army' which the Cabinet agreed to support in principle on 4 September 1951. The British economy also improved, if only temporarily, to the extent that it did not need to be bolstered by Marshall Aid.[104] Having obtained the American commitment to Europe, and an awareness of the dangers of Russian expansion in the Middle East, Britain was, initially, without American support when it was drawn into the Cold War in Asia through the Malayan insurgency in 1948. But despite the experience in China, and a consequent reluctance to become involved in Asia, the United States by the end of 1949 was taking over Britain's responsibilities in the area. It was a considerable achievement on the part of Bevin, and his Foreign Office officials, to help secure the American commitment to stop communist expansion in Asia outlined in NSC 48/2. In effect the United States once again was helping to pull British and French 'chestnuts out of the fire'. The British assessment was that nothing could be done in Asia without American participation. Though there were disagreements between the two countries, what differences in policy emerged were largely dictated by a consideration of American public opinion and Congress. Both Bevin and Morrison realized this limitation on the administration, and made allowances. Perhaps what was remarkable was the degree of unanimity evidenced by the governments of the two countries on how to manage the Cold War in Asia. This was largely due to the astute diplomacy of Bevin and his officials. That diplomacy helped to overcome both the considerable left-wing opposition to the American alliance in the Cabinet, and also to moderate American policy. Bevin and his officials perceived the Anglo-American special relationship as being of immeasurable significance. They also understood the importance of co-operation with the 'old' members of the Commonwealth. In Asia, Australia and New Zealand played their part. In the view of the Labour government their signing of the tripartite pact, ANZUS, with the United States was in line with the evolution of the modern

Commonwealth that individual Commonwealth countries should take the lead on behalf of the whole Commonwealth in areas where they themselves were especially concerned.

Notes: Chapter 8

1   Barker, *The British between the Superpowers*, pp. 196–7.
2   Australian Archives, Canberra, A1838/T184, 3123/5 Pt 1, J. P. Quinn to Secretary Department of External Affairs, no. 568, Secret, 28 June 1950.
3   A1838/T184, 3123/7/3, Department of External Affairs to Australian High Commissioner Wellington, Telegram no. 159, Secret, 4 July 1950; 5123/5 Pt 2, Department of External Affairs to Shaw, 13 July 1950.
4   Public Record Office, London, CAB 128/17, fol. 129, CM39(50)4, Secret, 27 June 1950.
5   Public Record Office, London, FO 371/84081, FK1022/36, R. E. Barclay to Younger, 28 June 1950.
6   FO 371/81655, AU1075/1, Foreign Office to Washington, Telegram no. 2980, Confidential, 30 June 1950.
7   FO 371/84091, FK1022/222G, Franks to Foreign Office, Telegram no. 2036, Particular Secrecy, July 1950.
8   CAB 128/18, fol. 6, CM42(50)3, Secret, 4 July 1950.
9   CAB 128/18, fol. 10, CM43(50)2, Secret, 6 July 1950.
10 CAB 128/18, fol. 37, CM50(50)3, Secret, 25 July 1950.
11 FO 371/84091, FK1022/208G, Minute by Dixon, Top Secret, 1 July 1950.
12 FO 371/84086, FK1022/111G, Bevin to Peking, Telegram no. 1027, Particular Secrecy, 15 July 1950.
13 FO 371/84091, FK1022/215G, Younger to Bevin, Top Secret, 11 July 1950.
14 CAB 128/18, fol. 44, CM52(50)2, Secret, 1 August 1950.
15 Public Record Office, London, FO 800/517, fol. 95, US/50/24, Bevin to Attlee, Secret, undated.
16 R. O'Neill, *Australia in the Korean War 1950–1953*, Vol. 1, *Strategy and Diplomacy* (Canberra, 1981), pp. 77–95.
17 A1838/T184, 3123/5 Pt 4, Office of the Australian High Commission in Pretoria to Secretary of External Affairs, no. 200, 9 August 1950.
18 FO 800/517, fos 106–9, US/50/33, Franks to Bevin, Telegram no 2233, Particular Secrecy, 16 August 1950.
19 Public Record Office, London, CAB 129/39, fos 242–3, CP(50)193, Memorandum by Bevin on Korea, Secret, 31 August 1950.
20 CAB 128/17, fos 58–60, CM55(50)3–7, Secret, 4 September 1950.
21 CAB 129/39, fos 219–20, CP(50)103, Memorandum by Bevin on Korea, Secret, 31 August 1950.
22 FO 371/84096, FK1022/318/G, Bouchier to Chiefs of Staff, 6 September 1950.
23 FO 371/84097, FK1022/324, Attlee to Bevin, Telegram no. 1357, Particular Secrecy, 21 September 1950.
24 FO 371/84097, FK1022/326/G, British Delegation New York to Foreign Office, Telegram no. COJA 131, Top Secret, 24 September 1950.
25 FO 371/84097, FK1022/328, Bevin to Attlee, Telegram no. 1156, Particular Secrecy, 22 September 1950.
26 FO 371/84097, FK1022/327/G, Jebb to Foreign Office, Telegram no. 1200, Particular Secrecy, 25 September 1950.
27 CAB 128/17, fol. 81, CM61(50)2, Secret, 26 September 1950.
28 FO 371/84098, FK1022/334, Attlee to Bevin, Telegram no. 1146, Particular Secrecy, 26 September 1950.

29 FO 371/84098, FK1022/361, Note by Tomlinson, Confidential, 26 September 1950.
30 A1838, 3123/5 Pt 5, Officer to Spender and Watt, Telegram no. 546, Secret, 25 September 1950.
31 A1838 T184, 505/14 Pt 1, Blakeney to Department of External Affairs, Telegram no. 149, Secret, 21 September 1950.
32 A1838, 3123/5 Pt 5, Officer to Watt, Telegram no. 557, Personal and Restricted, 27 September 1950.
33 CAB 129/39, fol. 85, CM62(50)5, Secret, 28 September 1950.
34 FO 371/84099, FK1022/373/G, Gascoigne to Foreign Office, Telegram no. 1371, Particular Secrecy, 3 October 1950.
35 FO 371/84100, FK1022/401/G, Foreign Office to Washington and New York, Telegram no. 4456, Particular Secrecy, 6 October 1950.
36 FO 371/84100, FK1022/402/9, Minute by J. S. H. Shattock, 7 October 1950.
37 CAB 128/17, fol. 89, CM63(50)4, Secret, 9 October 1950.
38 FO 800/517, fos 114–19, US/50/35, Minute by Dixon of conversation between Bevin and Charles Spofford and Mr Justice Holmes, Secret, 23 August 1950.
39 FO 800/465, fol. 246, R. E. Barclay to Dixon, 2 November 1950.
40 A1838, 3123/5 Pt 2, Resident Minister Australian High Commissioner's Office London to Menzies, Telegram no. 5202, Secret, 19 October 1950.
41 A1838, 88/1/10 Pt 4, External Affairs to Australian Consul General Shanghai, Telegram no. 326, Secret, 27 October 1950.
42 A1838, 88/1/10 Pt 4, Australian High Commissioner's Office London to Department of External Affairs, Telegram no. 5530, Immediate Confidential, 4 November 1950.
43 CAB 128/17, fol. 177, CM71(50)3, Secret, 6 November 1950.
44 CAB 128/17, CM72(50)5, Secret, 9 November 1950.
45 CAB 128/17, fol. 125, CM73(50)2, Secret, 13 November 1950.
46 P. N. Farrar, 'Britain's proposal for a buffer zone south of the Yalu in November 1950: Was it a neglected opportunity to end the fighting in Korea?', Journal of Contemporary History, vol. 18 (1983), pp. 327–51.
47 CAB 128/17, fos 144–5, CM78(50)1, Secret, 29 November 1950.
48 CAB 128/17, fol. 147, CM79(50)3, Secret, 30 November 1950.
49 CAB 128/17, fol. 150, CM80(50), Secret, 30 November 1950.
50 FO 800/465, fos 249–58, Fr/50/23, Record of meeting of Attlee and Bevin with French Prime Minister and Minister for Foreign Affairs, Top Secret, 2 December 1950.
51 FO 371/84107, FK1022/580/G, Bevin to Attlee, Telegram no. 5434, Particular Secrecy, 4 December 1950.
52 CAB 128/17, fos 167–8, CM85(50)3, Secret, 12 December 1950; FO 371/84104, FK1022/518/9, Minute by R. S. Millward, 1 December 1950.
53 A1838, 88/1/10 Pt 4, Quinn to A. S. Watt, no. 1131, Secret, 14 December 1950.
54 A1838, 88/1/10 Pt 4, Quinn to P. Shaw, Telegram no. 6562, Secret, 28 December 1950.
55 A1838/T184, 3123/5 Pt 7, Harrison to Spender, Telegram no. 20, Secret, 2 January 1951.
56 A426, 845/20, PMM(51) 3rd Mtg, Secret, 5 January 1951.
57 FO 800/517, fos 273–98, US351/1, Strachey to Bevin, Personal, undated; Draft memorandum by Strachey on Anglo-American relations, Top Secret and Personal, undated; Bevin to Strang, undated; Minute by Dixon, 6 January 1952; Minute by R. Makins, 8 January 1951; Minute by Strang, 8 January 1951; Barclay to Strang, 10 January 1951; Bevin to Strang, 11 January 1951.
58 FO 800/517, fos 299–304, US351/6, Bevin to Attlee, Top Secret, 12 January 1951.
59 CAB 128/19, fol. 13, CM3(51)3, Secret, 15 January 1951.

60 CAB 128/19, fol. 21, CM4(51)6, Secret, 19 January 1951.

61 CAB 128/19, fos 20–1, CM4(51)5, Secret, 18 January 1951.

62 CAB 128/19, fol. 39, CM8(51)1, Secret, 25 January 1951.

63 P. M. Williams (ed.), *The Diary of Hugh Gaitskell, 1945–1956* (London, 1983), pp. 229–32, diary, 2 February 1951.

64 CAB 128/19, fol. 47, CM10(51)3, Secret, 29 January 1951; fol. 54, CM11(51)7, Secret, 1 February 1951.

65 CAB 129/44, fol, 234, CO(51)46, Memorandum by Younger on Korea: the 38th parallel, Secret, 10 February 1951; A1838/T184, 3123/5 Pt 8, United Nations Division to Secretary Department of External Affairs, 13 February 1951.

66 CAB 128/19, fol. 47, CM10(51)3, Secret, 29 January 1951; fol. 117, CM23(51)1, Secret, 2 April 1951.

67 A426, 443/1/11 Pt 2, James Marjoribanks to Secretary Prime Minister's Department, Secret, 29 March 1951; A1838/T184, 3123/5 Pt 10, Marjoribanks to Secretary Prime Minister's Department, Secret, 28 March 1951; *FRUS* 1951(7), pp. 338–42, Memorandum of conversation by Nitze, Top Secret, 12 April 1951.

68 A426, 443/1/11 Pt 2, Marjoribanks to Secretary Prime Minister's Department, Secret, 29 March 1951.

69 CAB 128/19, fol. 113, CM22(51)5, Secret, 22 March 1951; fol. 134, CM27(51)1, Secret, 12 April 1951.

70 A426, 443/1/11 Pt 2, Williams to Menzies, Top Secret, 13 May 1951; A1838/T184, 3123/5 Pt 2, Australian Embassy Washington to Department of External Affairs, Telegram no. 793, Secret, 7 May 1951.

71 A1838/T184, 3123/5 Pt 2, Australian High Commissioner's Office London to Department of External Affairs, Telegram no. 2253, Secret, 26 April 1951; 3123/5 Pt 9, Australian Embassy Washington to Department of External Affairs, Telegram no. 387, Secret; Australian Mission to United Nations to Department of External Affairs, Telegram no. 205, Secret, 14 March 1951; A5954, Box 1697, Extract from British aide mémoire on political and economic sanctions against China, 13 May 1951.

72 CAB 128/19, fol. 225, CM46(51)2, Secret, 25 June 1951; fol. 229, CM47(51)2, Secret, 28 June 1951.

73 A5954, Box 1695, Australian Ambassador Washington to Department of External Affairs, Telegram no. 1124, Secret, 25 June 1951.

74 A1838/T184, 3123/5 Pt 13, Australian High Commission (External) London to Department of External Affairs, Telegram no. 5039, Secret, 13 September 1951.

75 A1838/T184, 3123/5 Pt 13, Australian High Commission (External) London to Department of External Affairs, Telegram no. 5560, Secret, 11 October 1951.

76 A1838, 532/6/3, Memorandum on Pacific Pact by Pacific division, 7 July 1950.

77 A5954, Box 1681, General impressions of a visit abroad in 1949 by Shedden, Secret, September 1949.

78 A1838, 535/3 Pt 5, Memorandum on Japanese peace settlement and Pacific Pact for Shaw, 27 October 1950.

79 A5954, Box 1813, Confidential annex to COS(51) 22nd Mtg, Top Secret, 31 January 1951.

80 A5799, 51/19, Australian Ambassador Washington to Minister for External Affairs, Telegram no. 108, Secret, 21 June 1951; CAB 129/44, fos 238–43, CP(51)47, Memorandum by Younger on Pacific Defence and Annex, Secret, 9 February 1951.

81 CAB 128/19, fol. 63, CM13(51)2, Secret, 12 February 1951.

82 CAB 129/45, fos 317–27, CP(51)64, Note by Attlee on Pacific defence and appendices, Secret, 27 February 1951.

83 CAB 128/19, fos 80-1, CM16(5)3, Secret, 1 March 1951.
84 CAB 129/45, fos 7-17, CP(51)16, Memorandum by Walker on Pacific defence and appendices, Secret, 9 March 1951; CAB 128/9, fol. 96, CM19(51)8, Secret, 12 March 1951.
85 National Library of Australia, Canberra, MS4875, Box 1, Shedden to Spender, Personal, 15 March 1951.
86 A5954, Box 1813, Shedden to Menzies, Top Secret and Personal, 11 May 1951.
87 National Library of Australia, Canberra, MS4936, Box 28, Series 1, Folder 233, Spender to Menzies, 4 September 1951.
89 A1838, 535/3 Pt 5, Memorandum on Japanese peace settlement and Pacific Pact for Shaw, 27 October 1950; CMJ(50)8, Report on Commonwealth working party on Japanese peace treaty 1-17 May 1950, Secret, 17 May 1950.
90 A1838, 480/8/7, Gascoigne to Foreign Office, 13 December 1950 (copy).
91 A426, 845/20, PMM(51) 6th Mtg, Secret, 9 January 1951.
92 MS4936, Box 28, Series 1, Folder 233, Spender to Menzies, 4 September 1951.
93 CAB 128/19, fol. 112, CM22(51)3, Secret, 22 March 1951.
94 CAB 128/19, fol. 149, CM30(51)4, Secret, 23 April 1951.
95 CAB 128/19, fol. 185, CM38(51)2, Secret, 29 May 1951.
96 CAB 129/45, fol. 372, CO(51)137, Memorandum by Morrison on Japanese peace treaty, 23 May 1951.
97 CAB 128/9, fol. 200, CM41(51)1, Secret, 7 June 1951.
98 CAB 129/46, fos 52-6, CP(51)158, Memorandum by Morrison on Chinese participation, Secret, 9 June 1951.
99 CAB 129/46, fos 52-6, CP(51)158, Memorandum by Morrison on Chinese participation, Secret, 9 June 1951.
100 CAB 129/46, fos 89-96, CP(51)166, Memorandum by Morrison on Japanese peace treaty, Secret, 19 June 1951.
101 A5799, 51/186, Australian Ambassador Washington to Minister of Defence, Telegram no. 1081, Secret, 18 June 1951.
102 A2031, 35, no. 244/1951, Minute by Defence Committee at meeting held on 2 August 1951, Secret.
103 CAB 128/20, fol. 53, CM60(51)3, Secret, 27 September 1951; C. Hosoya, 'Japan, China, the United States and the United Kingdom, 1951-2: the case of the "Yoshida Letter"', *International Affairs*, vol. 60 (1984), pp. 247-59.
104 Morgan, *Labour in Power*, pp. 409-61.

PART FIVE

The Cold War in Africa

9

The Significance of South Africa

In 1946 and early 1947 Attlee suggested that Britain should withdraw from the Middle East, and establish instead a line of defence stretching from Lagos to Kenya on the continent of Africa. Bevin argued, successfully, with the support of the Chiefs of Staff, that the Middle East was the shield for Africa, and at the time of the Cold War it could not be abandoned. That might enable Russia to establish its influence across the north of the continent, including French North Africa, and to reach the Atlantic. Russia could also penetrate southwards, and undermine Southern Africa, a principal source of British supplies and an area of immense strategic significance. Bevin and Attlee agreed on the need to keep the Russians out of Africa: they resisted, with the support of General J. C. Smuts, Russian efforts to get a trusteeship of a former Italian colony in Africa. Where the Prime Minister and the Foreign Secretary disagreed, however, was over the importance of the Middle East for the defence of Africa.[1]

Bevin, in his vision of Africa and the Middle East being inextricably linked, was helped by an unexpected source: the Nationalist government in South Africa which took power in 1948. Smuts, at the Commonwealth Prime Ministers' Conference in 1946, had declined to undertake defence commitments on behalf of South Africa: he spoke of the sense of nationalism in the Dominions.[2] The Nationalist government, however, was terrified of communism, particularly in Africa. It was a government voted in mainly by supporters nurtured on a hatred of the British and myths about the British occupation of the Cape and the Second Anglo-Boer War, 1899–1902. But the Cold War meant that the Nationalists drew a distinction between the British in South Africa, the English-speaking South Africans and a British government committed to stop Russian expansion. The new South African Prime Minister told his Commonwealth colleagues, meeting in London in April to discuss India's accession as a republic, that India's desire to continue as a member derived from 'factors less tangible but even more potent than the common allegiance to the Crown'. It was due partly to traditions, but even more to the consciousness of a common outlook and way of life, 'coupled with a sense of a community of interest'. Malan lauded the abitilty of the Commonwealth to adapt itself to changing circumstances and to respect freedom and liberty. The people of South Africa, he assured his fellow Prime Ministers, were fully conscious of the seriousness of the world situation and of the dangers ahead: 'All sections, with few exceptions, realise that South Africa cannot stand isolated, but must have friends and must find them generally, it is true, among the like-minded nations of the free world, but more especially too in the inner circle of the free and independent nations of the Commonwealth.' South Africa wanted to remain within the Commonwealth as long as that body remained true to its own spirit and basic principles. Within such an association, South Africa might 'ultimately find not only her international security and strength but also her complete national unity'.[3]

In many ways the history of the significance of the Commonwealth for Britain can be chartered in the story of Anglo-South African relations. That story also shows the immense significance of the Cold War for the foundation of what on the surface might have seemed an unlikely, if not impossible, alliance. With the Russian threat to Africa and the Middle East, South Africa, under an Afrikaner Nationalist government, became one of Britain's closest allies. The foundation of that relationship was laid by Attlee's Labour administrations.

In 1899 Joseph Chamberlain, the Secretary of State for the Colonies, and Sir Alfred Milner, the High Commissioner, fought to maintain British supremacy in South Africa. The Cabinet was told that the contest for supremacy was between 'the Dutch and the English': what was at stake was the position of Great Britain in South Africa, 'and with it the estimate formed of our power and influence in Colonies throughout the world'.[4] At the same time, in the Transvaal a memorandum by the State Attorney, J. C. Smuts, was accepted by the Volksraad: South Africa was to become a great state with an Afrikaner republic stretching from Table Bay to the Zambezi; the British were to be driven into the sea. [5] The second Anglo-Boer War, 1899–1902, was won by Britain, but in 1906–7 the new Liberal administration 'magnani-mously' granted responsible government first to the Transvaal and then to the Orange River Colony, effectively ensuring that South Africa would be ruled by Afrikaner Calvinists, and that it would be English-speaking South Africans and the non-European inhabitants that had to pay the price of this gesture. Milner, a great liberal statesman, had agreed to the insertion of a clause in the Treaty of Vereeniging – which ended the war – stating that the British government would not legislate for the blacks in the former Boer republics until these had achieved self-government. He regarded this as a mistake, but realized that without such a clause the war would have continued indefinitely. As early as 1901 Milner argued that any new self-governing confederation in South Africa could only be started with a British-minded majority. He gave precise calculations as to how this could be achieved, and the Afrikaners never forgot these whenever the question of British immigration was raised. Indeed, until the 1960s the 'race problem' in South Africa referred not to the black-white issue, but to relations between Afrikaners and English-speaking South Africans.[6]

With the formation of the Union of South Africa in 1910 English-speaking South Africans remained loyal to the imperial connection, but on the whole they followed the policy of conciliation advanced by the Boer War leaders, Smuts and Louis Botha. This meant that no English party emerged to balance the power of Afrikaner nationalism. Indeed during the First World War, the manhood of English-speaking South Africa was decimated on the fields of Flanders, and the natural leaders were lost.[7] Smuts, the man who had been behind the Afrikaner conspiracy to drive the British out of South Africa in 1899, became a great imperial and world statesman, and the 'darling' of English-speaking South Africa, which he effectively betrayed. In 1939 South Africa did enter the Second World War at Britain's side, but only with the connivance of Smuts, the British High Commissioner, and the Governor-General.[8] That left a deeply divided country, and Oswald Pirow, the Minister of Defence, predicted that the pendulum would swing back, and English-speaking South Africans would find themselves aliens in their own country.[9] During the Second World War the Purified Nationalist Party under Dr D. F. Malan emerged as the principal opposition, and many of its leaders had Nazi sympathies.[10] Almost as if in an attempt to maintain South Africa's loyalty to the Crown and Commonwealth it was chosen as the first Dominion the king should visit after the war. Indeed, it was in South Africa in 1947 that his daughter, Princess Elizabeth, celebrated her twenty-first bithday, and in a broadcast dedicated herself to 'the service of our great Imperial Commonwealth to which we all belong'. The Labour government in Britain declined the king's suggestion that he return early because of the crisis winter conditions. But it was English-speaking South Africa that cheered the royal family. A year later Malan was elected Prime Minister on the basis of a policy of white supremacy.[11] The Nationalists only secured power with the support of the more moderate Afrikaner pary under N. C. Havenga.

Smuts thought that they could not last: the alliance was too fragile. He told Philip J. Noel-Baker, the Secretary of State for Commonwealth Relations, on 14 June 1948 that the Nationalist victory could be attributed almost entirely to their attack on the liberal native (black) policy of Smuts's United Party. His deputy leader, Jan Hofmeyr, had used 'less guarded language' than he had, and so the Nationalists had been able 'to create prejudice in the minds of not only the Afrikaners but also some English Speaking people in the Union'. This victory against a liberal native policy was 'a misfortune both for the Union and for the world'. Smuts felt that his own native policy was the only answer to the propaganda of the communists among the natives into which the Russians were putting a great deal of effort. He also acknowledged that he had lost votes through his recognition of Israel. Many Afrikaners were traditionally anti-Semitic, and some English-speaking South Africans shared these sentiments, barring Jews from their country clubs. Others had been outraged by Zionists acts of terrorism against British conscript troops. Smuts felt, however, that Malan would behave in a most proper and constitutional manner as head of a commonwealth government. Malan had kept the republican issue out of the election 'and could not have afforded to bring it in because if he had, he would have lost the British vote which returned him to power'. Britain, Smuts felt, should be able to have more or less normal relations with Malan.[12]

It might have been thought that the Labour government in Britain would have been opposed to the policy of racial division that existed in South Africa even before the election of the Nationalists in 1948. But the spokesman on colonial affairs, Arthur Creech Jones, expressed a widely held sentiment that South Africa would become the leading influence in the African continent.[13] The new Labour government did its best to protect South Africa from criticism in the United Nations over the attempts to incorporate the mandated territory of South West

Africa and over its treatment of South African Indians involving legislation designed to delineate specific areas where Asians could buy property and to attempt to stop any further immigration from Asia.[14] Indeed in East and West Africa Britain was already pursuing the kind of policy which South Africa wanted to follow over Indian immigration, and was using similar arguments to justify it. In 1943, in British East Africa, it was agreed that a permanent system of control was needed to protect the interests of the African (black) population. Africans were taking an increased part in skilled employment and trade: they needed to be protected from immigrants, particularly Indians, who could compete with them both then and in the future. This was in line with the established policy of the British government, and with the provisions of the United Nations Charter dealing with colonial territories. In the case of Tanganyika there was an overriding obligation under the trusteeship agreement to give priority to the advancement of the inhabitants. Draft Bills were published in April 1946; amendments were made following comments from India but these did not endanger the general principle, and the Bills then became law. Subsequently objections were raised by New Delhi. In 1949 the Labour government envisaged similar legislation for Northern Rhodesia and Nyasaland; and it was already in operation in the Gold Coast by 1948, and a strengthening of restrictions was planned for Nigeria.[15]

There were open differences, however, between Britain and South Africa on the future of the High Commission territories, Basutoland, Swaziland and Bechuanaland. Geographically these formed part of South Africa, and the Act of Union of 1910 could be interpreted as envisaging their transfer from Britain to South Africa.[16] Both General J. B. M. Hertzog and Smuts raised this issue during their premierships, but were told that Britain was bound by pledges to make no change in the status of the territories without consulting the British Parliament, and the Conservative governments then in office felt that there was no chance of parliamentary consent to a transfer. When in London in April 1949 Malan raised the issue with Bevin, arguing that the matter had been provided for under the South Africa Act of 1910, and that nothing had been done for forty years, the Foreign Secretary told him that he could not hold out any hope, 'especially having regard to the fact that the fundamental principle associated with it was that we had to take into account the views of the local inhabitants and the native leaders'.[17] Malan said that it was a grave anomaly that there should be three territories geographically within the Union, economically entirely dependent on his country and yet wholly divorced from the authority of the South African government. He thought everyone was in agreement that the conditions in and development of the native (black) territories within South Africa were not only as good as but better than the conditions and development of the native population in any other part of Africa. Noel-Baker explained that the present Labour-dominated Parliament would be even more reluctant than previous Conservative ones to agree to the transfer of authority: there was no hope. In reply Malan hinted that under the agreement of 1910 South Africa could ask the Privy Council to order the transfer. But he did not want to take this action which would place the British government and parliament in 'a very difficult situation', and the Secretary of State for Commonwealth Relations was left with the impression that Malan would be unlikely to pursue this suggestion.[18] It should also be remembered that in 1950 the Labour government prevented Seretse Khama, the designated Chief of the Bamangwato of Bechuanaland, from returning to his country. While at Oxford Seretse Khama had flouted tribal custom and married a white English woman. At a time when the Nationalist government in South Africa was formalizing racial purity with the Mixed Marriages Act and the Immorality Act – which effectively forbade sexual intercourse between whites and other races – the issue of miscegenation was a real one in South Africa. But official white opinion in Southern Rhodesia also viewed the matter gravely.[19] It made the South African government even more conscious of the obvious dangers of territories within its borders which pursued racial policies at variance with its own.

At the beginning of the cold war period, when the Labour government's main preoccupation was stopping the advance of communism, the accession of the Nationalist government had immediate strategic implications for Britain; these, at the time, took priority. Although Washington was aware of the dangers in the Middle East, that area remained a Commonwealth responsibility. Bevin hoped for South African assistance there, as well as in halting any communist penetration of Africa.

As the British High Commissioner, Sir Evelyn Baring, reported in September 1948, the advent of the Nationalist government in South Africa might have appeared as a setback to Commonwealth co-operation in defence matters. He observed that its supporters were 'the heirs of a long tradition of anti-British feeling and activities': during the Second World War they had openly sympathized with Britain's enemies, and they were 'morbidly sensitive' on the subject of the Union's sovereign independence. But the Nationalists were, with good reason, terrified of communism. The South African defence force was entirely dependent on Britain for its equipment and its technical and service knowledge. And, unlike Hertzog and Pirow before the war, Malan and his colleagues were in 'complete sympathy' with the aims of British foreign policy. They were not hampered, as Smuts had been, by the attitude of the opposition. The High Commissioner advised that while it would be advisable to allow Pretoria to take the initiative, and also to avoid any appearance of attempting to rush them, there were grounds for hoping that, as practical men, the Nationalists might come to see that the interests and safety of South Africa would require some measure of co-operation on defence with Britain.[20]

By March 1949 British defence planning had reached the stage of reviewing the possibilities of armament and production within the Commonwealth that might be available in the event of war. It was decided to approach only the old dominions – South Africa, Canada, Australia and New Zealand – about bilateral discussions with Britain.[21] The South African government let it be known that it would willingly receive a visit from a small party of officers of the British planning staff, and the Minister of Defence, F. C. Erasmus, indicated to Baring that in any war with Russia Pretoria would adopt a favourable attitude towards requests concerning the use of South Africa as a transit base.[22]

But the British government had hints that the South African government was prepared to undertake even wider defence commitments. It was reported from the British embassy in Washington towards the end of 1948 that the South African ambassador at large, and a former High Commissioner in London, Charles te Water, had spoken to Robert A. Lovett, the American Under Secretary of State, about the possibility of South Africa's becoming a party to the North Atlantic Pact. Failing that, te Water suggested that the North Atlantic Pact be complemented by a South Atlantic Pact in which South Africa would participate. The Americans felt, however, that te Water was only speaking on his own initiative.[23] The Foreign and Commonwealth Relations Offices both, initially, had the mistaken impression that the attitude of the Nationalist government was one of aloofness. They felt that while Pretoria was generally favourably disposed to any arrangements Britain might be able to contribute to its own and Western security, South Africa would be unlikely to accept any defence commitments outside the African continent, and in the view of Baring would probably want to confine defence respon-sibilities to South African territory.[24]

On 28 March an 'inspired' leader in the semi-official Nationalist newspaper, *Die Burger*, explained Pretoria's thinking. Malan, it said, even before taking office, had made his view clear on South Africa's place in 'the present world upheaval'. Not only South Africa's sympathies, but its principles, made impossible an isolationist attitude towards the challenge which the might of Russia and the spread of communism held for Western civilization.No country had more to lose than South Africa by the world domination of Russian communism. While it might still be possible for a West European country to regard bolshevism as a temporary phenomenon, 'a communist conquest from without or within will mean the beginning of an endless night of barbarism for South Africa'.[25] The strengthening of an anti-communist West was in South Africa's interests. The question was what support South Africa could give in its particular circumstances.[26] Following this, Malan told Baring that while appreciating the regional nature of the North Atlantic Pact, he hoped an African Pact, 'something separate yet linked' to it, would become a possibility. Malan had in mind a pact signed by the European powers with the colonial dependencies in Africa, by the Union and by the United States involved through its connections with Liberia. Baring had spoken about this previously to D. D. Forsyth, an official retained from the Smuts administration. The reasoning behind the envisaged pact was that if Britain went to war against Russia, South Africa would probably give Britain considerable assistance, possibly extending even to the use of the Union Defence Force. But there would be Nationalists who would feel and say that, in 1949, as in 1914 and in 1939, South Africa had been dragged by Britain into a war not primarily its concern. But if South Africa were a signatory to a pact linked with the North Atlantic Pact, there would be no opposition as the Nationalists would feel that South Africa was joining not Britain alone but the entire Western world. Baring endorsed this argument, and said that Malan was in 'a very good mood': Britain should take advantage of it.

The High Commissioner also urged a hastening of the visit of the British defence mission: the government had moved so far 'in the right direction' that it was 'eager to talk as soon as possible to learn as much as possible from our people'. Baring warned, however, that the emphasis should be on the use of South Africa as a transit base rather than on the dispatch of South African troops outside the borders of the Union. It was also important to include someone to discuss internal security. Erasmus needed this to protect himself against his own followers: outside the Cabinet, planning war measures with Britain was still suspect, while measures to combat communist infiltration were popular. On the issue of industrial mobilization Malan and Erasmus had agreed that a member of Britain's war production staff could meet the equivalent South African committee.[27]

In the Commonwealth Relations Office C. G. L. Syers found this valuable evidence of a forward policy on the part of the South African government 'notable and welcome'. It could be a surprise to those who had expected the Nationalists to be 'obstinately isolationist'. But it was too late for Bevin to have talks in Washington with Dean Acheson, the American Secretary of State, on the South African Pact proposals.[28] Instead Sir Percivale Liesching urged the view of the Commonwealth Relations Office on Attlee that it was 'most important to take advantage of this favourable tide and to encourage to the full that co-operation between the United Kingdom and South Africa which is so essencial a part of our relationship as Members of the Commonwealth'.[29]

As Malan was in London for the Commonwealth Prime Ministers' Conference it was possible to discuss this and related issues with him personally. With this in mind Syers approached Sir M. Esler Dening of the Foreign Office about some association of South Africa with a prospective Middle Eastern collective security arrangement: South Africa would have a vital role between the area of the Atlantic Pact and the Middle Eastern security region as a transit centre and support base. Further, an informal arrangement of mutual guarantees between some or all African powers could be suggested, as could a special arrangement between South Africa and the Atlantic Pact powers under which South Africa would agree to provide military facilities to contribute to security in the mid-Atlantic area.[30] This thinking was in line with the reaction in South Africa to the signing of the North Atlantic Treaty. Malan welcomed it as a recognition of the failure of the United Nations. Smuts foresaw the treaty replacing the Security Council and being extended to Greece, Turkey, Western Germany and 'inevitably', Africa.[31] William Strang's weekly meeting of under secretaries, however, decided that there were difficulties in the way of a Middle Eastern Pact. Foreign Office officials also felt that if South Africa became a party to a pact with European powers, backed by the United States, it would no longer have to rely on the Commonwealth connection for security and inducement to remain within the Commonwealth might be weakened. Syers of the Commonwealth Relations Office, however, doubted this: South Africa was rather apprehensive about the United States. But Malan was not to be given a negative answer: it should be explained that the United States was essential to any pact and there were possible difficulties with Congress at that time; the visit of the British defence planning team to South Africa could help to prepare the way for any wider arrangements.[32]

Attlee saw Malan on 20 April, and asked Bevin to handle the South African Prime Minister.[33] Officials from the Colonial, Foreign and Commonwealth Relations Offices discussed the position the following day. F. E. Cumming-Bruce thought that Malan probably had a 'white' pact in mind; but might be prepared to consider one covering non-white countries as well. It was pointed out by A. B. Cohen that there were fundamental differences between Colonial Office Policy and the South African government on the question of arming 'native' troops; there could be grave political objections in African territories and the loyalty of African populations could be seriously undermined. The Chiefs of Staff, however, hoped not only for Union assistance in the defence of Southern Africa, but also for wider South African responsibilities over Egypt. In the end the meeting agreed to the suggestion from Dening that Malan should be convinced that South Africa's frontier was the Middle East. Tension between the Arab states and Israel, however, made the conclusion of any defence pact difficult.[34] There was also the danger of objections from India which could prejudice collaboration in South-East Asia.[35] Malan had a 'great regard' for Bevin, and so particular arrangements were made for him to see the Foreign Secretary on 27 April.[36] The South African Prime Minister was 'extremely anxious' to be associated with the Atlantic Pact. Bevin explained the problem of the traditional attitudes of the American Congress to colonial territories. Africa was a colonial territory and it would be impossible to get Congress to enter into any further arrangements at this stage.[37] Malan accepted this, but emphasized his conviction that South Africa was essential to the successful working of the Atlantic Pact, and to the defence of the Middle East, and he hoped that in some way it might be brought into the collective security system.[38] The Secretary for External Affairs, D. D. Forsyth, suggested that the Union convene a conference in Africa of representatives of those European countries which had territories in Africa south of the Sahara; the line of demarcation would exclude Egypt, Abyssinia and Spain. The subjects would be the question of the militarization of natives, and the mutual defence of Africa. The Nationalists opposed the arming of blacks, but Baring pointed to the difficulties of colonial powers with populations scarcely adequate for their own responsibilities.[39]

In June Charles te Water spoke in Athens of the Union aim to conclude a pact between African states and the neighbouring Mediterranean countries to complement the Atlantic treaty.[40] A British planning team paid a successful visit to South Africa. The size and type of South African forces which could be employed outside the Union in the event of a war against Russia was discussed. South Africa made no specific commitment, but the way was opened for further discussions on the planning level about the timing and manner of deployment of these forces. Further talks were also envisaged about industrial mobilization in the event of war. Then, in July, the Minister of Defence, F. C. Erasmus, and the Chief of the General Staff visited Britain, the United States and Canada to find out the cost of military hardware, This led to negotiations with Britain for the purchase of two destroyers, and equipment for the other two services.[41] The British naval facilities at Simonstown were also discussed. A solution to the problem of British control was seen in terms of an agreement bringing in the United States, and possibly other Atlantic powers. Bevin later intervened to oppose this suggestion: Britain in negotiating the Atlantic Pact had opposed its extension to Africa, and to approach any member on the Simonstown question would risk reviving the issue in Africa.[42]

Towards the end of 1949, following criticism from the United States about the lack of co-ordinated defence planning in Commonwealth countries, there was some discussion about a high level approach to the four old 'white' Dominions which had, of their own volition, gone to war alongside Britain in 1939. But fears that South Africa might revive the idea of an African Pact, and Australia and New Zealand that of a Pacific Pact, presented difficulties.[43] South Africa had helped with the Berlin airlift, sending sixty airmen, but the great Afrikaner nationalist 'ferment' generated by the celebrations surrounding the opening of the Voortrekker monument made it undesirable to raise any major questions with the Union at that time.[44] The new Secretary of State for Commonwealth Relations, Patrick Gordon Walker, further pointed out that in South Africa the Afrikaans-speaking element out-numbered the British and other European sections by 56 to 44 per cent. Like the French Canadians, the Afrikaner did not share the instinctive feeling of loyalty to Britain in a crisis shown by his fellow citizens of British stock – especially those who had recently arrived – and even those of British descent had inevitably lost some of that feeling in the third and fourth generation. Sacrifices for defence had to be shown to be in South Africa's interest. Indeed this lack of common descent was a contributory cause to Commonwealth countries' reluctance to undertake fresh defence commitments.[45]

It was decided that Bevin should make an individual approach to the South African representatives at the Commonwealth Conference at Colombo in January 1950. There Bevin told Forsyth and Paul Sauer that, following his success in securing an American interest in the Far East, the United States had shown a tendency to draw back from the Middle East, which remained an area of British responsibility. Russia was vulnerable to attack from that area, and Bevin thought it would be discouraged from aggression if it knew that it would meet with strong resistance there. South Africa would 'inevitably be concerned in what happened in the Middle East'. The Foreign Secretary hoped that Pretoria would take into account this particular problem. Sauer responded that his government was afraid that if trouble arose it would spread to Kenya and Tanganyika. South Africa would then be responsible for maintaining order in Africa from the Union northwards, and the question was how far up the continent the Union would be able to go. Harbour and other facilities would, of course, be available in South Africa itself. The Nationalists had a delicate political situation to handle, but Bevin need have no anxieties about the attitude of their government. In the last two wars only about half the (white) country had really participated, 'but if there was trouble with Russia, 90 per cent of the South African people would be wholeheartedly in it'.[46] On 15 June 1950 a letter from Erasmus indicated a much greater willingness by South Africa to assume defence commitments on the African continent and suggested a conference to discuss the extent of participation by Union forces in the event of war.[47]

It was then decided to extend the North Atlantic Treaty to Greece and Turkey. Following this, on 22 September 1950, Baring suggested to Liesching that South Africa could be associated with the work of NATO on the same basis.[48] Liesching, however, pointed to the difficulties: if military planning were to take place with South Africa by virtue of such an arrangement, Britain would have 'to open up the whole of our strategy in the Middle East with foreign countries in the context of NATO'. Neither London nor Pretoria would want that.[49] However, in May 1951 the Labour Cabinet still envisaged that NATO would be gradually expanded to include some of the other Commonwealth countries.[50] When Britain tried to form the Middle East Defence Organization, South Africa said it would join, but the idea collapsed as other

Commonwealth countries were not so enthusiastic, and in the end Britain's needs in the Middle East were partly met by further conversations with the Americans and the admission of Greece and Turkey to NATO.[51] In August 1951 Britain and South Africa sponsored a defence conference in Nairobi, but attempts to form a regional defence treaty for South and Central Africa failed because South Africa opposed the arming of blacks.[52]

South Africa was also of crucial significance for the Labour government's defence programme as a source of uranium. At the end of the war Smuts knew on a personal basis of the Anglo-Canadian atomic energy developments. South Africa was thought to have the largest uranium reserves in the world, and the United States relied on Britain to obtain it. Following a visit to London in June 1946 by Brigadier Basil Schonland, director of the South African Department of Scientific and Industrial Research (later director of Harwell), and Professor Tavener, director of the South African Government Metallurgical Laboratory, it was agreed to set up a purification plant in South Africa. At the end of 1950, after delays following the election of the Nationalists, and difficulties with the Americans, South Africa was informed about the Combined Policy Comittee and the Combined Development Agency, the prospects of atomic energy and nuclear power, and given special privileges including access to unclassified atomic energy work in Britain and the United States. Much of this collaboration remained between British and South African scientists: it was thought that Forsyth was the only Union official with any knowledge of atomic energy matters.[53]

Perhaps, however, it was economic links that provided the rock base of the Anglo-South African relationship. During the office of the Labour governments, 1945–51, South Africa proved to be one of the few countries with which Britain had a favourable balance of trade. Indeed South Africa, in 1947, gave Britain substantial assistance with a gold loan of £80 million and the people of the Union sent a gift of over £1 million. Harold Wilson, the President of the Board of Trade, stressed openly the importance of Britain's economic links with South Africa. South Africa was the world's main exporter of mineral products, some of which were of crucial strategic importance to Britain.[54] In 1950 about 47 per cent of the total production of gold was mined in South Africa. To mine this South Africa depended upon imports of black labour and also of capital. The labour came from the British High Commission territories, and the British colonial areas in Central Africa, and British investors traditionally met the capital requirements of the

South African gold mines – with handsome returns. Further discoveries of gold in the Orange Free State meant fresh opportunities for British investment. London saw 'a nice balance of interest': Britain wanted as much of South Africa's gold as it could get to strengthen the sterling area reserves; South Africa needed British capital. This 'mutual interdependence' formed the basis of a series of arrangements, and on 1 August 1950 'letters of understanding' were exchanged between Hugh Gaitskell and Eric Louw on behalf of the Union whereby South Africa would let Britain have £50 million of gold, plus, as before, any residual amount of that metal. South Africa, in return, would as usual be allowed to obtain capital in Britain. The background to all the financial contracts with South Africa was 'happy personal relations'.[55]

The various strands of the Labour government's policy towards the Union were drawn together in a paper presented to the Cabinet in September 1950. This overall consideration of Britain's relations with South Africa was prompted by developments in the United Nations over the treatment of Asians in South Africa, and the effective incorporation of South West Africa into the Union with the passing in 1949 of the South West Africa Amendment Act which gave whites in the mandate direct representation in the South African legislature. In 1946 South Africa had conducted a referendum in South West Africa, and claimed that 208,850 of the 'natives' in the territory favoured staying under the South African flag whereas only 33,250 were against this. Britain had accepted the result. In 1950 an advisory decision by the International Court of Justice found that the mandate was still in force, and that South Africa needed the consent of the United Nations to modify the status of the territory, but the court found that there was no obligation on South Africa's part to place the territory under the trusteeship system.[56]

It should also be remembered that, at this time, the Labour government was considering restricting the entry of immigrants from the black Commonwealth into Britain. The 'colour' question had been raised in 1947 when representatives of the armed forces had objected to difficulties created by black members. These were overruled on the grounds of the importance of Commonwealth co-operation in defence, and the need for personnel exchanges between members. In 1950 a Cabinet committee, concerned at the increasing numbers of black Commonwealth citizens arriving in Britain, had advised that these might form 'ghettos', not, like previous immigrants, accepting the British way of life but maintaining their own cultural and religious traditions, and becoming an alien community within the country.[57] The Labour Cabinet had to face the issue of 'colour' in Britain at a time when the 'apartheid' legislation was complicating its relations with South Africa. A committee of ministers, however, decided that apart from practical administrative measures to control immigration by stowaways and 'one-trip seamen' from colonial territories, the introduction of legislation to control immigration from the colonies would not be justified. The Cabinet accepted this on 22 February 1951.[58]

In the preparation of the paper for the Cabinet, the Commonwealth Relations, Foreign and Colonial Offices all made representations in line with their particular responsibilities. The paper was drafted in the Commonwealth Relations Office, largely by G. E. Crombie. He and his colleagues had some sympathy for South Africa's predicament. This was not altogether shared by the secretary of state, Gordon Walker, and was not reflected in the views of the Colonial Office officials concerned with the development of black territories. One Commonwealth Relations Office official, G. H. Baxter, even felt obliged to delete a suggestion for a paragraph on the reasons for South Africa's racial policy 'and the balancing factors that can be discerned'.[59] Baxter did, nevertheless, leave the observation that London would be more likely to influence Pretoria in the direction of more moderate policies if an appreciation were shown of the difficulties confronting the Union, rather than if Britain ignored these and merely condemned the South African policies. This point was endorsed by both R. R. Sedgwick and Sir Cecil Syers. Baxter further emphasized that Britain was not under any obligation either to associate itself with or to dissociate itself from the internal policies being pursued by a friendly country: if Britain and other governments were to follow the line of publicly condemning any aspect of other governments' domestic policies of which they disapproved, friendly relations would soon become impossible to maintain anywhere.[60] Sedgwick wanted to include the point that if South Africa left the Commonwealth, Southern Rhodesia would be left in an exposed position. While intensely loyal to Britain, its sympathies would be with South Africa on the racial issue, and the European community might conclude that its only hope of survival would be to join the Union. European settlers in neighbouring British colonies would want to follow.[61] Syers, agreeing with Sedgwick, also pointed to the danger of doing anything that 'would remove a foundation Member of the Commonwealth'.[62]

The Colonial Office at first only offered an 'office view' reached after Sir Thomas Lloyd had read the draft document. That view was that although the reasons given for maintaining good relations with South Africa were of major importance, there were other considerations of equal significance that the Cabinet should consider. First, any suspicion that Britain condoned or took a lenient view of South Africa's 'native' policies would 'immediately disturb African and Indian opinion in the African colonies, thus giving rise to a potentially serious threat to internal security in Africa, and it might also seriously compromise our relations with India and Pakistan both in the United Nations and generally in South East Asia, the Far East and East Africa'. Further, any suspicion that Britain was dealing with South Africa for reasons of imperial policy would embarrass Britain at a time when it was trying to persuade the United Nations of the 'enlightenment and progressiveness' of its colonial policies. London should explain its position on this clearly to Pretoria. There was concern that Britain might become isolated in its support of South Africa in the United Nations.[63] Both Crombie and Peter Hope of the Foreign Office thought these suggestions could be ignored: the Colonial Office proposals left 'too little room for manoeuvre', and it might be better not to associate the Colonial Secretary, James Griffiths, with the document.[64] The Foreign Office, however, welcomed the paper and suggested only minor amendments of the handling of the South West Africa issue. Kenneth Younger, the Minister of State, saw the draft before he left for New York.[65] Gordon Walker made some technical amendments on the South West Africa issue,[66] and by 25 September both the Colonial and Foreign Offices had agreed to the document, Griffiths reserving the right to make certain observations in Cabinet.[67]

The paper for the Cabinet, approved by the Commonwealth Relations, Foreign and Colonial Offices, explained that the election of the Nationalists had made the conduct of Britain's relations with South Africa 'a matter of some delicacy'. But there seemed no likelihood of Malan's party being overthrown in the near future. With the passing of Smuts and Hofmeyr, the opposition United Party lacked a first-class leader and a sufficiently challenging policy to counter the Nationalists' appeal to the electorate. The Nationalist policy that had created the greatest shock in their relations with the rest of the world was 'their programme of Apartheid – a stiffer form of the traditional South African policy of racial segregation'. The Nationalists' ultimate objective was the establishment of a republican, white and predominantly Afrikaner form of government which would 'ensure the domination of the white race and postpone as long as possible, if not for ever, the rise to power of the native population'. The republican aspect had been in abeyance, but the Nationalists were pressing their racial programme. Indeed, their strength derived from the general support for some form of racial segregation 'apparent among most sections of the white population, including those of British descent'. Opinion outside South Africa, including that in Britain, was hostile. Although Britain could not associate itself with many of the Nationalists' policies, it was important to preserve good relations with South Africa for the following reasons.

In the first place South Africa's goodwill was of particular importance to Britain 'from the general strategic and defence points of view'. If, as seemed likely, the Mediterranean were closed to Britain in any future war, the naval base at Simonstown where South Africa had granted Britain special rights would be indispensable to British shipping, and as a staging base for troops. The Union could also contribute considerable military forces, and Britain hoped to obtain a commitment from South Africa to send troops to the Middle East in the event of war. These would consist of one armoured division together with aircraft and naval forces. There were also deposits of uranium in the Union.

Secondly, the nationalists were 'staunchly anti-communist'. Malan had pledged South Africa's support in any war arising from Russian aggression. As recently as 9 September 1950 Malan, in Durban, had said South Africa would ally itself with the Commonwealth and other like-minded nations of the world in the event of a major war. Union aircrews had assisted in the Berlin blockade, and despite the unpopularity of the United Nations in South Africa, a squadron of the South African Air Force was joining the United Nations force in Korea.

Thirdly, South Africa was by far the largest producer of gold. It was of the utmost importance for the viability of the sterling area that Britain should be able to obtain a substantive part of the Union's gold output. South Africa was also an important market for British exports, and several hundreds of millions of pounds of British capital was invested there.

The draft paper pointed out that the High Commission territories were wholly dependent on the goodwill of South Africa. The final version simply admitted that South Africa could strangle them by withholding essential facilities.

Finally, Britain had obligations to South Africa as a fellow member of the Commonwealth, and even if South Africa became a republic Britain hoped it would remain within the Commonwealth. Though Britain had many points of difference with South Africa it had many in common, and 40 per cent of the white population was of British stock. The Commonwealth partnership relied on the principle of tolerance, and any attempt to secure complete identity of view between all its members would 'break up the association overnight'.

The document Gordon Walker signed went on to say that, despite difficulties and differences, relations with the Nationalist government had, in practice, been surprisingly good. The Nationalist leaders were parochial, and without much experience of the outside world. If relations were carefully handled they might modify their extreme views in response to world opinion. This was more likely if Britain showed appreciation of the problems confronting them, and did not simply adopt an attitude of condemnation. The Asians in South Africa did not want to be 'repatriated' to India. On this issue Britain had maintained an attitude of neutrality in the United Nations. While attempting reconciliation behind the scenes Britain should abstain in any resolution against South Africa 'of a strongly condemnatory character'. Moreover Pakistan had said that its relations with South Africa were good. The Foreign Office's legal advisers had some doubts about the ruling of the International Court of Jurists on South West Africa. Britain should try to prevent South Africa's isolation in the United Nations, though it could also try exerting direct pressure on Pretoria.

Overall, then, although Britain could not associate itself with South Africa's 'native' policies and apartheid, this view should be stated as politely as possible, and South Africa should not be antagonized. Together with the 'older' Commonwealth countries and the United States, Britain should try to exercise a moderating influence on disagreements between South Africa and other parties, while at the same time ensuring that Britain did not act as a mediator on its own. Britain should do all it could to retain South Africa as a member of the Commonwealth, preferably as one owing direct allegiance to the crown.[68]

When presenting this paper to the Cabinet on 28 September, Gordon Walker emphasized the 'special importance' of South Africa to Britain, and said that while it was advisable to avoid expressing sympathy with the 'native' policy of the Union, Britain should refrain from publicly condemning it. Griffiths was worried about South Africa's ambitions in other parts of Africa, and pointed to signs that Pretoria was encouraging the immigration of Afrikaners into Northern Rhodesia: the economic and strategic issue had to be weighed against British colonial interests in other parts of Africa. The Minister of Health, Aneurin Bevan, thought Britain might have to consider whether there was more to be lost than gained by its present association with the Union government. Despite these dissenting voices, the Cabinet was impressed with the general thrust of Gordon Walker's paper, and endorsed it.[69]

Towards the end of the year it was decided that Gordon Walker should visit Southern Africa, and in January and February 1951 he spent six weeks travelling there. He found South African politics 'extremely sharp and bitter'. In April 1951 he reported to the Cabinet that the Nationalist Party had many of the characteristics of 'a devoted movement of liberation': it used the Afrikaans language as a political weapon; it put its own people in every possible office; it believed unshakably in its cause. The leaders lived and dreamed politics, and their wives were as much in the movement as they were. The Nationalists were still fighting the Boer War – or rather they had just won it. Their enemy was not so much Britain as English-speaking South Africans, and they were taking a long delayed revenge for what they regarded as oppression. When they mentioned 'the war', they meant the Boer War. They felt the Afrikaner had no home but Africa. They resented the way 'the British can look to Britain'. The Afrikaner gloried in South Africa, and was 'filled with a desperate determination to keep it as his home and to be master in his own house'.

Gordon Walker did not like English-speaking South Africans. Perhaps their British upper middle class values offended his socialist sensibilities. He reported that he was 'extremely disappointed in the British in South Africa'. They considered the Boer War as their victory over the Afrikaners. For a generation they had been – and still were – 'very arrogant' and despised the Afrikaners. They reserved the jobs in the industries they controlled for 'British people'. They excluded Afrikaners from their clubs. Most serious of all, they failed to enter national public life. The British in South Africa deserved the 'persecution' now being visited on them by the Nationalists. The worst relations between black and white were in the cities dominated by the British – Johannesburg and Durban; but the best relations were in another British town, Port Elizabeth. The early English settlers were better than those who opened the gold mines and the sugar estates of Natal. The British still had considerable influence in business and through the press, but the Afrikaners were advancing.

Gordon Walker thought 'the best people in South Africa' the

Afrikaners in the United Party: they were well educated, self-confident and loyal to the British connection.

The Nationalists had contradictory objectives: they wished to pursue both an anti-black and an anti-British policy against the local population. Provided they concentrated on an anti-black policy, the Nationalists secured a great deal of British support in elections. The British population would vote against the Nationalists if they stressed their republicanism too strongly. Furthermore, the Nationalists' fear of Russian communism prevented any open breach with Britain. These anti-British (that is, anti-English-speaking South African) actions were confined to the domestic field. Gordon Walker found the 'appalling Voortrekker Monument' outside Pretoria typical of this. Designed as a national shrine, it was 'very ugly and rather hysterical', but completely Afrikaner; 'you would not know from seeing it that there were any British South Africans'. It emphasized the struggle between the Afrikaners and the blacks, and outside this 'national shrine' was a notice that non-Europeans were admitted only on Tuesdays. The Nationalists were placing their supporters in places of authority and in the police and army. Their strict application of bilingualism in effect excluded the British. They were rigging the electorate in their favour. The United Party was confident of winning the next election, but Gordon Walker thought they were wrong – provided that the Nationalists did not do something that involved a breach with Britain. He compared the Nationalists to the Irish Nationalists: 'they have a logic of their own that is grounded on emotions and hatreds that it is practically impossible for us to understand'.

Gordon Walker reported that policy towards the 'African Natives' was based on the theory of permanent exclusion of 'Africans' from any share in government and political rights. The theory of apartheid, however, involved the social and national development of Africans, and to some extent this was carried out in practice through funds raised by taxes on the whites. 'Very large areas' were set aside as 'Native reserves'. Asian leaders indicated that their people were not prepared to return to India where economic conditions were far worse than in the Union, and that they would accept residential, but not economic, segregation.[70]

Before leaving for South Africa, Gordon Walker had been apprised of London's attitude to Simonstown. It was anticipated that eventually Britain might have to come to some joint arrangement with the Union for sharing responsibility for maintaining and using the base. But there were 'powerful political considerations' which prevented considering this matter in detail.

Malan could be told of British difficulties in securing air requirements in Egypt vital to the safety of the Middle East and South Africa. Surrender of the Simonstown base would be a trump card for the Egyptians in these negotiations. At a time when the Union had 'committed' itself to the defence of Africa this would be prejudicial to South Africa's interests. It could also affect the Gibraltar issue in which there would be direct South African interest if forces were engaged in the Eastern Mediterranean.[71] Erasmus, however, never raised with Gordon Walker the matter of transfer of the base to South Africa.

In Southern Rhodesia, Gordon Walker found nothing to compare with the 'racial hatred and tension' in places like Johannesburg. The officials were ahead of public opinion, but the general attitude towards blacks was one of 'kindly superiority – the Africans must be helped but kept in their places'. The common electoral roll, based on a qualified franchise, meant that in around twenty-five years there should be African Members of Parliament. The English language test helped to exclude 'a number of undesirable Afrikaners'. The gravest problem was the pull towards Southern Africa: Gordon Walker was surprised at the readiness and desire to join the Union. South African immigrants were outnumbering those from Britain by two to one. There was an element in this immigration that was political: various organizations in the Union deliberately fostered this to bring Southern Rhodesia increasingly into South Africa's sphere of influence. The Prime Minister, Sir Godfrey Higgins, wanted to counter this by allowing unrestricted immigration from Britain and imposing quotas on 'other countries'.

In his report to the Cabinet Gordon Walker pointed to the 'appallingly difficult problems, for which there can be no simple solutions' in Britain's relations with South Africa. He recommended that one of Britain's prime aims should be to contain South Africa. This did not mean a hostile policy towards the Union; indeed Britain should be friendly. But it was necessary to prevent the spread of South Africa's influence and territorial sovereignty northwards. That would not be easy: South Africa was infinitely the most powerful political unit in Africa, and its strength was increasing. In East and Central Africa there were settled white populations that South Africa might hope to bring under its political leadership and protection. Britain had to balance a concern for the political advancement of the blacks with maintaining the loyalty of the whites in East and Central Africa who could, to avoid domination by blacks, throw in their lot with the Union resulting in the oppression of millions of blacks and terrible wars 'between a white-ruled Eastern Africa and a black-ruled Western Africa'. Southern Rhodesia would be the test case, and it should be one of Britain's cardinal policies to keep Southern Rhodesia out of the Union: that was 'the key-stone of the policy of containing South Africa'. People in Britain, particularly those in the Labour Party, would have to realize that Southern Rhodesia's native policy was not the same as that in South Africa; if this were not done Britain would succeed in making it so, and drawing Southern Rhodesia to South Africa. The question of closer association between Southern Rhodesia, Northern Rhodesia and Nyasaland posed the question whether Southern Rhodesia would go northwards or southwards. Apart from positively drawing Southern Rhodesia northwards, Britain should try to widen the gulf between Southern Rhodesia and South Africa by means of immigration policies, railway development and capital investment. The High Commission territories could also not be held unless they had behind them 'a solid block of British territory that is distinct from and independent of the Union'. Britain had to consider the reactions of South Africa to its policies in the High Commission territories, and had to 'refrain from those acts which would unite and inflame Union public opinions'. That was a luxury Britain could not afford. Recognition of Seretse Khama would have done just that, and gravely endangered British tenure in the territories, as would a decision to arm blacks there. Britain should announce its intention to keep the High Commission territories and refrain only from extreme actions that could provoke South Africa.

The Secretary of State for Commonwealth Relations argued that South Africa was very conscious of its need for British friendship, and there were in the Union powerful forces that positively desired to retain the British connection. Britain 'should be ready to develop those relations with the Union that bind her to us and make her unwilling to risk a break with us':

These relations are also in our direct interest. Chief amongst them come co-operation in defence and in economic matters. Also important is to give the Union what help and guidance we decently can at the United Nations. Those who argue that because we dislike the Union's Native policy we should ostracise her and have nothing to do with her completely fail to understand the realities of the situation. Such a policy would not only gravely harm us in the defence and economic fields it would also weaken our power to deter South Africa from foolhardy acts from fear of breaking with us. It would immediately and directly reduce our chances of holding the Territories, which form a vital part in any policy of containing and confining the Union's influence and territorial expansion in Southern Africa.[72]

In May 1951 Gordon Walker reiterated his arguments about Southern Rhodesia to the Cabinet, and argued for a closer association in Central Africa.[73] In July Baring reported reliably that Malan had said that if Britain allowed Seretse Khama to return to Bechuanaland with his white wife 'the consequences would be deplorable'. South Africa would have to take 'very early action', and resort to economic measures. Malan thought he would have a united South Africa behind moves to force transfer. Developments in the Gold Coast, where Kwame Nkrumah was emerging as the leader backed by an 'illiterate' black electorate, would mean that many English-speaking South Africans would support the Nationalists on the incorporation of the High Commission territories.[74]

A few months later the Labour government was voted out of office. The Conservatives immediately set about implementing the policy towards South Africa laid down by their socialist predecessors. In November 1951 the new Secretary of State for Commonwealth Relations recommended the Central African Federation as the only effective means of resisting Afrikaner pressure on these territories. Afrikaner immigration into Southern Rhodesia made the situation urgent; in Northern Rhodesia the situation was probably even more serious, and in the absence of effective action it was probable that in the 1953 general election Afrikaners would obtain half the European seats on the Northern Rhodesian Legislative Council. South Africa was dominant economically, and the Nationalists had expansionist aims. A British bloc of territories in Central Africa was necessary to counter this.[75] In December he argued that while Britain could not transfer the High Commission territories to South Africa, they were at Malan's mercy. A bad quarrel with the Union would not only prejudice co-operation in defence and trade but might lose Britain the territories. The issue required 'the most careful handling'.[76]

The Cabinet Paper of September 1950, and the report by Gordon Walker of his visit to Southern Africa early in 1951, laid down the fundamentals of British policy towards South Africa that were, with fluctuations, pursued for the following thirty years. With the election of the Nationalists, it was Attlee's Labour government that perceived South Africa's strategic and economic importance for Britain, and the need to maintain contact to ameliorate the policy of apartheid. At the same time it was thought essential to prevent

South Africa spreading northwards and expanding the Afrikaner influence – ensured by the policy of the British Liberal government of 1906–7 – and the possible 'oppression' of millions of blacks. In the late 1960s the United States, under President Richard Nixon and Henry Kissinger, embarked on a similar policy.[77] The Cold War in Africa meant that South Africa became part of the English-speaking alliance, even though its leaders did not speak English as their first language. The apparent threat of communist penetration was such that Afrikaner nationalists were prepared to co-operate intimately with a British Labour government. London considered such a relationship in its own 'direct interest'.

Notes: Chapter 9

1 See Chapters 4 and 5 above.
2 Public Record Office, London, CAB 133/86, PMM (46) 18th Mtg, Confidential Annex, 22 May 1946.
3 Australian Archives, Canberra, A5954, Box 1685, PMM (49) 1st Mtg, Secret, 22 April 1949; PMM (49) 2, Memorandum of statement by Malan on 22 April 1949, Secret, 22 April 1949.
4 Public Record Office, London CAB 41/25, no. 18, Salisbury to Victoria, 8 September 1899.
5 Transvaal Archives, Pretoria, Leyds Archives, 192(1), GR1293/99, Memorandum on military situation, 4 September 1899; Minutes. See also R. Ovendale, 'Profit of patriotism: Natal, the Transvaal, and the coming of the Second Anglo-Boer War', *Journal of Imperial and Commonwealth History*, vol. 8 (1980), pp. 209–34 at pp. 225–7.
6 See N. Mansergh, *South Africa 1906–1961, the Price of Magnanimity* (London, 1962), *passim*.
7 See E. A. Walker, *A History of Southern Africa*, 3rd edn (London, 1959), pp. 558–69.
8 Ovendale, '*Appeasement' and the English Speaking World*, pp. 300–6.
9 O. Pirow, *James Barry Munnik Hertzog* (Cape Town, 1958), p. 246.
10 J. Barber, *South Africa's Foreign Policy 1945–1970* (London, 1973), pp. 9–11.
11 See C. Cross, *The Fall of the British Empire: 1918–1968* (London, 1968), pp. 256–61.
12 Public Record Office, London, DO 35/3138, G2110/22, Record by Noel-Baker of conversation with Smuts, Secret, 14 June 1948; for an evaluation of the 1948 election see W. K. Hancock, *Smuts, the Fields of Force 1919–1950* (Cambridge, 1968), pp. 497–510; for the Palestine issue see R. Ovendale, 'The Palestine policy of the British Labour government, 1945–6', *International Affairs*, vol. 55 (1979), pp. 409–31, and 'The Palestine policy of the British Labour government 1947: the decision to withdraw', *International Affairs*, vol. 56 (1980), pp. 73–93; for Hofmeyr's position see A. Paton, *Hofmeyr* (Cape Town, 1964), pp. 475–505.
13 Cross, *The Fall of the British Empire*, pp. 238–9.
14 On the Indian question see Hancock, *Smuts, the Fields of Force*, pp. 450–72; see generally Barber, *South Africa's Foreign Policy*, pp. 23–42.
15 DO 35/2752, F2077/1, Brief prepared in Colonial Office of Malan's visit to Britain, April 1949, and sent to J. J. S. Garner and K. A. East.
16 L. M. Thompson, *The Unification of South Africa 1902–1910* (Oxford, 1960), pp. 271–8.
17 DO 35/2752, F2077/1, fol. 33, Record by Bevin of conversation with Malan on 27 April 1949.

18 DO 35/2752, fol. 30, Memorandum by Noel-Baker of meeting at Foreign Office on 27 April 1950.
19 Cross, *The Fall of the British Empire*, p. 258; Barber, *South Africa's Foreign Policy*, pp. 112–13.
20 DO 35/2752, Baring to Commonwealth Relations Office, 27 September 1948 (extract).
21 DO 35/1752, Commonwealth Relations Office to British High Commissioners, Telegram Z no. 19, Top Secret, 24 March 1949.
22 DO 35/2752, Baring to Defence (A) Department, Telegram no. 108, Top Secret, March 1949.
23 DO 35/2752, IGI/49, F. R. Hoyer-Millar to Gladwyn Jebb, Top Secret, 3 January 1949.
24 DO 35/2752, 223/1074/72G, Stuckburgh for Jebb to Hoyer-Millar, Top Secret, 18 January 1949; Cumming-Bruce to Holdgate, 12 January 1949; Lamour to Noel-Baker, 30 March 1949.
25 Do 35/2752, Noel-Baker to Leif Egeland (South African High Commission, London), March 1949.
26 DO 35/2752, Translation of leader in *Die Burger*, 28 March 1949.
27 DO 35/2752, D/104, Baring to Sir Percivale Liesching, Top Secret, 31 March 1949.
28 DO 35/2752, Syers to Liesching, 8 April 1949.
29 DO 35/2752, Liesching to L. N. Helsby, 8 April 1949.
30 DO 35/2752, Syers (drafted by Cumming-Bruce) to Dening, Top Secret, 11 April 1949; Minute by Cumming-Bruce, 7 April 1949.
31 DO 35/2752, Baring to Noel-Baker, no. 13, 7 April 1949.
32 DO 35/2752, Dening to Syers, Top Secret, 14 April 1949.
33 DO 35/2752, M88/49, Attlee to Bevin, 20 April 1949.
34 DO 35/2752, F2077/1, Note of a meeting at Commonwealth Relations Office, Secret, 21 April 1949; Appendix A, Possible association of South Africa in an international collective security arrangement.
35 DO 35/2752, fol. 23, Summary of meeting at Commonwealth Relations Office, 21 April 1949.
36 DO 35/2752, Patricia Llewellyn-Davies to R. D. C. McAlpine, 26 April 1949.
37 DO 35/2752, fol. 33, Record by Bevin of conversation with Malan, 27 April 1949.
38 DO 35/2752, fol. 30, Memorandum by Noel-Baker of meeting at Foreign Office, 27 April 1949.
39 DO 35/2752, Minute by Liesching of conversation with Forsyth, 26 April 1949.
40 DO 35/2752, *South Africa*, 4 June 1949.
41 DO 35/2277, fol. 7, Annex to CP(49) (draft), Contribution to Commonwealth defence made by other Commonwealth countries, Top Secret.
42 DO 35/2752, F2077/1, W4891/4/68G, Bevin to Christopher Addison, 24 October 1949.
43 DO 35/2277, Note of a talk on 28 October of defence planning with Australia, New Zealand and South Africa, 2 November 1949.
44 DO 35/2277, Draft paper for Cabinet on defence burdens and the Commonwealth by Patrick Gordon Walker, December 1949.
45 DO 35/2277, fol. 9, Memorandum by Gordon Walker for draft Cabinet paper first revise on defence burdens and the Commonwealth, Top Secret, December 1949.
46 DO 35/2752, F2077/1, fol. 38, Record of a meeting at Temple Trees, Colombo, on 14 June 1950, Top Secret.
47 DO 35/2277, D2000/99, fol. 19, Note for Gordon Walker, Top Secret, received 26 July 1950.
48 DO 35/2752, F2077, fol. 42, Baring to Liesching, Telegram, Personal and Top Secret, 22 September 1950.

49 DO 35/2752, fol. 44, Liesching to Baring, Top Secret, 2 October 1950.
50 Public Record Office, London, CAB 128/19, fol. 175, CM36(51)2, Secret, 22 May 1951.
51 Fitzsimons, *The Foreign Policy of the British Labour Governments*, pp. 164–5.
52 J. E. Spence, *The Strategic Significance of Southern Africa* (London, 1970), p. 11.
53 DO 35/2494, D3450/62, Atomic energy exchange of technical information between South Africa, United Kingdom and United States, Top Secret; fol. 3, Rumbold to J. M. C. James, 24 August 1950; R. C. C. Hunt to L. D. J. Wakely, Secret, 13 January 1951; Rumbold to Hunt, Secret, 10 June 1952; M. M. Gowing assisted by L. Arnold, *Independence and Deterrence: Britain and Atomic Energy, 1945–1952*, Vol. 1 (London, 1974), pp. 8, 146, 333–5, 355, 378–83.
54 Barber, *South Africa's Foreign Policy*, pp. 36, 66–70.
55 DO 35/2672, Financial relations between the Union of South Africa and the United Kingdom, Secret, December 1950; 2670, Enquiries in IMF Gatt re UK-SA gold sales arrangements, Secret.
56 Barber, *South Africa's Foreign Policy*, pp. 26–31, 76–9.
57 CAB 128/10, CM51(47)3, Secret, 3 June 1947; 17, 15 June 1950.
58 CAB 128/19, fol. 77, CM15(51)4, Secret, 22 February 1951.
59 DO 35/3839, U3030/14, Garner to Sedgwick, Baxter and Syers, 16 September 1950; Minute by G. H. Baxter, 19 September 1950.
60 DO 35/3839, Minutes by Baxter, 19 September 1950; Sedgwick, Syers, undated.
61 DO 35/3839, Minute by Sedgwick, 19 September 1950.
62 DO 35/3839, Syers to Garner, 25 September 1950.
63 DO 35/3839, 25/55/1/50, W. G. Wilson to G. E. Crombie, Secret, 20 September 1950.
64 DO 35/3839, Crombie to Garner, 21 September 1950.
65 DO 35/3839, C. P. Hope to Crombie, Personal, 13 September 1950; Crombie to Garner, 21 September 1950.
66 DO 35/3839, Minute by Gordon Walker, 24 September 1950.
67 DO 35/3839, Crombie to Garner, 23 September 1950; Minutes by Crombie, 25 September 1950.
68 DO 35/3839, CP(50)214(draft), Memorandum by Gordon Walker on relations with South Africa, Secret; Public Record Office, London, CAB 129/42, fos 54–6, CP(50)217, Memorandum by Gordon Walker on relations with South Africa, Secret, 25 September 1950.
69 DO 35/3839, CM62(50), Secret, 28 September 1950 (extract).
70 CAB 129/45, fos 224–30, CP(51)109, Memorandum by Gordon Walker on visit to Southern Africa, Secret, 16 April 1951.
71 DO 35/3885, W2380/24/2, fol. 39, FA3, Memorandum on Simonstown, December 1950.
72 CAB 129/45, fos 224–30, CP(51)109, Memorandum by Gordon-Walker on visit to Southern Africa, Secret, 15 April 1951.
73 CAB 129/45, fol. 278, CP(51)122, Memorandum by Griffiths and Gordon Walker on closer association in Central Africa, Secret, 3 May 1951.
74 CAB 129/47, fol. 6, CP(51)227, Memorandum by Gordon Walker on solution in South African High Commission territories, Secret, 25 July 1951.
75 CAB 129/48, fos 37–8, C(51)11, Memorandum on closer association in Central Africa, Confidential, 9 November 1951.
76 CAB 129/48, fol. 203, C(51)49, Memorandum on transfer of the High Commission territories, Secret, 17 December 1951.
77 See R. Ovendale, 'The United States and Southern Africa: an evolving foreign policy', *Interstate* (1976–7), pp. 26–36.

PART SIX

Conclusions

10

Defence Policy and Global Strategy

Like Neville Chamberlain's policy for the 'appeasement' of Europe in the late 1930s, myths and legends have proliferated about the origins of the Cold War. 'Inevitability' has been invoked; 'ineluctable forces' mentioned; 'accident' offered as an explanation. The Cold War was a name, given in hindsight, to what appeared as a Russian threat, first to some British, and then afterwards to American statesmen. The phrase, in inverted commas, began to appear in British official minutes around 1948. By 1949 it was accepted, and written in small letters. The Cold War did not only cover Europe; and, on the Western side, it was not just an American affair. Views like these have often been proliferated for political or national ends. In the years immediately after the end of the Second World War, the Cold War was almost global in scale, extending across Europe and Asia, penetrating the Middle East and Africa.

It was the British Foreign Secretary Ernest Bevin who was the architect of the Western alliance that was formed to deter the threat. He had served under Churchill in the wartime coalition government. Churchill, from the end of 1943, saw Russia as the real problem rather than Germany. His difficulty was trying to get the Americans to appreciate that. Bevin, within a few days of taking office, satisfied some Foreign Office officials that he was going to continue Churchill's policy. Though virtually bankrupt, Britain was still an imperial and world power. The Labour government was determined that it should remain so. It was necessary to prevent the United States from withdrawing into isolation, and to make that country realize what appeared to be the reality of the Russian menace. The most pressing problem seemed Europe as, with its armies in occupation, Russia consolidated its control. Initially Bevin had problems: the American Secretary of State, James F. Byrnes, continued Roosevelt's policy of accommodation towards Russia. But Bevin was helped by Frank Roberts in the British embassy in

273

Moscow. Roberts's diagnosis of Russian expansionism was similar to that of Bevin; indeed Roberts both provided Bevin with the specific analyses the Foreign Secretary needed and worked with his old friend George Kennan on formulating what became known later as the doctrine of containment. At that time, especially when Walter Bedell Smith arrived as American ambassador, the British and American embassies in Moscow virtually functioned as a single unit. Early in January 1946 Truman also changed his mind about the Russians. British and American policy after that had similar objectives. But, of course, there was no American commitment.

By early 1946 Bevin had the long-term aim of reviving the old wartime Anglo-American alliance. Initially, it seemed only possible to do this on the level of military co-operation. By the end of 1946 that was well under way. Co-operation was close, except in the atomic field. And there was the suspicion that Britain could not always rely on the United States. The Foreign Office was accused by some State Department officials of spreading propaganda that the United States was a 'conglomerate of ill-assorted groups'. Truman's Palestine policy, dictated by Zionist pressure groups and a fear of electoral punishment, convinced British ministers that the United States could be an uncertain ally. Its President was prepared to sacrifice what Britain considered the vital interests of Western security on the altar of domestic politics. William Strang's Permanent Under Secretary's Committee, which in 1949 outlined the basis of British foreign policy, warned that the hyphenate culture in the United States and its influence on American elections could endanger Britain's position as an ally. But, as Strang's committee pointed out, Britain had no option other than to rely on the United States. The Commonwealth and the nations of Western Europe between them were not strong enough to deter Russia. Britain, however, could not have a dependent relationship with the United States. The ministers who decided to go ahead and build Britain's atomic bomb appreciated this. Besides Truman's Palestine policy, there had been the sudden cancellation of Lend Lease. Britain had to maintain an independence.

Bevin's policy in Europe at times appeared hesitant and uncertain. It was largely the policy of the Foreign Secretary. At times he used Foreign Office officials, as he did in his battle with Attlee in December 1946 and January 1947. Sometimes he relied on his principal private secretaries, particularly Pierson Dixon and Frank Roberts. Bevin was an opportunist. His timing was good. He reacted to the Harvard speech and organized Europe in preparation for Marshall Aid. He initiated the Western Union and the North Atlantic Treaty Organization.

But Bevin's vision extended far beyond Europe. As he told the Commonwealth Prime Ministers at Colombo in 1950, Britain was a world power. The Foreign Secretary outlined his global strategy to Marshall in December 1947. The democratic nations had to get together to meet the Russian threat. Britain, the European democracies, the United States and the Dominions should co-operate. They did not have to have a formal alliance. It could be a loose association. Though no admirer of Neville Chamberlain, Bevin had the same objectives. In a time of crisis Britain had to rely on the United States and the 'old' Dominions. Bevin had an even lower opinion of the Europeans that did Chamberlain. By May 1950 he had refined his ideas: Britain and Western Europe had to be able to rely on the full support of the English-speaking democracies of the Western hemisphere. Seemingly Bevin did not think that the West Europeans could provide much. In August 1950 he said that people in Britain were pinning their faith 'on a policy of defence on a Commonwealth-U.S.A. basis – an English-speaking basis'. Britons who had been bombed by Germans during the war could not rely on them for defence: if the Germans wanted to help that was all right. The French were defeatist. 'Reliance must be placed on America and the Commonwealth.'

In practice Bevin started to implement this vision at the Commonwealth Prime Ministers' Conference of 1948. There was general agreement amongst the 'old' Dominions about the nature of the Russian threat. South Africa, under a new Afrikaner Nationalist government, was particularly co-operative. The Nationalists, though nurtured on a hatred of English-speaking South Africans, feared communism and were prepared to work closely with Britain as an ally to meet the apparent threat in Africa, and the shield of Africa, the Middle East. The Labour government decided that for economic, strategic and other reasons a close relationship between Britain and South Africa was in Britain's direct interests. Though the South African leaders did not speak English as their first language, South Africa too became part of Bevin's scheme for the English-speaking alliance. The Nationalist Prime Minister, D. F. Malan, had a particularly high opinion of Bevin. After Bevin's death, Patrick Gordon Walker outlined the specific terms of Britain's mutually interdependent relationship with South Africa, cemented with the Cold War.

The Commonwealth was of particular significance for the defence of the Middle East. Throughout the period of the Labour governments that area was of cardinal importance for Britain's defence. Together with the defence of the United Kingdom itself, it was vital for Britain's security. In the Chiefs of Staff papers on defence policy and global strategy of 1950 and 1951 the line was extended to part of the European continent. South Africa was, on the whole, willing. Australia, however, was torn. That Pacific country had difficulty accepting a British defence policy and global strategy which stated that the retention of Malaya in a hot war, though crucial, was not vital. Washington assured Canberra that the United States Navy could look after the Pacific, and that it wanted Australia to go to the Middle East which it considered a Commonwealth responsibility. But Australia was difficult to convince. Bevin was personally identified with British policy in the Middle East. He hoped to establish a relationship with Arab states on an equal footing based on mutual interests. But he was shackled by Palestine and the conflicting claims of Britain's military requirements as insisted on by the Chiefs of Staff, and the American domestic interest as perceived by Truman and dictated by the Zionists. In the end, however, it was Menachem Begin's terrorism that forced the British withdrawal. That made the Egyptian base seem even more crucial. Bevin's policy of a mutually interdependent relationship was changed by Morrison and Shinwell. After Bevin's death, Britain's policy in the Middle East appeared more high-handed. At the end of 1947 the Americans had agreed that Britain's position should be supported in that area. During the Iranian oil crisis the British government did not always feel that the Americans were doing that. Attlee, however, told the Cabinet just before the fall of his second government that Britain could not risk a break with the Americans on this issue. In the end the Labour government worked with the pashas rather than the peasants in the Middle East in an attempt to preserve a sort of British suzerainty over an area which Britain had acquired, almost absent-mindedly, between 1917 and 1922, but which between 1945 and 1951 was considered vital for Britain's very survival.

Britain also hoped that the Pacific Dominions would play a role in Asia. At different times both New Zealand and Australia had bombers stationed in Malaya. By 1951 Australia was paying £900,000 towards the defence effort there. But the Malayan attitude to the 'White Australia' policy meant that Malaya had to remain within the British command structure in the Cold War, even though it was envisaged that in a hot war it would most likely be under an American command. The Malayan insurgency made the Cold War in Asia a reality for Britain in 1948. But it was

Indochina that was considered the key. In their paper on defence policy and global strategy of June 1950 the Chiefs of Staff argued:

> The front line of the cold war in Asia lies in Indo-China. If that front gives way it is only a matter of time before Siam and Burma fall under communist influence. In that event our difficulties in Malaya would become almost insuperable and ultimately communism would probably prevail throughout Malaya and the Archipelago. Nothing is more important than to make sure that the French restore order and establish a stable and ultimately friendly government in Indo-China.[1]

Malcolm MacDonald, the British Commissioner General in South-East Asia, enunciated the domino theory long before President D. D. Eisenhower. Indeed domino theory thinking motivated British policy in Europe at the time of the Marshall Plan. At the beginning of 1949 the Foreign Office decided that something had to be done about the communist threat to South-East Asia. London had been conscious of this at the end of the Second World War: in 1946 Lord Killearn was asked to make an assessment of Moscow's influence in the area. The communist insurgency in Malaya and the deteriorating situation in Indochina made the situation more pressing. Britain could not do anything on its own. The Foreign Office thought that only the United States could stop the communist advance in Asia. After the experience of supporting Nationalist China – where it had given everything possible in terms of money and weapons and support short of fighting a land war in Asia – the United States refused, initially, to become involved in Asia. British policy for Asia was developed in the Foreign Office and by Strang's Permanent Under Secretary's Committee. It was put across to the Americans by Bevin. In mounting this policy Britain had to take American sensibilities over the recognition of Communist China carefully into account: in the United States important foreign policy issues could again be decided by domestic considerations. In November 1949 George Kennan's Policy Planning Staff was shown an edited version of the Strang committee's policy for South-East Asia. At the end of December Truman endorsed NSC 48/2, a document outlining an American policy set to stop communist expansion in Asia, which reflected a remarkable congruence of views with Strang's policy paper. After that the United States started supporting the French position in Indochina. In effect, in an area of traditional British and French interest, the United States was once again 'pulling British and French chestnuts' out of the fire. In many ways Britain had been the instigator, if not the initiator, of this policy.

With the American stand over the Korean crisis in June 1950 the *pax Britannica* became, in effect, the *pax Americana*. To Britain it seemed that the United States was finally prepared to face up to its worldwide responsibilities. Though the Chiefs of Staff were reluctant to send troops, Britain did so lest the Americans felt lonely in carrying out their great new task. When it seemed that the United States did not have a policy, Britain was quick to find one for it. The change of the intention of the Korean operation from being merely to repel the aggressor north of the 38th parallel, to one of bringing about a united Korea, was Britain's initiative. Britain organized the United Nations resolution endorsing the crossing of the 38th parallel. When the Communist Chinese entered and there were reverses, the British Cabinet was told that whatever might be said in the House of Commons, Britain was just as responsible as the United States. The Americans did not go over to an Asia first policy. During the early stages of the Korean crisis Bevin secured a change in the nature of the American commitment to Europe: the United States became more than just committed to go to Europe's defence, it became part of Europe's defence. In December 1950 Attlee and Truman agreed on what was, in effect, a Europe first policy. The British Prime Minister also understood that Truman had said that, except in the case of an attack on the United States, Truman regarded the atomic bomb as the possession of Britain, Canada and the United States and would consult the allies before using it. The American public had a slightly different version, but not much was made of that at the time. Bevin was worried that the deterrent threat of the bomb, so successfully used during the Berlin crisis, would be lost. It was Bevin, ill and dying, with the able assistance of Strang and other Foreign Office officials, who managed to quell the anti-American revolt led by John Strachey and seemingly even supported by Lord Mountbatten early in January. When Bevin was 'incoherent' on his sickbed later that month Hugh Gaitskell took over. Attlee initially stood in the middle. But what won was the policy decided on by Strang's committee. Britain, the countries of the Western Union and the Commonwealth – even if such an alliance were possible – could not stand up to the communist threat on their own. The full participation of the United States was 'essential to sustain the free world which Soviet Russia is trying to undermine'. What Britain had to do was to 'exert sufficient control over the policy of the well-intentioned but inexperienced colossus on whose co-operation our safety depends'.

London felt that it did that. The Labour government also felt that it was helped in this by the responsibilities undertaken by Australia and New Zealand working with the United States in the Pacific. The tripartite security pact, ANZUS, was regarded by Attlee and most of his colleagues as being in line with their idea of the evolution of the modern Commonwealth in which member states would take the lead in areas of their particular interest. The Labour government was also satisfied with the Japanese treaty: Morrison found Dulles most co-operative and felt that Truman's ambassador allowed Britain to contribute a great deal to the treaty.

Bevin and the Chiefs of Staff saw the Middle East and Africa as being interlinked: the Middle East in the Cold War was the shield of Africa. Russia had to be kept out of that area of rich resources, strategic and material, and be stopped from interfering with the important communications lines that ran around and through the continent. Bevin was attached to Africa: in 1946 he wanted to build Britain's nuclear reactor on the Victoria Falls. He liked the idea of a defence line running from Lagos to Kenya, but not, of course, at the expense of the defence of the Middle East. Attlee, and strategists like Basil Liddell-Hart wanted Britain to withdraw from the Middle East to a defence line in Africa. Attlee persisted in arguing this case again and again. It was difficult for Bevin, the Chiefs of Staff and Foreign Office officials to disillusion the Prime Minister. But then the Prime Minister was prepared at one point, despite his distrust of Russia and his view of its tsarist imperialist policy, to accommodate Russia. He had to be told that Britain did not have a defence line in Africa: it existed only on paper. It was hoped that there would be a support base in Southern Africa. But that was just anticipation. In 1951 the British defence equipment sent to the so-called 'Kenya road' base lay rotting and rusting. But what Britain did have was a close relationship with South Africa. Defence discussions had shown a great willingness on the part of the Nationalist government to co-operate in the defence of Africa and the Middle East in the face of the communist menace. The South Africans did not even raise the question of the return of the Simonstown base. The Smuts government had never been so forthcoming on matters of defence. For Britain it was the fortuitous election of the Afrikaner Nationalist government in 1948, with its phobic fear of communism, that made the Anglo-South African relationship, based on mutual interdependence, a reality. That relationship was the basis of Britain's handling of the Cold War in Africa.

A problem for the Labour government was to enunciate a defence policy to match a foreign policy based on the assumption that Britain was a world power. The impact of Hiroshima and Nagasaki did not have an immediate effect on the planning of the Chiefs of Staff. Perhaps this was realistic. Until the late 1940s there were not many atomic bombs anyway, and some of them were not usable. It was early in 1948 that defence appreciations began to take the bomb seriously, and it was only after the Russians had exploded a bomb that the papers on defence policy and global strategy began to consider its full impact, and even to make provision for the time when the manned bomber would no longer be used. In the immediate postwar years British defence thinking concentrated, in a traditional way, on the defence of the United Kingdom, and the area seen as being of cardinal importance as a base, for communication lines and as a source of oil, the Middle East. The Chiefs of Staff did not want to leave Palestine. Britain had to have a military presence there as a front base for the huge Suez base. To give up the Egyptian base was almost unthinkable. The require-ments of the Chiefs of Staff in the Middle East, until September 1947, dictated Britain's foreign policy in the area. In December 1946 both Attlee and Bevin wanted to give up the Palestine mandate. The Chiefs of Staff persuaded them otherwise. In the end Bevin kept the Chiefs of Staff waiting outside when, after the hanging of the two British sergeants and the booby-trapping of their bodies, he was convinced that the British public would not tolerate a British presence in Palestine any more and the Cabinet agreed to a British withdrawal. Bevin commented that if the military wanted to go back to Palestine, they would have to go back in ''elicopters'. Transjordan could not provide a base suitable for British requirements. Cyprus was the only British sovereign territory in the area: Enosis, or union with Greece, was in the air. Egypt became all the more important, but under the Anglo-Egyptian treaty Britain could only stay there until 1956 anyway. Somehow the Egyptians had to be made to agree to allow Britain to return in time of emergency. If the Egyptians refused, Britain would have to plan to do so anyway. It was agreed with the Americans that the Middle East was an area of Commonwealth responsibility. Britain tried to secure definite commitments from South Africa, New Zealand and Australia. Canada declared that the Americans would expect them to co-operate in their sphere of action and was not interested. But Commonwealth commitment, beyond a planning stage, was difficult to get. Before it fell, Attlee's government tried to involve the Egyptians on an equal footing with the scheme for the Middle East Command. But the Egyptians just wanted Britain out and turned it down. At that time Britain refused to get out.

The Chiefs of Staff did not like the idea of British land forces fighting on the European continent again. Air and naval support for the West European democracies was acceptable. But the memories of Mons and Dunkirk lingered. When Montgomery raised the issue of committing British land forces to the European continent to hold the Russians on a line in Germany in a future war, he met with considerable opposition. That was 1948. In March 1950 the Defence Committee finally agreed that, in the event of war, two British divisions would be sent to Europe. They would take three months to arrive, and would only go if the line were holding. The military inclined to the view that next time the Europeans should do their own fighting. The West Germans would have to be rearmed. On 4 September 1951 the Cabinet agreed, in principle, to the idea of a 'European army'.

In planning for defence policy and global strategy with the Americans it was agreed that Asia and the Pacific were an American sphere. Even that area of traditional British interest, South-East Asia, was in the view of the Chiefs of Staff in 1950 and 1951 'critical' but not 'vital'. This appreciation disturbed Britain's Australian allies. Slim tried to reassure the Australians, with an eye to their participation in the defence of the Middle East, that Britain would fight for Malaya. That was the British line at the Commonwealth Defence Ministers' meeting in London in June 1951. Shinwell reiterated this in August. But it was obvious to the Australians that there was a caveat: British support troops would be dependent on the requirements of other theatres. Malaya was not 'vital' in the same way as the Middle East. Presumably what is the crucial British defence paper on the issue, 'The Threat to Malaya', is closed 'indefinitely' on instructions of Her Majesty's Government.

In 1952 the Chiefs of Staff revised Britain's global strategy. Far-reaching changes over the previous two years made this necessary. The allies were, in 1952, in a position to launch a devastating atomic attack on Russia at the very outset of a war. That had to be well known to the Kremlin. Russia with its widely spread frontiers and the vast expanse of its territories could not protect itself against an attack of this nature. So, it was unlikely that Russia would deliberately start a war. Rather it would concentrate its efforts on a prolonged Cold War. But the West had to be prepared for a world war since, even though Russia might not want one, circumstances could arise that would make war unavoidable. In considering what preparations to make for war, it was necessary to take into account three major developments: the increased accuracy and power of atom bombing; the advent of the small atom bomb for tactical use;

and the economic situation. In its opening stages a world war was likely to be an all-out affair, lasting perhaps only a few weeks; during that time Britain, though not defeated, would be very seriously mauled by Russia's 'atom attack'. At the same time, the allied attack on Russia, which would be considerably more powerful, was likely to throw Russia into complete confusion and might well knock Russia out. But Russia would probably succeed in this stage in overrunning most of Europe. During the second stage, it was envisaged that those countries 'which had not taken a hammering', such as the United States, would 'turn the tables on Russia and in due course complete her defeat'. Australia would make a major contribution during the second stage. The Chiefs of Staff had decided that it was economically impossible to prepare and build up the necessary reserves for a prolonged war. Efforts had to be concentrated on producing forces and equipment for an intense, all-out conflict of short duration. In the view of the Chiefs of Staff in the cold war period, the main effort had to be directed to the prevention of world war. In the Cold War, Europe had to be given top priority, with the Far East next and after that the Middle East. In hot war Europe should remain a top priority, but the Middle East should be given priority above the Far East owing to the importance of communications through the Middle East, its oil and the 'necessity to prevent Communism from spreading throughout Africa'.[2]

The foundation stone of British policy during this period was, as Strang's committee suggested, the Anglo-American special relationship. This was sustained and revived by men and women in bureaucracies on both sides of the Atlantic who spoke the same language, and, in most cases, enjoyed a common heritage. Some of the Americans concerned had been educated at Oxford under a scheme established by the great imperialist Cecil John Rhodes for fostering co-operation in the English-speaking world. Some of the Britons had American family connections and felt at home in the United States anyway. Bevin, at the end of 1946, explained to Molotov that the two leading 'Anglo-Saxon' – perhaps a loose and inaccurate term – nations were just able to get on with one another in a natural sort of way. At the top personal relations were not especially good. Bevin in particular, but Attlee as well, never forgave Truman for pursuing a policy in Palestine in the interests of his own re-election at a time when British soldiers were being murdered in Palestine. Later Bevin could not understand Truman's insensitivity over the question of the 1 million Arab refugees. But it was through the skilful diplomacy of officials, both British and

American, that the Palestine issue was kept outside the deepening current of the Anglo-American special relationship. From London, Lewis Douglas, the American ambassador, warned Washington of the danger of Palestine policy undermining the basis of American policy in Europe which rested on the co-operation of a friendly and well-disposed Britain. Douglas appreciated Bevin's difficulties: he sent a personal note to the Foreign Secretary thanking him for his 'understanding and tolerance'. Bevin appreciated how helpful Douglas had been.[3] At the end of 1945 British and American officials in Moscow were worried by the animosity Bevin and Byrnes felt for each other. They hoped that the two men would keep it on a personal basis. Bevin and Marshall, however, were frank with each other, and there seems to have been a friendship based on trust and liking. The two men exchanged books: Marshall enjoyed George Orwell's *Animal Farm*. Those two men did a great deal to foster the Anglo-American special relationship at a time when Americans were discovering hyphenate identities that challenged a concept of 'Anglo-Saxondom'. In Washington Oliver Franks was particularly sensitive to the exigencies of American opinion, and offered shrewd advice to London.

If the Anglo-American special relationship was the foundation stone of British foreign policy, the co-operation of the old 'white' Dominions who had gone to war at Britain's side in 1939 of their own volition was an essential part of the structure. As the British Commonwealth became the Commonwealth, London drew a distinction between the 'kith and kin' Dominions and the new Asian members. In 1949 this was evident with the bilateral defence discussions. In 1950, with the outbreak of the Korean conflict, this was formalized, and a distinction was drawn between the full and frank information sent to South Africa, Canada, Australia and New Zealand, and that going to the new Asian members who were considered a potential security risk. The defence relationship with Australia and New Zealand was close: a British representative was usually present at all discussions affecting the security of the ANZAM area, that part of the world stretching roughly from just below Thailand across Indonesia to the islands around Australia's coast line and on into the Pacific – the exact boundaries of the area varied from time to time as a result of discussions with the Americans particularly at Pearl Harbor early in 1951. The relationship between the 'old' Commonwealth statesmen and their British counterparts was good. St Laurent played a vital role, in Britain's interest, in the formation of the North Atlantic Treaty Organization. Sidney George Holland of New Zealand was intensely loyal to the imperial connection: New Zealand felt that its links with the crown had strengthened not weakened with the passing of time. Menzies, though he fostered the American connection which London saw as essential anyway and a part of the evolution of the modern Commonwealth, remained a loyal 'British subject'. Even the Afrikaner Nationalist Prime Minister of South Africa, Dr D. F. Malan, was a great admirer of Bevin, and care was taken to ensure that he saw the Foreign Secretary privately on his visit to London in 1949. The background to Britain's financial contacts with South Africa was 'happy personal relations'; Hugh Gaitskell and Eric Louw apparently liked one another. On the atomic side the relationship was especially close and there was collaboration between British and South African scientists. A South African, Brigadier Basil Schonland, at one time the director of the South African Department of Scientific and Industrial Research, became the director of Harwell. Personal contacts like these helped Britain to forge one of the closest relationships it had with any country with Afrikaner Nationalist South Africa. With the perception of the British Chiefs of Staff in 1952 of the 'necessity to prevent Communism from spreading throughout Africa', the relationship, founded by Attlee's administration, deepened.

Whatever ideas Bevin might have had about closer West European co-operation from 1945 onwards, he made it clear to the Americans and the Commonwealth that he did not want Britain as part of Europe. In 1950 he angrily said that Britain was not just another Luxembourg, it had a very special position. When the issue of American aid for Europe was first raised Bevin even hoped that that would be Anglo-American administered. But such a scheme was unacceptable to the Americans. Bevin resented bitterly unofficial American pressure for Britain to become part of Europe, and told Marshall so, despite the assurances that this was not the policy of the American administration. When it seemed that this might be the policy of the American administration in 1950, Bevin fought it resolutely. The British people were pinning their faith on a defence alliance between the 'old' Dominions, Britain and the United States. The West European countries were not reliable. In any case Bevin disliked the French approach to European unity: formal written constitutions were simply not British. The Foreign Secretary told this to the Commonwealth Prime Ministers. At the Colombo Conference in 1950 Bevin said that Britain would 'resist ill-considered plans for the integration of the UK economy with that of other European countries'. Britain formally refused to accept the French approach in the Schuman Plan of 1950. A gulf opened up between France and Britain. It is not clear that the Europeans wanted Britain in anyway.[4]

Bevin attempted to create the English-speaking alliance to counter the threat of Russia. The Chiefs of Staff, from the end of the Second World War, considered Russia as the only really serious potential enemy. They designed a defence policy and a global strategy to cope with what was increasingly seen as a menace to British security both in a cold war and a hot war situation. By 1952 the priorities had changed slightly: the Far East had priority in the Cold War though the Middle East retained that position in a hot war, partly because of the need to stop communism from spreading through Africa. It was also anticipated that in a hot war Britain would be seriously mauled in a Russian 'atom attack'. Until 1952 planning and defence preparations envisaged a fairly protracted war. For instance, it was thought that it would be two years before the Americans would be able to send troops to reinforce the Middle East. In 1952, with the new Conservative government and the further development of atomic weapons, contingency planning changed. It was decided that it was economically impossible to prepare for a prolonged war: instead forces had to be produced for a short, intense conflict. Russia knew a great deal about Britain's cold war plans during Attlee's Labour administration. One agent, Donald Maclean, was present at the Pentagon talks in 1948 that led to the formation of the North Atlantic Treaty Organization. Another, Guy Burgess, was on the Far Eastern desk and not only presumably forwarded the crucial report of Strang's committee on that area to the Russians, but also saw documents of some significance giving the American analysis of Russian aid to Communist China prior to the outbreak of the Korean War.[5] Burgess and Maclean defected in May 1951. But other agents, including Kim Philby, remained.[6] It seems that Russia had penetrated the British High Commission in Cairo in the 1920s and 1930s.[7] Perhaps Russia still had agents there in the late 1940s.

Burgess and Maclean, together with Kim Philby who worked as a senior British Secret Service officer in liaison with the Central Intelligence Agency in Washington, were products of a particular British school system and Trinity College, Cambridge. A West End play by Julian Mitchell, *Another Country*, has analysed the conformity demanded by part of the public school system, and the connection between the alienation created by this, and the social exclusion suffered by homosexuals, with betrayal of king and country. The actress Coral Browne met Burgess in Moscow in the 1950s: his life did not seem any better there. She played herself in John

Schlesinger's brilliant film of the encounter, *An Englishman Abroad*.

That hierarchical education system produced many of the bureaucrats and ministers who initially perceived the Russian threat that later became known as the 'Cold War', and devised the British policy to meet it. Of course, its principal architect, Bevin, was proud of his working-class background and had little formal education. Emmanuel Shinwell who, as Minister of Defence, urged a strong policy against the Russians came from a similar background. Attlee, however, went to Haileybury College and University College, Oxford. Kenneth Younger and Hugh Gaitskell were both at Winchester and New College, Oxford about the same time. Patrick Gordon Walker attended Wellington College and Christ Church, Oxford, often considered the 'aristocrats'' college; Philip Noel-Baker went to Kings College, Cambridge. The permanent under secretary Orme Sargent attended Radley and entered the Foreign Office at the age of 22. His successor, William Strang, went to Palmer's School, 'one of the leading grammar schools in the country',[8] and University College, London. One of Britain's 'pro-consuls' of the time, Lord Killearn, enjoyed Eton and then went to the Foreign Office when he was 23. The other, Malcolm MacDonald, the son of a former British Prime Minister, was a product of Bedales School, Petersfield, and Queen's College, Oxford. Bevin's influential principal private secretaries both attended Cambridge: Frank Roberts, born in Argentina, went to Bedales, Rugby and then Trinity College; Pierson Dixon went to Bedford School and then Pembroke College. Frank Roberts married the daughter of Sir Said Shoucair Pasha, the financial adviser to the Sudan government. Archibald Clark Kerr (later Lord Inverchapel), Roberts's chief in Moscow and later ambassador in Washington, also married a woman from abroad, a Chilean, twenty-three years after he had entered the diplomatic service. Clark Kerr was 'privately educated'.

Sir Alexander Cadogan, Britain's ambassador at the United Nations and permanent under secretary from January 1938 to February 1946, went to Eton and Oxford. Those concerned with European affairs had Establishment backgrounds. Examples are: Nigel Ronald, Winchester and Magdalen College, Oxford; Henry Ashley Clarke, Repton and Pembroke College, Cambridge; Duff Cooper, Eton and New College, Oxford. Lord Halifax who remained in the Washington embassy for a while had been viceroy in India, and had been to Eton, Christ Church, Oxford, and was a fellow of All Souls. One of his successors, Oliver Franks, went to Bristol Grammar School and Queen's College, Oxford. Gladwyn

Jebb was a product of Eton and Magdalen College, Oxford. Sir Ralph Stevenson, an influential ambassador both in China and Egypt, attended Wellington College and University College, Oxford. Egypt was almost an Oxford prerogative: other officials who were particularly influential there were: Sir Ronald Campbell, Eton and Magdalen College; R. J. Bowker, Charterhouse and Oriel. Probably the most influential official on Palestine was Sir Harold Beeley: Highgate and Queen's College, Oxford. He was later British ambassador in Egypt. Sir M. Esler Dening, probably the most important man on the Far Eastern desk, enlisted in the Australian Imperial Forces in 1915 at the age of 18. Five years later he entered His Majesty's Consular Service and served in Tokyo. In 1952 he was appointed British ambassador to Japan. His subordinates on the Asian desks came from Establishment backgrounds: Robert H. Scott, Queen's Royal College, Trinidad, and New College, Oxford; John O. Lloyd, Marlborough and Clare College, Cambridge.

Besides Gordon Walker, all the principal British officials who developed the crucial British policy towards South Africa were also mainly public school–Oxbridge products. Of course there was nothing unusual or exceptional in that. It just reflected the recruiting system of the time. In the Colonial Office there was Sir Thomas Lloyd (Rossall, Royal Military Academy, Woolwich, and Caius College, Cambridge), and A. B. Cohen who went to Malvern and Trinity College, Cambridge. What bureaucratic opposition there was to the South African policy came from these men. The Cabinet document was drafted by G. E. Crombie in the Commonwealth Relations Office. He went to Fettes College, Edinburgh, and Aberdeen University, and in 1965 was appointed British High Commissioner in the Gambia. His colleague, F. E. Cumming-Bruce, who later became High Commissioner in Nigeria, went to Shrewsbury School and Trinity College, Cambridge. Sir Cecil Syers and George Herbert Baxter were both Oxford products: the former attended St Paul's and Balliol, the latter Manchester Grammar School and New College. Sir Percivale Liesching, who later became High Commissioner in South Africa, went to Bedford School and Brasenose College, Oxford. His predecessor, Sir Evelyn Baring, like Gordon Walker and Gaitskell, was educated at Winchester and New College. The Deputy High Commissioner in South Africa, R. R. Sedgwick, went to Westminster and Trinity College, Cambridge.

These men, largely from establishment backgrounds, did not undermine what prospect there might have been for a socialist foreign policy. Indeed, on the European side, with the exception of

Roberts and Dixon, they do not even seem to have been particularly influential.[9] These men were not the whizz-kids and wonder-boys of a later generation. They were career officials with a good education, and though psychologically some might have been damaged by a Spartan school system (apart from Burgess and Maclean there does not seem to be any evidence of this), many were considerable scholars with first-class degrees in history from either Oxford or Cambridge and fellows of their colleges. They came from a considerable number of different schools – though Eton and Winchester were obviously favourites – and although New College and Trinity College, Cambridge predominate, they were educated in a fairly wide spread of Oxbridge colleges. In many ways, the most influential figure of all, William Strang, whose committee laid down the principles of British foreign policy in 1949, attended a grammar school and University College, London. The age structure was conventional: those at the top were older than those at the bottom. Some apparently did not belong to clubs. It seemed to have been a convention anyway that Labour politicians either did not belong to clubs, or did not let it be known that they belonged to clubs. Career officials in the foreign service, however, appear to have favoured the Travellers: Strang, Killearn, Ronald, Sedgwick, Liesching and Cumming-Bruce all belonged. The Atheneum and the Oxford and Cambridge also attracted a few. On the surface, at any rate, there is no indication of school friends going through university together, and into the diplomatic or foreign service. It is possible that nepotism did exist, and that people from the same background favoured others from the same background, but there does not seem to be any conclusive proof. The recruiting system favoured an elite, but some did penetrate the barriers. It produced an efficient and dedicated organization. It was through the shrewd diplomacy of these men that Britain maintained the illusion of great power status. They were also able to exercise a restraining influence on the new colossus on the scene, the 'inexperienced' but powerful United States. The Americans, too, appreciated their expertise. These men oversaw with great skill, and perhaps a little regret, the transformation from the *pax Britannica* to the *pax Americana*.[10]

Many, including Halifax, Cadogan, Duff Cooper, Jebb, Mac-Donald, Killearn, Ronald, Roberts, Sargent, Strang and J. M. Troutbeck, had served in Neville Chamberlain's administration, Foreign Office and diplomatic service. When faced with a crisis two British statesmen, separated by a decade and largely supported by their bureaucracies, Chamberlain and Bevin, had the same vision of British defence policy and global strategy: what was needed was the English-speaking alliance.

Notes: Chapter 10

1 Australian Archives, Canberra, A426, 429/24, P. A. McBride to Menzies, Top - Secret, 24 October 1950.
2 Australian Archives, Canberra, A5954, Box 1793, COS(S)52(5th Mtg), Minute of staff conference, Top Secret, 30 May 1952.
3 Public Record Office, London, FO 800/515, fol. 137, US/48/52, Douglas to Bevin, 20 August 1948; fol. 138, US/48/53, Bevin to Douglas, 21 August 1948.
4 G. Warner, 'The Labour governments and the unity of Western Europe, 1945–51', in Ovendale (ed.), *The Foreign Policy of the British Labour Governments*, pp. 61–82; J. W. Young, *Britain, France, and the Unity of Europe, 1945–1951* (Leicester, 1984).
5 R. Ovendale, Letter to *The Times*, 10 February 1981, p. 13, col. d; P. Hennessy, 'Burgess knew US analysis of Russian aid', *The Times*, 2 February 1981, p. 2.
6 K. Philby, *My Silent War* (London, 1968).
7 G. Brook-Shepherd, *The Storm Petrels. The First Soviet Defectors, 1928–1938* (London, 1977), pp. 80–1, 110–11.
8 W. Strang, *Home and Abroad* (London, 1956), p. 26.
9 Morgan, *Labour in Power*, p. 236.
10 *Who's Who 1946* (London, 1946); *Who's Who 1949* (London, 1949); *Who's Who 1966* (London, 1966).

Bibliography

(A) MANUSCRIPT SOURCES

AUSTRALIA

Canberra

Australian Archives
(a) Cabinet
     A4638
(b) Defence Committee
     A2031, A5799
(c) Department of External Affairs
     A1838
(d) Prime Minister
     A426
(e) Shedden Papers
     A5954

National Library of Australia
(a) Sir Frederick Eggleston Papers
     MS423
(b) Sir John Latham Papers
     MS1009
(c) Sir Robert Menzies Papers
     MS4936
(d) Sir Percy Spender Papers
     MS4875

BRITAIN

Cambridge

Churchill College, Cambridge
Alexander of Hillborough Papers
Attlee Papers
Halifax Papers

London

British Library
Oliver Harvey Diaries

British Library of Political and Economic Science
Dalton Papers
McKay Papers
James Meade Diaries

Public Record Office
(a) *Bevin Papers*
     FO 800
(b) *Cabinet*
     CAB 41; CAB 42; CAB 65; CAB 66; CAB 128; CAB 129; CAB 131;
     CAB 133
(c) *Colonial Office*
     CO 537; CO 733
(d) *Defence*
     DEFE 4; DEFE 6
(e) *Dominions Office (Commonwealth Relations Office)*
     DO 35
(f) *Foreign Office*
     FO 371; FO 381; FO 954
(g) *Prime Minister's Office*
     PREM 4; PREM 8

Oxford

Western Manuscripts Department, Bodleian
Attlee Papers

SOUTH AFRICA

Pretoria

Transvaal Archives
Leyds Archives

UNITED STATES

Burlington, Vermont

Guy W. Bailey Library, University of Vermont
Senator Aiken Papers
Governor Ernest Gibson Jr Papers
Warren R. Austin Papers

Charlottesville, Virginia

Alderman Library, University of Virginia
J. Rives Childes Papers
Louis Johnson Papers
Edward R. Stettinius Jr Papers

Clemson, South Carolina

Robert Muldrow Cooper Library, Clemson University
James F. Byrnes Papers

Hyde Park, New York

Franklin D. Roosevelt Library
Harry L. Hopkins Papers
Henry M. Morgenthau Jr Papers
Samuel I. Rosenman Papers
Anna Eleanor Roosevelt Papers
Franklin D. Roosevelt Papers
War Refugee Board: Records 1944–5

Independence, Missouri

Harry S. Truman Library
Dean Acheson Papers
Clark M. Clifford Papers
Jonathan Daniel Papers
Elsey Papers
Edward Jacobson Papers
Herschel V. Johnson Papers
Howard McGrath Papers
Harry S. Truman Papers: Foreign Affairs Files
   Official Files: United Nations Special Committee on Palestine
   President Secretary's Files: Palestine – Jewish Immigration
   General Files: American Christian Palestine Committee
               American Zionist Emergency Council
               Jews May 1944
               Jews
               Eddie Jacobson
               United Nations Relief and Work Agency
               for Palestine Refugees in Near East
               Zionist Organizations
               Zionist Organization of America
   MHCD 184: Correspondence between Merriam and Henderson
   MHDC 250: Material on Palestine donated by E. M. Wright, Department of State Official
   MHDC 259: Epstein Correspondence
   PPF 1296: Alex F. Sachs Files
   PPF 1395: Rabbi Samuel Thurman Files
   PPF 2513: Herbert H. Lachman Files
   Rosenman Files
   Henry L. Stimson Diaries
   Copies of Papers in the Weizmann Archives, Rehovoth, Israel, Relating to Relations between the United States and Palestine and Israel 1945–52

Oral Histories: Mathew J. Connelly; George M. Elsey; Mark Ethridge; Loy E. Henderson; John D. Hickerson; Max Lowenthal; Evan M. Wilson

Lexington, Virginia

George C. Marshall Library, Virginia Military Institute
Marshall S. Carter Papers
George C. Marshall Papers
Kenneth W. Condit, *The History of the Joint Chiefs of Staff. The Joint Chiefs of Staff and National Policy*, Vol. 2, *1947–1949* (Historical Division, Joint Secretariat, Joint Chiefs of Staff, 22 April 1976)
Op-35-ohn Ser 000687P35(SC)EF52, Papers relating to the Chiefs of Staff, Xerox
WDCSA 381, Papers relating to Security, Xerox
Secretary's Weekly Summaries, 19 May 1947–3 January 1949, Xerox 2055
Record Group 59, General Records of the Department of State, Records of Charles E. Bohlen 1942–52, Xerox 2061
Record Group 59, Department of State, Policy Planning Staff
United States National Security Council: Papers of the National Security Council, Xerox
United States Joint Chiefs of Staff, White House Records of Fleet Admiral William D. Leahy, 1942–49

Princeton, New Jersey

Princeton University Library
Bernard M. Baruch Papers
John Foster Dulles Collection
Louis Fischer Papers
James V. Forrestal Diaries
George Kennan Papers
Arthur Krock Papers
Adlai E. Stevenson Papers
Harry Dexter White Papers
The John Foster Dulles Oral History Collection: Robert R. Bowie; Herbert Brownell; James F. Byrnes; Andrew W. Cordier; Hugh S. Cumming, Jr; Thomas E. Dewey; Clarence Dillon; C. Douglas Dillon; Allen Dulles; Eleanor Lansing Dulles; Ernest A. Goss; Raymond A. Hare; W. Averell Harriman; Loy W. Henderson; John D. Hickerson; Douglas G. Mode; Harold Stasson; Thomas E. Stephens; James P. Richards

Washington, District of Columbia

Georgetown University Library
Robert F. Wagner Papers

Library of Congress Manuscript Division
Emmanuel Celler Papers
Tom Connally Papers
W. S. Culbertson Papers

Felix Frankfurter (Zionism) Papers
Theodore F. Green Papers
Jessup Papers
James M. Landis Papers
Francis Bowes Sayre Papers
Lawrence A. Steinhart Papers

National Archives
Record Group 59, General Records of the Department of State, Decimal Files 1945–19, 501.BB Palestine; 711, 741, 867N; OSS Bureau of Intelligence Research; Records of Charles E. Bohlen 1942–52; Office of Near Eastern Affairs Palestine; Records of Policy Planning Staff 1947–53; Records Relating to Palestine, Palestine Reference 'book' of Dean Rusk, 15 February–19 April 1948

Washington National Records Centre (Suitland, Maryland)
Record Group 0000319 Entry 00082 Army Staff Intelligence (G2) Library 'C File' 1946–51
Record Group 84 Entry 57A-446 (Cairo Embassy)
Record Group 84 Entry 59A543 Pt 5, '00 Palestine (London Embassy Files)
Record Group 165 G2 Regional File 1933–44, Palestine 2800–900

(B) A SHORT LIST OF FURTHER READING

Anderson, T. H., *The United States, Great Britain, and the Cold War 1944–1947* (Columbia, Miss., 1981).
Attlee, C. R., *As It Happened* (London, 1954).
Barber, J., *South Africa's Foreign Policy 1945–1970* (London, 1973).
Barclay, R. E., *Ernest Bevin and the Foreign Office* (London, 1975).
Barker, E. *The British between the Superpowers* (London, 1983).
Bethell, N., *The Palestine Triangle: The Struggle between the British, the Jews and the Arabs, 1935–48* (London, 1979).
Boardman, R., *Britain and the People's Republic of China 1949–74* (London, 1976).
Buckley, R., *Occupation Diplomacy: Britain, the United States and Japan* (Cambridge, 1982).
Bullock, A., *Ernest Bevin. Foreign Secretary 1945–1951* (London, 1983).
Cross, C., *The Fall of the British Empire: 1918–1968* (London, 1968).
Dilks, D. (ed.), *Retreat from Power: Studies in Britain's Foreign Policy of the Twentieth Century* (London, 1981).
Dixon, P., *Double Diploma: the Life of Sir Pierson Dixon, Don and Diplomat* (London, 1968).
Dobbs, C. M., *The Unwanted Symbol: American Foreign Policy, the Cold War, and Korea, 1945–1950* (Kent, Ohio, 1981).
Donoughe, B. and G. W. Jones, *Herbert Morrison: Portrait of a Politician* (London, 1973).
Eayrs, J., *In Defence of Canada. Peacemaking and Deterrence* (Toronto, 1972).
Eayrs, J., *In Defence of Canada. Growing up Allied* (Toronto, 1980).
Eden, A., *The Reckoning* (London, 1965).
Epstein, L. D., *Britain – Uneasy Ally* (Chicago, 1954).

Fitzsimons, M. A., *The Foreign Policy of the British Labour Government, 1945–1951* (Notre Dame, Ind., 1953).

Foot, M., *Aneurin Bevan: A Biography*, Vol. 2, *1945–1960* (London, 1973).

Gardner, R. N., *Sterling-Dollar Diplomacy* (London, 1969).

Gladwyn, H. M. G. J., *The Memoirs of Lord Gladwyn* (London, 1972).

Glubb, J. B., *A Soldier with the Arabs* (London, 1957).

Glubb, J. B., *Britain and the Arabs: A Study of Fifty Years, 1908–1958* (London, 1959).

Goldsworthy, D., *Colonial Issues in British Politics, 1945–1961: From 'Colonial Development' to 'Wind of Change'* (Oxford, 1971).

Gordon, M. R., *Conflict and Consensus in Labour's Foreign Policy, 1914–1965* (Stanford, Calif., 1969).

Gowing, M. M. assisted by L. Arnold, *Independence and Deterrence: Britain and Atomic Energy, 1945–1952*, 2 vols (London, 1974).

Harris, K., *Attlee* (London, 1982).

Hathaway, R. M., *Ambiguous Partnership. Britain and America 1944–1947* (New York, 1981).

Hayter, W., *A Double Life* (London, 1974).

Hazlehurst, C. and C. Woodland, *A Guide to the Papers of British Cabinet Ministers 1900–1951* (London, 1974).

Henderson, N., *The Birth of NATO* (London, 1982).

Hudson, W. J., *Australia and the Colonial Question at the United Nations* (Sydney, 1970).

Iriye, A., *The Cold War in Asia. A Historical Introduction* (Englewood Cliffs, NJ, 1974).

Ismay, Lord, *The Memoirs of Lord Ismay* (London, 1960).

Jones, B., *The Russia Complex: the British Labour Party and the Soviet Union* (Manchester, 1977).

Jones, P., compiler, *Britain and Palestine: Archival Sources for the History of the British Mandate* (Oxford, 1979).

Judd, D., *King George VI 1895–1952* (London, 1982).

Kaiser, R. G., *Cold Winter, Cold War* (London, 1974).

Kennedy, P. M., *The Realities behind Diplomacy: Background Influences on British External Policy, 1865–1980* (London, 1981).

Kimche, J. and D., *Both Sides of the Hill: Britain and the Palestine War* (London, 1960).

Krug, M. M., *Aneurin Bevan: Cautious Rebel* (London, 1961).

Kuniholm, B. R., *The Origins of the Cold War in the Near East: Great Power Conflict and Diplomacy in Iran, Turkey and Greece* (Princeton, NJ, 1980).

Lee, J., *My Life with Nye* (London, 1980).

Lewin, R., *The Chief: Field Marshal Lord Wavell, Commander-in-Chief and Viceroy 1939–1947* (London, 1980).

Louis, W. R., *The British Empire in the Middle East 1945–51. Arab Nationalism, the United States, and Postwar Imperialism* (Oxford, 1984).

Low, D. A. (ed.), *Congress and the Raj: Facets of the Indian Struggle 1917–1947* (London, 1977).

Luard, D. E. T., *Britain and China* (London, 1962).

Macmillan, H., *Tides of Fortune, 1945–1955* (London, 1969).

McIntosh, A. *et al.*, *New Zealand in World Affairs*, Vol. 1 (Wellington, 1977).

McMahon, R. J., *Colonialism and the Cold War: The United States and the Struggle for Indonesian Independence, 1945–1949* (Ithaca, NY, 1981).

McNeill, W. H., *America, Britain and Russia. Their Co-operation and Conflict 1941–1946* (London, 1953).

Manderson-Jones, R. B., *The Special Relationship: Anglo-American Relations and Western European Unity 1947–1956* (London, 1972).

Mansergh, N., *Survey of British Commonwealth Affairs; Problems of Wartime Cooperation and Postwar Change, 1939–1952* (London, 1958).

Mansergh, N., *The Commonwealth Experience* (London, 1959).

Mansergh, N., *South Africa 1906–1961, the Price of Magnanimity* (London, 1962).

Medlicott, W. N., *British Foreign Policy since Versailles 1919–1963*, 2nd edn (London, 1968).

Mee, C. L., Jr, *Meeting at Potsdam* (London, 1975).

Meehan, E. J., *The British Left Wing and Foreign Policy: A Study of the Influence of Ideology* (New Brunswick, NJ, 1960).

Messer, R. L., *The End of an Alliance: James F. Byrnes, Roosevelt, Truman, and the Origins of the Cold War* (Chapel Hill, NC, 1982).

Millar, T. B., *Australia in Peace and War. External Relations 1788–1977* (London, 1978).

Monroe, E., *Britain's Moment in the Middle East 1914–1971* (London, 1981).

Montgomery, B. L., *The Memoirs of Field-Marshal the Viscount Montgomery of Alamein* (London, 1958).

Moon, Penderel (ed.), *Wavell: The Viceroy's Journal* (Oxford, 1973).

Moore, J. H. (ed.), *The American Alliance: Australia, New Zealand and the United States, 1940–1970* (Melbourne, 1970).

Moran, C. M. W., *Winston Churchill. The Struggle for Survival, 1940–1965* (London, 1966).

Morgan, K. O., *Labour in Power 1945–1951* (Oxford, 1984).

Mosley, L., *The Last Days of the British Raj* (London, 1961).

Nagai, Y. and A. Iriye (eds), *The Origins of the Cold War in Asia* (New York, 1977).

Nicholas, H. G., *Britain and the United States* (London, 1963).

Northedge, F. S., *Descent from Power: British Foreign Policy 1945–1973* (London, 1974).

Northedge, F. S. and A. Wells, *Britain and Soviet Communism: the Impact of a Revolution* (London, 1982).

O'Neill, R., *Australia in the Korean War, 1950–1953*, Vol. 1, *Strategy and Diplomacy* (Canberra, 1981).

Ovendale, R., *'Appeasement' and the English Speaking World. Britain, the United States, the Dominions and the Policy of 'Appeasement', 1937–1939* (Cardiff, 1975).

Ovendale, R. (ed.), *The Foreign Policy of the British Labour Governments, 1945–1951* (Leicester, 1984).

Ovendale, R., *The Origins of the Arab-Israeli Wars* (London, 1984).

Pearson, L. B., *Mike. The Memoirs of the Rt. Hon. Lester B. Pearson*, Vol. 1, *1897–1948* (Toronto, 1972).

Pearson, L. B., edited by J. A. Munro and A. I. Inglis, *Mike. The Memoirs of the Right Honourable Lester B. Pearson*, Vol. 2, *1948–1957* (Toronto, 1973).

Perham, M., *Colonial Sequence, 1949 to 1969: A Chronological Commentary upon British Colonial Policy in Africa* (London, 1970).

Philips, C. H. and M. D. Wainwright (eds), *The Partition of India: Policies and Perspectives 1935–1947* (London, 1970).

Pierre, A. J., *Nuclear Politics: the British Experience with an Independent Strategic Force 1939–1970* (London, 1972).

Porter, B. E., *Britain and the Rise of Communist China: A Study of British Attitudes, 1945–1954* (London, 1967).

Reid, E., *Time of Fear and Hope: The Making of the North Atlantic Treaty 1947–1949* (Toronto, 1977).

Rendel, Sir G., *The Sword and the Olive. Recollections of Diplomacy and the Foreign Service, 1913–1954* (London, 1957).

Roberts, H. L. and P. A. Wilson (eds), *Britain and the United States. Problems in Co-operation* (London, 1953).

Ross, G. (ed.), *The Foreign Office and the Kremlin. British Documents on Anglo-Soviet Relations 1941–45* (Cambridge, 1984).

Rothwell, V. H., *Britain and the Cold War, 1941–1947* (London, 1982).

Rubin, B., *The Great Powers in the Middle East 1941–1947: The Road to the Cold War* (London, 1980).

Sharp, T., *The Wartime Alliance and the Zonal Division of Germany* (Oxford, 1975).

Sherwin, M. J., *A World Destroyed: The Atomic Bomb and the Grand Alliance* (New York, 1975).

Shinwell, E., *Lead with the Left: My First Ninety-Six Years* (London, 1981).

Shlaim, A., *The United States and the Berlin Blockade, 1948–1949: A Study in Crisis Decision-Making* (Berkeley, Calif., 1983).

Shlaim, A. et al., *British Foreign Secretaries since 1945* (Newton Abbott, 1977).

Smith, F. E. (Lord Birkenhead), *Halifax: The Life of Lord Halifax* (London, 1965).

Spence, J. E., *The Strategic Significance of South Africa* (London, 1970).

Spencer, R. A., *Canada in World Affairs. From UN to NATO 1946–1949* (Toronto, 1959).

Spender, P., *Exercises in Diplomacy. The ANZUS Treaty and the Colombo Plan* (Sydney, 1969).

Stephens, M., *Ernest Bevin: Unskilled Labourer and World Statesman 1881–1951* (London, 1981).

Strang, W., *Home and Abroad* (London, 1956).

Stueck, W. W., *The Road to Confrontation: American Policy toward China and Korea, 1947–1950* (Chapel Hill, NC, 1981).

Sutch, W. B., *The Quest for Security in New Zealand 1840 to 1966* (Wellington, 1966).

Sykes, C., *Crossroads to Israel* (London, 1965).

Thorne, C., *Allies of a Kind: the United States, Britain and the War against Japan, 1941–1945* (London, 1978).

Watt, A., *The Evolution of Australian Foreign Policy 1938–1965* (Cambridge, 1967).

Watt, D. C., *Succeeding John Bull. America in Britain's Place 1900–1975* (Cambridge, 1984).

Wheeler-Bennett, J., *King George VI, his Life and Reign* (London, 1958).

Williams, F., *Ernest Bevin, Portrait of a Great Englishman* (London, 1952).

Williams, F., *A Prime Minister Remembers: The War and Post-War Memoirs of the Rt. Hon. Earl Attlee* (London, 1961).

Williams, P. M. (ed.), *The Diary of Hugh Gaitskell 1945–1956* (London, 1983).

Wittner, L. S., *American Intervention in Greece, 1943–1949* (New York, 1982).
Wood, E. F. L. (Lord Halifax), *Fullness of Days* (London, 1957).
Woodhouse, C. M., *The Struggle for Greece 1941–1949* (London, 1976).
Xydis, S. G., *Greece and the Great Powers, 1944–1947* (Thessaloniki, 1963).
Yergin, D., *Shattered Peace* (Boston, Mass., 1977).
Young, J. W., *Britain, France, and the Unity of Europe, 1945–1951* (Leicester, 1984).

Index

Abadan 91

Abdullah, Emir (later King) of Jordan 89, 92, 96, 106, 110

Abyssinia. *See* Ethiopia

Acheson, Dean: agreement with Bevin on consultation 194, 199, 200; alerts Miall to Marshall's impending Harvard speech 64; conditions for recognizing China 205; explains neutralizing of Formosa Straits 203; interdepartmental co-ordinating committee 63; ministerial talks with UK and France 170; prepares for aid to Greece 49; Nationalist Chinese support questioned by Bevin 195-6; SE Asia discussions with Bevin 158, 160; on US China policy 187, 193; on US Pacific policy 166; warns of danger of Greek guerilla victory 59; 59, 63, 64; work on Atlantic Pact 156

Addison, Lord 227

Aden 91, 107

Afghanistan 38, 49, 159

Alanbrooke, Viscount. *See* Brooke, Sir Alan

Albania 78

Alexander, A. V. 53, 69, 79, 103, 233

Alexandretta 127

Ali Khan, Liaqat 81

Allen, Roger 199

Amethyst, HMS 191

Amman 96

Anglo-American: agreement on consultation 194, 195; alliance 46, 47, 60, 80, 206, 213, 224, 274; armaments standardization 41, 45, 46, 47, 49; co-operation 31, 45, 61, 69, 274; differences on Czechoslovakia 13, on Far East 226; difficulties over China 200-1, 206; Eastern Europe policy 31; 'fraternal association' 40; military assistance in Indo-China 157; military strength 13; reciprocal use of ports 46; Refugee Commission 95; rift possible over Palestine 110; secret Far East talks 158; solidarity against Russia 45; special relationship 53-4, 80, 206, 215, 227, 282-3

Anglo-Boer War 245, 246-7

Anglo-French: alliance 61-2; approach on Western Union 67-8; economic union proposed 66; military staff conversations 62

Anglo-Soviet: occupation of Iran 34, 41; Treaty (1942) 44-5

Animal Farm 283

Annam 142, 179

ANZAM area 129, 171, 177, 283; ANZUS 230, 279, 233, 238

Aqaba 96, 110

Aquitania, RMS 30

Arab: alliances 106-7; armies enter Palestine 109; disquiet over Jewish immigration 101; friendship with Britain 51, 105, 112, 131; – Israeli war 110; Legion 91, 106, 136; nationalism 89, 133, 139; opinion and Israeli offers of defence help 131, 132; reaction to Palestine problems 102, 103; refugees 110, 282; resentment at possible partition of Palestine 109

Arabism 92

Argentina 14, 108, 120

Arnold, Thomas 89

Ashton-Gwatkin, F. 4

Asia: British policy 214-15, 225; Cold War 21, 117, 133, 237; Commonwealth countries 164; communist advance 206, 237, 277; defence priority 118; democracy 164; free peoples 200; security 74; suspicion of USA 215; US policy 169. *See also* South-East Asia.

Atlantic: Charter 6; North 134; Pact 77, 82, 113, 156, 167; security system 74-5. *See also* North Atlantic Treaty Organization.

atomic bomb: British 61, 134; common to Allies 31, 223, 278; development 31, 285; effect on British strategy 91; B-29 aircraft 79, 80; effect on USSR 35-6, 133; possible use in Korea 213, 221-2, 223, 282; Russian weapon 285; on UN agenda 35; used on Japan 19; US monopoly 77

atomic energy 31-2, 61, 79-80, 81

Attlee, Clement: accompanies Churchill to Potsdam 16; announces Indian independence 54; approaches Truman about atomic development 31-2; asks Truman to delay Palestine statement 101; attitude to Russia 16; becomes Prime Minister 16; on Chinese acceptance of Hong Kong retention 190; on communist threat

Liberia 108, 109, 252
Libya 129
Liesching, Sir Percivale 253
Life 38
Lindsay, Sir Ronald 4
Lippmann, Walter 59, 66
Lloyd, J. O. 155, 161-2, 166, 287
Louw, Eric 81, 258, 284
Lovett, Robert A. 60, 68, 77, 110, 251
Lowenthal, Max 109
Luxembourg 76, 108
Lydda 91

MacArthur, Gen. Douglas 197, 216, 218, 220, 228-9, 236
MacDonald, Malcolm 4, 152, 156-7, 161, 168, 196-7, 200, 277, 288
Maclean, Donald 285, 288
McMahon Act 32-3
Macmillan, Harold 6
McNeil, Hector 227
Mafrak 96
Malan, D. F.: Africa Pact proposals 252, 254; arms co-operation with UK 252; attitude to UK 248, 250, to USSR 252; elected Prime Minister 248; High Commission Territories issue 249-50; Korea military aid 214; London visit 245-6, 249; on NATO extension 252, 254; proposes conference 254; on Seretse Khama case 267; on South Africa's role 251-2; UN 'failure' 253
Malaya: Australian unpopularity 164, 171, 175, 178, 276; Australian view 124-5; British presence 159; Chinese population 196, 198; crisis 130; defence priority 125, 137; dollar earnings 176; insurrection 176, 179, 198, 199, 202, 217, 237, 276; Lincoln bombers 176; rubber 229; security zone 74, 171
Malraux, André 147
Manchuria 218
Maniulsky, Dimitri 147
Mao Tse-Tung 148, 152, 154, 173, 186-7
Marshall, Gen. George C.: Harvard speech 64; opposes operations with political purposes 13; persuades Bevin to allow mission to stay in Greece 60; reaction to Bevin's plan for association of democracies 66; tells Stalin of US aid plans 62-3; Secretary of State 45
Marshall Aid 20, 147
Menon, K. P. S. 173
Menzies, Sir Robert 118, 122, 129-30
Mexico 108
Miall, Leonard 64
Middle East: abortive Defence Organ-

ization 253, 256-7; American commercial penetration 93, 97; Arab-Israeli War 110; Australian role 172; base for counter-offensive 70; British and Commonwealth responsibility 92, 136-7, 256, 275-6; British paramountcy 89-114, 139; British policy 53, 90; Command 117-39; defence 98, 158; deterioration of UK position 130-1; economic and social policy 92; military bases 119-20; nationalism 133; oil 97, 99, 282; peacetime garrison 136; possible USSR air offensive 135; Russian threat 67, 94, 99; 'shield of Africa' 275; South African interest 118, 256; special meeting 126-7; strategic importance 68, 71, 90, 91, 97, 110-11, 118, 122, 135; token forces 127, 136; US reinforcements 285
Mikolajczyk, Stanislaw 8-9, 11, 3
Milner, Sir Alfred 246-7
Mollet, Guy 219-20
Molotov, Vyacheslaw: 'peace offensive' exchanges with Bedell Smith 77; Polish policy deplored by Churchill 8, 10; told by Truman that 'one-way street friendship' was not wanted 14
Monroe Doctrine 33
Montgomery, FM Sir B. L.: European army principle 281; talks with US Chiefs of Staff 46: Moscow visit 44
Moran, Lord 7
Morrison, Herbert 16, 131, 227, 229, 237
Mountbatten, Earl 225, 278
Munich crisis 4-5
Mussadiq, Mohammed 130
Mutual Aid 19

Nagasaki 19
Nehru, Jawaharlal 81, 155, 167, 190, 217
nepotism 288
Netherlands: colonial empire 11, 130, 145, 151, 231; extension of Anglo-French alliance to 62; inclusion in Marshall Plan 64; recognizes Indonesian independence 214-15; wish to delay recognition of China 198
New Zealand: bombers stationed in Malaya 276; elections 198; frigates sent to Far East 212; Hankey's visit 3; Middle East defence 125, 129, 136-7, 232; 'old White' dominion 118, 215, 283; 'Peter Pan' dominion 166; role in Pacific defence 232; solidarity with Commonwealth 165-6, 283; South-East Asia policy 155, 163, 175-6; strategic planning talks 82, 119, 129
Nigeria 249